ЛОМОНОСОВЪ

Anthology of Russian Literature

From the Earliest Period to the Present Time

By

Leo Wiener

Assistant Professor of Slavic Languages at Harvard University

IN TWO PARTS

From the Tenth Century to the Close of the
Eighteenth Century

G. P. Putnam's Sons

New York and London

The Knickerbocker Press

1902

The Knickerbocker Press, New York

TO MY FRIEND AND COLLEAGUE
ARCHIBALD CARY COOLIDGE
THIS WORK IS
GRATEFULLY DEDICATED

PREFACE

THE time is not far off when the Russian language will occupy the same place in the curriculum of American universities that it now does in those of Germany, France and Sweden. A tongue that is spoken by more than one hundred million people and that encompasses one-half of the northern hemisphere in itself invites the attention of the curious and the scholar. But the points of contact between the Anglo-Saxon and Slavic races are so many, both in politics and literature, that it is a matter of interest, if not yet of necessity, for every cultured person of either nationality to become well acquainted with the intellectual and social life of the other. In Russia, the English language is steadily gaining in importance, and not only the universities, but the gymnasiums as well, offer courses in English. In England and America there are many signs of a similar interest in their Russian neighbour, though at present it expresses itself mainly in the perusal of Russian novels in translations that rarely rise above mediocrity. There is also a growing demand for a fuller treatment of Russian Literature as a whole, which even Prince Wolkonsky's work cannot satisfy, for the reason that only a small fraction of the nineteenth-century writers, and hardly anything of the preceding periods, is accessible to the reader for verification. It is the purpose of this Anthology to render a concise, yet sufficient, account of Russian Literature in its totality, to give to the English reader who is not acquainted with any other language than his own a biographical, critical and bibliographical sketch of every important author, to offer representative extracts of what there is best in the language in such a manner as to give a correct idea of the evolution of Russian Literature from its remotest time. The selections have been chosen so as to illustrate certain important historical events, and will be found of use also to the historical student.

In the preparation of this work, I have availed myself of many native sources, to which I shall express my indebtedness by a general declaration that I have with profit perused the monumental works of Pýpin and the authors on whom he has drawn in the preparation of his history of Russian Literature. To give variety, I have reproduced such of the existing translations as are less objectionable. In my own translations, for which alone I am responsible, I have attempted to render minutely the originals, with their different styles, not excepting their very imperfections, such as characterise particularly the writers of the eighteenth century. Only where the diction is inexpressibly crude, as in Pososhkóv's writings, or the text corrupt, as in the *Word of Ígor's Armament*, have I made slight deviations for the sake of clearness.

Russian words are transliterated differently by every translator: some attempt to give English equivalents, which, even if they were correctly chosen (they seldom are), cannot possibly give an idea of the phonetic values in Russian; others follow the simpler method of an etymological transliteration of letter by letter, but needlessly encumber the words with diacritical marks and difficult consonant combinations. The method pursued here, though far from ideal, recommends itself for its simplicity. Where the Russian and English alphabets are practically identical, the corresponding letters are used; in the other cases, the combinations are made with *h*, for which there is no corresponding sound in Russian; for the guttural vowel *y* is used, which does also the duty of the English *y* in *yes*. There can be no confusion between the two, as the guttural *y* before or after a vowel is extremely rare. It is useless for anyone without oral instruction to try to pronounce Russian words as the natives do. The nearest approach will be attained if the consonants be pronounced as in English (*g* always hard, *zh* as *z* in *azure*, *r* always rolled, *kh*, guttural like German *ch* in *ach*), and the vowels always open as in Italian (*a* as *a* in *far*, *e* as *e* in *set*, *o* as *o* in *obey*, or a little longer when accented, *u* as *oo* in *foot*, or a little longer when accented, *y* between consonants is guttural, which it is useless to attempt and had better be pronounced like *i* : *i. e.*, like *i* in *machine* or *bit*, according to the accent). The accents are indicated throughout the work. Accented *é* is frequently pronounced as *yó*, but it would be useless to indicate all such cases. It has not been found practicable to spell Russian names uniformly when their English forms are universally accepted.

It will not be uninteresting to summarise all that Englishmen and Americans have done to acquaint their countrymen with the language and literature of Russia.

When Russia was rediscovered by England in the middle of the sixteenth century and the Muscovy Company established itself at Moscow, there was naturally a demand for Englishmen who could speak Russian. There are frequent references in native reports to Englishmen who spoke and wrote Russian fluently and who were even used as ambassadors to the Muscovite Tsars. It was also an Englishman, Richard James, who, in 1619, made the first collection of Russian popular songs. In 1696, the first Russian grammar was published by the Oxford University Press, though its author, Ludolf, was not an Englishman by birth. In the eighteenth century, there seems to have been in England no interest in Russia except as to its religion, which received consideration from certain divines. An exception must be made in the case of W. Coxe, who in his *Travels in Poland, Russia, Sweden and Denmark*, 1st edition, London, 1784, gave an excellent account of Russian Literature from German and French sources. In 1821, Sir John Bowring startled his countrymen with his *Specimens of the Russian Poets*, which for the first time revealed to them the existence of a promising literature. Though his knowledge of Russian was quite faulty, as his translations prove, yet he put the poems into such pleasing verses that they became deservedly popular. A second edition followed the same year, and a second part two years later.

The impulse given by Sir John Bowring found a ready response in the periodic press of that time. In 1824 the Westminster Review brought out an article on *Politics and Literature of Russia,* which gave a short review of eighteenth-century literature. In 1827, R. P. Gillies gave a good sketch of *Russian Literature* in vol. i of the Foreign Quarterly Review, based on the Russian work of Grech. The same year, the Foreign Review brought out a short account, and the next year an elaborate article on *Russian Literature and Poetry,* also after Grech, which for some decades formed the basis of all the articles and chapters dealing with the same subject in the English language. The Foreign Quarterly Review brought out similar matter in vol. viii, xxi, xxiii, xxix, xxx. But more interesting than these, which are nearly all fashioned after some Russian articles, are the excellent literary notes in every number, that kept the readers informed on the latest productions that appeared in Russia. There seems hardly to have been a public for these notes in England, and indeed they get weaker with the twenty-fourth volume, and die of inanity in the thirtieth. This early period of magazine articles is brought to an end by *Russian Literary Biography*, in vol. xxxvi (1841) of the Westminster Review.

The example set by Sir John Bowring found several imitators. We have several anthologies, generally grouping themselves around Púshkin, for the first half of the century: W. H. Saunders, *Poetical Translations from the Russian Language,* London, 1826; [George Borrow], *The Talisman, with Other Pieces,* St. Petersburg, 1835; W. D. Lewis, *The Bakchesarian Fountain, and Other Poems,* Philadelphia, 1849. The Foreign Quarterly Review brought out in 1832 translations from Bátyushkov, Púshkin, and Rylyéev, and in Blackwood's Edinburgh Magazine for 1845 T. B. Shaw gave some excellent translations of Púshkin's poems. Other articles, treating individual authors, will be mentioned in their respective places.

While these meagre accounts of Russian Literature, at second hand, and the scanty anthologies were appearing, there was published in the Biblical Repository of Andover, Mass., in 1834, the remarkable work by Talvi, the wife of Dr. Edward Robinson, entitled: *Historical View of the Languages and Literatures of the Slavic Nations*, and this was republished in book-form, and enlarged, in New York, in 1850. Though there existed some special works by Slavic scholars, Talvi's was the first to encompass the whole field in a scholarly and yet popular manner. It is authoritative even now in many departments that have not been overthrown by later investigations, and it is a matter of surprise that none of the later English writers should have based their Russian Literatures on this important work, or should have proceeded in the path of Slavic studies which she had so beautifully inaugurated. There is no excuse for G. Cox's translation of F. Otto's *History of Russian Literature, with a Lexicon of Russian Authors*, which appeared at Oxford in 1839, and adds a number of its own inaccuracies to the blunders of the German original. Nor is there any notice taken of Talvi in [C. F. Henningsen's] *Eastern Europe and the Emperor Nicholas*, London, 1846, which gives a chapter on Russian Literature, mainly on Púshkin.

In the sixties W. R. Morfill began to translate some poems from the Russian, and towards the end of that decade, but especially in the next, Ralston published his excellent studies on the Folksongs and Folktales and Krylóv, and in the Contemporary Review, vols. xxiii and xxvii, two articles on the *Russian Idylls*. The magazines that in the seventies reviewed Russian Literature got everything at second hand, and are of little value: National Quarterly Review, vol. xxiv (1872); Catholic World, vol. xxi (1875); Harper's Magazine, 1878. Of books there were issued: Sutherland Edwards's *The Russians at Home*, London, 1861, a very useful work for contemporary literature, and F. R. Grahame's *The Progress of Science, Art and Literature in Russia*, London [1865], which contains a great deal of interesting material badly arranged and ill-digested. The chapter on Literature in O. W. Wahl's *The Land of the Czar*, London, 1875, is unimportant.

Since the eighties there have appeared a number of translations from good foreign authors bearing on Russian Literature: Ernest Dupuý, *The Great Masters of Russian Literature in the Nineteenth Century*, translated by N. H. Dole, New York [1886]; E. M. de Vogüé, *The Russian Novelists*, translated by J. L. Edmands, Boston [1887]; Dr. George Brandes, *Impressions of Russia*, translated by S. C. Eastman, New York, 1889; E. P. Bazán, *Russia: Its People and its Literature*, translated by F. H. Gardiner, Chicago, 1890.

The following more or less original works will be found useful: W. R. Morfill, *Slavonic Literature*, London, 1883, and *The Story of Russia*, New York and London, 1890; also his *The Peasant Poets of Russia* (Reprint from Westminster Review), London, 1880; C. E. Turner, *Studies in Russian Literature*, London, 1882, and before, in Fraser's Magazine for 1877; Ivan Panin, *Lectures in Russian Literature*, New York and London, 1889; *Memorials of a Short Life: A Biographical Sketch of W. F. A. Gaussen* (chapter on *The Russian People and their Literature*), London, 1895; Prince Serge Wolkonsky, *Pictures of Russian History and Russian Literature* (Lowell Lectures), Boston, New York and London, 1897; K. Waliszewski, *A History of Russian Literature*, New York, 1900, but this work must be used with extreme caution, on account of the many inaccuracies it contains. W. M. Griswold's *Tales Dealing with Life in Russia*, Cambridge, 1892, is a fair bibliography of all the prose translations that have appeared in the English language before 1892. But few anthologies have of late seen daylight: C. T. Wilson, *Russian Lyrics in English Verse*, London, 1887; John Pollen, *Rhymes from the Russian*, London, 1891 (a good little book); E. L. Voynich, *The Humour of Russia*, London and New York, 1895. The periodical " Free Russia," published in London since 1890, contains some good translations from various writers and occasionally some literary essay; but the most useful periodic publication is " The Anglo-Russian Literary Society," published in London since 1892, and containing valuable information on literary subjects, especially modern, and a series of good translations from contemporary poets. Nor must one overlook the articles in the encyclopedias, of which those in Johnson's Cyclopedia are especially good.

Very exhaustive statements of the modern literary movement in Russia appear from year to year in the Athenæum. More or less good articles on modern literature, mainly the novel, have appeared since 1880 in the following volumes of the periodical press: Academy, xxi and xxiii; Bookman, viii; Chautauquan, viii and xxii; Critic, iii; Current Literature, xxii; Dial, xx; Eclectic Magazine, cxv; Forum, xxviii; Leisure Hours, ccccxxv; Lippincott's, lviii; Literature, i; Living Age, clxxxv; Nation, lxv; Public Opinion, xx; Publisher's Weekly, liv; Temple Bar, lxxxix.

In conclusion, I desire to express my gratitude to my friends and colleagues who have aided me in this work: to Prof. A. C. Coolidge, for leaving at my disposal his collection of translations from the Russian, and for many valuable hints; to Dr. F. N. Robinson, for reading a number of my translations; to Prof. G. L. Kittredge, to whom is largely due whatever literary merit there may be in the introductory chapters and in the biographical sketches. I also take this occasion to thank all the publishers and authors from whose copyrighted works extracts have been quoted with their permission.

CONTENTS

xiv
Contents

Contents

xvi   Contents

Contents

A SKETCH OF RUSSIAN LITERATURE

A SKETCH OF RUSSIAN LITERATURE

OF the many Slavic nations and tribes that at one time occupied the east of Europe from the Elbe and the headwaters of the Danube to Siberia, and from the Ionic Sea to the Baltic and White Seas, some have entirely disappeared in the ruthless struggle with a superior German civilisation; others, like the Bulgarians and Servians, have paled into insignificance under the lethargic influence of the Crescent, to be fanned to life again within the memory of the present generation by a breath of national consciousness, which is the result of the Romantic Movement in European literature; others again like the Bohemians and Poles, rent asunder by fraternal discord and anarchy, have forfeited their national existence and are engaged in an unequal battle to regain it. Of all the Slavs, Russia alone has steadily gathered in the lands of the feudal lords, to shine at last as a power of the first magnitude among the sisterhood of states, and to scintillate hope to its racial brothers as the "Northern Star."

The unity of the Russian land was ever present to the minds of the writers in the earliest days of the appanages. The bard of the *Word of Igor's Armament* and Daniel the Palmer made appeals to the whole country and prayed for all the princes in the twelfth century, and for upwards of four centuries Moscow has been the centre towards which the outlying districts have been gravitating. Yet, in spite of so continuous and well-defined a political tendency, Russia is the last of the Slavic nations to have evolved a literature worthy of the name. Bohemia had a brilliant literature

3

of the Western stamp as early as the thirteenth century; Bulgaria had made a splendid start three centuries before, under the impulse of the newly introduced religion; the Servian city of Ragusa, receiving its intellectual leaven from its Italian vicinage, invested Petrarch and Dante with Servian citizenship in the fifteenth century, and, shortly after, gloried in an epic of a Gundulić, and in a whole galaxy of writers; Poland borrowed its theology from Bohemia, took an active part in the medieval Latin literature, and boasted a golden age for its native language in the sixteenth century. Russia produced an accessible literature only in the second half of the eighteenth century, became known to Western Europe not earlier than the second quarter of the next, and had not gained universal recognition until within the last twenty-five years.

In the case of the Western and Southern Slavs, a community of interests, whether religious or social, has led to an intellectual intercourse with their neighbours, from whom they have received their models for imitation or adaptation. Without a favourable geographical position, or some common bond with the external world, no nation can have a healthy development, especially in the incipient stage of its political existence. Blatant Slavophiles of fifty years ago heaped reproach on the reforms of Peter the Great, on the ground that they were fashioned upon Western ideals, and that he had retarded the evolution of Russia according to its inherent Slavic idea. There still survive men of that persuasion, though a comparative study of Russian literature long ago demonstrated that every step in advance has been made by conscious or unconscious borrowings from abroad. If there was a Russian literature previous to the introduction of Christianity, it certainly stood in some kind of relation to the literatures of the neighbours. The few extant treaties with the Greeks for that period show unmistakable Byzantine influences, and the Russian Code of Yaroslàv, with its purely Norse laws, dates from a time when the Varyágs had not yet disappeared in the mass of the Slavic majority.

With the introduction of Christianity, Russia, instead of

entering into closer communion with the rest of the world, was separated from it even more securely than before, and soon after, an intellectual stagnation began that lasted very nearly to the end of the seventeenth century. Various causes combined to produce this singular effect. Chief of these was its geographical position. Living in the vast eastern plain of Europe, which in itself would have been productive of a larger life, the Russian tribes had civilised neighbours on one side only. On the north they were separated from the Swedes by rude Finnish tribes; on the south, they had for centuries to contend against all the nomads, Pechenyegs, Cumanians, Khazars, who slowly proceeded from Asia to central Europe to become lost in the nations to the south of the Carpathians and in the Balkan peninsula; in the east the Finns of the north met the Tartars of the south, and behind them lay unprofitable Asia. On the north-west, it is true, was the civilised Teutonic Order, but the inveterate hatred between these Germans and the Slavs prevented any intercommunication from that quarter. There was left Poland, through which Russia might issue into Europe; but savage Lithuania was wedged in between the two, so as to reduce still more the line of contact with the West. When Lithuania became civilised, and a part of Poland, the latter had grown suspicious of the youthful Ilyá of Múrom who "had sat thirty years upon the oven," and enunciated a political maxim that either Russia would have to become Polish, or else Poland Russian. Knowing that there was no other exit for Russia, Poland permitted no light to reach it from the West. When England began to communicate with Russia in the sixteenth century, King Sigismund made an earnest appeal to Queen Elizabeth to stop sending skilled mechanics, lest the Colossus should awaken and become a danger to Europe.

These external causes of Russia's aloofness were still more intensified by a systematic determination of Russia to keep out the Catholic contamination that would come from intercourse with Europe. This was a direct outgrowth of its adoption of Christianity from Byzantium, instead of Rome.

Cyril and Methodius, the apostles to the Slavs, were themselves Bulgarians from Macedonia. When they first carried the new religion to Moravia and later to Bulgaria, they, no doubt, preached and wrote in the dialect with which they were most familiar. This innovation of preaching the gospel in another than one of the three sacred languages was a necessary departure, in order to win over the troublesome Slavs to the north of Byzantium. Though at the end of the ninth century the various dialects were already sufficiently dissimilar to constitute separate languages, yet they were not so distant from each other as to be a hindrance to a free intercommunication. When, a century later, Christianity was introduced into Russia from Constantinople, Bulgarian priests and bookmen were the natural intermediaries, and the Bulgarian language at once became the literary medium, to the exclusion of the native tongue. Soon after, the Eastern Church separated from Rome, and the Greek-Catholic clergy inculcated upon their neophytes an undying hatred of the Latins, as the Romanists were called. In Moscow, the slightest deviation from the orthodox faith was sufficient cause for suspecting a Romanist heresy, and anathemas against Roman-Catholics were frequent, but at Kíev, where the contact with Poland was inevitable, the disputes with the Latins form a prominent part of ecclesiastical literature. To guard the country against any possible contagion, the punishment of Russians who crossed the border, in order to visit foreign parts, was so severe, that few ever ventured out of the country. The seclusion of Russia was complete.

Even under these difficulties, literature and the arts might have flourished, if Constantinople had been able to give to the new converts even its degraded Byzantine culture, or if there had not been other powerful causes that militated against a development from within. In the west of Europe the Latin language of the Church did not interfere with an early national literature. Latin was the language of the learned, whether clerical or lay, and mediated an intellectual intercourse between the most distant members of the universal faith. At the same time, the native dialects had received an impulse before the introduction of Christianity, often under the influence of Rome, and they were left to shift for themselves and to find their votaries. The case was quite different in Russia. The Bulgarian language, which was brought in with the gospel, at once usurped on the native Russian to the great disadvantage of the latter. Being closely related to the spoken Russian, Bulgarian was easily acquired by the clergy, but it was not close enough to become the literary language of the people. On the one hand, this new gospel language could at best connect Russia with Byzantium by way of Bulgaria; on the other, Russian was looked down upon as a rude dialect and was discouraged, together with every symptom of the popular creation which was looked upon as intimately connected with ancient paganism.

This Bulgarian language was not long preserved in its purity. Detached from its native home, it was immediately transformed in pronunciation, so as to conform to the spoken Russian; thus, for example, it at once lost its nasals, which were not familiar to the Russian ear. In the course of time, words and constructions of the people's language found their way into the Church-Slavic, as the Bulgarian was then more properly called. Naturally, many words, referring to abstract ideas and the Church, passed from the Bulgarian into the spoken tongue. Thus, the two dialects, one the arbitrary literary language, the other, the language of every-day life, approached each other more and more. At the present time, the Russian of literature contains a large proportion of these Church-Slavic words ; the language of the Bible and the liturgy is the Church-Slavic of the sixteenth century, which differs so much from the original Bulgarian that, though a Russian reads with comparative ease this Church-Slavic, he has to study Bulgarian as a German would study Old German. This Church-Slavic of the Russian redaction has also been, and still is, in part, the ecclesiastical language of the other Greek-Catholic countries of the Slavs.

Some time passed before Russia could furnish its own

clergy. All the leading places in the Church were at first
filled with Bulgarians and Greeks who were steeped in
Byzantine religious lore. The Church at Constantinople
stood in direct opposition to the classical traditions of
Greece. These were not separated from the old heathenism,
and to the luxury and voluptuousness of medieval Greece,
which was ascribed to classical influences, the Church
opposed asceticism and self-abnegation. Monasticism was
preached as the ideal of the religious life, and arts and
sciences had no place in the scheme of the Church. Theology and rhetoric were the only sciences which the hermit
practised in his cell, in the moments that were free from
prayer and self-castigation. And it is only the Church's
sciences that ancient Russia inherited from Byzantium.
The civil intercourse between the two countries was very
slight, and the few Russian ecclesiastics who visited Mount
Athos and the Holy Land brought back with them at best a
few legends and apocryphal writings. The Byzantine influence at home showed itself in a verbal adherence to the Bible
and the Church Fathers, and an occasional attempt at pulpit
oratory in the bombastic diction of contemporary Greece.

Not a science penetrated into ancient Russia. Historically
the rest of the world did not exist for it, and geographically
it was only of interest in so far as it came into contact with
Russia: Russia knew more of Tartars and Cumanians than
of Germany or France. Arithmetic, not to speak of mathematics, and physics, medicine and engineering, were unknown before the sixteenth century, and then only when a
few foreigners practised these arts in the capital and at the
Court. The only literature that reached Russia was the
legendary lore of the South and West, through Bulgaria and
Poland, generally at a time when it had long been forgotten
elsewhere : thus, the Lucidarius and Physiologus were accepted as genuine bits of zoölogical and botanical science,
long after sober knowledge had taken possession of the universities of the world. The literature of Russia before Peter
the Great is by no means meagre or uninteresting, but it
lacks an important element of historical continuity; in fact,

it is devoid of every trace of chronology. What was written in the twelfth century might with equal propriety be the product of the sixteenth, and *vice versa*, and the productions of the earliest time were copied out as late as the seventeenth century, and relished as if they had just been written. Where a certain literary document has come down to us in a later copy, it is not possible to date it back, unless it contains some accidental indication of antiquity. In short, there was no progress in Russia for a period of six or seven centuries, from the tenth century to the seventeenth.

In this achronism of literary history, there may, however, be discerned two periods that are separated from each other by the first invasion of the Tartars. Previous to that momentous event, Kíev formed the chief intellectual and political centre of the Russian principalities. Here the Norse traditions, which had been brought by the Varyág warriors, had not entirely faded away in the century following the introduction of Christianity, and the Court maintained certain relations with the rest of the world, as in the case of Yaroslav, who was related, by the marriage of his children, to the Courts of Norway, France, Germany and Hungary. On the other hand, Vladímir's heroes were celebrated abroad, and Ilyá of Múrom is not unknown to German tradition and the Northern saga. Not only its favourable geographical position, but its climate as well, inspired the inhabitants of Kíev with a greater alacrity, even as the Little-Russians of to-day have developed less sombre characteristics than the Great-Russians of the sterner north. It is sufficient to compare the laconic instructions of Luká Zhidyáta in the commercial Nóvgorod with the flowery style of Serapión's sermon, or the dry narrative of the northern chronicles with the elaborate adornment of the stories in the chronicles of Néstor and Sylvester, to become aware of the fundamental difference between the two sections of Russia. The twelfth century, rich in many aspects of literature, including that beautiful prose poem of popular origin, the *Word of Ígor's Armament*, gave ample promise of better things to come. Similarly, the bylínas of the Vladímir cycle, the best and most numerous of all that are preserved, point to an old poetic tradition that proceeded from Kíev.

The fact that these bylínas have been lately discovered in the extreme north-east, in the Government of Olónetsk, while not a trace of them has been found in their original home, has divided the scholars of Russia into two camps. Some assert that all the Russians of Kíev belonged to the Great-Russian division, and that the Tartar invasion destroyed most of them, and caused the rest to migrate to the north, whither they carried their poetry. The Little-Russians that now occupy the south of Russia are supposed by these scholars to have come from Galicia to repeople the abandoned places. The Little-Russians themselves claim, with pardonable pride, to be the direct descendants of the race that gave Russia its Néstor and the bard of the *Word of Igor's Armament.* There are weighty arguments on both sides, and both the Great-Russians, with whom we are at present concerned, and the Little-Russians, or Ruthenians, who have developed a literature in their own dialect, claim that old literature as their own.

The terrible affliction of the Mongol invasion marks, on the one hand, the beginning of the concentration of Russia around Moscow, and, on the other, accentuates more strongly the barren activities of the Russian mind for the next few centuries. Historians have been wont to dwell on the Tartar domination as the chief cause of Russian stagnation, but the calmer judgment of unbiassed science must reject that verdict. It is true, the Tartars carried ruin to all the Russian land, but after every successful raid, they withdrew to their distant camps, ruling the conquered land merely by exacting tribute and homage from its princes. The Tartars in no way interfered with the intellectual and religious life of the people; on the contrary, they mingled freely with the subject nation, and intermarriages were common. It has already been pointed out that the germ of unprogressiveness was older than the invasion, that the Byzantine religious culture was the real cause of it. That Moscow was even less progressive than Kíev is only natural. All its energies were bent on political aggrandisement, on throwing off the hated Tartar yoke, and it was farther removed from Europe than the more fortunate southern metropolis. All these conditions were unfavourable to the practice of the gentler arts.

The religious lore of ancient Russia was derived from the gospel, which was hardly ever accessible in continuous form, but only as an *aprakos*, *i. e.*, as a manual in which it was arranged according to the weekly readings. This was supplemented by two peculiar versions of the Old Testament, the *palæas*, in which passages of the Bible were intermingled with much apocryphal matter, and which originally had served as controversial literature against the Jews, and to prove the coming of Christ; there was no translation of the whole Old Testament, and as late as the eighteenth century a priest referred to the *palæa* as to Holy Writ. Prayers to saints, lives and legends of saints, with moral instructions, complete the list of the religious equipment that Russia received from Byzantium. One of the oldest Russian manuscripts, the *Collection of Svyatosláv*, made for Svyatosláv of Chernígov in 1073, is a copy of a similar production, translated from the Greek for Simeón of Bulgaria. It is an encyclopedia of ecclesiastic and moral themes, culled from the Church Fathers, among whom John Chrysostom is most prominent. Later, there were many similar collections, known under the names of *The Golden Beam*, *Emerald*, *Golden Chain*, and so forth.

By the aid of this literature and such Greek models as were accessible to the priests, were produced the sermons that have come down to us in a large number, and a few of which, like those of Cyril of Túrov and Serapión, do not lack literary polish, and are not inferior to Western pulpit oratory of the same period. Whenever the preachers turned to praise the princes, as in the case of Ilarión who eulogised Vladímir, they had in mind only their orthodox Christianity, for religion was the all-absorbing question. Similarly, when Vladímir Monomákh wrote his *Instruction* to his children, he composed it according to the model given in Svyatosláv's *Collection*. Sermons and Instructions, from the introduction of Christianity to the middle of the eighteenth century, form one of the most important ingredients of Collections, and served as models for *Spiritual Testaments* even in the eighteenth century. Sylvester's *Domostróy* belongs to the same type, though what in Vladímir was the enthusiasm and earnestness of the new faith, has in this later document become a series of external observances. Formalism and adherence to the dead letter characterise the whole period of Russian unprogressiveness, and remained the characteristic of the Church at a much later time, in spite of the enlightened labours of a Feofán or Platón; and it was the same formalism that caused the schism of the raskólniks, who saw in Nikón's orthographical corrections of the corrupt Bible text an assault upon the orthodox religion.

Only a small proportion of the literature of ancient Russia was produced outside the ranks of the clergy. There were few literate persons who were not priests or monks; for there hardly existed any schools during this whole period, and even princes could not sign their names. The influence of the lettered priest was paramount, and if he was at all equal to the task of composing readable sermons, these were eagerly sought for by all who could read them. When, in the sixteenth, and still more in the seventeenth century, rays of light began to penetrate into Moscow, the chief and most dangerous task of instruction fell to the share of those preachers who had come in contact with Polish learning at Kíev; in the days of Peter the Great, Feofán Prokopóvich was an important factor in the civilisation of Russia, and in the beginning of the nineteenth century the sermons of Platón still form an integral part of literature.

To the student of comparative literature the semi-religious lore, which finds its expression in the apocrypha, is of vastly greater interest. The poetical creative activity of the people, combining with the knowledge of religious lore, has ever been active in producing spurious legendary accounts of matters biblical. The book of Enoch and the Talmud disseminated such legends in regard to the Old Testament long before the birth of Christianity. The Russian apocryphal literature is rich in legendary accounts of the creation of the world, the confession of Eve, the lives of Adam, Melchisedec, Abraham, Lot, Moses, Balaam, the twelve patriarchs, David, and particularly Solomon. Much more extensive is the store of legends from the New Testament. The birth of the Holy Virgin is dilated upon in the gospel of Jacob, the childhood of Christ is told in the gospel of Thomas, while a fuller story of Pilate's judgment of Christ and of Christ's descent into Hell is given in the old gospel of Nicodemus. Lazarus, Judas, and the twelve apostles have all their group of legends, but the Assumption of the Virgin Mary and the Judgment-day were the most popular. The list is far from being exhausted, and only a small part of the material has been scientifically investigated and located. Most of these stories travelled by the customary road over Bulgaria from Byzantium. As they have also reached the west of Europe, the investigator of their Western forms has to look into Byzantine sources; but as many of the legends have been preserved in the Slavic form, and when they have disappeared from the Greek, or as fuller redactions are to be met with in the North, he cannot well afford to overlook the Slavic sources. The *index librorum prohibitorum* of Russia, fashioned after the Greek, includes all such apocrypha as were current at the time of the composition of the first *index*. The clergy were continually preaching against them, yet their efforts were useless, especially since they themselves were at the same time drawing extensively on the apocryphal accounts of the *palæas*, lives of saints, etc.

There is this vast difference in the literature of this kind as it was current in Russia and in the West. Elsewhere the legends were early seized upon by the fancy of the poets, were clothed in the conventional garb of verse, remodelled, combined, beautified, until they became the stock in trade of literature, while the memory of the unadorned story had entirely faded from the popular consciousness. Dante's *Divine Comedy* is an illustration of how transformed the legends had become at a very early date. In Russia nothing of the kind has taken place. With the usual achronism of its literature, legends of the eleventh and eighteenth centuries live side by side, or mingle in the same version, and they have undergone no other change than corruption of misunderstood passages, transposition of motives, modernisation of language. The religious songs that a mendicant may be heard singing at the present time in front of a church are nothing but these old legends, almost in their primitive form.

Nearly allied to the apocryphal stories are the profane legends that form the subject-matter of so much of European medieval literature. The stories of Alexander the Great, the Trojan War, Digenis Akritas, Barlaam and Josaphat, Calilah-wa-Dimnah, are as common in Russian literature as in that of France or Germany. Byzantium is the immediate source of most of these legends both for the East and the West, but there are also many motives in the Russian stories that were derived from the West through Servia and Bulgaria. It is not yet quite clear how these stories came to travel in a direction opposite to the customary route of popular tales; no doubt the crusades did much to bring about an interchange of the oral literature of the nations. In the West, these stories have furnished the most beautiful subjects for medieval poetry, but as before, the Russian stories have not found their way into polite literature. They have either remained unchanged in their original form, or, being of a more popular character than the religious legends, have adapted themselves to the style of folktales, as which they have been preserved.

It is not unlikely that many of these tales were brought back from Palestine, the common camping-ground of the Christian nations during the crusades. Pilgrimages to the Holy Land began soon after the introduction of Christianity into Russia, and in the twelfth century we have the first account of such a journey, from the pen of the abbot Daniel. None of the later accounts of Palestine and Constantinople compare in interest with the simple narrative of Daniel the Palmer, after whose *Pilgrimage* they are fashioned and whose very words they often incorporated in their *Travels*. The purpose of all these was to serve as incitements to religious contemplation. There is but one account of a journey to the west of Europe. It was undertaken by the metropolitan Isidor who, in 1437, attended the Council of Florence. A few years later Afanási Nikítin described his journey to India, which was one of the earliest undertaken by Westerners in the same century; but while Vasco de Gama and Columbus were revolutionising the knowledge of geography, and were making the discovery of a route to India the object of mercantile development, Nikítin's report, important though it was, had absolutely no effect upon dormant Russia.

As there existed no external geography, so there was no external history. But fortunately for Russia, a long series of chronicles have saved historical events from oblivion. The earliest chronicle, that of Néstor, was the model for all that followed. Excepting the history of Kúrbski, who had come into contact with Western science through the Polish, and Krizhánich, who was not a Russian, there was no progress made in the chronological arrangement of historical facts from Néstor to Tatíshchev, while in style and dramatic diction there is a decided retrogression. The promise held out by the historian of the twelfth century was not made good for six hundred years. Néstor and Sylvester, the continuator, were of the clerical profession, and naturally the religious element, richly decked out with legend, folktale and reports of eye-witnesses, is the prevailing tone throughout the whole production. The Bible and the Byzantines, Hamartolos and John Malalas, serve as models for the fluent style of this production, but the vivid, dramatic narrative bears witness to considerable talent in the author. At first only the cities of Kíev, Nóvgorod and Súzdal, and Volhynia seem to have possessed such chronicles; but those that are preserved show traces of being composed of shorter accounts of other individual places. In the following centuries, most of the larger cities and monasteries kept chronological records of important events, and with the centralisation of Russia about Moscow there also appeared a species of Court chroniclers whose dry narration is often coloured in favour of the tsarate.

All this mass of literature is essentially ecclesiastic, and hardly any other could raise its head against the constant anathemas of the Church. No prohibition of the priests was strong enough to obliterate the craving for a popular literature, for no school, no science, was opposed to the superstition of the people, which therefore had full sway. The best the Church was able to do for the masses was to foster a "double faith," in which Christianity and paganism lived side by side. We shall see later how this state of affairs has been favourable to the preservation of an oral tradition up to the present time. Yet, but for the *Word of Ígor's Armament*, and its imitation, the *Zadónshchina*, no one could have suspected that the elements of a natural, unecclesiastic literature were present in ancient Russia.

This *Word of Ígor's Armament* is unique. It was composed at a time when Russia was already well Christianised, yet the references to Christianity are only sporadic, whereas the ancient pagan divinities and popular conceptions come in for a goodly share of attention. There are some who are inclined to see in this production a forgery, such as Hanka concocted for Bohemian literature, or Macpherson for Celtic, for the absence of any later works of the kind seems to be inexplicable. But this absence need not surprise us, for no such work could have been written at a later time outside the Church, which alone was in possession of a modicum of learning. It must be assumed that the bard of the *Word* represents the last of a bygone civilisation that had its firm footing in the people, but stood in a literary relation to the singers of the Norsemen; for there is much in the *Word* that reminds one of the Northern sagas. The tradition of the bard came to an end with this last production, but his manner, corrupted and twisted by a wrongly understood Christianity, lived on in the folksong of the people; hence the remarkable resemblance between the two.

But for the inertia of the Russian Church and people, it would not have been necessary to wait until a Peter the

Great violently shook the country into activity, for long before his time glimpses of European civilisation reached Moscow. In the fifteenth century, we have found metropolitan Isidor travelling to the Council of Florence, to cast his vote in favour of a union of the Churches under Rome. In the same century foreigners began to arrive in Moscow to practise medicine or architecture, or to serve in the Russian army; in the time of Iván the Terrible there was already a considerable foreign colony in Moscow, and its influences upon individual Russians were not rare. Iván the Terrible himself made several attempts to get skilled mechanics from the West, but his efforts were generally frustrated by Poland and the Germans of the Baltic provinces.

The most important points of contact with the West were in the Church itself, through Kíev and Western Russia. These outlying parts of Russia had early come into relation with Poland, and their unyielding orthodoxy had been mellowed by the prevailing scholasticism of the Polish theology. In the academy of Kíev, Greek and Latin grammar, theology and rhetoric were taught, while these sciences—especially grammar, even though it were Slavic grammar—were looked upon at Moscow as certain expressions of heresy. The correction of the corrupt church books, which in itself was advocated by priests who had imbibed the Kíev culture, made the presence of learned men—that is, of such as knew grammar enough to discover orthographical mistakes—an absolute necessity. In the reign of Alexis Mikháylovich, Kíev monks were called out for the purpose of establishing a school, and only in 1649 was the first of the kind opened. This innovation divided the churchmen into two camps,— those who advocated the Greek grammar, and those who advocated the Latin,—that is, those who would hear of nothing that distantly might remind them of the Latins, and those who were for a Western culture, even though it was to be only the scholastic learning already abandoned in he rest of Europe. The battle between the two was fought to the death. Those who were in favour of the Latin were generally worsted, and some of the most promising of them

were imprisoned and even capitally punished; but men like
Medvyédev, and later Simeón Pólotski, laid the foundation
for an advancement, however gradual, which culminated in
the reforms of Peter the Great.

Where a few individuals gained some semblance of Western culture, they could not write freely at home, and had to
develop their activities abroad. Kúrbski, who for a long
time stands alone as an historian, wrote his *History* in Poland, and it remained without any influence whatsoever at
home; its very existence was not known before our own
times. The same thing happened with Kotoshíkhin, whose
description of Russia was known to the learned of Sweden,
but the original of which was unknown until its accidental
discovery by a Russian scholar of the nineteenth century.
So, while the ferment of reform began much earlier than the
eighteenth century, it would have been indefinitely delayed,
causing many a bloody battle, if the Gordian knot had not
been cut by Peter the Great in favour of the West.

II.—THE FOLKLORE

In the Russian terminology, the *people* includes all the
elements of society that are not covered by the term *intelligence*. This latter is a comprehensive designation of all the
classes that have some education and can give intelligent
opinions on social, political and cultural themes. The vast
majority of the nation are the *people* in the narrower sense,
and it is essentially the characteristic of the democratic nineteenth century to regard the intellectual life of this people as
worthy of consideration. This is true of the world at large,
but, in Russia, preoccupation with the people, down to the
lowest strata of society, has become a dominating note in
literature. Whatever other causes may have been active in
creating this strong sentiment,—and they will be discussed
in a later chapter,—the strongest impulse to such a people-
worship was received from the unexpected and undreamt-of
wealth of that popular literature which has been unearthed
by the diligent labours of a few investigators.

In the eighteenth century, the term *people* had a wider significance. All those who did not belong to polite society, that is, all those who were not dignitaries or functionaries of a higher order, were the *people*, and at first the literati were included in that general appellation. Literature was entirely in the service of the higher classes, whom it was intended to amuse and eulogise; there was no other audience, and writers had to direct their attention to filling the demand, as hirelings of princes, and as pamperers of the pseudo-classic taste and Voltairism which held sway in refined society. Though frequently originating from the people, these writers dissevered all connection with it, for they had no longer any interests in common. With a few occasional exceptions, the people had no place in literature, and the inflated style that prevailed in prose and poetry was so far removed from the language of the people that the written literature could exert little influence upon the popular mind, and if there existed anything of a traditional nature among the lower classes, it was little, if at all, contaminated by literary influences. Whatever it had received from bygone ages was transmitted to the nineteenth century and collected just in time, before its certain disintegration.

This disregard for the enormous majority of the people was an inheritance of ancient Russia, before the reforms of Peter the Great. We have already seen with what unintelligent severity the Church persecuted every creation of a popular nature. As the nation consisted of the Church and the people, so, also, everything that was not directly of a Christian tendency was un-Christian and therefore tabooed. True Christianity could never take possession of the people that was not intelligent enough to discern what was religion and what not, and the result was that " double faith " in which, in spite of the persistent endeavours of the clergy, the old heathenism showed through the varnish of the new faith. The anathemas of the Church against " pagan rites," which included the singing of harmless songs, continue down to the eighteenth century.

In the general unprogressiveness of the whole country,

the agricultural classes, that constituted the bulk of the people, have remained unchanged for centuries. Russia was as much a country of raw products in the eighteenth century as in the twelfth, and barter and tribute in kind were common until a very late time. The life of the peasant has always moved in the same primitive conditions. Nothing whatsoever has been added to his physical and intellectual existence since the introduction of Christianity, and the latter itself did not much affect his spiritual life. He has remained essentially the same through the ages. The love of singing and story-telling that characterises him to-day has, no doubt, been his characteristic for centuries, and as the memory of the untutored man is much better than that of the lettered, he has been able to transmit orally to our own day the stock of his ancient songs and tales. The folklore of Russia, more than that of any Western nation, bridges over the chasm between the most distant antiquity and the present. It is an inheritance of the past, the more precious because it has been transmitted by an unsophisticated class, whereas in the West the people has come to a great extent under the influence of the literary caste.

When the folklore of Russia first became accessible to scholars, the adherents of the mythological theory of the origin of popular tales and songs, which had been enunciated by Grimm, set out at once to expound the epic songs and fairy tales as purely mythical symbols of a pre-Christian era. It was assumed that the songs and stories had come down to us in an almost unchanged text from the most remote antiquity, and that they were the representatives of a distinctly Russian conception. In the meantime, Benfey and his followers have pointed out that the fairy tales of Europe are traceable to their Indian home, whence they have wandered to the most remote regions, crossing and recrossing each other, and mingling in a variety of ways. Even the casual song that bears every appearance of native origin is frequently identical with similar songs in distant quarters; so, for example, Professor Child has brought together a vast number of similar motives from the whole world in his monumental work on the English and Scotch Ballads. Under the stress of these discoveries, the greater part of the mythological ballast had to be thrown overboard, and Russian folklore was brought into direct relations with the rest of the world.

It has been a rude disappointment to those who believed in an autochthonous development of the bylínas, to discover that they are often variations of similar accounts in foreign literatures; that, for example, the story of Sadkó the Merchant has been found to be identical with a French story; similarly, the ceremonial songs are not all of native growth. The study of comparative literature is of recent development, at least so far as Russian sources are concerned, and only a small part of the material has been properly located; but this much can even now be asserted,—that the folklore of Russia is much more intimately connected with that of Europe and Asia than is the written literature of the old period. Much of the apocryphal matter came through the South Slavic countries; many stories and songs must have wandered by way of Poland to White-Russia, and hence farther into the interior. Anciently there could have been an interchange of motives between Germany and Russia in the cities of Nóvgorod and Pskov, which stood in commercial relations with the towns of the Hansa, while earlier the Northern saga may have left some traces during the domination of the Norse. But one of the investigators, Stásov, and after him Potánin, have stoutly maintained that most of the stories of the Russian epic cycle came with the Tartars directly from Asia.

If we admit all possible borrowings from the West and the East, Russian folklore is still of unique interest to the student of literature on account of the evident traces of great antiquity which it has preserved. The same cause that kept the written literature of Russia at a low level and destroyed all appreciable chronology has been active in the traditional literature, and has saved it from violent transformations. It cannot be asserted that any one song has come down to us in its original shape. The change of the spoken language naturally affected the stories and songs, and many a word that has become obsolete has been superseded, or preserved in an unrecognisable form.   Contemporary facts of history have been introduced in the place of older ones, as when the heroes of the cycle of Vladímir are made to fight the Tartars. Motives have become mingled by superposition of related stories, or by accretion of foreign material.   But never has the people wilfully transformed, corrupted, added or taken away.   Though individuals continually produced new songs and stories, yet they moved in narrowly prescribed traditional limits, and the moment these passed to the people and became its common possession, they suffered only the accidental changes just spoken of.   The task of separating later and adventitious elements from the bulk of this literature has only begun, and when that is accomplished, the past of Russia will be reproduced much more clearly than that of other countries of Europe, because an achronous period separates the last two centuries from the tenth.

Only one epic, the *Word of Ígor's Armament*, has survived from antiquity.   That others existed, the bard assures us when he tells of princes, for a period of a whole century, whom Boyán, an older singer, had celebrated.   This precious relic is not only interesting for its intrinsic poetical merit, permitting us to guess the possibilities of the Russian untutored mind before the introduction of the repressive Byzantinism, but it serves as a guide in redating much of the oral literature of the present day.   In the bylínas, the ceremonial songs, the fairy tales, we continually come upon passages that are constructed in the same manner as in the *Word*, and the popular poetry of to-day and the writings of the whole old period contain many identical phrases and illustrations.

The epic songs, or bylínas, have been discovered in out-of-the-way places in the swampy region of the Government of Olónetsk.   It has puzzled all the investigators to explain why the memory of Vladímir and his heroes should have lived so long in these distant regions when every recollection of them has entirely disappeared in Kíev, the scene of all their deeds.   Throughout these epic songs there is evidence of their southern origin, yet nothing whatsoever is known of them in the south of Russia. Various explanations have been attempted, but the most wide-spread is that the Great-Russians of the south had been exterminated by the Tartars, and that the few who survived had taken refuge in the north, while the present inhabitants of the south have come from the south-east and represent a different tribe. There seems, however, to be a more plausible explanation. Considering that the *Word of Ígor's Armament* has not survived except in writing, and that there are no old epics living in the mouths of the people, except in inaccessible regions, it is natural to assume that no longer poem, nor a cycle of poems, which demanded a great amount of mental exertion and a special class of singers, could outlive the persecution of the Church, and that only where the people were separated from the rest of the world by impassable swamps and forests, and where, therefore, the influence of the Church was of necessity weakest, was it possible for the class of traditional bards to maintain itself.

There is ample evidence that these epics were based on historical events, and that they belong to the same category as the historical songs, of which a number have been recorded from the seventeenth century and later. The oldest are those that Richard James had written down in 1619; they were composed by some popular bard immediately after the incidents which they relate. Later historical songs deal with Peter the Great, while the song collections contain many others that range in time from Iván the Terrible to the nineteenth century. The manner of all these is identical, and strongly reminds us of the epic songs. From this it may be inferred that the bylínas were separate songs, composed by contemporary bards, and that their present condition is merely due to that series of corruptions to which all orally transmitted literature is subject.

In the *Word*, Germans, Venetians, Greeks and Moravians are made to sing the glory of Svyatosláv. This is certainly not a mere adornment of speech, but rests on the actual fact of a lively intercommunication between the East and the

West before the introduction of Christianity and in the first
century following it. Thus, the chief hero of the Vladímir
cycle, Ilyá of Múrom, was known to German song and the
Northern saga, where he is often mentioned. It has also
been found that many of the heroes are real personages
whose names are recorded in chronicles. Yet, though Vladímir is made the centre of the Kíev cycle, his heroes seem to
range over two or three centuries; from this we may conclude
that poetical activity continued for a long time, and that it
is only a later tradition that has grouped all the interesting
events around the famous Vladímir. Originally, there must
have been a number of cities of prominence around which
separate epics centred, but in time they were transferred to
the three great cities, Kíev, Nóvgorod and Moscow, where
the national life had its fullest development.

In the ceremonial songs, antiquity is even better preserved
than in the epics, and quite naturally. The epics arose on
special occasions, were adapted to transitory historical incidents, and only the most favourable conditions of seclusion
could save them from entire oblivion. Not so the ceremonial songs. These belonged to a heathen religion, contained a mythological element, and were part and parcel of
the people's belief and customs. The chief labour of the
Church consisted in battling against the survivals from
heathenism; but all it accomplished was to ensure an existence for the Christian tenets by the side of the traditional
customs. The pagan festivities were merged in the corresponding holidays of the Church, but the old games, rites
and songs went on as before. In time, the meaning of all
the customs connected with the seasons, marriage, death, was
forgotten, but the simple ditties were easily remembered,
though frequently transferred to other occasions. Had
there existed in the Russian Middle Ages any incitement to
the introduction of new songs, the old ones would have been
abandoned long ago; but city life was weakly represented
in the country, most of the towns hardly differing from
agricultural settlements, and the city song, which always
plays havoc with the country tunes, had little chance to

spread.   City life is of quite recent growth in Russia, and industrialism, which is only now developing under our very eyes, draws many forces away from the plough; when these return to the village, they bring with them the refrains of the modern opera, and degraded street ballads.   The same lowering of the popular poetry has been caused in the nineteenth century by the soldiers who have come in contact with the city.   The result of this is the complete disappearance of popular song from some districts, and its gradual dying out in others.   Should this tendency continue with any regularity, a new kind of folksong will result, but in the meanwhile there is produced an uninteresting chaos.

The freer form of the prose story and the fairy tale, which are bound by neither verse nor tune, makes them more subject to change than the ceremonial song.   Whatever their original meaning may have been, they have been preserved as mere stories to amuse.   Though they frequently deal with mythical beings who had some special meaning, they have all an equal value, and one tale is as good as another; consequently they easily combined with each other, and new elements were continually added to them.   The prose story is, therefore, less local and even less national: it travels far and wide, and may turn up in any corner of the globe. The Russian peasant is a good story - teller, witty and dramatic; hence he has added much local colouring to all the flotsam of fairyland, and the folktales of Russia have a distinct flavour of their own, and are relished even more than the popular tales of the West.   The absence of a book influence on these stories shows itself in simplicity of narration and lack of a moral; the latter is particularly the case in the animal tales, which, contrary to the usual stories of the kind, contain no explicit instruction.

In the nineteenth century, the popular element enters more and more into the literary productions, but a proper beginning has hardly been made in utilising the extremely rich store of Russian folklore.   When the Romantic spirit held sway over the West, Russia had not yet collected its songs and popular stories, and a Zhukóvski had to imitate

Western models, in order to make Romanticism accessible. Púshkin divined more correctly the value of the native stories, and made excellent use of the tales of his nurse. Otherwise, only sporadic use has been made of the folktale in literature. One of the best literary rifacimentos is the collection of all the stories told about the Fox, which Mozharóvski has brought together in one long, connected series.

III.—THE EIGHTEENTH CENTURY

The Court at Moscow had come into contact with foreign ideas ever since the days of Iván the Terrible. The "German Suburb," as the foreign colony was called, was itself a piece of the West, transplanted into the semi-barbarous capital, and foreigners of necessity occupied various posts in the Government. Germans, Greeks, and especially Englishmen were employed as ambassadors and foreign agents, and in the seventeenth century it was not rare to find Westerners as teachers of Russian youths. At the same time, clergymen from Kíev carried ever more and more the Polish scholasticism and rhetoric to the most orthodox city, and with it came the weak reflection of Western culture. Alexis Mikháylovich became fascinated by the theatre, and a German troupe and even English comedians played before the Tsar; among these early plays was a crude rifacimento of Marlowe's *Tamerlane*. Sophia went one step further, and had a Russian translation of Molière's *Médecin malgré lui* performed in her apartments. Even poetry of an European type had made its appearance before Kantemír, though only in the mediocre syllabic versification of a Karión Istómin and a Simeón Pólotski. Yet the progress was very slow, and the historian of Peter's time, Tatíshchev, had figured out that at the rate at which it was proceeding, it would take Russia seven generations, or more than two hundred years, to be equal in civilisation to the rest of Europe.

Then Peter appeared. He found around him weak tendencies to reform, but hardly any men to help him carry them out, and no institutions of any kind on which to engraft the new knowledge he had brought with him from Holland and Germany. There was no native scientific literature whatsoever; there were no terms in which to express the truths which he and his disciples had learned; there was no established language even for educated people. Peter united in his person the extreme of practical sense with the idealism of youth; while bent on introducing mechanical sciences for the advancement of his country, he at the same time carried on a correspondence with the philosopher Leibniz, and favoured the introduction of every branch of literature. With an indomitable will he wanted to merge savage Russia into the liberal West, and he frequently used savage means to attain his end.

Peter's idea of conviviality consisted in getting drunk in a room filled with tobacco smoke, as he had known it in the taverns of Holland, and the whole aspect of literature of his period is that of a crude democracy, such as he advocated in his own circle. In whatever he or his followers wrote there is a tone of rough simplicity, practical liberalism, and the ardour of manful youth. Everything that could be useful to the State and nation received his equal attention. He familiarised his people with the German and Dutch jurists, who were translated under his care, and with text-books on the most necessary sciences and arts; he corresponded with German, French and English scholars on the subject of establishing universities and academies; he invited actors from Slavic Austria to play in his theatre; and superintended the translation of Ovid, of encyclopedias, and of romances. In this burning activity there could be no such a thing as a literary school; everything was welcome, provided it advanced his cherished reforms.

There was no time to waste on the mere externals of language. The authors of the day had to grope their way as best they could. Some interlarded their style with hybrid words from all the tongues of Europe; others wavered between a purely Slavic and a more or less Russianised language, and Peter the Great, though he was fond of a display of Dutch words, could use a very idiomatic style. While

Stefán Yavórski and Feofán Prokopóvich charmed their congregations with elegant sermons in which Byzantine rhetoric and Western eloquence had the fullest sway, Tatíshchev laboured to find the proper expressions for the historical truths which he had well learned in the West, and the peasant Pososhkóv dimly guessed the economic problems that presented themselves to the country, vainly trying to clothe them in an intelligible language.

Peter did not live to see the fruition of his endeavours in literature. The time was too short to produce any good writers, and though *belles-lettres* were encouraged, the whole attention of the best minds was absorbed in the acquisition of the most-needed information. Knowledge was the watchword of Peter's time, and the desire for knowledge was so great that even later Lomonósov and Tredyakóvski thought no hardships too great, to gain the coveted instruction. It is characteristic of the times, that these two poets in the new style walked to Moscow to enter school, one from the extreme north, the other from the extreme south. A mighty task fell to the lot of the generation that had been born in the days of the great Tsar. They had to transfer the whole European culture to Russian soil and to discover a means of expressing it. Kantemír, whose education was of an European type, chose the ready model of French verse in which to write his satires, wrestling to say in Russian what he thought out in French. Tredyakóvski discovered the proper versification for his native tongue, but his diligence and good sense did not make up for his barren poetical talent. Sumarókov, single-handed, created the drama, while Lomonósov fostered the ode, settled grammar and created Russian science.

The intermediate period between the death of Peter the Great and the accession of Catherine II. was not one that would in itself have encouraged people to take to literature, which was looked down upon as the handmaid of the mighty, if the writers had not inherited an insatiable love of knowledge. The rough and sincere manner of the Tsar had given way to a flimsy imitation of the Court at Versailles. With the introduction of Western civilisation, the Empresses Anna and Elizabeth took over only the mere external appearance, the love of pleasure, a luxury that was incompatible with their rude surroundings. Literary men had no public to write for, except the degraded courtiers who might flatter themselves that they were the Mæcenases of that literature for which, in their hearts, they cared very little. Odes by which one might gain a favour, solemn addresses written to order, tragedies to be furnished by such and such a date, epigrams of a flippant turn,—these were the verses that the courtiers wanted, and they were furnished in sufficient quantity. Though Lomonósov was more intimately acquainted with Günther than with Boileau, yet he, like his contemporaries, found himself compelled to favour the introduction of the French pseudo-classic style, which was the only one that high society knew anything about. From chaos and no literature at all, Russia was of necessity forced to cultivate the unnatural imitation of what was supposed to be classic antiquity, before it knew anything about that antiquity, and before it had tried itself in simpler fields. The literature of that period was consequently unreal, stilted, distant.

This pseudo-classicism continued to flourish to the end of the century, though a new spirit had taken possession of men's minds in the reign of Catherine. This Empress had educated herself in the school of the great philosophers who, in the second half of the eighteenth century, were the dominating spirits in European literature. She corresponded with Voltaire, had not only studied Montesquieu, but embodied his *Esprit des Lois* in her famous instruction for a new code of laws, invited d'Alembert to be her son's tutor,—in short, she was in sympathy with the humanitarian movements of the encyclopedists. She planned reforms on a magnificent scale,—though but few of them were executed, as her theories were only academic and had little reference to existing conditions. Though she planned, with the help of Diderot, a complicated educational system, yet there were no more schools at the end of her reign than at the beginning,

and the freedom of the press was curtailed much more
in the second half of her rule than in the first. So long as
there were no disturbing elements at home, and things went
to her liking, she was pleased to favour the liberalism which
had spread over Europe, and had found its advocates at
other Courts. Her idealism was of a purely intellectual
character, and her humanitarian views as she had expressed
them in her *Instruction* were good and harmless so long as
they remained on paper. The moment she was disturbed in
her philanthropy by the rebellion of Pugachév at home, and
when, later, she was still more startled by the events of the
French Revolution, which it became the fashion to ascribe
to the philosophy of Voltaire, she recanted her liberalism,
and tried to crush all intellectual progress that had grown
strong in the earlier part of her reign. The best authors
were ruthlessly persecuted: Radíshchev was banished to
Siberia for his advocating the very theories which she had
propounded in her *Instruction ;* Nóvikov's philanthropic
activity was sufficient cause for his imprisonment, and it
was fortunate for Knyazhnín that he was dead when his
Vadím of Nóvgorod made its appearance.

Yet, Russian literature owes much to Catherine, who, at
least in the first part of her enlightened absolutism, encouraged a healthy development of Letters, often through her
own example. Her own writings familiarised her people
with the best thought of Europe, and as before her Racine
and Boileau, so now Voltaire, Beccaria, Montesquieu, were
upon the lips of all. Literature had begun in imitations of
foreign models, and hardly a trace of anything original is to
be found in the eighteenth century; but even a superficial
Voltairism was preferable to the more distant pseudo-classicism of the preceding reigns, for, though most of its human-
itarianism was spurious and its culture skin-deep, it led a
few more gifted individuals to a clearer perception of actual-
ities, to a fuller interest in that which was immediate and
around them, and, in the end, to true culture.

The most promising influence on Russian literature was
the one which Addison and the English satirical journals

began to exert on Catherine and on nearly all the writers of the day. The *Spectator*, the *Guardian*, and the *Tatler* had found a host of imitators in continental Europe, and satirical journals sprang up in astonishing abundance. It is not likely that Catherine became acquainted with the English originals. Her knowledge came rather through German and French translations; and the many passages from these English journals that found their way into Russia after the fifties were likewise generally derived at second hand. In any case, Addison and the satirical journals took deep root in Russian soil, and a long series of similar productions, from 1769 to 1774, had a very salutary effect on the drama and on those writings in which contemporary manners are held up to the scorn and ridicule of the people. Catherine herself, the founder of the first of these journals, had only the intention of practising this kind of literature for purposes of good-natured banter, and she was rather shocked when she discovered that her example had given Nóvikov and his adherents a weapon for attacking all the negative sides of contemporary civilisation. Without having wished it, Catherine gave into the hands of the disaffected a means of concentrating themselves around a name, a standard,—and public opinion became a factor in literature.

Patronage of the mighty was as much a goal towards which authors aimed in the days of Catherine as in the previous half-century, and the Empress regarded it as her privilege and duty to draw literary talent to the Court, by giving them government positions and lavish gifts. Derzhávin, Fon-Vízin, Bogdanóvich, Kostróv, Petróv, all were attracted to her as the central luminary. *Felítsa* was the keynote of what Derzhávin purported to be a new departure in the writing of odes, but it was in reality an old laudatory theme with an application of fashionable liberalism, and *Felítsa* remained the watchword of a generation of poets that gyrated around the throne. At the same time, Catherine made a seeming appeal to public opinion by her comedies and satires. If Nóvikov took her in earnest, and responded to her invitation by making a stand against her lukewarm satire by a systematic arraignment of vice in every form, he soon found it necessary in his next literary venture, the *Painter*, to appease her suspicion and anger by a fulsome praise of the Empress. Underneath this outward dependence upon the Court's opinion, literary coteries were, however, beginning to come into existence, and the dramas of the day received their impulse from their writings, and in their turn were beginning to look to others than the Court for their approval.

These coteries were concentrated around the Masonic lodges, where, under the pledge of secrecy, an exchange of ideas could take place, and which, consequently, Catherine hated more and more. This Freemasonry was in itself under English influence, whence were taken the ceremonial and the organisation. It is said that Freemasonry first made its appearance in Russia under Peter the Great; later it came also under German influence, had its wide-spread connections in Europe, and, under the guise of mysterious practices, discussed the means of spreading popular education, doing unstinted charity, and ensuring freedom of thought. In the uncertain and superficial state of culture which then prevailed in Russia, much that these men did was unreal and irrelevant: they lost themselves in the mystical speculations of the Martinists and the Rosicrucians, and wasted their time in an unprofitable symbolism. But it is sufficient to read the biography of a Nóvikov to perceive that their efforts for the advancement of science and useful knowledge were more real than those of the cultivated and more materialistic Catherine. If Catherine had made the press free, she also persecuted those who had availed themselves of the privilege against her pleasure; if her mouth spoke fine sentiments, her heart was closed against their realisation. But Nóvikov, in the silence of his mysticism, made Russia's past accessible to the scholar, founded the book trade, and took a practical interest in the common people by giving them useful books to read. This Nóvikov, and the unfortunate Radíshchev, whose book is even now prohibited in Russia, and Shcherbátov, who preferred the rough old times to the flighty

manners of the day,—that is, the writers who were at outs
with existing conditions,—were the carriers of a new spirit
which, though not characteristically Russian, was akin to it
in that it devoted itself with ardour to the treatment of
burning questions from a native standpoint. Two of these
writers, Shcherbátov and Nóvikov, were Slavophiles in the
best sense of the word.

We shall now make the balance-sheet of the eighteenth-
century literature in the separate departments, and see what
residuum it bequeathed to the nineteenth century.

In the scholastic style of the Middle Ages it became a
settled practice to dedicate books to powerful persons, and
to address them with eulogies on all solemn occasions. Polish influence had made this kind of poetry popular at Kíev,
and Simeón Pólotski introduced it in Moscow in time to sing
the glory of the new-born Peter. Lomonósov's activity
began with an ode, and Tredyakóvski, Sumarókov, Petróv
and a host of minor poets, if that name can be applied to
writers of soulless rhymed adulation, proceeded in the beaten
track of "ecstatic" poetry, until Dmítriev gave it the death-
blow by his *What Others Say*. The only positive value lay
in the odes of Lomonósov in which he described phenomena
of nature, and those of Derzhávin, who, following his example, made similar use of them as, for example, in his *Ode
to the Deity*. His *Felítsa*, which marked the disintegration
of the "ecstatic ode," left its effect in the lighter epistolary
poetry of his contemporaries, like Kostróv, and may even be
traced in the playful productions of the next generation.

The epic is akin to the ode, in that it is a kind of rapturous
eulogy on some momentous event in history. In the mad
intoxication with foreign pseudo-classic ideals there could be
no place for a proper understanding of native history; hence
the flatulent epics of Kheráskov, admired though they were,
could be of no lasting merit. The other epics dealt with
foreign subjects. Tredyakóvski's *Telemachiad* could only
amuse as a piece of poetical ineptitude, and a pleasure-loving
public of the times of Catherine II. was more inclined to go
into raptures over Apuleius's *Golden Ass* which, having

passed through a French transformation, appeared as a
species of mock-heroic in Bogdanóvich's *Psyche*. Púshkin
still took delight in it, and his earlier productions of this
kind have something of Bogdanóvich's manner. Máykov's
Elíséy, which is really superior to the *Psyche*, was not so well
received because he introduced too freely the popular element, for which at that time there could be no appreciation.

Lyrics (in the narrower sense of poems expressing the individual emotion of the writer) can have a place only where
the conditions are favourable to the formation of individual
feelings, where well-defined conceptions of nature and man
are common to a certain class of society or to the whole
nation. Nothing of the kind could exist in Russia throughout the greater part of the eighteenth century, when everything was only external veneer, and no lyrics made their
appearance until the last quarter, when, under the influence
of a thorough acquaintance with Horace and the French
lyricists, some fine verses were produced by Bogdanóvich,
Kapníst, Derzhávin, Dmítriev, Neledínski-Melétski. Most
of these poems only appeared in the nineteenth century, and
all belong to that intermediate stage of literature which was
represented by Karamzín and Dmítriev and which, in spirit,
no longer continues the tradition of the days of Catherine.

Krylóv's fables are justly celebrated as among the best
literature that Russia evolved in the last century; but they
are only the culmination of a series of fables, most of them
adaptations from La Fontaine and Gellert, in which nearly
all the poets tried their skill. By 1700, there had been current in Russia three translations of Esop's *Fables*, and
Pólotski had imitated a number of such as he knew. Here
again we see the utter inability of the writers of the eighteenth century to make use of a popular motive. Nothing
is more common in the oral literature of the people than
fables, especially animal fables, yet they had to borrow their
themes from abroad. Sumarókov's fables make, with rare
exceptions, unprofitable reading; Máykov struck a few times
a proper note, and Khémnitser alone, though he followed
Gellert closely, is still read with pleasure on account of the

simplicity of his tales.   Dmítriev, as before, belongs to another period.

Modern Russian poetry practically begins with the satires of Kantemír, and satires, with their adjunct, comedy, have remained down to our day the most prominent part of *belles-lettres;* only, whereas their usual purpose is to provoke laughter, in Russia tears are their more appropriate due. Under the systematic, though arbitrary and capricious, persecution of the censorship, writers have evolved the art of telling a bitter truth by means of satire which by its outward appearance generally escapes the scrutinising attention of the usually dull censor, but the esoteric meaning of which is quite comprehensible to the whole class of readers.   In the days of Peter the Great, with his violent reforms, direct command was more effective than a satire which but few could unravel, and Kantemír's *Satires*, in spite of their literary value, are mere exotics.   Catherine thought this species of essays a good medium for a gentle reproof, but Nóvikov more correctly divined their office, and much later Gógol and Shchedrín brought them to great perfection along the path indicated by him.

The same causes which prevented the formation of a Russian epic and of lyric poetry throughout the greater part of the eighteenth century militated against the evolution of a native tragedy.   Theatrical performances had been given ever since the days of Alexis, but these were mainly Mysteries and Moralities that had long been forgotten in the West, or crude plays and harlequinades by German, Italian and English travelling comedians.   Thus, a taste had been formed for the drama when Sumarókov was ordered to organise the first Russian theatre, though there did not exist the elements for a native stage.   Sumarókov furnished pseudo-classic tragedies as readily as he manufactured any other kind of poetry, and his conceit of being the Russian Racine indicates whence he took his models.   Neither Knyazhnín's nor Ózerov's borrowing of incidents from Russian history could make their tragedies real: they were accessible only to those who were steeped in French culture.   Not so comedy. Comedy stands in direct relation to satire, and it has taken firm root in Russian soil. Catherine herself wrote a number of dramatised satires, and Fon-Vízin's *Brigadier* made its appearance just as satire began to occupy an important place in the public eye. Fon-Vízin, Griboyédov and Gógol are only the greatest of the long series of dramatists, who in the eighteenth and nineteenth centuries used comedy as a weapon for attacking the corruption of officials, superficiality in education and the brutality of the serf-owners. Here was an opportunity to introduce a native element, which becomes for the first time prominent in Ablesímov's comic opera.

Though Western novels reached Russia in indifferent translations long before the end of Catherine's reign, yet there was no proper soil for them until Radíshchev came under the influence of the English writers, especially of Sterne, and Karamzín, on the verge of the century, introduced sentimentalism into literature. Throughout the whole eighteenth century, little earnestness was shown in literary pursuits. Prose suffered more than poetry, for prose demands a more assiduous and constant attention than verse. It was left for the nineteenth century to settle the prose diction appropriate to the Russian language. In this neglect of cultivating an elegant prose style is to be found the main reason for a very extensive literature of memoirs which were not originally meant for publication, but were intended as mere records for the use of posterity. The restriction of free speech was another powerful factor in encouraging this species of historical revelation. In these memoirs, the student of manners and history and literature will find much better material for a correct appreciation of the eighteenth century than in the exotic literature of the upper classes. The emptiness of the superficial French culture, which was prevalent in Russia, became apparent only to those who, like Tatíshchev, Shcherbátov, and Nóvikov, busied themselves with the study of native history. The progress which history made from Tatíshchev to Karamzín is the most prominent feature in the evolution of the native literature. By the historians was laid the real foundation for a native science and interest in the people. It was quite natural for these men to turn away from the disheartening corruption of manners which was introduced from abroad, and to find inspiration in their own past. They, consequently, were the first Slavophiles, though as yet in the gentler sense of the word. They did not preach a turning away from European culture, as did their later spiritual descendants, but a more organic welding of the new life with the Russian reality.

THE OLDEST PERIOD

THE OLDEST PERIOD

Treaty with the Greeks (911)

Néstor's Chronicle contains three treaties made with the Greeks in the tenth century. It is evident, from the manner of their composition, that the chronicler quoted some extant documents which were probably translated by some Bulgarian from the original Greek. These treaties are interesting as being the earliest specimens of writing in Russia and as having been composed before the introduction of Christianity.

WE of the Russian nation, Karly, Inegeld, Farlof, Veremud, Rulav, Gudy, Ruald, Karn, Frelav, Ryuar, Aktevu, Truan, Lidulfost, Stemid, who were sent by Olég, the Russian Grand Prince, and the illustrious boyárs who are under his rule, to you, Leo and Alexander and Constantine, the Greek Emperors and great autocrats by the grace of God, to confirm and proclaim the amity which has existed for many years between the Christians and Russians, by the will of our princes and by the order of all those in Russia who are under his rule. Our illustrious Prince has often thought, more persistently than the others who have desired to maintain and proclaim the amity in God which has been between Christians and Russia, that not only with mere words, but also in writing and with a solemn oath made over our armour, ought such amity be proclaimed and confirmed, according to our faith and law. The following are the articles that we wish to establish in the faith of God and in love:

In the first place, we will make an agreement with you Greeks to love each other with our souls and as much as is in our power, and we will not permit, as far as is in our power, that harm or damage be done to any of you by those who are under the rule of our illustrious princes, but we will try, according to our ability, to preserve for ever and ever, unbroken and undisturbed, the amity which we profess both in words and in writing under oath. Likewise you Greeks shall preserve the same love to our illustrious Russian princes and to all who are under the rule of our illustrious Prince unpolluted and unchanged for ever and all time.

Under the head which is called damages we will agree as follows: Whatever may be made manifest in regard to a grievance, let the information of such grievance be accurate, and let not him be believed who begins the action; and let not that party take an oath if he deserve no belief; but if one swear according to his religion, let there be a punishment if perjury be found.

If a Russian kill a Christian, or a Christian a Russian, let him die where the murder has been committed. If he who has committed murder run away, then if he be possessed of property, let the nearest in kin to the murdered person receive that part which is his by law, and let the wife of the murderer have as much as belongs to her by law. If he who has committed the murder be destitute and have run away, let the case stand against him until he be found, and then he shall die.

If anyone strike another with a sword or beat him with a drinking vessel, let him for such striking or beating pay five litras of silver according to the Russian law. If the offender be destitute, let him pay as much as he can, and let him take off his upper garment which he wears, and besides let him swear according to his religion that there is no one to help him, and let the case against him forthwith be dropped.

If a Russian steal something from a Christian, or a Christian from a Russian, and the thief at the time when he commits the theft be caught by him who has lost the article, and the thief struggle and be killed, let not his death be avenged by either Christians or Russians, but let him who has lost take back what belongs to him. If a Russian despoil a Christian, or a Christian a Russian, by torture or by a show of force, or if he take anything away from a member of the druzhína, let him pay back threefold.

If a boat be cast by a great wind upon a strange shore, where there be any of our Russians, and someone come to furnish the boat with its belongings, we will take the boat through all dangerous places until it has smooth sailing. If such a boat cannot be returned to its place, on account of storm or impassable places, we Russians shall see the oarsmen off safe with their goods, if the accident happens near Greek land. But if the same happen near Russian land, we will take the boat to Russian territory, and let them sell the belongings of the boat and what else of the boat they can sell, and when we Russians shall go to Greece, with merchandise or with an embassy to your Emperor, the proceeds from the sale of the belongings of the boat shall be forwarded without hindrance. Should any man of the boat be killed, or beaten, by us Russians, or should anything be taken away, the wrongdoers shall be punished as above.

Should a Russian slave be stolen, or run away, or be sold by force, and a Russian make complaint of it, and the fact be ascertained in regard to the slave, then let him be returned to Russia. And if the merchants should lose a slave and make complaint thereof, let them search for him and let him be returned; should anyone prevent making such a search, then the local magistrate shall be responsible for him.

If a criminal should return to Greece from Russia, let Russia institute a complaint to the Christian Empire, and let the same be returned to Russia, even against his will.

All these things the Russians are to do to the Greeks, wherever such things may happen. To make the peace established between the Christians and Russians firm and lasting, we ordered this document to be written by John upon two charts and to be signed by the Emperor's and our own hand before the blessed cross and in the name of the holy Trinity and our one, true God, and to be proclaimed and to be delivered to our ambassadors. And we have sworn to your Emperor according to the law and custom of our nation, as being God's own creatures, not to depart, or let anyone else of our land depart, from the established treaty of peace and amity. This document we gave to your Empire in order to confirm the treaty on both sides and to confirm and proclaim the peace in your country, September the second, the fifteenth week, in the year from the creation of the world 6024 (911).

Luká Zhidyáta. (First half of XI. century.)

Luká Zhidyáta or Zhiryáta, was bishop of Nóvgorod from 1036–1060. All we have from him is his *Instruction*, which is written in a coarse, unadorned style, and is nothing more than a sententious statement of gospel teachings. The Nóvgorod style, as it appears in its chronicles, is always laconic and businesslike. Zhidyáta was evidently instructing a congregation that had not long been converted and that was not yet firm in the fundamental teachings of Christianity.

INSTRUCTION TO HIS CONGREGATION

Above all, brothers, we Christians must keep the command to believe in one God who is worshipped in the Trinity, in the Father, the Son, and the Holy Ghost, as the holy apostles have taught, and the holy fathers have confirmed. I believe in one God, and so forth. Believe also in the resurrection, and the eternal life, and the everlasting torment of the sinful. Be not slow in going to church, and to the morning, noon and evening masses. When you are about to lie down in your room, make your obeisance to God. Stand in church in the fear of the Lord, speak not, nor think of worldly matters, but pray to God with all your thought that He may forgive you your sins. Live in friendship with all men, but particularly with your brothers, and let there not be one thing in your hearts, and another upon your lips. Dig not a grave under your brother, lest God throw you into a worse one. Be righteous, and flinch not from laying down your head for the sake of truth and God's Law, that God may count you among the saints. Be patient with your brothers and with other men, and do not repay evil for evil; praise each other that God may praise you.

Cause no strife that you may not be called a son of the devil, but make peace that you may be a son of God. Judge your brother neither in speech, nor in thought, but think of your own sins, that God may not judge you. Be thoughtful and merciful to strangers, to the poor and to prisoners, and be merciful to your servants. It is not proper for you, O brothers, to have devilish games, nor to speak unseemly words. Be not angry, and rail not at anyone; in danger be patient and rely upon God. Rave not, be not haughty; remember that to-morrow we shall be stench and worms. Be humble and gentle, and obediently do the commands of God, for in the heart of the proud sits the devil, and the word of God will not stick to him. Honour old people and your parents. Swear not in the name of God, nor curse anyone else, nor swear by him. Judge rightly, receive no reward, give not in usury. Fear God, honour the Prince; first serve the Lord, then your master. With all your heart honour the priest of God, and honour the servants of the Church. Kill not, steal not, lie not, bear not false witness, hate not, envy not, calumniate not . . ., drink not out of season to intoxication, but in measure. Be not angry, nor harsh. Rejoice with those who rejoice, and be sad with the sad. Do not eat abominations; celebrate the holy days. The peace of the Lord be with you. Amen!

The Russian Code. (XI. century.)

The first draught of the *Russian Code*, or the *Rússkaya Právda*, as it is called in Russian, is ascribed to Yarosláv the Wise, the son of Vladímir, Grand Prince of Kíev. He is supposed to have given it to the Nóvgorodians, whose Prince he had been, for their active participation in the war that he waged against Svyatopólk in order to maintain himself on the Kíev throne. This Code is the oldest extant among all the Slavs. It was evidently borrowed from the laws of the Scandinavians, and in most points almost coincides with the old English laws of the same period. This is not surprising, for the druzhína was originally composed of Norsemen ; besides, Yarosláv stood in direct communication with the west of Europe : thus, one of his daughters was married to Harald of Norway ; another was the wife of Andrew, King of Hungary; a third was married to Henry of France ; and two of his sons had taken German princesses for wives.

If a man[1] kill a man, let him be avenged by his brother, or father, or son, or nephew. If there is no one to avenge him, let the price on his head be 70 grívnas,[2] if he be a prince's man, or a prince's thane's[3] man. If he be a Russ,[4] or henchman, or merchant, or a boyár's thane, or swordsman,[5] or hapless man,[6] or Slovene,[7] let the price on his head be 40 grívnas. After Yaroslár, his sons Izyaslár, Svyatoslár, Vsévolod, and their men Kusnyáchko, Perenyég, and Nikifór, came together and did away with the blood revenge, but substituted weregild for it, but in everything else his sons left as Yaroslár had decreed.

If one strike another with the unsheathed sword, or with the haft, the prince's fine[8] for the offence is 12 grívnas. If one strike another with a rod, or cup, or horn, or the blunt edge of a sword, also 12 grívnas; but if the offence be committed in warding off a sword blow, he shall not be fined. If one strike a man's hand, and the hand fall off, or dry up, or if he cut off a foot, or eye, or nose, the fine is 20 grívnas, and 10 grívnas to the maimed man. If one cut off another man's finger, 3 grívnas fine, and to the maimed man one grívna of kúnas.

If a bloodstained or bruised man comes to the court, he

---

[1] That is, an older member of the prince's druzhína, also called *boyárs;* the younger members were called *hrid, i. e.,* Norse "hirðr," henchman, or youth, or simply *druzhína.*

[2] A *grívna* was originally a unit of weight, about a pound, then only half a pound, and less. About seven *grívnas* of *kúnas* were equal to one *grívna* of silver; a *kúna* means "marten's skin," which formed the smaller denomination of money; one *grívna* was equal to twenty *nogátas.*

[3] The Russian is *tiún,* which is the Norse *tjonn;* the Old English *thane* is of the same origin and has almost the same significance.

[4] A Russ was a Scandinavian who did not bear arms; a Scandinavian who bore arms was a Varyág.

[5] The prince's guardsman and inspector of the sword trial.

[6] A "hapless man" was more particularly applied to a son of a priest who could not read, a freedman, an indebted merchant, all Russians at the death of a prince.

[7] Inhabitants of Nóvgorod.

[8] The fine was paid to the prince's treasury.

need not bring any witnesses, but the fine shall be 4 grívnas; but if he have no marks upon him, let him bring a witness. If both parties complain, let him who has begun pay 6 kúnas. If the bloodstained man be he who has begun the quarrel, and there are witnesses to the quarrel, let his bruises be his reward.[1] If one strike another with the sword, but kill him not, the fine is 3 grívnas, and to the sufferer a grívna for his wound for medicaments; if he kill him, there is the usual weregild. If a man pushes another, either to him, or from him, or strikes him in his face, or beats him with a rod, and there are two witnesses, the fine is 3 grívnas.

If one mounts another man's horse, without having asked permission, the fine is 3 grívnas. If one loses his horse, or arms, or wearing apparel, and announces his loss in the market-place, and later recognises his property in his town, he may take it back, and the fine of 3 grívnas is paid to him. If one recognises what he has lost, or has been stolen from him, either a horse, or apparel, or cattle, let him not say: "This is mine!" but let him go before the judge who will ask: "Where did you get that?" and the fine will be on him who is guilty; and then he will take that which belongs to him, and the fine shall be likewise paid to him. If it be a horse-thief, let him be turned over to the prince for banishment; if it be a shop-thief, his fine shall be 3 grívnas.

If one gives money on interest, or money as a loan, or grain, let him have witnesses, and then receive as has been agreed.

If a hired servant runs away from his master, he becomes a slave; but if he goes to collect his money, and does so openly, or runs to the prince or the judges on account of injury done him by his master, he is not enslaved, but gets his right.

If a master has a farm servant, and his war horse be lost, the servant shall not pay for it; but if his master gives him, who receives his measure of grain, a plough and harrow, he

---

[1] That is, if the bruised man make complaint, and it be found that he had started the quarrel, he receives no monetary reward for his bruises, but has justly been punished by his wounds.

shall pay for any damage to them.   But if the master sends him on his own business, and they be damaged while he is away, he shall not pay for them.

If a free peasant assault another without the prince's permission, the fine is 3 grívnas to the prince, and one grívna of kúnas for the wounds.   If he assault a prince's or boyár's man, the fine is 12 grívnas, and a grívna for the wounds.   If one steal a boat, the fine is 6 kúnas, and the boat is to be returned; for a seafaring boat, 3 grívnas, and for a warboat, 2 grívnas; for a smack, 8 kúnas, and for a barge, a grívna.

If ropes be cut in somebody's hunting-ground, the fine shall be 3 grívnas, and a grívna of kúnas for the ropes.   If one steal in the hunting-ground a falcon, or hawk, the fine is 3 grívnas, and to the owner one grívna; for a dove–9 kúnas, for a chicken–9 kúnas, for a duck–20 kúnas, for a goose–20 kúnas, for a swan–20 kúnas, and for a crane–20 kúnas.   And if hay or timber be stolen–9 kúnas, and the owner receives 2 nogátas for each waggonload stolen.

In one puts fire to a barn, he is to be banished and his house confiscated; first the damage is to be made good, and then the prince shall banish him.   The same, if he put fire to a house.   And who maliciously injures a horse or beast, the fine is 12 grívnas, and for the damage one grívna.

Ilarión, Metropolitan of Kíev.   (XI. century.)

Hilarion (in Russian Ilarión) was made metropolitan of Kíev in 1050.   An extant sermon, to which is added the *Eulogy on St. Vladímir* and *Exposition of Faith*, witnesses to his acquaintance with classical Greek, and is one of the best examples of ancient Russian pulpit eloquence.

EULOGY ON ST. VLADÍMIR

Rome sings the praises of Peter and Paul, through whom it believes in Jesus Christ, the Son of God; Asia, Ephesus and Patmos praise John the Theologue; India, Thomas; Egypt, Mark.   All countries and cities and men honour and glorify their teacher who has taught them the orthodox faith.   Let us also, according to our power, praise with humble praises our teacher and instructor, who has done great and wondrous things, the great Khan of our land, Vladímir, the grandson of old Ígor, the son of the glorious Svyatosláv, who ruling their days in courage and valour have become famous in many lands, and are remembered and honoured even now for their victories and power, for they did not rule in a poor and unknown country, but in Russia, which is known and celebrated in all the corners of the earth.

A good testimony to your piety, O blissful one, is that holy church of St. Mary, the Mother of God, which you have builded on an orthodox foundation, and where your valiant body now resteth, awaiting the archangel's trumpets. A very good and fine testimony is also your son George whom God has made an heir to your power, who does not destroy your institutions, but confirms them; who does not diminish the benefactions of your piety, but increases them; who does not spoil but mend, who finishes what you have left unfinished, as Solomon has completed the works of David; who has builded a large and holy God's temple to His Allwisdom, to sanctify your city; who has embellished it with all beautiful things, with gold and silver and precious stones and sacred vessels, so that the church is a wonder to all surrounding lands, and so that no like can be found in all the north, from east to west; who has surrounded your famous city of Kíev with grandeur as with a crown; who has turned over your people and city to the holy, all-glorious Mother of God; who is ever ready to succour Christians, and for whom he has builded a church with golden doors in the name of the first holiday of the Lord of the Holy Annunciation, so that the kiss which the archangel will give to the Virgin may also be on this city. To Her he says: "Rejoice, blissful one, the Lord is with you!" but to the city: "Rejoice, faithful city, the Lord is with you!"

Arise, honoured dead, from your grave! Arise, shake off your sleep, for you are not dead, but sleep to the day of the common resurrection. Arise! You are not dead, for it is not right for you to die, who have believed in Christ who

is the life of the whole world.   Shake off your sleep, lift your
eyes, that you may see with what honours the Lord has
showered you above, and how you live unforgotten upon
earth through your son!   Arise!   Look at your son George,
see your entrails, your beloved one, see him whom God has
brought out of your loins, see him adorning the throne of
your land, and rejoice, and be glad!   Then also see your
pious daughter-in-law Iréna, see your grandchildren, and
great-grandchildren, how they live and are cared for by God,
how they keep your piety according to your tradition, how
they partake of the sacrament of the holy church, how they
praise Christ, how they bow before His name!   See also your
city beaming in its grandeur!   See your blossoming churches,
see the growing Christianity, see the city gleaming in its
adornment of saintly images, and fragrant with thyme, and
re-echoing with hymns and divine, sacred songs!   And seeing all this, rejoice and be glad, and praise the good God,
the creator of all this.

Vladímir Monomákh (Monomachos).   (1053–1125.)

Vladímir was Grand Prince of Kíev from 1113–1125.   As his *Instruction to his Children* shows, and as the chronicles witness, he was
a very learned man for his time.   From the letters of the metropolitan Nikifór to the Prince we also learn that he strictly carried out the
rules which he brought to the attention of his posterity : he often
slept on the ground, discarded sumptuous garments, and only on rare
occasions wore the insignia of his office.   He was well versed in
Byzantine literature, for his *Instruction* is not only after the fashion
of older Byzantine *Testaments*, but many passages are taken directly
from the writings of Basil the Great.   This *Instruction* is one of the
most remarkable productions of early Russian literature, especially
on account of the liberal spirit that pervades it, as compared, for example, with a similar, somewhat earlier document by St. Stephen of
Hungary.   This latter fact has served the Slavophiles as an important argument for the superiority of the Slavic spirit over that of the
west of Europe.   The *Instruction* is included in Néstor's Chronicle
under the year 1096, but it has been conclusively proved that it is the
work of Vladímir.   Parts of the *Instruction* are translated in A. P.
Stanley's *Lectures on the History of the Eastern Church*, London,
1861 (and often afterwards), and in N. H. Dole's *Young Folks' History of Russia*, Chicago, 1895.

HIS INSTRUCTION TO HIS CHILDREN

Being ill and about to seat myself in the sleigh,[1] I have considered in my soul and have praised God for having preserved me, sinful man, to this day. Do not make light of this instruction, my children, or anyone else who may hear it, but if it please any of you children, take it to heart, and give up indolence, and begin to work.

Above all, for the sake of the Lord and your own souls, have the fear of the Lord in your hearts by doing unstinted charity, for that is the beginning of all good. If this instruction should not please any of you, be not angry but say thus: "Starting out on a distant journey and about to seat himself in the sleigh, he spoke this insipidity."

My brothers' messengers met me on the Vólga and said: "Hasten to us that we may drive out the sons of Rostisláv,[2] and take away their patrimony, and if you go not with us, we shall stand alone, and you will be alone." And I said: "Even though you may be angry, I cannot go with you and transgress the cross." And having sent them away, I picked up a psalter in my sorrow, opened it, and these words were before me: "Why are you sad, my soul? Why are you grieved?" and so forth. And then I picked out words here and there, and put them in order, and I wrote: "If the latter things do not please you, accept the former. . . ."

Forsooth, my children, consider how kind and overkind God, the lover of men, is. We men, who are sinful and mortal, wish to avenge ourselves and immediately to spill the blood of him who has done us any wrong; but our Lord, who rules over life and death, suffers our transgressions above our heads, nay to the very end of our lives, like a father, now loving, now chastising his child, and again fondling it. Our Lord has likewise shown us how to be victorious over our foe, how to assuage and conquer him with three good acts: with repentance, tears and charity. It is not hard, my children, to keep this command of the

[1] Karamzín remarks that the dead were always taken away in sleighs, whether in winter or summer.

[2] Volodár, Prince of Peremýshl, and Vasílko, Prince of Terebóvl.

Lord, and you can rid yourselves of your sins by those three acts, and you will not forfeit the kingdom of heaven. And, I beg you, be not slack in the performance of the Lord's commands, and do not forget those three acts, for neither solitude, nor monkhood, nor hunger, such as many good people suffer, is hard to bear, but with a small act you may gain the favour of the Lord. What is man that Thou shouldst remember him?

Thou art great, O Lord, and Thy works are wonderful, and human understanding cannot grasp all Thy miracles! And again we say: Thou art great, O Lord, and Thy works are wonderful, and Thy name be blessed and praised for ever and through all the earth! For who would not praise and glorify Thy power and Thy great miracles and goodness that are evident in this world: how by Thy wisdom the heaven is builded, how the sun, the moon, the stars, darkness and light, and the earth is placed on the waters, O Lord! How the various animals, birds and fishes are adorned by Thy foresight, O Lord! And we also wonder at the miracle, how that He has created man from the dust, how different the forms of human faces are, how if you look at the whole world, you will not find all made in one image, but the face of each according to God's wisdom. And we wonder also how the birds of the sky come from the south, and do not remain in one country, but both the weak and the strong fly to all lands, by the will of God, in order to fill the woods and fields. All these God has given for the use of man, for food and enjoyment.

Listen to me, and if you will not accept all, heed at least half. If God should mollify your hearts, shed tears over your sins and say: "As Thou hast shown mercy to the harlot, the murderer and the publican, even thus show mercy to us sinners." Do this in church and when you lie down to sleep. Fail not to do so a single night. If you can, make your obeisance to the ground; if your strength gives out, do it thrice; in any case, be not slack in it, for with this nightly obeisance and singing man conquers the devil and frees himself from the sins he has committed during the day.

When you are riding and have no engagement with any-one, and you know no other prayer, keep on repeating secretly: "Lord, have mercy upon me!" for it is better to say this prayer than to think idle things. Above all, forget not the destitute, but feed them according to your means, and give to the orphan, and protect the widow, and allow not the strong to oppress the people. Slay neither the righteous, nor the wrongdoer, nor order him to be slain who is guilty of death, and do not ruin a Christian soul.

Whenever you speak, whether it be a bad or a good word, swear not by the Lord, nor make the sign of the cross, for there is no need. If you have occasion to kiss the cross with your brothers or with anyone else, first inquire your heart whether you will keep the promise, then kiss it; and having kissed it, see to it that you do not transgress, and your soul perish. As for the bishops, priests and abbots, receive their benediction in love, and do not keep away from them, but love them with all your might, and provide for them, that you may receive their prayers to God. Above all, have no pride in your hearts and minds, but say: "We are mortal, alive to-day, and to-morrow in the grave. All that Thou hast given us, is not ours, but Thine, and Thou hast en-trusted it to us for but a few days." Put away no treasure in the earth, for that is a great sin.

Honour the elders as your father, and the younger ones as your brothers. Be not slack in your houses, but watch everything: Do not rely upon your thane, nor your servant, lest those who come to see you should make light of your house and of your dinner. If you start out to a war, be not slack, depend not upon your generals, nor abandon your-selves to drinking and eating and sleeping. Put out the guards yourselves, and lie down to sleep only after you have placed the guards all around the army, and rise early. Do not take off your armour in haste, without examination, for man perishes suddenly through his negligence. Avoid lying and drunkenness and debauchery, for body and soul perish from them.

Whenever you travel over your lands, permit not the servants, neither your own, nor a stranger's, to do any damage in the villages, or in the fields, that they may not curse you. Wheresoever you go, and wherever you stay, give the destitute to eat and to drink. Above all honour the stranger, whencesoever he may come, whether he be a commoner, a nobleman or an ambassador; if you are not able to honour him with gifts, give him food and drink, for these travellers will proclaim a man to all the lands, whether he be good or bad. Call on the sick, go to funerals, for we are all mortal, and pass not by a man without greeting him with kind words. Love your wives, but let them not rule you.

But the main thing is that you should keep the fear of the Lord higher than anything else. If you should forget this, read this often; then shall I have no shame, and all will be well with you. Whatever good you know, do not forget it, and what you do not know, learn it; just as my father had learned, staying at home, five languages,[1] for this makes one honoured in other lands. Indolence is the mother of all vices: what one knows, one forgets, and what one does not know, one does not learn. While doing good, be not negligent in any good act, first of all in regard to the Church. Let not the sun find you in bed. Thus my father of blessed memory did, and thus do all good, perfect men. Having prayed to God at daybreak, he, noticing the rising sun, praised God in joy and said: "Thou hast made me see, Christ, O Lord, and Thou hast given me this beautiful light!" and again: "Lord, add years to my years that I may repent my sins and, improving my life, may praise God." And thus he did when he seated himself to take counsel with the druzhína, or to judge people, or when he went on the chase, or out riding, or laid himself down to sleep: but sleep has been intended by the Lord for the afternoon, when both beasts and birds and men rest themselves.

And now I shall tell you, my children, of my labours which I have performed either in my expeditions or on the

---

[1] Karamzín surmises that he knew Greek, Norse, Pólovts (Cumanian) and Hungarian, besides Russian.

chase these thirteen years. First I went to Rostóv [1] through
the country of the Vyátiches,[2] whither my father sent me
when he himself went to Kursk; next I went to Smolénsk
[follows an account of his expeditions]. . . . Altogether
I have made eighty-three long journeys and I cannot recall
how many shorter ones. I have made peace with the
Pólovtses twenty times lacking one, both with my father
and without him, giving away much of my cattle and garments. I have liberated from their shackles royal princes
of the Pólovtses as follows . . .

I have undergone many hardships in the chase. Near
Chernígov I have with my own hand caught ten or twenty
wild horses in the forests, and I have besides caught elsewhere many wild horses with my hands, as I used to travel
through Russia. Two aurochses threw me and my horse
with their horns; a stag butted me with his horns; an elk
trampled me under his feet, and another butted me with his
horns. A boar took away the sword at my side; a bear bit
me into my knee covering; a grim animal [wolf] leaped at
my loins and threw me with my horse: and yet God has
preserved me. I have often fallen from my horse, I twice
injured my head and frequently hurt my hands and feet in
my youth, being reckless of my life and not sparing my
head. Whatever there was to be done by my servants, I
did myself, in war and in the chase, in daytime and at night,
in the summer heat and in winter, without taking any rest.
I depended neither on the posádniks[3] nor the heralds, but
did all myself, and looked after my house. In the chase I
looked myself after the hunting outfit, the horses, the
falcons and the sparrow-hawks. Also have I not permitted
the mighty to offend the poor peasants and the destitute
widows, and I have myself looked after the church property
and the divine service.

Think not ill of me, my children, nor anyone else who
may read this, for I do not boast of my daring, but praise

[1] In the Government of Yaroslávl.
[2] A Slavic tribe settled on the river Oká.
[3] Burgomasters.

God and proclaim His goodness for having preserved me, sinful and miserable man, for so many years from the hour of death, for having made me, miserable one, active in the performance of all humane acts. Having read this instruction, may you hasten to do all good acts and praise the Lord with His saints. Fear neither death, my children, nor war, nor beast, but do what behooves men to do, whatever God may send you. Just as I have come out hale from war, from encounters with animals, from the water, and from my falls, even so none of you can be injured or killed, if it be not so ordained by God. And if death come from the Lord, neither father, nor mother, nor brothers can save you. Though it is good to take care of oneself, yet God's protection is better than man's.

Abbot Daniel, the Palmer. (Beginning of XII. century.)

Pilgrimages to the Holy Land began in Russia soon after the introduction of Christianity, but Daniel the abbot is the first who has left an account of his wanderings. Nothing is known of the life of this traveller, but from internal evidence it may be assumed that he visited Palestine soon after the first crusade, from 1106–1108. From his mention of none but princes of the south of Russia it is quite certain that he himself belonged there. In a simple, unadorned language, Daniel tells of his wanderings from Constantinople to the Holy Land and back again. Characteristic is his patriotic affection for the whole Russian land and his mention of all the Russian princes in his prayers,—a rather surprising sentiment for the period when Russia was nothing but a heterogeneous mass of appanages. None of the Western accounts of pilgrimages to Palestine surpass in interest that of the Russian palmer of that period, if they at all equal it.

OF THE HOLY LIGHT, HOW IT DESCENDS FROM HEAVEN UPON THE HOLY SEPULCHRE

Here is what God has shown to me, His humble and unworthy servant, Daniel the monk, for I have in truth seen with my own sinful eyes how the holy light descends on the life-giving grave of the Lord our Saviour, Jesus Christ. Many pilgrims do not tell rightly about the descent of the holy light: for some say that the Holy Ghost descends to the Sepulchre of the Lord in the shape of a dove, and others say that a lightning comes down and lights the lamps over the Sepulchre of the Lord. But that is not true, for nothing is to be seen, neither dove, nor lightning, but the divine Grace descends invisibly, and the lamps over the Sepulchre of the Lord are lit by themselves. I shall tell about it just as I have seen it.

On Good-Friday after vespers they rub the Sepulchre of the Lord clean, and wash the lamps that are above it, and fill them with pure oil without water, and put in the wicks which are not lit, and the Sepulchre is sealed at the second hour of night. And not only these lights, but those in all the other churches in Jerusalem are extinguished.

On that very Good-Friday I, humble servant, went in the first hour of the morning to Prince Baldwin and made a low obeisance to him. When he saw me making the obeisance, he called me kindly to him and said to me: " What do you wish, Russian abbot ?" for he had known me before and loved me much, being a good and simple man, and not in the least proud. And I said to him: " Sir Prince, I beg you for the sake of the Lord and the Russian princes, let me also place my lamp over the Holy Sepulchre for all our princes and for all the Russian land, for all the Christians of the Russian land!"

The Prince gave me permission to place my lamp there and readily sent his best man with me to the œkonomos of the Holy Resurrection and to him who has charge of the Sepulchre. Both the œkonomos and the keeper of the keys to the Holy Sepulchre ordered me to bring my lamp with the oil. I bowed to them with great joy, and went to the market-place and bought a large glass lamp which I filled with pure oil without water, and carried it to the Sepulchre. It was evening when I asked for the keeper of the keys and announced myself to him. He unlocked the door of the Sepulchre, told me to take off my shoes, and led me bare-footed to the Sepulchre with the lamp which I carried with my sinful hands. He told me to place the lamp on the Sepulchre, and I put it with my sinful hands there where are the illustrious feet of our Lord Jesus Christ. At his head stood a Greek lamp, on his breast was placed a lamp of St. Sabbas and of all the monasteries, for it is a custom to place every year a Greek lamp and one for St. Sabbas. By the grace of God the lower lamps lighted themselves, but not a single one of the lamps of the Franks, which are hung up, was lighted up. Having placed my lamp upon the Sepulchre of our Lord Jesus Christ, I bowed before the worshipful grave, and with love and tears kissed the holy and glorious place where lay the illustrious body of our Lord Jesus Christ. We came out of the Holy Sepulchre with great joy, and went each to his cell.

Next day, on the Holy Saturday, in the sixth hour of the day, people gather before the church of the Resurrection of Christ; there is an endless number of people from all countries, from Babylon and Egypt and Antioch, and all the places about the church and about the crucifixion of the Lord are filled. There is then such a crowd inside and outside the church that many are crushed while waiting with unlit candles for the church doors to be opened. Within, the priests and people wait until Prince Baldwin's arrival with his suite, and when the doors are opened all the people crowd in, and fill the church, and there is a large gathering in the church and near Golgotha and near Calvary and there where the Lord's cross had been found. All the people say nothing else, but keep repeating: " Lord, have mercy upon us!" and weep aloud so that the whole place reverberates and thunders with the cries of these people. The faithful shed rivers of tears, and if a man's heart were of stone, he could not keep from weeping, for then everybody looks within himself, remembers his sins, and says: " Perchance on account of my sins the Holy Ghost will not descend!" And thus all the faithful stand with tearful countenances and contrite hearts. Prince Baldwin himself stands there in great fear and humility, and a torrent of tears issues from his eyes; and his suite stand around him, opposite the grave and near the great altar.

In the seventh hour of the Saturday Prince Baldwin

started with his suite from home for the Sepulchre, and they all walked barefooted. The Prince sent to the abbey of St. Sabbas for the abbot and his monks. And I went with the abbot and the monks to the Prince, and we all bowed before him. He returned the abbot's greeting. The Prince ordered the abbot of St. Sabbas and me, humble servant, to come near him, and the others to walk before him, but the suite behind him. We arrived at the western doors of the church of the Lord's Resurrection, but such a mass of people barred the way that I could not enter. Then Prince Baldwin ordered his soldiers to drive the crowd away by force, and they opened a way through the mass of the people up to the very Sepulchre, and so we were able to pass by.

We arrived at the eastern doors of the Sepulchre. The Prince came after us, and placed himself at the right side, near the partition of the great altar, opposite the eastern doors, where there was a special elevated place for the Prince. He ordered the abbot of St. Sabbas and his monks and orthodox priests to stand around the Sepulchre, but me, humble servant, he ordered to stand high above the doors of the Sepulchre, opposite the great altar, so that I could look into the doors of the Sepulchre: there are three of these doors and they are locked and sealed with the royal seal. The Latin priests stood at the great altar. At about the eighth hour of the day the orthodox priests above the Sepulchre, and many monks and hermits who had come, began to sing their vesper service, and the Latins at the great altar chanted in their own way. I stood all the time they were singing and watched diligently the doors of the Sepulchre. When they began to read the prayers of the Holy Saturday, the bishop walked down with his deacon from the altar and went to the doors of the Sepulchre and looked through the chinks, but as he did not see any light, he returned to the altar. When they had read the sixth prayer, the bishop went again with his deacon to the door of the Sepulchre, but he did not see anything within. Then all the people sang in tears: " Kyrie, eleison!"

When it was the ninth hour of the day, and they had begun to sing, " To the Lord we sing," a small cloud suddenly came from the east and stopping over the uncovered middle of the church, came down in a rain over the Holy Sepulchre and gave us who were standing around the tomb a good drenching. And then suddenly the holy light glimmered in the Sepulchre, and then a mighty, bright brilliancy burst forth from it. Then the bishop came with four deacons and opened the doors of the Sepulchre and, taking a candle from the Prince, went inside the tomb and lighted it. After coming out again, he handed the candle to the Prince. The Prince remained standing in his place, and held the candle with great joy. From that candle we lighted all our candles, and from ours all the other candles were lighted.

This holy light is not like any earthly fire, but quite different: it burns with a bright flame like cinnabar. And all the people stood with their burning candles and wept for great joy all the time they saw the divine light. He who has not seen the great joy of that day cannot believe one who is telling about it, although good and faithful men believe it all and with pleasure listen to the account of this divine light and of the holy places, for the faithful believe the great and small things alike, but to an evil man truth is crooked. But to me, humble servant, God, and the Holy Sepulchre, and my whole suite, Russian men from Nóvgorod and Kíev, are my witnesses: Syedesláv Ivánkovich, Gorodisláv Mikhálkovich, the two Kashkíchs and many others know me and my narration.

But let us return to our story. When the light shone up in the Sepulchre, the singing stopped, and all cried aloud: " Kyrie, eleison!" Then they all went out of the church in great joy and with burning candles, watching them carefully against gusts of wind, and going home they all lighted the candles in their churches with that holy light, and finished the singing in their own churches. But in the large church of the Sepulchre the priests end the singing without the people. We went with the abbot and the monks to our monastery, carrying the burning candles, and after finishing our vesper singing, we went to our cells praising the Lord who had shown us His grace. . . .

After three days I went to the keeper of the keys of the Holy Sepulchre and said to him: "I should like to take away my lamp!" He received me with much kindness, took me alone into the Sepulchre, and walking in, I found my lamp still burning with the holy light. I bowed before the Holy Sepulchre and kissed the glorious place where once lay the illustrious body of our Lord Jesus Christ. Then I measured the length, the width and the height of the Sepulchre, for one is not allowed to measure it in presence of others. After having honoured the Lord's Sepulchre as much as I could, I gave the keeper a little something and a blessing. He, seeing my love for the Holy Sepulchre and kindness to himself, removed a little the boards at the head of the Sepulchre and broke off a small piece of rock from it which he gave to me after I had solemnly sworn to him that I would not tell anyone in Jerusalem about it. I bowed to the Sepulchre and to the keeper, took my lamp which was still burning, and went away with great joy, having been enriched by the grace of God, carrying in my hand a gift from the holy place and a token from the Holy Sepulchre. And thus rejoicing at the treasures which I had acquired, I went back to my cell.

EPILOGUE

I made my pilgrimage in the reign of Grand Prince Svyatopólk Izyaslávich, the grandson of Yarosláv Vladímirovich of Kíev. God is my witness, and the Holy Sepulchre, that in all those holy places I did not forget the Russian princes and their wives and children, nor the bishops, abbots, boyárs, nor my spiritual children, nor all the Christians, but that I remembered them everywhere. And I also thank God that He has enabled me, humble servant, to inscribe the names of the Russian princes in the monastery of St. Sabbas, where they are mentioned even now in their services. . . .

May the benediction of the Lord, of the Holy Sepulchre and of all the holy places be on all who read this message with faith and love! For they will receive their reward from God equally with those who have made pilgrimages to the holy places. Blessed are those who have not seen and yet believe! Abraham came into the promised land through faith, for indeed faith is equal to good deeds. For the Lord's sake, brothers and fathers, do not accuse my simplicity and rudeness, and do not make light of this writing; not on my account, but on account of the holy places, honour it in love, that you may receive your reward from the Lord our God, and our Saviour Jesus Christ, and may the God of peace be with all of you unto eternity. Amen!

Cyril, Bishop of Túrov. (XII. century.)

Little is known of the life of this remarkable preacher. He was born at Túrov, Government of Minsk, about the year 1130, where his parents were wealthy people. Having become a monk, he distinguished himself by his austere asceticism and great piety. At the request of the Prince of Túrov he was made bishop. Eight or nine of his sermons and some prayers have come down to us in manuscript. His eloquence stands alone in the whole ancient period of Russian literature. Though other preachers followed Byzantine models in their sermons, yet none carried the flowery Greek symbolism so far, or wrote in so fluent a language.

FROM A SERMON ON THE FIRST SUNDAY AFTER EASTER

The Church needs a great teacher and a wise orator to properly celebrate the holiday, but we are poor in words and dim in mind, not having the fire of the Holy Ghost,—the enjoyment of words useful to the soul; yet for the love of my brethren who are with me, we shall say something about the renewal of the Lord's resurrection. In the past week of the Easter there was joy in heaven, and terror in the nethermost regions, a renewal of life and liberation of the world, a destruction of hell and victory over death, a resurrection of the dead, and annihilation of the enticing power of the devil; a salvation of the human race by the resurrection of Christ; an impoverishment of the Old Testament and enslavement of the Sabbath; an enrichment of the Church of Christ, and enthronement of the Sunday.

Last week there was a change of all things, for the earth was opened up by heaven, having been purified from its satanic impurities, and the angels with their wives humbly served at the resurrection. All creation was renewed, for no longer are the air, the sun, the fire, the springs, the trees, thought to be gods; no longer does hell receive its due of infants sacrificed by their fathers, nor death its honours, for idolatry has come to an end, and the satanic power has been vanquished by the mystery of the cross. The Old Testament has become impoverished by the rejection of the blood of calves and sacrifices of goats, for Christ has given Himself to the Lord as a sacrifice for all. And with this, Sunday ceased to be a holiday, but the Sunday was sanctified on account of the resurrection, and Sunday is now supreme, for Christ arose from the dead on that day. . . .

To-day the heavens have been cleared from the dark clouds that enshrouded them as with a heavy veil, and they proclaim the glory of God with a clear atmosphere. . . .

To-day the sun rises and beams on high, and rejoicing warms the earth, for there has arisen for us from the grave the real sun, Christ, and He saves all who believe in Him. To-day the moon descends from its high place, and gives honour to the greater lights. The Old Testament, as had been prophesied, has stopped with its Sabbath, and with its prophets gives honour to the Testament of Christ with its Sunday. To-day the winter of sin has stopped in repentance, and the ice of unbelief is melted by wisdom. To-day spring appears spruce, and enlivens all earthly existence; the stormy winds blow gently and generate fruits, and the earth, giving nurture to the seed, brings forth green grass. For spring is the beautiful faith in Christ which, through baptism, produces a regeneration of man, and the stormy winds are the evil, sinful thoughts that, being changed to virtue through repentance, generate soul-saving fruits; but the earth of our being, having received the Word of God like a seed, and, passing through an ecstatic labour, through the fear of Him, brings forth a spirit of salvation.

To-day the new-born lambs and calves frisk and leap about joyfully and returning to their mothers gambol about, so that the shepherds, playing on their reeds, praise Christ in joy. The lambs, I say, are the gentle people from among the pagans, and the calves—the idolaters of the unbelieving countries who, having accepted the Law through Christ's incarnation and the teachings of the apostles and miracles, and having returned to the holy Church, suck the milk of its teachings; and the teachers of Christ's flock, praying for all, praise Christ, the Lord, who had collected all the wolves and sheep into one herd.

To-day the trees send forth buds and the fragrant flowers bloom, and behold, the gardens already emit a sweet odour, and the workers labouring in hope acclaim Christ the giver of fruits. We were before like the trees of the forest that bear no fruit, but to-day the faith of Christ has been grafted on our unbelief, and those who already held to the roots of Jesse have burgeoned with the flowers of virtue and expect through Christ a regeneration in heaven, and the saints who labour for the Church expect a reward from Christ. To-day the ploughman of the Word leads the oxen of the Word to the spiritual yoke, sinks the plough of baptism into the furrows of thought and deepening them to furrows of repentance plants in them the spiritual seed and rejoices in the hope of future returns. To-day everything old has taken an end, and all is new for the sake of the resurrection. To-day the apostolic rivers are full, and the pagan fish let out their broods, and the fishermen, having examined the depth of the divine incarnation, drag in full nets into the Church. . . . To-day the industrious bees of the monastic order show their wisdom and set all to wonder, for living in the wilderness and providing for themselves, they astonish both angels and men, just as the bee flies upon the flowers and forms combs of honey in order to furnish sweetness to man and what is needed in the church. . . .

To-day there is a feast of regeneration for the people who

are made new by the resurrection of Christ, and all new
things are brought to God: from heathens, faith; from good
Christians, offerings; from the clergy, holy sacrifices; from
the civil authorities, God-pleasing charity; from the noble,
care for the Church; from the righteous, humility; from the
sinners, true repentance; from the unhallowed, a turning to
God; from the hating, spiritual love.

Néstor's Chronicle. (XII. century.)

Néstor was born about 1056, and at the age of seventeen entered
the monastery of the Grottoes at Kíev. In 1091 he was commissioned
to find in the Grottoes the mortal relics of Theodosius, the founder
of the monastery. Having performed this task he wrote a life of the
founder. He died about 1146. To this Néstor has been ascribed
the authorship of the chronicle which in one of the manuscripts of
the fourteenth century bears the title: *The stories of bygone years,
whence the Russian land began, who first reigned at Kíev, and how
the Russian land was formed.* It has, however, been proved that
only a small part of the chronicle belongs to him, and that the last
editor of the whole was the abbot Sylvester, the continuator of
Néstor's Chronicle for the twelfth century.

The chronicle contains the reports of important facts in the life of
the princes, arranged in chronological order. The author, or authors,
being of the clerical profession, the influence of Christianity shows
itself throughout in the use of a biblical diction. This is especially
the case where Byzantine chronographers, whose influence on all the
early Russian chronicles is unmistakable, and church and monastery
notes are the source of the historical narrative. But popular stories,
legends and accounts of eye-witnesses also play an important part in
the composition of the work, and in these the diction is more
dramatic and natural. The chronicle covers the period from 862 to
1110, and is exceedingly valuable as the chief source for the history
of Russia for the time described. It has not come down to us in the
original, but has reached us in copies of the fourteenth century, of
which the Laurentian manuscript, copied by the monk Laurentius for
Dimítri Konstantínovich, Prince of Súzdal, is the most important.

THE BAPTISM OF VLADÍMIR AND OF ALL RUSSIA

In the year 6495 (987), Vladímir called together his
boyárs and city elders, and said to them: "There have

come to me Bulgarians who said: 'Accept our religion!'
Then came the Germans, and they praised their religion;
after them came the Jews.' But after them came the Greeks,
who spoke slightingly of all the other religions, but praised
their own. They spoke much about the beginning of the
universe and the existence of the whole world. They are
cunning of speech, and talk so pleasantly that it is a pleasure
to hear them. They say that there is another world, and
that if anyone enters into their faith, he would live after his
death, and would not die for eternity; but that if he accepts
any other faith, he would burn in the other world. Now,
what counsel do you give me? What is your answer?''

And the boyárs and elders said: "You know, O Prince,
that nobody detracts his own, but praises it. If you are
anxious to find out the truth, you have men whom you can
send out to see how they all serve God.''

And the speech pleased the Prince and all people. They
selected good and clever men, to the number of ten, and
said to them: "Go first to the Bulgarians and inquire into
their religion!'' And they went, and saw their abominable
deeds and worshipping in shrines, and returned to their
land. Vladímir said to them: "Go now to the Germans,
find out there also, and thence go to Greece!''

And they went to Germany and, having seen their divine
service, they came to Constantinople, and went to the Emperor. The Emperor asked them what they had come for,
and they told him all as it was. Having heard this, the
Emperor was glad, and gave them a banquet on that very
day. Next morning he sent to the Patriarch saying: "Some
Russians have come to find out about our faith; so have the
church and clergy in order, and yourself don the holy garments, that they may see the glory of our God.''

Having heard this, the Patriarch called together the clergy
to celebrate the day according to the custom, and he had the
censers lighted, and arranged the singing and the choir.
The Emperor went with them to church, and they were
placed in a prominent place where they could see the beauty

¹ The Khazars, a Tartar tribe that professed the Mosaic Law.

of the church, hear the singing and archiepiscopal ministration, and watch the attendance of the deacons in the divine service. They were surprised, and marvelled, and praised their service. And the Emperors Basil and Constantine called them and said to them: "Go to your land!" and they sent them away with many gifts and honours.

They came back to their country, and their Prince called together his boyárs and old men. Said Vladímir: "The men we have sent away have come back. Let us hear what has happened!" And he said: "Speak before the druzhína!" and they spoke: "When we were in Bulgaria, we saw them worshipping in the temple, where they talk in the shrine and stand without their girdles. Having made their obeisance, they sit down and look around hither and thither like madmen, and there is no joy among them, only sadness and a great stench: their religion is not good. And we came to Germany, and we saw many ceremonies in their temples, but of beauty we saw none. We went to Greece, and they took us where théy worship their God, and we do not know whether we were in heaven or upon earth, for there is not upon earth such sight or beauty. We were perplexed, but this much we know that there God lives among men, and their service is better than in any other country. We cannot forget that beauty, for every man that has partaken of sweetness will not afterwards accept bitterness, and thus we can no longer remain in our former condition." And the boyárs answered and said: "If the Greek religion were bad, your grandmother Ólga, who was the wisest of all men, would not have accepted it." And Vladímir answered and said: "Where shall we receive our baptism?" But they answered: "Wheresoever it may please you!"

Next year, the year 6496, Vladímir went with his warriors against Korsún,[1] a Greek city, and the Korsúnians shut themselves up in the city. Vladímir was encamped at the side of the city nearest the harbour, at one shot's distance from it, and they fought valiantly in the city, and Vladímir

[1] The ancient Tauric Chersonese; this later city was not built on the ancient site, but near Sebastopol.

beleaguered it. The townspeople were weakening, and Vladímir said to them: "If you do not surrender, I shall stay here, if need be, three years." They paid no attention to it, and Vladímir drew up his soldiers, and ordered them to build a rampart to the city. While they were asleep, the Korsúnians undermined the city wall, and, stealing the dirt which they had thrown up, carried it into the city, and deposited it there. The soldiers again filled up the rampart, and Vladímir remained there.

A Korsún man, by the name of Nastás, shot an arrow upon which was written as follows: "It is by the wells that are behind you in the east, that the water is led by pipes into the city; dig them up, and stop the supply!" Hearing this, Vladímir looked to the heavens and said: "If it shall come to pass, I will be baptised," and immediately he ordered the pipes to be dug up, and the water was intercepted. The people were exhausted with thirst, and they surrendered themselves. Valdímir entered the city with his druzhína, and he sent word to the Emperors Basil and Constantine: "I have taken your famous city. I hear you have a sister who is still a maiden. If you will not give her to me for a wife, I shall do unto your city as I have done unto this."

And they heard the tsar, and were sad, and gave the following answer: "It does not behoove Christians to give in marriage to a pagan. If you will receive the baptism, you shall get her, and you will receive the kingdom of heaven, and will be of one faith with us. If you do not wish to do so, we cannot give you our sister."

Hearing this, Vladímir said to the messengers of the Emperors: "Tell your Emperors that I will be baptised, that I have inquired before these days into your faith, and am pleased with your belief and divine service, from what the men that had been sent by us have told me."

Which when the Emperors heard, they were glad and persuaded their sister, by the name of Anna, and sent to Vladímir saying: "Receive the baptism, and then we will send our sister to you."

But Vladímir answered: "Let them come with your sister to baptise me!"

The Emperors obeyed, and sent their sister and a few high officers and presbyters. She did not want to go: "It is as if I were going into captivity," she said. "It were better if I died here." And her brothers said to her: "Perchance God will through you turn the Russian land to repentance, and free Greece from a dire war. Do you not see how much evil the Russians have caused to the Greeks? If you will not go, they will do even thus to us." They persuaded her with difficulty. She boarded a boat, kissed her relatives under tears and went across the sea. She arrived at Korsún, and the Korsúnians met her with honours, and led her into the city and seated her in the palace.

By God's will, Vladímir was at that time ailing with his eyes, and he could not see, and was much worried. The empress sent to him saying: "If you want to be rid of your disease, be baptised at once. If not, you will not be rid of it."

Hearing this, Vladímir said: "If it will be so in truth, then indeed your Christian God is great." And he ordered to baptise him. The bishop of Korsún with the priests of the empress received Vladímir as a catechumen and baptised him, and the moment he laid his hands upon him, he regained his eyesight. When Vladímir saw this sudden cure, he praised God and said: "Now have I for the first time found the real God!" When his druzhína perceived this, many were baptised. He was baptised in the church of St. Basil, and that church is situated in Korsún, there where the Korsúnians have their market-place. Vladímir's palace by the church is standing up to the present day. The palace of the empress is beyond the altar. After the baptism he led the empress to the betrothal. Those who do not know right say that he was baptised in Kíev; others say in Vasilév; others again say otherwise.

After that, Vladímir took the empress and Nastás, and the Korsún priests with the holy relics of Clement and Phœbus, his disciple, and church vessels, and images, for his own use.

He built a church in Korsún on the hill which they had thrown up in the middle of the city from the dirt they had carried away, and that church is still standing there. Going away, he took along with him two brass statues and four brass horses which stand to-day behind the church of the Holy Virgin, and which the ignorant think to be of marble. He gave as a marriage price Korsún back to the Greeks, for the sake of the empress, and went back to Kíev.

Upon his return, he ordered the idols to be cast down, and some to be cut to pieces, and others to be consumed by fire; but Perún he had tied to the tail of a horse, and dragged down the hill over the Boríchev [1] to the brook, and placed twelve men to strike him with rods, not as if the wood had any feeling, but as a scorn to the devil who had in that way seduced people, that he might receive his due punishment from men. As he was dragged along the brook to the Dnieper, the unbelievers wept over him, for they had not yet received the holy baptism, and he was cast into the Dnieper. Vladímir stood by, and said: "Should he be carried anywhere to the banks, push him off, until he has passed the rapids, when you may leave him!" They did as they were told. When he passed the rapids, and was let loose, the wind carried him on a sandbank, which is named from this "Perún's Bank," and is called so to this day.

After that Vladímir proclaimed throughout the whole city: "Whosoever will not appear to-morrow at the river, whether he be rich or poor, or a beggar, or a workingman, will be in my disfavour." Hearing this, people came gladly and with joy, and said: "If this were not good, the Prince and boyárs would not have accepted it." Next morning Vladímir went out with the priests of the empress and of Korsún to the Dnieper, and there came together people without number. They went into the water, and stood there up to their necks, and some up to their breasts, but the younger nearer the shore, and others held the younger ones, while the grown people waded into the water. And the priests stood there and said the prayers; and there was a joy in heaven and

[1] A suburb of Kíev.

upon earth at the sight of so many saved souls, but the devil groaned, and said: "Woe to me! I am driven away from here. Here I had intended to have my habitation, for here are no apostolic teachings, and they do not know God, and I rejoiced in the worship with which they served me. And now I am conquered by ignorant people and not by apostles and martyrs. I shall no longer reign in these lands."

Having been baptised, the people went to their houses. Vladímir was happy for having, himself and his people, found God, and looking up to heaven he said: "God, Thou hast created heaven and earth! Guard these Thy new people, and let them, O Lord, find out the real God, such as the Christian people know Him. Strengthen the true and constant faith in them, and help me, O Lord, against my foe, that relying upon Thee and Thy power, I may escape his ambush!"

The people having been baptised, they all went to their homes, and Vladímir ordered churches to be built, and to place them there where formerly stood the idols. He built the church of St. Basil on the hill where stood the idol Perún and the others, to whom the Prince and others used to bring sacrifices. And he began to locate churches and priests over the towns, and to lead people to baptism in all towns and villages. He sent out men to take the children of noblemen, and to put them out for book instruction; but the mothers of those children wept for them, for they were not yet firm in their faith, and they wept for them as for the dead.

The Kíev Chronicle. (XII. century.)

The Kíev Chronicle is a continuation of Néstor's Chronicle, from 1111–1201, and describes mainly the acts of the principality of Kíev. The best manuscript of this chronicle is from the monastery of St. Ipáti, near Kostromá, and dates from the end of the fourteenth, or the beginning of the fifteenth, century. The passage given below is selected to illustrate the historical account of the same incident contained in the *Word of Igor's Armament*.

THE EXPEDITION OF ÍGOR SVYATOSLÁVICH AGAINST THE PÓLOVTSES[1]

In the year 6693 (1185). At that time Ígor, the son of Svyatosláv, the grandson of Olég, rode out of Nóvgorod on the 23rd of April, which was on a Tuesday, having taken with him his brother Vsévolod from Trubétsk, and Svyatosláv Ólgovich, his nephew, from Rylsk, and Vladímir, his son, from Putívl, and Yaroslav had sent him, at his request, Olstín Oléksich, the grandson of·Prokhór, with Kovúans[2] from Chernígov. They proceeded slowly, collecting their druzhína, for their horses were very fat. As they were going towards the river Donéts, Ígor looked one evening at the sky, and he saw the sun standing there like a moon, and he said to his boyárs and druzhína: "Do you see this omen?"

They looked up, and having noticed it, hung their heads, and said: "Prince, this is not a good omen!"

But Ígor said: "Brothers and druzhína! Nobody knows God's mystery, and God is the creator of mystery, as well as of all His world; but we shall find out in time whether God means our good or our evil."

Having said this, he forded the Donéts and came to the river Oskól, where he waited for two days for his brother Vsévolod who was marching by another road from Kursk; thence they proceeded to Sálnitsa. There came to them the guards whom they had sent out to reconnoitre; they said: "We have seen the army of the enemy; they were riding rapidly: either you ride fast, or we had better return home, for the time is not propitious."

But Ígor consulted his brothers and said: "If we return without fighting, our shame will be greater than death. Let us proceed with God's aid!"

Having said this, they travelled through the night, and the next day, which was a Friday, they met the army of the Pólovtses at noontime. When they saw them, they were

[1] For notes consult the *Word of Ígor's Armament* (p. 80 *et sqq.*).
[2] A Finnish tribe.

without their tents, for they had left them behind them, but
the old and young were all standing on the other side of the
river Syuurlí. The Russians arranged their six troops as
follows: Ígor's troop was in the middle, to his right was the
troop of his brother Vsévolod, and to the left that of his
nephew Svyatosláv; in front of him was placed his son Vladímir, and Yaroslav's Kovúans, and a third troop of archers
was in front of them, and they were selected from the troops
of all the princes; that was the position of their troops.

And Ígor spoke to his brothers: " Brothers! We have
found what we have been looking for, so let us move on
them!" And they advanced, placing their faith in God.
When they came to the river Syuurlí, the archers galloped
out from the troops of the Pólovtses, sent each an arrow
against the Russians, and galloped back again, before the
Russians had crossed the river Syuurlí; equally the Pólovtses
who stood farther away from the river galloped away. Svyatosláv Ólgovich, and Vladímir Ígorevich, and Olstín with
his Kovúans, and the archers ran after them, while Ígor
and Vsévolod went slowly ahead, and did not send forward
their troops; but the Russians ahead of them struck down
the Pólovtses. The Pólovtses ran beyond their tents, and
the Russians, having come as far as the tents, plundered
them, and some returned in the night with their booty to
the army.

When the Pólovtses had come together, Ígor said to his
brothers and men: "God has given us the power to vanquish
our enemy, and honour and glory to us! We have seen the
army of the Pólovtses that it is large, and I wonder whether
they have all been collected. If we now shall ride through
the night, what surety is there that all will follow us next
morning? And our best horsemen will be in the meantime
cut down, and we will have to shift as best we can."

And Svyatosláv Ólgovich spoke to his uncles: " I have
driven the Pólovtses a long distance, and my horses are
played out; if I am to travel on to-day, I shall have to fall
behind on the road," and Vsévolod agreed with him that it
was best to rest.

Ígor spoke: "Knowing this, it is not proper to expose ourselves to death," and they rested there.

When the day broke on the Saturday, the troops of the Pólovtses began to appear like a forest. The Russian princes were perplexed, and did not know whom to attack first, for there was a numberless host of them. And Ígor said: "See, I have collected against me the whole land: Konchák, Kozá Burnovích, Toksobích, Kolobích, Etebích, and Tertrobích." And seeing them, they dismounted from their horses, for they wished to reach the river Donéts by fighting, and they said: "If we remain on horseback, and run away, and leave our soldiers behind, we will have sinned before God; but let us die or live together!" And having said this, they all dismounted and fought on foot.

By the will of God, Ígor was wounded, and his left arm was disabled, and there was a great sorrow in his troop; and they captured his general, having wounded him in front. And they fought that day until evening, and many were the wounded and killed in the Russian army. They fought till late into the night, and when the Sunday began to break, the Kovúans became confused and ran away. Ígor was at that time on horseback, for he was wounded, and he followed them up, trying to bring them back to the army. Seeing that he had gone far away from his people, he took off his helmet so that they might recognise him and might return to the army, and he rode back to his troop. But no one returned, except Mikhálko Gyúrgevich who had recognised the Prince. The trouble was, no one, except a few of the rank and file and boyárs' youths, had thoroughly mingled with the Kovúans, for they were all busy fighting on foot; among these, Vsévolod excelled in bravery. As Ígor was approaching his troop, the Pólovtses crossed his path and made him prisoner within an arrow's shot from his troop. While Ígor was held captive, he saw his brother fighting mightily, and in his heart he implored for his own death that he might not see his brother fall dead; but Vsévolod was fighting until he had no weapons left in his hands, and they were fighting around a lake.

It was on the day of the holy Sunday that the Lord
brought down His anger upon them, and changed joy into
weeping, and instead of pleasure gave them sorrow, on the
river Kayála. And Ígor spoke: " I now recall my sins before the Lord my God, for I have caused much slaughter and
bloodshed in the Christian land, and did not spare the
Christians, but took by storm the town of Glyébov near
Pereyáslavl. Then innocent Christians suffered no small
measure of evil, for fathers were separated from their children, brother from brother, friend from friend, wives from
husbands, and daughters from their mothers, and all was
confused in captivity and sorrow. The living envied the
dead, and the dying rejoiced because they had like holy
martyrs received their trial by fire in this life; old men were
killed, young men received fierce and inhuman wounds, men
were cut to pieces. All this I have done, and I am not
worthy to live; to-day the revenge of the Lord has reached
me. Where is now my beloved brother? Where is now
the son of my brother? Where is the child of my loins?
Where are the counselling boyárs, where are the brave men,
the ranks of the soldiers? Where are the horses and costly
weapons? Am I not separated from all that, and has not
the Lord given me fettered into the hands of the pagans?
The Lord has repaid me for my lawlessness and my mean-
ness, and my sins have this day come down upon my head.
The Lord is just, and His judgments are right, and I have
nothing in common with the living. I see to-day others receiving the crown of martyrdom, but why can I not, guilty
one, suffer for all of them? But Lord my God! Do not reject me to the end, but as Thy will, O Lord, is done, so also
is Thy mercy to us, Thy slaves! "

The battle being over, the Pólovtses scattered, and went
to their tents. Ígor was captured by the Targólaus, by a
man named Chilbúk; his brother Vsévolod was taken by
Román Kzich, Svyatosláv Ólgovich by Eldechyúk of the
Boburchéviches, and Vladímir by Kópti of the Ulashéviches.
Then Konchák took care of Ígor on the battlefield, for he
was wounded. Of the many prisoners taken but few could

run away, God being willing, for it was not possible for anyone to escape, being surrounded on all sides by the Pólovts
army as with mighty walls; and yet there escaped about
fifteen of us Russians, and fewer Kovúans, but the rest were
drowned in the sea.

At that time Grand Prince Vsévolod's son Svyatosláv had
gone to Koráchev[1] to collect warriors in the upper lands,
wishing in the summer to go to the Don against the Pólovtses. When Svyatosláv returned and was at Nóvgorod
Syéverski, he heard that his brothers had gone against the
Pólovtses, without his knowledge, and he was displeased.
Svyatosláv was travelling in boats, and when he arrived in
Chernígov, Byelovolód Prosóvich came to him and told him
what had happened with the Pólovtses. When Svyatosláv
heard that, he sighed much and, wiping off his tears, he
said: "O beloved brothers and sons and men of the Russian
land! Oh, that God would grant me to crush the pagans!
But they, impulsive in their youth, have opened the gates
into the Russian land. The will of the Lord be on everything! However sorry I was for Ígor, I am more sorry for
Ígor, my brother!"

After that Svyatosláv sent his son Olég and Vladímir into
the Posémie,[2] for when the cities of the Posémie heard of the
disaster, they were disturbed, and there was a sorrow and
heavy anguish upon them, such as had never before been in
the whole Posémie, in Nóvgorod Syéverski and in the whole
district of Chernígov. They had heard that their princes
had been taken prisoners, and the druzhína had been captured, and killed; and they became restless, as if in turbid
water, and the cities revolted, and many had no care for
their relatives, but they renounced their souls, weeping
for their princes. After that Svyatosláv sent to David of
Smolénsk, saying: "We had intended to go against the
Pólovtses, and pass the summer on the Don; but now the
Pólovtses have vanquished Ígor, and his brother with his
son; now come, brother, to protect the Russian land!" And

[1] Town in the country of the Vyátiches.
[2] The country along the river Sem.

David came to the Dnieper, and there arrived also other help, and they stopped at Trepól, but Yarosláv collected his troops at Chernígov.

The pagan Pólovtses, having conquered Ígor and his brothers, were filled with great conceit, and they gathered all their tribes against the Russian land. And there was a strife among them, for Konchák said: "Let us march against Kíev, where our brothers and our Grand Prince Bonyák were cut down!" But Kza said: "Let us go against the Sem, where their wives and children are left, an easy booty for us; we shall sack their cities without danger!" And thus they divided into two parts. Konchák went against Pereyáslavl. He besieged the city, and they fought the whole day. At that time Vladímir Glyébovich was the Prince of Pereyáslavl. He being bold and a mighty warrior, rode out of the city and rushed against the enemy, and then a few men of his druzhína were emboldened, and they fought valiantly. Many Pólovtses surrounded them. Then the others, seeing their Prince hard pressed, rushed out of the city, and saved their Prince, who was wounded with three spear thrusts. This good Vladímir rode back into the city heavily wounded, and he wiped the sweat from his brave face, having fought doughtily for his country.

Vladímir sent word to Svyatosláv, and to Rúrik, and to David: "The Pólovtses are at my gates, help me!" Svyatosláv sent word to David, who stood at Trepól with his Smolénsk troop. The men of Smolénsk held a council, and said: "We have marched to Kíev to fight in case there is a war there; but we cannot look for another war, for we are worn out." Svyatosláv hurried to the Dnieper with Rúrik and other troops, against the Pólovtses, and David went away with his Smolénsk men. When the Pólovtses heard this, they went away from Pereyáslavl, but on their way they attacked Rímov. The Rímovans shut themselves up in the city; having climbed the rampart, two wicker structures gave way with all their men, God having so willed, and broke in the direction of the enemy. Terror fell upon the city people. Some of them sallied from the city and kept up a running fight into the Rímov swamps, and thus escaped capture; but those who remained in the city were all taken prisoners. Vladímir sent again to Svyatosláv Vsévolodich and Rúrik Rostislávich, imploring them to come to his aid. But they were tardy in coming, having waited for David with his Smolénsk troop, and thus they did not get there in time to meet the Pólovtses. Having taken the city of Rímov, the Pólovtses returned to their homes, loaded down with booty. The princes went back to their homes, and they were very sad, and they were sorry for Vladímir Glyébovich, for he was struck down with mortal wounds, and they were sorry for the Christians that had been taken prisoners by the pagans. . . .

The other Pólovtses were going by another road to Putívl. Kza had a large host with him; they laid waste the country, burnt the villages, and also burnt the castle near Putívl, and returned home again.

Ígor Svyatoslávich was that year with the Pólovtses, and he said: "According to my deserts have I received defeat at Thy hands, my Lord, and not the daring of the pagans has broken the might of Thy servants. I do not complain of my suffering, for I have been punished for my misdeeds." The Pólovtses, respecting his leadership, did not do him any harm, but placed over him fifteen guards of their sons, and five lords' sons, in all twenty. They gave him permission to go where he wanted, and he went a-hunting with the hawk, and there were with him five or six of his servants. His guards obeyed him and honoured him, and whithersoever he sent them, they did his command without grumbling. He had brought with him a priest from Russia, with all the divine service, for he did not know the divine will, and he thought he would have to stay there for a long time. But the Lord delivered him for the many prayers of the Christians which they sent up to heaven, and the many tears which they shed for him. While he was among the Pólovtses, there was a man there, himself a Pólovts, by the name of Lavór; he having a blessed thought said: " I will go with you to Russia!" At first Ígor had no confidence in him,

but had a high opinion of his own manliness, for he did not
intend to take the man and run with him into Russia; he
said: "For glory's sake I did not then run away from my
druzhína, and even now will I not walk upon an inglorious
road."

But there were with him the son of the thousand-man and
his equerry, and they pressed him and said: "Go, O Prince,
back to Russia, if the Lord will deliver you!" But the time
was not propitious. As we said before, the Pólovtses returned from Pereyáslavl, and Ígor's advisers said to him:
"You harbour a proud thought and one that is not pleasing
to God; you do not intend to take the man and run with
him, but why do you not consider that the Pólovtses will
return from the war, and we have heard that they will slay
all the princes and all the Russians, and there will be no
glory for you, and you will lose your life." Prince Ígor
took their advice to heart, being afraid of the return of the
Pólovtses, and bethought himself of flight. He was not
able to run away either in daytime or at night, for the
guards watched him, but he found an opportune time at the
setting of the sun. And Ígor sent his equerry to Lavór,
saying: "Cross on the other side of the Tor with a led
horse," for he intended to fly to Russia with Lavór. At
that time the Pólovtses were drunk with kumys; and it was
towards evening when his equerry came back and told him
that Lavór was waiting for him. Ígor arose frightened and
trembling, and bowed before the image of the Lord and the
honourable cross, and said: "Lord, knower of hearts! If
Thou, Master, wilt save me, unworthy one,"—and he took
the cross and the image, lifted the tent's side, and crawled
out. His guards were gambling and feasting, for they
thought that the Prince was asleep. He arrived at the river,
waded across, and mounted the horse; thus they both rode
by the tents.

This deliverance the Lord granted on a Friday, in the
evening. He then walked eleven days to the town of
Donéts, and thence he went to his Nóvgorod, and they were
much rejoiced. From Nóvgorod he went to his brother

Yaroslív in Chernígov, to ask for help in the Posémie. Yaroslív was glad to see him, and promised him aid. Ígor travelled thence to Kíev to Grand Prince Svyatosláv, and Svyatosláv was glad to see him, as was also Rúrik.

The Word of Ígor's Armament. (End of XII. century.)

No other production of Russian antiquity has roused so much interest in Russia and abroad as this version of Ígor's expedition by an unknown poet of the end of the twelfth century. Thirty-five translations into modern Russian, numerous translations into Little-Russian, Polish, Bohemian, Servian, Bulgarian, Hungarian, German, French, witness to the enormous popularity this production has attained. The historical background of the poem is found in the recital from the Kíev Chronicle, which is given on pp. 71–80. The disasters which befell Ígor and his army are probably told with better effect in that prosaic version; but the superior value of the *Word* lies in its being a precious relic of the popular poetry of the end of the twelfth century, such as no other nation can boast of. The *Nibelungenlied* and the *Chanson de Roland* are chiefly productions of a literary character, while the *Word* bears every evidence of representing the untutored labour of a popular bard.

Who the author was, when he lived, for whom he sang, are all unanswered questions, but from internal evidence we glean that he sang for his contemporaries while Ígor was still alive. From his apostrophe to Yaroslív Osmomýsl, who died in 1187, we may infer that the poem was written before that year, and it is not unlikely, from his vivid description of the battle at the Kayála, that he was an eye-witness of the expedition which took place in 1185. From the absence of biblical references it is generally assumed that the author was not a member of the clerical profession. Here, however, various difficulties arise. It is quite incomprehensible why there should be so many references to pagan divinities at a time when Christianity had been deep-rooted in Russia for fully two centuries; why, except for the evident imitation of many passages in the *Zadónshchina*, there should be no reference to the poem by any medieval writer, and why only one copy of so remarkable a work should have been preserved. If this poem came so very near being lost to posterity, how many other remarkable productions of that early period have disappeared? It is not at all impossible that there existed an extensive popular poetry, of which only the barest traces have come down to us. This suspicion is strengthened by the emphatic mention by the author of the *Word* of a poet Boyán who had lived before his days.

A copy of the poem was discovered by Count A. I. Músin-Púshkin, Procurator-General of the Holy Synod, in 1795. He it was who in rummaging St. Petersburg bookstalls had discovered the manuscript of Néstor's Chronicle. From a monk he procured a collection of eight pieces, the fifth of which was this poem. He published the *Word*, as this poem is called in the manuscript, in 1800, with a modern Russian translation. The manuscript itself was burnt in the Moscow conflagration of 1812. The poem has since been edited a countless number of times, and equally large is the mass of critical essays to explain the many dark and corrupt places of what now must pass for the original. When we consider that there are not less than six versions of the *Word* in French, it seems strange that it is now first rendered into English in its entirety. There is an imperfect translation of a small part of it in H. H. Munro's *The Rise of the Russian Empire*, Boston and London, 1900.

I

Were it not well for us, O brothers, to commence in the ancient strain the sad story of the armament of Ígor,[1] Ígor son of Svyatosláv? And let the song be told according to the accounts of the time, and not according to the cunning of Boyán[2] the Wise, for Boyán the Wise, when he wished to make a song, soared with his thoughts in the tree, ran as a grey wolf over the earth, flew as a steel-grey eagle below the clouds. When he recalled the strife of former time, he let loose ten falcons o'er a flock of swans, and every swan each touched sang first a song: to old Yarosláv,[3] to brave Mstisláv[4] who slew Redédya before the Kasóg army, to fair

[1] Ígor was the son of Svyatosláv Ólgovich of Nóvgorod Syéverski, and grandson of Olég of Tmútorokan.

[2] From the references to the princes whose praise he sang, it is evident that he lived at the end of the eleventh and the beginning of the twelfth centuries. Nothing else is known of this famous poet.

[3] Yarosláv, the son of Vladímir, lived from 1019-1054: he was the author of the Russian Code (see p. 45).

[4] Mstisláv, Prince of Tmútorokan, was the brother of Yarosláv († 1036). In 1022 he killed in duel the giant Redédya, chief of the Kasógs who dwelt between the Black and Caspian seas, and conquered their country.

Román Svyatoslávich.[1]   But Boyán, O brothers, did not let
loose ten falcons on a flock of swans, but laid his inspired
fingers on the living strings, and they themselves sounded
the glory to the princes.

Let us begin, O brothers, this tale from Vladímir[2] of old
to the late Ígor who strengthened his soul by his valour,
and sharpened it by the courage of his heart, and having
filled himself with a manly spirit, led his valiant army for
the land of Russia into the country of the Pólovtses.[3]

II

Then ıgor looked up to the bright sun, and saw that he
had covered in darkness[4] all his warriors.   And Ígor spoke
to his druzhína: " O brothers and druzhína!   It is better to
be cut to pieces than to be made a captive!   Let us, O
brothers, mount our swift horses that we may behold the
beautiful Don! "

A strong desire filled the Prince's soul to drink from the
great Don, and his eagerness blinded him to the evil omen.

" For I wish," he said, " to break the spear on the border
of the Pólovts land together with you, sons of Russia!   I
want to lay down my head, and drink with my helmet from
the Don! "

O Boyán, nightingale of ancient time!   It were for you
to spell this army, soaring like a nightingale over the tree
of thought, flying like an eagle below the clouds, stringing
together words for the deeds of that time, racing over
Troyán's[5] footsteps over fields to the mountains.   You

[1] Román was a brother of Ígor's grandfather Olég; he was killed
by the Pólovtses in 1079.

[2] Vladímir the Great, father of Yaroslav.

[3] A Turkish tribe, related to the Pechenyégs, who called themselves
Cumanians.   They occupied the south of Russia as far as Hungary.

[4] See account of the eclipse in the Chronicle (p. 72).

[5] Troyán is counted among the ancient Russian divinities in *The
Holy Virgin's Descent into Hell* (p. 97); but evidently he is also a
reminiscence of the Roman Emperor Trajan, whose ramparts and
roads are still to be traced along the Danube.

ought to have sung a song to Ígor, his grandson: "Not a
storm has driven the falcons over the broad fields: flocks of
crows hasten to the great Don." . . . Or you might
have sung thus, inspired Boyán, grandson of Velés [1]:

"'The horses neigh beyond the Sulá [2]; glory resounds in
Kíev; trumpets blare in Nóvgorod [3]; the standards are at
Putívl [4]; Ígor waits for his beloved brother Vsévolod. And
Vsévolod, the Grim Aurochs, spoke to him: "My only
brother, my only light, glorious Ígor, we are both sons of
Svyatosláv! Saddle, O brother, your swift steeds, for mine
are ready for you, having been saddled in advance at Kursk!
My Kurians are tried warriors, nurtured by the sound of
trumpets, rocked in helmets, fed at the point of the spear.
The roads are known to them; the ravines are familiar to
them; their bows are drawn; their quivers open, their
swords — whetted. They race over the fields like grey
wolves, seeking honour for themselves, and glory for their
Prince."

III

Then Prince Ígor stepped into the golden stirrup and
galloped over the clear field. The sun barred his way in
darkness; night groaning with the cries of birds awoke him;
beasts howled, and Div [5] called in the top of a tree, sending
the news to the unknown land, to the Vólga, the Sea border, [6]
the Sulá country, Surózh [7] and Korsún, [8] and to you, idol of
Tmútorokan! [9] But the Pólovtses hastened by untrodden

[1] The god of the flocks, *i. e.*, of wealth and abundance. It is not
quite clear why the poet is called his grandson.

[2] Tributary of the Dnieper.

[3] Nóvgorod Syéverski, Ígor's capital, in the Government of
Chernígov.

[4] The appanage of Ígor's son Vladímir, in the Government of Kursk.

[5] A bird of ill-omen; according to some, divinity of darkness.

[6] The border of the Black Sea.

[7] The Ázov Sea.

[8] The ancient Tauric Chersonese, near the modern Sebastopol.

[9] An ancient city of the Khazars, on the eastern shore of the Ázov
Sea, on the peninsula of Tamán. It became a Russian possession in
the tenth century.

roads to the great Don; the carts creaked at midnight, like swans let loose.

Igor leads his soldiers to the Don: the birds in the thicket forbode his misfortune; the wolves bristle up and howl a storm in the mountain clefts; the eagles screech and call the beasts to a feast of bones; the foxes bark for the crimson shields. O Russian land, you are already beyond the mound![1] Night is long and murky; the dawn withholds the light; mist covers the fields; the nightingale's song is silent; the cawing of the crows is heard. The Russians bar the long fields with their crimson shields, seeking honour for themselves and glory for the Prince.

IV

Early in the morning, on the Friday, they crushed the pagan Pólovts host, and, spreading like arrows over the field, seized fair Pólovts maidens, and with them gold and gold-worked stuffs and costly velvet; with cloaks and coats and Pólovts lace they bridged their way over bogs and muddy places. A red flag, white pennon, red panache, silver cross-beam, for the brave son of Svyatosláv![2] . . . Olég's valiant brood has flown afar and dreams in the field! They thought not to offend the falcon, gerfalcon, nor you, black raven, pagan Pólovts! But Gza ran like a grey wolf, with Konchák[3] in his track, to the great Don.

V

Very early the next morning a bloody dawn announces the day. Black clouds come from the sea and try to veil four suns,[4] while blue lightnings quiver through them. There

---

[1] A frequently recurring sentence, the meaning of which seems to be : You are lost beyond redemption !

[2] The trophies won by Ígor.

[3] Gza and Konchák, khans of the Pólovtses, were the leaders of the expedition. See p. 77.

[4] The four suns are : Ígor, his brother Vsévolod, his son Vladímir of Putívl, and his nephew Svyatosláv Ólgovich of Rylsk.

is to be a mighty thunder, and the rain is to go down in arrows by the great Don! There spears will be broken; there swords will be blunted against Pólovts helmets on the Kayála,[1] by the great Don. O Russian land, you are already beyond the mound!

Behold the winds, Stribóg's[2] grandchildren, blow arrows from the sea on Ígor's valiant army. The earth groans, the rivers flow turbid; dust covers the fields; the banners whisper. The Pólovtses come from the Don, and from the sea, and from all sides: the Russian army recedes. The devil's children fill the field with their cries, but the brave Russians line it with their crimson bucklers.

Grim Aurochs Vsévolod! You stand in the van; you pour arrows on the warriors; you thunder with steel swords against their helmets. Wherever you, Aurochs, lead, gleaming with your golden helmet, there fall the heads of the pagan Pólovtses, their Avar[3] helmets cloven by your tempered swords, Grim Aurochs Vsévolod! What wound does he brook, O brothers, having forgotten his honours and manner of life, and Chernígov town, his paternal golden throne, and the caresses of his sweetheart, Glyeb's fair daughter,[4] and the habits and customs of his home?

VI

Troyán's age is past, gone are the years of Yaroslâv; past are the expeditions of Olég,[5] the son of Svyatosláv. That Olég had fostered discord with his sword, and had sowed arrows over the land. In Tmútorokan city he stepped into the golden stirrup. Great Yaroslâv, that was, heard the

---

[1] Tributary of the Don.   [2] God of the winds.

[3] Descendants of the Avars still live between Georgia and Circassia.

[4] Her name was Ólga.

[5] Olég is the grandfather of Ígor. The poet here recalls former encounters with the Pólovtses. Not having been able to agree with his uncles, Izyasláv who had occupied the throne in Kíev, and Vsévolod who had his appanage of Chernígov, Olég escaped to Román the Fair of Tmútorokan, and decided to get his rights by means of arms. He led three times the Pólovtses into Russia (in 1078, 1079 and 1094).

tocsin,[1] and Vsévolod's son Vladímir closed his ears all the
days at Chernígov.[2] But Glory brought Borís,[3] the son of
Vyacheslár, before the judgment seat and bedded him,
brave young prince, on the green feather grass of the steppe,
through Olég's offence. . . .

Then, in the days of Olég Gorislávich,[4] feuds were sown
and grew, and Dazhbóg's[5] grandchildren perished, and the
years of men were shortened by the discord of the princes.
In those days the warriors rarely walked behind the plough
in the Russian land, but the ravens croaked as they divided
the dead bodies, and crows chattered, flying to the banquet.
Such were the wars and expeditions then, but the like of
this war was never known.

VII

From early morning until evening, from evening until
daylight fly tempered arrows, thunder the swords against
the helmets, resound the steel spears in a strange field,
within the country of the Pólovtses. The black earth beneath the hoofs was sown with bones, and watered with
blood, and a harvest of sorrow went up in the Russian land.

What noise is that, what din, so early in the morning before dawn ? Ígor leads his army ; he is sorry for his beloved
brother Vsévolod. They fought a day, they fought another[6];
upon the third at noon fell the standards of Ígor. The

[1] That is, in the other world.

[2] Vladímir Monomákh hastened to his father's aid. See his *Instruction*, p. 55.

[3] Olég and his cousin, Borís, were at that time absent from Chernígov. When they arrived and opposed themselves to the superior
force of Izyaslár, Olég advised Borís to surrender ; but he would not
listen and made an attack upon his uncle's army and was killed.

[4] Olég is called the son of "Góre," *i. e.*, woe.

[5] The Russians are sons of Dazhbóg, the god of the sun, while the
enemy are the "devil's children."

[6] The first day the Russians defeated the Pólovtses ; the next, the
Pólovtses defeated the Russians ; on the third day, which was a
Sunday, the Kovúans ran away, and at noon Ígor was made prisoner.
See the Chronicle, p. 74.

brothers separated on the bank of the swift Kayála.   Here
there was not enough of bloody wine; here the brave Russians ended the feast: they gave their host their fill to drink,
and themselves fell for the Russian land.   The grass withered
from sorrow, and the trees in anguish bent down to the
earth.[1]

VIII

There befell a hapless hour, O brothers!   Already had the
wilderness covered Russia's hosts, when Mischief arose in
the hosts of Dazhbóg's grandchildren: she walked as a
maiden in Troyán's land,[2] splashed her swan pinions in the
blue sea,[3] and splashing them in the Don, recalled heavy
times.

Through the feuds of the princes ruin came from the
pagans, for brother spoke to brother: "This is mine and
that is mine also," and the princes said of trifling matters,
"They are important," and created discord among themselves; and the pagans came from all sides victorious into
the Russian land.

Oh, far has the falcon[4] flown, driving the birds by the sea,
but Ígor's brave army will rise no more!   Konchák called,
and Gza raced over the Russian land, hurling fire from
a flaming horn.[5]   Russian women wept, saying: "No
longer will our thoughts reach our dear ones, nor shall we
ever see them with our eyes, nor be adorned with tinkling
gold and silver!"

And Kíev groaned under its sorrow, and Chernígov on
account of its misfortunes.   Sadness spread over the Russian
land, and a heavy gloom.   The princes fostered discord
among themselves, and the pagans victoriously overran the
country, receiving tribute, a squirrel[6] from each house.

It is Ígor and Vsévolod, Svyatosláv's brave sons, who
through their discord had wakened dishonour which their

[1] Nature sympathises with the Russians.
[2] That is, far away ; see note 5, p. 82.   [3] The Sea of Ázov.
[4] That is, Ígor ; the Pólovtses are the birds.
[5] The Chronicle says the Pólovtses hurled the Greek fire.
[6] A silver coin.

father, Svyatosláv [1] of Kíev, the great, the mighty had, put
to sleep: he had invaded the Pólovts land and had carried
terror to them, with his mighty armies and tempered swords;
had levelled their hills and ravines, ruffled their rivers and
lakes, dried up their streams and swamps; and, like a whirlwind, had snatched pagan Kobyák [2] away from his mighty,
steel-clad Pólovts army by the Ázov Sea, until Kobyák fell
in Kíev city, in the council-room of Svyatosláv. Germans,
Venetians, Greeks and Moravians sing the glory of Svyatosláv, but blame Prince Ígor who had merged his wealth in
the Kayála, the Pólovts river, and had filled it with Russian
gold. Here Ígor was unseated from his golden saddle and
placed upon the saddle of a slave.

IX

The city walls were silent, and merriment was dead.
Svyatosláv saw a troubled dream: "In Kíev on the mount
you enveloped me last night," he said, "in a black shroud
on a bed of yew; they poured out to me blue wine mixed
with bitterness; from empty quivers they showered large
gems upon my lap, and tried to comfort me. Already are
there boards without a cross beam in my hall of gold, and all
night have the devilish crows been cawing." [3] . . . .

The boyárs spoke to the Prince: "Prince, sorrow has
enthralled your mind. Two falcons flew from their paternal
throne of gold to find the city of Tmútorokan, and anxious
to drink from the Don with their helmets. The falcons'
wings have been clipped by the pagan swords, and they
have been enmeshed in iron fetters. On the third day it
was dark: two suns were dimmed, [4] two red torches went

---

[1] This Svyatosláv, the son of Vsévolod Ólgovich, had been the
Prince of Chernígov. He was Grand Prince of Kíev from 1174-1194.
He had to give up his throne twice, but in 1181 ascended it for the
third time. He is called Ígor's and Vsévolod's father by seniority,
though he was only their uncle by relationship.

[2] The Russians obtained a famous victory over the Pólovtses, of
whom 7000 were taken prisoners, in 1184.

[3] A series of evil omens.   [4] Ígor and Vsévolod.

out, and with them two young moons, Olég [1] and Svyatosláv, were shrouded in darkness. On Kayála river darkness veiled the day: the Pólovtses had invaded the Russian land, like a litter of lynxes. . . . Fair Gothic [2] maidens sing upon the shore of the blue sea, tinkling with the Russian gold: they sing the times of Bus, recall Sharokán's [3] revenge. But we, your druzhína, are anxious for the feast.''

Then great Svyatosláv uttered golden words, mingled with tears: '' Oh, my nephews, Ígor and Vsévolod! Too early did you begin to strike the land of the Pólovtses with your swords, and to seek glory for yourselves. You were vanquished ingloriously, for ingloriously have you spilled the blood of the pagans! Your brave hearts are forged with hard steel and tempered in daring exploits. See what you have done with my silvery hair! I no longer see with me my mighty, warlike brother Izyasláv with his Chernígov druzhína. . . . They overwhelmed their enemies with dirks, not bearing bucklers, but raising a warcry and resounding the glory of their forefathers. But you spoke: ' We alone will vanquish! Let us ourselves gain the future glory, and share the glory of our fathers!' Why should not an old man feel young again? When the falcon is moulting, he drives the birds far away, and allows not his nest to be hurt. But alas, the princes will not aid me! My years have turned to nothing. At Rim [4] they cry under the swords of the Pólovtses, and Vladímir [5] groans under his wounds. Bitterness and sorrow has befallen the son of Glyeb!''

[1] Probably the son of Ígor ; but he was only eleven years old during the expedition.

[2] Descendants of the Goths who had settled along the Black Sea had been found and described as late as the sixteenth and even seventeenth centuries in the Crimea and in the Tamán peninsula.

[3] These Gothic girls evidently sang the exploits of Pólovts princes. Sharokán had made an incursion into Russia in 1107, but he was defeated and had to flee. In 1111 Sharokán returned with an immense army to avenge his defeat.

[4] Now Rómen, in the Government of Poltáva.

[5] Vladímir of Pereyáslavl. See the Chronicle, p. 78.

x

Grand Prince Vsévolod![1] Fly from afar not only in thought, but come to protect your paternal throne: for you could dry up the Vólga[2] with your oars, and empty the Don with your helmets. If you were here, a Pólovts slave-girl would be worth a dime, and a man-slave—half a rouble.[3] And you know, together with the brave sons of Glyeb, how to hurl the Greek fire on land.

You, Grim Aurochs Rúrik and David![4] Did not your golden helmets swim in blood? Did not your valiant dru- zhína bellow like aurochses, when they were wounded by tempered swords in a strange field? Put your feet, O lords, into your golden stirrups to avenge the insult to the Russian land, the wounds of Ígor, the valiant son of Svyatosláv!

Yaroslav Osmomýsl of Gálich![5] You sit high upon your throne wrought of gold, propping with your iron-clad army the Carpathian mountains, barring the king's path, closing the gates of the Danube, hurling missiles higher than the clouds, sitting in judgment as far as the Danube. Your thunders pass over the land, and you hold the key to the gates of Kíev; sitting on your paternal throne, you slay the sultans in their lands. Slay, O lord, Konchák, the pagan villain, to avenge the Russian land, the wounds of Ígor, the valiant son of Svyatosláv!

And you, valiant Román[6] and Mstisláv! A brave

[1] Vsévolod Yúrevich, Prince of Súzdal, whose father, Yúri Dol- gorúki, had been Grand Prince at Kíev.

[2] In 1183 Vsévolod made an expedition against the Bulgarians of the Vólga; he went down the Vólga as far as Kazán, and then proceeded on foot.

[3] That is, if Vsévolod were there, he would be so victorious against the Pólovtses as to lower the price of Pólovts slaves.

[4] The sons of Rostisláv Mstislávich, and great-grandchildren of Vládímir Monomákh.

[5] Yaroslav Osmomýsl († 1187) was the Prince of Gálich, which in his days extended as far as the Prut and the Danube and included part of Moldavia. His daughter was Ígor's wife.

[6] Román Mstislávich († 1205), Prince of Volhynia, twice occupied the throne in Gálich. He fought successfully against the Lithuanians

thought carries you into action.[1] You fly high in your onslaught, like a falcon circling in the air, about to swoop
down upon the birds. You wear iron hauberks under Latin
helmets, and the earth has trembled from you in many a
pagan land: the Lithuanians, Yatvyágans, Deremélans and
Pólovtses threw down their warclubs and bent their heads
under those tempered swords. But now, O Prince, Ígor's
sun is dimmed,—the tree, alas, has shed its leaves. Along
the Ros[2] and the Sulá the Pólovtses have sacked the towns,
but Ígor's brave army will rise no more. The Don calls you,
O Prince, and the other princes to victory!

Olég's sons have hastened to the war. Íngvar and
Vsévolod,[3] and the three sons of Mstisláv,[4] a mighty winged
brood! Not by the lot of war have you acquired power. Of
what good are your golden helmets, and Polish warclubs and
shields? Bar the enemy's way with your sharp arrows, to
avenge the Russian land, the wounds of Ígor, the valiant son
of Svyatosláv!

XI

The Sulá no longer flows with a silvery stream by Pereyáslavl town,[5] and the Dviná flows turbid by mighty Pólotsk,
agitated by the pagans. Izyasláv,[6] Vasílko's son, alone

and Yatvyágans, and when he was Prince of Gálich he saved Constantinople from the impending danger of a Pólovts and Pechenyég
invasion. The Chronicle says of him: "He rushed against the
pagans like a lion, raged like a lynx, and destroyed them like a
crocodile, and crossed their lands like an eagle, for he was as brave
as an aurochs," and "The Pólovtses used to frighten their children
with his name."

[1] Mstisláv was probably the brother of Íngvar and Vsévolod, mentioned below.

[2] Tributary of the Dnieper.

[3] The sons of Yarosláv Izyaslávich, Prince of Lutsk, who was
Grand Prince of Kíev in 1173.

[4] Román, Svyatosláv and Vsévolod, sons of Mstisláv, great-grandchildren of Vladímir Monomákh.

[5] The Pólovtses divided among themselves the towns along the
Sulá. See the Chronicle, p. 77.

[6] Izyasláv's appanage was Goródno, in the Government of Minsk,
hence farther down "The trumpets blare at Goródno."

made his sharp swords ring against the Lithuanian helmets, outstripping the glory of his grandfather Vsesláv, but himself was worsted by Lithuanian swords, and fell under crimson shields, upon the bloodstained grass. Lying on his death-bed, he spoke[1]: "O Prince, the birds have covered your druzhína with their wings, and the beasts have lapped their blood." There was not present the brother Bryachisláv, nor the other, Vsévolod; alone he lost the pearl soul out of his valiant body through the golden necklace. The voices were subdued, merriment died away. The trumpets blare at Goródno.

Yarosláv and all grandchildren of Vsesláv![2] Furl your standards, sheath your blunted swords, for you have leaped away from your grandfather's glory! You have with your discords invited the pagan hosts against the Russian land, against the life of Vsesláv, for through your strife has come the enslavement by the Pólovts land.

In the seventh age of Troyán,[3] Vsesláv cast his lot for his beloved maiden.[4] He bestrode his horse, and galloped to the city of Kíev, and with the thrust of the spear possessed himself of golden-throned Kíev. He galloped hence as a grim beast to the south of Byélgorod,[5] and disappeared in the blue mist; next morning he clanked with the battering-ram, and opened the gates of Nóvgorod; he shattered the glory of Yarosláv,[6] and raced as a wolf to the Nemíga from Dudútki.[7]

[1] Izyasláv addresses himself.

[2] These are opposed to the brave Izyasláv, who is also a descendant of Vsesláv. Vsesláv Bryachislávich, Prince of Pólotsk, was, in 1064, defeated by Izyasláv and his brothers on the Nemíga; later he was enticed by Izyasláv to Kíev, where he was imprisoned. In 1067 Izyasláv was driven out by the Kíevans, and Vsesláv was made Grand Prince. Izyasláv attacked Vsesláv at Byélgorod, but the latter fled to Pólotsk.

[3] The exact meaning of the "seventh age of Troyán" is not known; some distant time is designated.

[4] That is, for Kíev.   [5] Ten versts from Kíev.

[6] Tributary of the Svísloch, in the Government of Minsk.

Near Nóvgorod.

On the Nemíga, ricks are stacked with heads, and they flail with tempered chains; the body is placed on the threshing-floor, and the soul is winnowed from the body. Not with grain were sown the bloody banks of the Nemíga, but with the bones of Russian sons.

Prince Vsesláv sat in judgment over his people, apportioned cities to the princes, but himself raced a wolf[1] in the night, and by cockcrow reached from Kíev to Tmútorokan, and as a wolf crossed the path of great Khors.[2] When they rang the bell in the church of St. Sophia for matins, early in the morning at Pólotsk, he heard the ringing in Kíev. Though his cunning soul could pass into another body, yet he often suffered woe. Thus wise Boyán of old has justly said: "Neither the cunning, nor the agile, nor the swift bird can escape the judgment of the Lord!"

Oh, the Russian land must groan as it recalls the former days and the ancient princes! It was not possible to nail Vladímir to the hills of Kíev[3]: now there are standards of Rúrik, and others of David.[4]   .   .   .

XII

Yaroslávna's[5] voice is heard; like a cuckoo in a lonely spot she calls plaintively in the morning: "I will fly," she says, "like a cuckoo along the Danube,[6] will wet my beaver sleeve in the river Kayála, will wipe off the Prince's bloody wounds on his manly body!"

Yaroslávna weeps in the morning at Putívl town on the wall, saying: "O wind, mighty wind! Why, master, do you blow so strong? Why do you on your light wings carry the Khan's arrows against the warriors of my beloved one?

[1] The chronicles and popular tradition make Vsesláv a werewolf and a sorcerer.

[2] Another name for Dazhbóg, the god of the sun.

[3] That is, for ever to retain Vladímir in Kíev.

[4] Now there is discord.

[5] Evfrosíniya (Euphrosyne), daughter of Yaroslác Osmomýsl of Gálich, Ígor's second wife.

[6] A standing formula for rivers in general, here the Kayála.

Is it not enough for you to blow on high below the clouds, rocking the ships on the blue sea? Why, master, have you dispersed my happiness over the grass of the steppe?"

Yaroslávna weeps in the morning at Putívl town on the wall, saying: "O famous Dnieper, you have pierced the rocky mountains across the country of the Pólovtses! You have rocked on your waves the boats of Svyatosláv as far as the army of Kobák.[1] Fondly bring to me, master, my sweetheart, that I may not in the morning send tears after him out to sea."

Yaroslávna weeps in the morning at Putívl town on the wall, saying: "Bright, three times bright sun, you give warmth and joy to all! Why, master, have you thrust your burning beams on the warriors of my beloved one? Why have you in the waterless plain dried up their bows, and sealed their quivers in sorrow?"

XIII

The sea is agitated at midnight: mists are borne in the darkness. God shows to Ígor a way out of the land of the Pólovtses into the country of Russia to his father's golden throne. The evening twilight has gone out. Ígor sleeps; Ígor is awake: Ígor in his thought measures the plains from the great Don to the small Donéts. His steed is ready at midnight. Ovlúr whistles beyond the river, gives a sign to the Prince,—Prince Ígor will be no more!

The earth resounded, the grass rustled, the Pólovts tents trembled. But Ígor raced like an ermine in the reeds, like a white duck over the water; he jumped on a swift steed, dismounted as a light-footed wolf, and hastened to the plain of the Donéts; and as a falcon flew through the mist, killing geese and swans for his breakfast and dinner and supper. When Ígor flew as a falcon, Ovlúr raced as a wolf, shaking off the cold dew, for they had worn out their swift steeds.

The Donéts spoke: "Prince Ígor, great is your honour, and the grief to Konchák, and joy to the Russian land!"

[1] Expedition of 1184.

Ígor spoke: "O Donéts, great is your honour, having rocked the Prince on your wave, having spread out for him the green grass on your silver banks, having cloaked him with warm mists under green trees. You have guarded him as a duck on the water, as a gull on the waves, as a mallard in the air. Not thus the river Stúgna[1]: though having a scanty stream, it has swallowed other brooks, and has spread the floods over the bushes. To the young Prince Rostisláv the Dnieper has closed its dark banks. Rostisláv's mother weeps for the young Prince. The flowers faded in their sorrow, and the trees bent in anguish to the ground."

It is not magpies that are in a flutter: Gza and Konchák ride in Ígor's track. Then the raven did not croak, the jackdaws were silent, the magpies did not chatter, only leaped from branch to branch. The woodpeckers indicated the road to the river by their pecking; the nightingales announced the day by their merry song.

Said Gza to Konchák: "Since the falcon is flying to his nest, let us shoot the fledgling[2] with our golden darts."

Said Konchák to Gza: "Since the falcon is flying to his nest, let us enmesh the fledgling with a fair maiden!"

And Gza spoke to Konchák: "If we enmesh him with a fair maiden, we shall have neither the young falcon, nor the fair maiden, and the birds will attack us in the Pólovts plain."

XIV

Boyán has said: "Hard it is for you, O head, to be without your shoulders; ill it is for you, O body, to be without a head." Even so is the Russian land without Ígor.

The sun shines in the heaven,—Prince Ígor in the land of

[1] A swampy river in the Government of Kíev. Rostisláv Vsévolodo-vich, the son of Vsévolod and Anna, the daughter of a Pólovts Khan, and the brother of Vladímir Monomákh. After an unsuccessful attack upon the Pólovtses, he escaped from captivity by jumping into the Stúgna, but being in heavy armour he was drowned.

[2] Vladímir, the son of Ígor, who was also taken captive. He really married Konchák's daughter and returned with her to Kíev in 1187.

Russia! Maidens sing at the Danube: their voices are carried over the sea to Kíev. Igor rides over the Boríchev,[1] to the church of the Holy Virgin of Pirogóshch. The country is happy, the towns rejoice; they sing songs to the elder princes, and then to the younger. Let us sing the glory of Igor Svyatoslávich, of Grim Aurochs Vsévolod, Vladímir Igorevich! Hail, princes and druzhína, who battle for the Christians against the pagan host! Glory to the princes and the druzhína! Amen!

The Holy Virgin's Descent into Hell. (XII. century.)

In spite of the prohibition of the Church, apocryphal literature reached Russia from Byzantium by way of Bulgaria, and not only spread all over Russia as a possession of the people, but even crept into ecclesiastical literature, serving frequently the same purpose as the writings of the Church Fathers. These apocryphal productions, of which there is a very large number, held sway over the people from the twelfth to the seventeenth century, and even now form the background of many popular tales and songs, especially of those of the "wandering people" and beggars. One of the most beautiful stories of this kind is *The Holy Virgin's Descent into Hell*, the Russian manuscript of which goes back to the twelfth century. Similar stories were also current in Italy, where there were colonies of Bulgarian Manicheans, who were most active in disseminating them. Dante was, no doubt, acquainted with them when he wrote his *Divine Comedy*.

The Holy Virgin wished to see the torments of the souls, and She spoke to Michael, the archistrategos: "Tell me all things that are upon earth!" And Michael said to Her: "As you say, Blessed One: I shall tell you all things." And the Holy Virgin said to him: "How many torments are there, that the Christian race is suffering?" And the archistrategos said to Her: "Uncountable are the torments!" And the Blessed One spoke to him: "Show me, in heaven and upon earth!"

Then the archistrategos ordered the angels to come from the south, and Hell was opened. And She saw those that

[1] The slope of the mountain near Kíev, where to-day is the suburb of Podól.

were suffering in Hell, and there was a great number of men and women, and there was much weeping. And the Blessed One asked the archistrategos: "Who are these?" And the archistrategos said: "These are they who did not believe in the Father and the Son and the Holy Ghost, but forgot God and believed in things which God has created for our sakes; they called everything God: the sun and the moon, the earth and water, beasts and reptiles. They changed Troyán, Khors, Velés, Perún[1] to gods, and believed in evil spirits. They are even now held in evil darkness, therefore they suffer such torments."

And She saw in another place a great darkness. Said the Holy Lady: "What is this darkness, and who are those who dwell therein?" Spoke the archistrategos: "Many souls dwell in this place." Spoke the Holy Virgin: "Let the darkness be dispersed that I may see the torment." And the angels who watched over the torment answered: "We have been enjoined not to let them see light until the coming of your blessed Son who is brighter than seven suns." And the Holy Virgin was saddened, and She raised Her eyes to the angels and looked at the invisible throne of Her Father and spoke: "In the name of the Father and the Son and the Holy Ghost! Let the darkness be taken off that I may see this torment."

And the darkness was lifted, and seven heavens were seen, and there dwelt there a great multitude of men and women, and there was loud weeping and a mighty noise. When the Holy Virgin saw them, She spoke to them, weeping tears: "What have you done, wretched and unworthy people, and what has brought you here?" There was no voice, nor an answer from them. And the watching angels spoke: "Wherefore do you not speak?" And the tormented said: "Blessed One! We have not seen light for a long time, and we cannot look up." The Holy Virgin looking at them wept bitterly. And the tormented, seeing Her, said: "How

---

[1] Pagan divinities. For Troyán, see note on p. 82; Khors, the god of the sun (*cf.* note on p. 93); Velés, the god of abundance (*cf.* note on p. 83); Perún, the god of thunder (see p. 70).

is it, Holy Virgin, you have visited us? Your blessed Son came upon earth and did not ask for us, nor Abraham the patriarch, nor Moses the prophet, nor John the Baptist, nor Paul the apostle, the Lord's favourite. But you, Holy Virgin and intercessor, you are a protection for the Christian people." . . . Then spoke the Holy Virgin to Michael the archistrategos: "What is their sin?" And Michael said: "These are they who did not believe in the Father and the Son and the Holy Ghost, nor in you, Holy Virgin! They did not want to proclaim your name, nor that from you was born our Lord Jesus Christ who, having come in the flesh, has sanctified the earth through baptism: it is for this that they are tormented here." Weeping again, the Holy Virgin spoke to them: "Wherefore do you live in error? Do you not know that all creation honours my name?" When the Holy Virgin said this, darkness fell again upon them.

The archistrategos spoke to Her: "Whither, Blessed One, do you want to go now? To the south, or to the north?" The Blessed One spoke: "Let us go out to the south!" And there came the cherubim and the seraphim and four hundred angels, and took the Holy Virgin to the south where there was a river of fire. There was a multitude of men and women there, and they stood in the river, some to their waists, some to their shoulders, some to their necks and some above their heads. Seeing this, the Holy Virgin wept aloud and asked the archistrategos: "Who are they that are immerged up to their waists in the fire?" And the archistrategos said to Her: "They are those who have been cursed by their fathers and mothers,—for this the cursed ones suffer torment here." And the Holy Virgin said: "And those who are in the fiery flame up to their necks, who are they?" The angel said to Her: "They are those who have eaten human flesh,—for this they are tormented here." And the Holy One said: "Those who are immerged in the fiery flame above their heads, who are they?" And the archistrategos spoke: "Those are they, Lady, who holding the cross have sworn falsely." . . . The Holy One spoke to the archistrategos: "I beg you this one thing, let me also enter, that I may suffer together with the Christians, for they have called themselves the children of my Son." And the archistrategos said: "Rest yourself in paradise!" And the Holy One said: "I beg you, move the hosts of the seven heavens and all the host of the angels that we may pray for the sinners, and God may accept our prayer and have mercy upon them. I beg you, order the angelic host to carry me to the heavenly height and to take me before the invisible Father!"

The archistrategos so ordered, and there appeared the cherubim and seraphim and carried the Blessed One to the heavenly height, and put Her down at the throne of the invisible Father. She raised Her hands to Her blessed Son and said: "Have mercy, O Master, upon the sinners, for I have seen them, and I could not endure: let me be tormented together with the Christians!" And there came a voice to Her and said: "How can I have mercy upon them? I see the nails in my Son's hands." And She said: "Master! I do not pray for the infidel Jews, but for the Christians I ask Thy forgiveness!" And a voice came to Her: "I see how they have had no mercy upon my children, so I can have no mercy upon them."

Spoke again the Holy One: "Have mercy, O Master, upon the sinners,—the creation of Thine own hands, who proclaim Thy name over the whole earth and even in their torments, and who in all places say: "Most Holy Lady, Mother of God, aid us!" Then the Lord spoke to Her: "Hear, Holy Mother of God! There is not a man who does not praise Thy name. I will not abandon them, neither in heaven, nor upon earth." And the Holy Virgin said: "Where is Moses, the prophet? Where are all the prophets? And you, fathers, who have never committed a sin? Where is Paul, God's favourite? Where is the Sunday, the pride of the Christian? And where is the power of the worshipful cross through which Adam and Eve were delivered from their curse?" Then Michael the archistrategos and all the angels spoke: "Have mercy, O Master, upon the sinners!" And Moses wept loud and said: "Have mercy upon them,

O Lord! For I have given them Thy Law!" And John wept and said: "Have mercy, O Master! I preached Thy gospel to them." And Paul wept and said: "Have mercy, O Master! For I carried Thine epistles to the churches."

And those that were in the darkness heard of this, and they all wept with one voice and said: "Have mercy upon us, Son of God! Have mercy upon us, King of all eternity!" And the Master said: "Hear all! I have planted paradise, and created man according to my image, and made him lord over paradise, and gave him eternal life. But they have disobeyed me and sinned in their selfishness and delivered themselves to death. . . . You became Christians only in words, and did not keep my commands; for this you find yourselves now in the fire everlasting, and I ought not to have mercy upon you! But to-day, through the goodness of my Father who sent me to you, and through the intercession of my Mother who wept much for you, and through Michael, the archistrategos of the gospel, and through the multitude of my martyrs who have laboured much in your behalf, I give you from Good Thursday to the holy Pentecost, day and night, for a rest, and you praise the Father and the Son and the Holy Ghost!" And they all answered: "Glory be to Thy goodness! Glory to the Father and the Son and the Holy Ghost, now and for ever!"

Daniel the Prisoner. (XIII. century.)

For some unknown reason Daniel had been imprisoned in an island in the Lake of Lach, in the Government of Olónetsk. He seems to have belonged to the druzhína of Yaroslár Vsévolodovich of Pereyáslavl, who died in 1247 as Grand Prince of Vladímir. That is all that is known about the life of this layman, one of the few in the old period whose writing has come down to our times. The begging letter which he addressed to the Prince is composed of incorrectly quoted biblical passages and popular saws and proverbs; many of these he drew from an ancient collection, *The Bee*, in which moral subjects are arranged in chapters. In their turn, Daniel's saws have largely entered into the composition of a very popular collection of the same kind, *The Emerald*.

LETTER TO PRINCE YAROSLÁV VSÉVOLODOVICH

We will blare forth, O brothers, on the reasoning of our mind, as on a trumpet forged of gold. We will strike the silver organs, and will proclaim our wisdom, and will strike the thoughts of our mind, playing on the God-inspired reeds, that our soul-saving thoughts might weep loud. Arise, my glory! Arise, psalter and cymbals, that I may unfold my meaning in proverbs, and that I may announce my glory in words. . . . Knowing, O lord, your good disposition, I take refuge in your customary kindness, for the Holy Writ says: Ask and you shall receive. David has said: There is no speech nor language, where their voice is not heard. Neither will we be silent, but will speak out to our master, the most gracious Yarosláv Vsévolodovich.

Prince my lord! Remember me in your reign, for I, your slave, and son of your slave, see all men warmed by your mercy as by the sun; only I alone walk in darkness, deprived of the light from your eyes, like the grass growing behind a wall, upon which neither the sun shineth nor the rain falleth. So, my lord, incline your ears to the words of my lips, and deliver me from all my sorrow.

Prince my lord! All get their fill from the abundance of your house; but I alone thirst for your mercy, like a stag for a spring of water. I was like a tree that stands in the road and that all passers-by strike;—even thus I am insulted by all, for I am not protected by the terror of your wrath, as by a firm palisade.

Prince my lord! The rich man is known everywhere, even in a strange city, while the poor man walketh unseen in his own. The rich man speaketh and all are silent, and his words are elated to the clouds; but let the poor man speak out, and all will call out to him, for the discourse of those is honoured whose garments are bright. But you, my lord, look not at my outer garb, but consider my inner thoughts, for my apparel is scanty, and I am young in years, but old in mind, and I have soared in thought like an eagle in the air.

Prince my lord! Let me behold your fair face and form. Your lips drop honey; your utterances are like paradise with its fruit; your hands are filled with gold of Tharsos; your cheeks are a vessel of spices; your throat is like a lily dropping myrrh—your mercy; your look is as the choice Lebanon; your eyes are like a well of living water; your belly is like an heap of wheat, feeding many; your head riseth above my head. . . .

Prince my lord! Look not at me as a wolf at a lamb; but look at me as a mother at her babe. Look, O lord, at the birds of the air, that neither plough, nor sow, nor gather into granaries, but rely upon God's kindness. Let not your hand be closed against giving alms to the needy. For it is written: Give to him who asketh of you, open to him who knocketh, that you may not forfeit the kingdom of heaven. For it is also written: Confide your sorrow to the Lord, and He will nurture you until eternity. Deprive not the needy wise man of his bread, but extol him to the clouds, like pure gold in a dirty vessel; but the silly rich man is like a silken pillow-case stuffed full of straw.

Prince my lord! Though I am not a valiant man in war, yet am I strong in words, and I cull the sweetness of words, mixing them, as sea-water in a leather bottle, and wind them and adorn them with cunning parables, and I am glib of speech and . . . my lips are pleasing, like a stream of the river rapids.

Prince my lord! As an oak is strong by the multitude of its roots, thus is our city under your domination. The helmsman is the head of the vessel, and you, Prince, are the head of your people. I have seen an army without a prince; —you might say: a big beast without its head. Men are the heads of women, and princes—of men, and God—of the prince. As the pillow-case that is adorned with silk makes a pleasant appearance, even thus you, our Prince, are glorified and honoured in many lands through the multitude of your men. As the net does not hold the water, but keeps a multitude of fish, even thus you, our Prince, keep not the wealth, but distribute it among the strong, making them brave, for you will gain gold and cities through them. Hezekiah, the King of the Jews, boasted before the messengers of the King of Babylon, when he showed them the treasure of his gold. But they answered: " Our kings are richer than you, not with the treasure of gold, but with a multitude of brave and wise men." (For men will gain gold, but gold will not gain men.) Water is the mother of the fish, and you are Prince of your people. Spring adorns the earth with flowers, and you, Prince, adorn us with your mercy. The sun alone warms with its rays, and you, Prince, adorn and revive with your mercy.

Prince my lord! I have been in great distress, and have suffered under the yoke of work: I have experienced all that is evil. Rather would I see my foot in bast shoes in your house than in crimson boots in the court of a boyár. Rather would I serve you in homespun than in purple in the court of a boyár. Improper is a golden ring in the nose of a swine, and a good garment upon a peasant. Even if a kettle were to have golden rings in its handles, its bottom would not escape blackness and burning. Even thus a peasant: let him be ever so haughty and insolent, he will not escape his blemish, the name of a peasant. Rather would I drink water in your house, than mead in the court of a boyár; rather would I receive a roasted sparrow from your hand than a shoulder of mutton from the hand of a bad master.

Often has my bread, earned by work, tasted as wormwood in my mouth, and my drink I have mingled with tears. Serving a good master, you gain your liberty in the end, but serving a bad master, you only gain an increase of your labour. Solomon has said: Better is one wise man than ten brave men without understanding; better is one clever man than ten rulers of cities. Daniel has said: A brave man, O Prince, you will easily acquire, but a wise man is dear; for the counsel of the wise is good, and their armies are strong, and their cities safe. The armies of others are strong, but without understanding, and they suffer defeat. Many, arming themselves against large cities, start out from smaller towns; as Svyatosláv, the son of Ólga, said on his way to

Constantinople to his small druzhína: "We do not know, O brothers, whether the city is to be taken by us, or whether we are to perish from the city: for if God is with us, who is against us?" . . .

Not the sea draweth the ships, but the winds; even thus you, O Prince, fall not yourself into grieving, but counsellors lead you into it. Not the fire causeth the iron to be heated, but the blowing of the bellows. A wise man is not generally valiant in war, but strong in counsel; so it is good to gather wise men around you. It is good to pasture horses in a fertile field (and to fight for a good prince). Often armies perish through lack of order. If the armies are strongly placed, they will, though they be defeated, make a good running fight; thus Svyatopólk, who was guilty of killing his brothers, was so fortified, that Yarosláv barely overcame him at night. Similarly Bonyák the Scurfy through cunning routed the Hungarians at Gálich: when the latter fortified themselves behind ramparts, the first scattered like hunting men over the land; thus they routed the Hungarians, and badly defeated them.

Prince my lord! I have not been brought up in Athens, nor have I studied with the philosophers, but I have pored over books, like a bee over all kinds of flowers: from them have I gathered sweetness of speech, mingling wisdom with it, as sea-water in a leather bottle. . . .

Serapión, Bishop of Vladímir. (XIII. century.)

Serapión had been abbot of the monastery of the Grottoes in Kíev, and in 1274 he was made bishop of Vladímir and Súzdal. He died in 1275. We have five of his sermons, which are distinguished for a certain simple, stern eloquence. The thirteenth century produced very few writers, and Serapión's sermons have an additional interest because they contain references to the Tartar invasion.

A SERMON ON OMENS

The Lord's blessing be with you!

You have heard, brothers, what the Lord Himself has said in the gospel: in the last years there will be signs in the

sun, in the moon, and in the stars, and earthquakes in many
places, and famine. What had been foretold by the Lord
then, is now fulfilled in our days.[1] We have seen many
times the sun perished, the moon darkened, and the stars
disturbed, and lately we have seen with our own eyes the
quaking of the earth. The earth, firm and immovable from
the beginning by the order of God, is in motion to-day,
trembling on account of our sins, being unable to bear our
lawlessness. We did not obey the gospel, did not obey the
apostles, nor the prophets, nor the great luminaries, I mean
Basil and Gregory the theologues, John Chrysostom, and
the other holy fathers, by whom the faith was confirmed,
the heretics repelled, and God made known to all the nations. They have taught us without interruption, but we
are living in lawlessness.

It is for this that God is punishing us with signs and
earthquakes. He does not speak with His lips, but chastises
with deeds. God has punished us with everything, but has
not dispelled our evil habits: now He shakes the earth and
makes it tremble: He wants to shake off our lawlessness and
sins from the earth like leaves from a tree. If any should
say that there have been earthquakes before, I shall not
deny it. But what happened to us afterwards? Did we not
have famine, and plague, and many wars? But we did not
repent, until finally there came upon us a ruthless nation, at
the instigation of God, and laid waste our land, and took
into captivity whole cities, destroyed our holy churches, slew
our fathers and brothers, violated our mothers and sisters.
Now, my brothers, having experienced that, let us pray to
our Lord, and make confession, lest we incur a greater wrath
of the Lord, and bring down upon us a greater punishment
than the first.

Much is still waiting for our repentance and for our con-
version. If we turn away from corrupt and ruthless judgments, if we do away with bloody usury and all rapacity,
thefts, robbery, blasphemy, lies, calumny, oaths, and denun-

[1] These disturbances of nature are mentioned in the Chronicle under
the year 1230.

ciations, and other satanic deeds,—if we do away with all
that, I know well that good things will come to us in this
life and in the future life. For He Himself hath said: Turn
to me, and I will turn to you. Keep away from everything, and I will withhold your punishment. When will
we, at last, turn away from our sins? Let us spare ourselves
and our children! At what time have we seen so many sudden deaths? Many were taken away before they could care
for their houses; many lay down well in the evening and
never arose again. Have fear, I pray you, of this sudden
parting! If we wander in the will of the Lord, God will
comfort us with many a comfort, will cherish us as His sons,
will take away from us earthly sorrow, will give us a peaceful exit into the future life, where we shall enjoy gladness, and
endless happiness with those who do the will of the Lord.

I have told you much, my brothers and children, but I
see our punishments will not be diminished, nor changed.
Many take no heed, as if they weened themselves to be immortal. I am afraid that the word of God will come to pass
with them: If I had not spoken to them, they would not
have sinned; but now they have no excuse for their sin.
And I repeat to you, if we do not change, we shall have no
excuse before the Lord. I, your sinful pastor, have done
the command of God in transmitting His word to you.

The Zadónshchina. (XIV. century.)

The *Zadónshchina, i. e.,* The Exploits beyond the Don, has come
down in two versions, and is an interesting poetical account of the
battle at Kulikóvo (1380). The *Word of Ígor's Armament* had
taken a strong hold on the author, who seems to have been a certain
Sofóniya of Ryazán. Not only are there many parallels in the two
poems, but whole passages are bodily taken from the older text, with
corruption of some phrases, the meaning of which was not clear to
the author of the *Zadónshchina*.

THE ZADÓNSHCHINA

Let us go, O brothers, into the midnight country, the lot
of Japheth,[1] the son of Noah, from whom has risen the most

[1] The Byzantine chronographers generally begin their accounts
with Noah ; so does Néstor, who follows those sources.

glorious Russia; let us there ascend the Kíev mountains, and look by the smooth Dnieper over the whole Russian land, and hence to the Eastern land, the lot of Shem, the son of Noah, from whom were born the Chinese,[1] the pagan Tartars, the Mussulmans. They had defeated the race of Japheth on the river Kayála.[2] And ever since, the Russian land has been unhappy, and from the battle of the Kálka[3] up to Mamáy's defeat it has been covered with grief and sorrow, weeping and lamenting its children. The Prince and the boyárs, and all the brave men who had left all their homes, and wealth, and wives, children, and cattle, having received honour and glory of this world, have laid down their heads for the Russian land and the Christian faith.

Let us come together, brothers and friends, sons of Russia! Let us join word to word! Let us make the Russian land merry, and cast sorrow on the eastern regions that are to the lot of Shem! Let us sing about the victory over the heathen Mamáy, and an eulogy to the Grand Prince Dmítri Ivánovich and his brother,[4] Prince Vladímir Andréevich! . . . We shall sing as things have happened, and will not race in thought, but will mention the times of the first years; we will praise the wise Boyán,[5] the famous musician in Kíev town. That wise Boyán put his golden fingers on the living strings, sang the glory of the Russian princes, to the first Prince Rúrik, Ígor Rúrikovich and Svyatosláv, Yaropólk, Vladímir Svyatoslávich, Yarosláv Vladímirovich, praising them with songs and melodious musical words.—But I shall mention Sofóniya of Ryazán, and shall praise in songs and musical words the Prince Dmítri Ivánovich and his brother, Prince Vladímir Andréevich, for their bravery and

[1] The original has a word derived from *Khin*, which seems to be identical with " China," and is used in general for Asiatics.

[2] See pp. 75 and 89.

[3] The battle with the Tartars at the river Kálka took place in 1224.

[4] Vladímir Andréevich was the cousin of Dmítri Donskóy, the son of Iván II.

[5] In the text the word is *boyarin*, *i. e.*, " boyár," evidently a corruption of Boyán, which is one of the proofs of the Zadónshchina being a later imitation of the *Word of Ígor's Armament*.

zeal was for the Russian land and the Christian faith. For this, Grand Prince Dmítri Ivánovich and his brother, Prince Vladímir Andréevich, sharpened their hearts in bravery, arose in their strength, and remembered their ancestor, Prince Vladímir of Kíev, the tsar of Russia.

O lark, joy of beautiful days! Fly to the blue clouds, look towards the strong city of Moscow, sing the glory of Grand Prince Dmítri Andréevich! They have risen like falcons from the Russian land against the fields of the Pólovtses. The horses neigh at the Moskvá; the drums are beaten at the Kolómna; the trumpets blare at Serpukhóv; the glory resounds over the whole Russian land. Wonderfully the standards stand at the great Don; the embroidered flags flutter in the wind; the gilded coats of mail glisten. The bells are tolled in the vyéche[1] of Nóvgorod the Great. The men of Nóvgorod stand in front of St. Sophia, and speak as follows: "We shall not get in time to the aid of Grand Prince Dmítri Ivánovich." Then they flew together like eagles from the whole midnight country. They were not eagles that flew together, but posádniks[2] that went out with 7000 men from Nóvgorod the Great to Grand Prince Dmítri Ivánovich and to his brother Vladímir Andréevich.

All the Russian princes came to the aid of Grand Prince Dmítri Ivánovich, and they spoke as follows: "Lord Grand Prince! Already do the pagan Tartars encroach upon our fields, and take away our patrimony. They stand between the Don and Dnieper, on the river Mechá.[3] But we, lord, will go beyond the swift river Don, will gain glory in all the lands, will be an object of conversation for the old men, and a memory for the young."

Thus spoke Grand Prince Dmítri Ivánovich to his brothers, the Russian-princes: "My dear brothers, Russian princes! We are of the same descent, from Grand Prince Iván Danílovich.[4] So far we brothers have not been in-

---

[1] Popular assembly of Nóvgorod.
[2] Burgomasters or governors of Nóvgorod.
[3] Tributary of the Don.
[4] Iván Kalitá, 1328–1340.

sulted either by falcon, or vulture, or white gerfalcon, or this dog, pagan Mamáy.''

Nightingale! If you could only sing the glory of these two brothers, Ólgerd's sons,[1] Andréy of Pólotsk and Dmítri of Bryansk, for they were born in Lithuania on a shield of the vanguard, swaddled under trumpets, raised under helmets, fed at the point of the spear, and given drink with the sharp sword. Spoke Andréy to his brother Dmítri: ''We are two brothers, sons of Ólgerd, grandchildren of Gedemín, great-grandchildren of Skoldimér. Let us mount our swift steeds, let us drink, O brother, with our helmets the water from the swift Don, let us try our tempered swords.''

And Dmítri spoke to him: ''Brother Andréy! We will not spare our lives for the Russian land and Christian faith, and to avenge the insult to Grand Prince Dmítri Ivánovich. Already, O brother, there is a din and thunder in the famous city of Moscow. But, brother, it is not a din or thunder: it is the noise made by the mighty army of Grand Prince Dmítri Ivánovich and his brother Prince Vladímir Andréevich; the brave fellows thunder with their gilded helmets and crimson shields. Saddle, brother Andréy, your good swift steeds, for mine are ready, having been saddled before. We will ride out, brother, into the clear field, and will review our armies, as many brave men of Lithuania as there are with us, but there are with us of the brave men of Lithuania seven thousand mailed soldiers.''

Already there have arisen strong winds from the sea; they have wafted a great cloud to the mouth of the Dnieper, against the Russian land; bloody clouds have issued from it, and blue lightnings flash through them. There will be a mighty din and thunder between the Don and the Dnieper, and bodies of men will fall on the field of Kulikóvo, and blood will flow on the river Nepryádva, for the carts have already creaked between the Don and Dnieper, and the pagan Tartars march against the Russian land. Grey wolves

[1] These Lithuanian Princes had acknowledged the sovereignty of Moscow.

howl: they wish at the river Mechá to invade the Russian land. Those are not grey wolves: the infidel Tartars have come; they wish to cross the country in war, and to conquer the Russian land. The geese have cackled and the swans have flapped their wings,— pagan Mamáy has come against the Russian land and has brought his generals. . . .

What is that din and thunder so early before daybreak? Prince Vladímir Andréevich has reviewed his army and is leading it to the great Don. And he says to his brother, Grand Prince Dmítri Ivánovich: "Slacken not, brother, against the pagan Tartars, for the infidels are already in the Russian land, and are taking away our patrimony!" . . .

The falcons and gerfalcons have swiftly flown across the Don, and have swooped down on the many flocks of swans: the Russian princes have attacked the Tartar might, and they strike with their steel lances against the Tartar armour; the tempered swords thunder against the Tartar helmets on the field of Kulikóvo, on the river Nepryádva. Black is the earth under the hoofs, but they had sowed the field with Tartar bones, and the earth was watered with their blood, and mighty armies passed by and trampled down hills and fields, and the rivers, springs and lakes were turbid. They uttered mighty cries in the Russian land . . . and they vanquished the Tartar horde on the field of Kulikóvo, on the river Nepryádva.

On that field mighty clouds encountered, and in them lightnings frequently flashed, and terrible thunders clapped: it is the Russian brave warriors who were engaging the pagan Tartars for the great insult, and their mighty gilded armour glistened, and the Russian princes thundered with their tempered swords against the Tartar helmets. . . .

At that time neither soldiers nor shepherds called in the field near the Don, in the land of Ryazán, but only ravens croaked for the sake of the bodies of the dead, so that it was a terror and a pity to hear: for the grass was watered with blood, and the trees were bent to the ground with sorrow, and the birds sang pitiful songs. All princesses and wives of the boyárs and generals wept for the slain. Fedósya, the wife of Mikúla Vasílevich,[1] and Mary, the wife of Dmítri, wept early in the morning at Moscow, standing on the city wall, and spoke as follows: "Don, Don, you are a swift river, and have cut through stone walls, and flow through the land of the Pólovtses! Bring back my beloved one to me!" . . .

All over the Russian land there spread joy and merriment: the Russian glory was borne through the land, but shame and destruction came on the pagan Tartars, evil Mussulmans. . . . The Grand Prince by his own bravery and with his druzhína vanquished pagan Mamáy for the sake of the Russian land and the Christian faith. The pagans deposited their own arms under the Russian swords, and the trumpets were not sounded, their voices were silent. Mamáy galloped away from his druzhína, howled like a grey wolf, and ran away to the city of Khafest.[2] . . .

Afanási Nikítin. (XV. century.)

Nikítin set out about 1468 for India, whence he returned in 1474. He wrote out an account of his many adventures, which is interesting for its sober though rather one-sided narration. It stands alone in the old Russian literature as the writing of a layman bent on a commercial enterprise. His *Travel to India* has been translated by Count Wielhorsky for the Hakluyt Society.

TRAVEL TO INDIA

I, poor sinner, brought a stallion to the land of India; with God's help I reached Junir all well, but it cost me a hundred roubles.

The winter began from Trinity day, and we wintered at Junir and lived there two months; but day and night for four months there is but rain and dirt. At this time of the year the people till the ground, sow wheat, tuturegan (?), peas, and all sorts of vegetables. Wine is kept in large skins (?) of Indian goats. . . .

Horses are fed on peas; also on kichiris, boiled with sugar and oil; early in the morning they get shishenivo. Horses

---

[1] A thousand-man of the Russian army.

[2] Probably a mistake for Kaffa in the Crimea.

are not born in that country, but oxen and buffaloes; and these are used for riding, conveying goods, and every other purpose.

Junir stands on a stony island; no human hand built it—God made the town. A narrow road, which it takes a day to ascend, admitting of only one man at a time, leads up a hill to it.

In the winter, the people put on the fata, and wear it around the waist, on the shoulders, and on their head; but the princes and nobles put trowsers on, a shirt and a caftan, wearing a fata on the shoulders, another as a belt round the waist, and a third round their head.

O God, true God, merciful God, gracious God!

At Junir the Khan took away my horse, and having heard that I was no Mahommedan, but a Russian, he said: "I will give thee the horse and a thousand pieces of gold, if thou wilt embrace our faith, the Mahommedan faith; and if thou wilt not embrace our Mahommedan faith, I shall keep the horse and take a thousand pieces of gold upon thy head." He gave me four days to consider, and all this occurred during the fast of the Assumption of our Lady, on the eve of our Saviour's day (18th of August).

And the Lord took pity upon me because of His holy festival, and did not withdraw His mercy from me, His simple servant, and allowed me not to perish at Junir among the infidels. On the eve of our Saviour's day there came a man from Khorassan, Khozaiocha Mahmet, and I implored him to pity me. He repaired to the Khan into the town, and praying him delivered me from being converted, and took from him my horse. Such was the Lord's wonderful mercy on the Saviour's day.

Now, Christian brethren of Russia, whoever of you wishes to go to the Indian country may leave his faith in Russia, confess Mahomet, and then proceed to the land of Hindostan. Those Mussulman dogs have lied to me, saying I should find plenty of our goods; but there is nothing for our country. All goods for the land of Mussulmans, as pepper and colours, and these are cheap.

The rulers and the nobles in the land of India are all Khorassanians. The Hindoos walk all on foot and walk fast. They are all naked and bare-footed, and carry a shield in one hand and a sword in the other. Some of the servants are armed with straight bows and arrows.

Elephants are greatly used in battle. The men on foot are sent first, the Khorassanians being mounted in full armour, man as well as horse. Large scythes are attached to the trunks and tusks of the elephants, and the animals are clad in ornamental plates of steel. They carry a citadel, and in the citadel twelve men in armour with guns and arrows.

There is a place Shikhbaludin Peratyr, a bazaar Aladinand, and a fair once a year, where people from all parts of India assemble and trade for ten days. As many as 20,000 horses are brought there for sale from Beder, which is 20 kors distant, and besides every description of goods; and that fair is the best throughout the land of Hindostan. Everything is sold or bought in memory of Shikbaladin, whose fête falls on the Russian festival of the Protection of the Holy Virgin (1st October).

In that Aland (Aladinand?) there is a bird, gukuk, that flies at night and cries gukuk, and any roof it lights upon, there the man will die; and whoever attempts to kill it will see fire flashing from its beak. Wild cats rove at night and catch fowls; they live in the hills and among stones. As to monkeys, they live in the woods and have their monkey knyaz, who is attended by a host of armed followers. When any of them is caught they complain to their knyaz, and an army is sent after the missing; and when they come to a town they pull down the houses and beat the people; and their armies, it is said, are many. They speak their own tongues and bring forth a great many children; and when a child is unlike its father or its mother, it is thrown out on the highroad. Thus they are often caught by the Hindoos, who teach them every sort of handicraft, or sell them at night, that they might not find their way home, or teach them dancing.—From *India in the Fifteenth Century*, in the Hakluyt Society Publications, London, 1857.

Apocryphal Legends about King Solomon.
(XV. century.)

Among the many apocryphal stories of the Old Testament that were current in Russia the largest number centre about King Solomon. They are mostly derived from Byzantine sources which, in their turn, are often based on Jewish apocryphal accounts; thus the *Story of Kitovrás* (evidently transformed from Centaurus) is also given in the Talmud. Kitovrás is mentioned in Russian literature in the fourteenth century, but the following passage is from a manuscript of the fifteenth.

THE STORY OF KITOVRÁS

Then came Solomon's turn to learn about Kitovrás. He found out that his habitation was in a distant wilderness. Solomon, in his wisdom, prepared a steel rope and a steel hoop, and on this he wrote an incantation in the name of God. And he sent his best boyár with his men, and ordered them to take with them wine and mead, and the fleece of sheep. And they came to the appointed place, and behold, there were three wells, but he was not there. By the instruction of Solomon, they emptied the three wells, and closed the springs with the fleeces of the sheep, and filled two of the wells with wine, and the third one with mead, but they themselves hid themselves nearby, for they knew that he would come to the wells to drink water. And he came, for he was very thirsty, and he lay down to drink, but seeing the wine, he said: "Nobody becomes wise from drinking wine." But as he was very thirsty, he said again: "You are the wine that gladdens the hearts of men," and he emptied all three wells, and lay himself down to sleep. The wine heated him up, and he fell into a deep sleep. Then the boyár approached him, put the hoop upon his neck, and tied the steel rope to him. When Kitovrás awoke, he wanted to tear himself loose. But Solomon's boyár said to him: " The name of the Lord is upon you with a prohibition "; and he, seeing the name of the Lord upon him, went meekly along.

His habit was not to go by the crooked road, but by the straight road; and when he arrived in Jerusalem, they levelled the road for him, and palaces were destroyed, for he would not go by the crooked road. They came to the house of a widow. She wept loud, and she begged Kitovrás with the following words: ". I am a poor widow." He turned around the corner, without leaving the street, and he broke a rib, and said: "A gentle word breaks bones, but a harsh word rouses anger." As he was led through the market-place, he heard a man say: " Is there not a shoe that will wear seven years?" and Kitovrás laughed out loud. And he saw another man who was telling fortunes, and he laughed; and he saw a wedding ceremony, and he wept. . . .

Solomon asked Kitovrás: "Wherefore did you laugh at the man that asked for a shoe that would last seven years?" And Kitovrás answered: " As I looked at him, I saw that he would not live seven days." And Solomon said: " Wherefore did you laugh at the fortune-teller?" And Kitovrás said: "He was telling people hidden things, and he did not himself know that a gold treasure was right under him." And the King said: " Go and find out!" They went, and they found that it was so. And the King said: " Wherefore did you weep when you saw the wedding?" And he said: " I felt sorry for the groom, for I knew he would not live another thirty days." And the King had the matter investigated, and he found that it was so.

Andréy Mikháylovich Kúrbski.   (1528–1583.)

Kúrbski was a descendant of the Yarosláv princes who, as he was proud of mentioning, derived their origin from the great Vladímir. At twenty years of age he took part in an expedition against Kazán, and a few years later he distinguished himself at the storming of that Tartar city. Iván the Terrible personally decorated him for his valour in these and other expeditions against the Tartars, and sent him with an army to Livonia to operate against the Livonian order. In 1563 Kúrbski lost an important battle against Poland. Fearing a terrible vengeance from the cruel Tsar, not only for this defeat, but also for having belonged to the party of Sylvester and Adáshev, he fled to Poland, where he was received with open arms by King Sigismund. As soon as he had reached the city of Volmar, then in the hands of the Lithuanians, he sent his faithful servant Váska Shibánov with an epistle (here given) to the Tsar. Iván, upon learning from Shibánov that the letter he brought him was from the traitor Kúrbski, struck the sharp point of his staff through the messenger's foot and ordered him to read its contents. Shibánov did so, without expressing any pain, though he was bleeding profusely.

Kúrbski had belonged in Moscow to the circle of the enlightened churchman Maksím the Greek, who believed in the importance of profane studies. Kúrbski had acquired some knowledge of Latin and Greek, which he perfected in his exile. In Poland he devoted himself to literary studies, translating Chrysostom and Eusebius, and writing a series of four epistles to Iván the Terrible, and others to other prominent personages in Poland. His greatest merit consists in his having written a *History of Iván the Terrible*, which is the first work in the Russian language to deserve the name of history; for, while the older chronicles gave accounts of events, Kúrbski subordinated them to a general idea which runs through the whole work.

THE STORMING OF KAZÁN

If I wrote everything that took place around the city, there would be a whole book of it. But it is worth mentioning that they used charms against the Christian army by which they caused a great rainstorm. From the beginning of the siege, and when the sun just began to rise, there walked out upon the walls of the city, in our sight, now their old men, now their women, and they began to howl satanic words, all the time waving their garments to our army and turning around in an improper manner. Then there arose a wind, clouds were formed, however clear the day may have begun, and there came such a downpour of rain that all the dry places were changed into bogs and filled with water. And this happened only over our army, and not elsewhere, so that it did not proceed from the condition of the atmosphere.

Seeing this, the Tsar was advised to send to Moscow for the wood from the Saviour's cross, which is worked into the rood that always lies near the crown of the Tsar. With God's aid, they reached Moscow in a very short time, travelling by water to Nízhni Nóvgorod in swift Vyátka boats, making the journey in three or four days, and from Nóvgorod to Moscow by fast relays. When the rood was brought, into which is worked the wood from the Saviour's cross on which our Lord Jesus Christ suffered in the flesh for men, the presbyters made a procession with Christian ceremonies and blessed the water according to church use; through the vivifying power of the cross, the pagan charms disappeared from that very hour completely.   .   .   .

At the end of the seventh week [1] of the city's investment, we were ordered to prepare the next day before daybreak for a general assault.   This was to be the signal: when the powder would explode and would demolish the wall, which had previously been undermined and under which forty-eight barrels of powder had been placed.   More than half of the infantry was ordered to the assault, a third of the army, or a little more, remaining in the field to guard the Tsar.   We were ready early in the morning, as we were ordered, about two hours before daybreak.   I was sent to make the assault at the lower gate, above the river Kazán, and I had with me twelve thousand soldiers.   At the four sides of the city were placed strong and brave men, some of them with large detachments.   .   .   .   The Tsár of Kazán and his senators had been informed about all this, and they were prepared against us, as we against them.   .   .   .

Then God helped us! My brother was the first to mount upon the city wall by a ladder, and other brave soldiers were with him.   Hacking and spearing the Mussulmans about them, they climbed through the windows of the great tower, and from the tower they rushed down to the large city gate. The Mussulmans turned their backs on the gate and ran up the high hill to the Tsar's court, which was strongly fortified with a high fence, between palaces and stone mosques.   We after them to the Tsar's palace, even though we were burdened with our armour and many brave men had wounds on their bodies, and very few were left to fight against them. Our army which was left outside of the city, seeing that we were within and that the Tartars had run away from the walls, rushed into the city,—and the wounded that were lying on the ground jumped up, and the dead were resur-

[1] The siege of Kazán began on August 23, and the city was taken October 2, 1552.

rected.   And not only they, but those in the camp, the cooks
and those that had been left to watch the horses, and others
who follow with merchandise, all ran into the city, not to
fight, but to plunder: that place was indeed full of the rich-
est booty, gold and silver and precious stones, and it teemed
with sable furs and other costly things.

LETTER TO IVÁN THE TERRIBLE

To the Tsar, glorified by God, who had once been illustrious in orthodoxy, but who now, through our sins, has become the adversary of both.   Those who have sense will
understand how that your conscience is corrupt even beyond
what is found among the infidels. . . .   I have not allowed before my tongue to utter any of these things, but
having suffered the bitterest persecution from you, and from
the bitterness of my heart I shall speak to you a little.

Why, O Tsar, have you struck down the mighty in Israel?
Why have you delivered to various deaths the generals given
to you by God, and why have you spilled their victorious,
saintly blood in the temples of the Lord, at your royal banquets? Why have you stained the thresholds of the churches
with the blood of the martyrs, and why have you contrived
persecutions and death against those who have served you
willingly and have laid down their lives for you, accusing
good Christians of treason and magic and other unseemly
things, and zealously endeavouring to change light into
darkness and to call bitter what is sweet?

Of what crime have they been guilty, O Tsar, and with
what have they angered you, O Christian vicar? Had they
not, through their bravery, destroyed haughty kingdoms,
and made those subservient to you by whom our forefathers
had been once enslaved? Have not the strong German cities
been given to you by God, through their wise foresight? Is
that the way you have rewarded us, poor men, by destroying
us altogether? Do you, O Tsar, deem yourself to be immortal? Or are you carried away by an unheard-of heresy
and imagine that you will not have to appear before the

Supreme Judge, the godlike Jesus, who will judge the whole world, but especially cruel tormentors? He, my Christ, who sits on the throne of the cherubim, at the right of the Supreme Power upon high,—will be the judge between you and me.

What evils and persecutions have I not suffered from you! And what misery and torment have you not caused me! And what mean calumnies have you not brought down on me! So many various miseries have befallen me that I cannot count them all to-day: my heart is still oppressed with sorrow on account of them. But I shall say this much: I have been deprived of everything, and through you I am exiled from God's own country. I did not implore with gentle words, did not entreat you with tearful sobs, did not, through the clergy, beg for any favour from you, and you have repaid me good with evil, and my love with an irreconcilable hatred.

My blood, which has been spilled for you like water, cries to my Lord against you! God sees our hearts: I have diligently searched my mind, have invoked the testimony of my conscience, have looked inwardly, have rummaged, and have not found myself guilty before you in anything. I have all the time led your army, and have brought no dishonour upon you: by the aid of the Lord's angel, I have obtained brilliant victories to your glory, and never have your armies turned their backs to the enemy, but he has always been gloriously vanquished to your honour. And this I did not in one year, nor in two, but through a long series of years, and with much toil and patience. I always defended my country, and little saw of my parents, nor was I with my wife. I was continually out on expeditions, in distant cities, against your enemies, and suffered much want and sickness, to which my Lord Jesus Christ is a witness. I have frequently been covered with wounds from the hands of the barbarians, in many battles, and all my body is covered with sores. But all this, O Tsar, is as if it had not been, and you have shown me your relentless fury and bitter hatred which is more fiery than a furnace.

I wanted to tell you in order all my warlike exploits that I had performed to your honour, my Christ aiding me, but I did not do so, as God knows them better than man can, for He gives rewards for all this, nay even for a glass of cold water; besides, I know that you know all that as well. Know also this, O Tsar, that you will not behold my face again in this world before the glorious coming of Christ. Nor imagine that I will forgive you what has happened: up to my death will I continually cry out against you in tears to the uncreated Trinity in which I believe, and I call to my aid the Mother of the Prince of the Cherubim, my hope and intercessor, the Virgin Mary, and all the saints, God's elect, and my forefather, Prince Feódor Rostislávich, whose body is incorrupt, having been preserved for many years, and emits an aromatic odour from his grave and, by the grace of the Holy Ghost, causes miraculous cures, as you, O Tsar, well know.

Do not imagine, O Tsar, in your vanity that those who have been innocently struck down by you, and who are imprisoned and unjustly banished by you, have all perished; do not rejoice and boast your vain victory. Those who have been slain by you stand before the throne of God and ask for vengeance against you; and those of us who are imprisoned or unjustly banished from our country cry day and night to God! Though in your pride you may boast of your evil power in this temporal, transitory world, and invent instruments of torture against the race of Christians, and insult and tread under foot the image of the angel, with the approbation of your flatterers and companions of your table and with the approbation of your boyárs who make your body and soul to perish . . . yet this my letter, which is wet with tears, I shall order to be placed in my tomb, in order to go with you before the judgment seat of my Lord Jesus Christ. Amen.

Written in Volmir, a city of my lord, King August Sigismund, from whom I hope favours and comfort for all my sorrows, through his royal kindness, the Lord aiding me.

Iván the Terrible. (1530–1584.)

Iván the Terrible united the qualities of a great ruler with those of a most cruel tyrant. In his long epistles to Kúrbski he develops a strong sarcastic vein and defends himself with specious arguments, quoting copiously from the Bible and the Church Fathers. He denies his cruelty, but admits the execution of traitors, who, in his case, form an enormous category.

LETTER TO PRINCE KÚRBSKI

Our God, the Trinity, who has existed since eternity but now as Father, Son, and Holy Ghost, has neither beginning nor end; through Him we live and move about, through Him kings rule and the mighty write laws. By our Lord Jesus Christ the victorious standard of God's only Word and the blessed Cross which has never been vanquished have been given to Emperor Constantine, first in piety, and to all the orthodox tsars and protectors of orthodoxy and, in so far as the Word of God has been fulfillen, they, in eagle's flight, have reached all the godly servants of God's Word, until a spark of piety has fallen upon the Russian realm. The autocracy, by God's will, had its origin in Grand Prince Vladímir, who had enlightened all Russia through the holy baptism, and the great Tsar Vladímir Monomákh, who had received memorable honours from the Greeks, and the valiant great Tsar Alexander Névski, who had obtained a great victory over the godless Germans, and the praiseworthy great Tsar Dmítri, who had obtained a great victory over the Hagarites beyond the Don, then it passed to the avenger of wrongs, our ancestor, the great Tsar Iván, the gatherer of the Russian land from among the ancestral possessions, and to our father of blessed memory, the great Tsar Vasíli, until it reached us, the humble sceptre-bearer of the Russian empire.

But we praise God for the great favour He has shown me in not permitting my right hand to become stained by the blood of my race: for we have not snatched the realm from anyone, but by the will of God and the blessing of our ancestors and parents, were we born in the realm, were brought up there and enthroned, taking, by the will of God and the blessing of our ancestors and parents, what belonged to us, and not seizing that which was not ours. Here follows the command of the orthodox, truly Christian autocrat, the possessor of many kingdoms,—our humble, Christian answer to him who was an orthodox, true Christian and a boyár of our realm, a councillor and a general, but now is a criminal before the blessed, vivifying cross of the Lord, a destroyer of Christians, a servant of the enemies of Christianity, who has departed from the divine worship of the images and has trodden under foot all sacred commands, destroyed the holy edifices, vilified and trampled the holy vessels and images, who unites in one person Leo the Isaurian, Constantine Kopronymos and Leo of Armenia, — to Prince Andréy Mikháylovich Kúrbski, who through treachery wanted to become a ruler of Yaroslávl.

Wherefore, O Prince, if you regard yourself to have piety, have you lost your soul? What will you give in its place on the day of the terrible judgment? Even if you should acquire the whole world, death will reach you in the end! Why have you sold your soul for your body's sake? Is it because you were afraid of death at the false instigation of your demons and influential friends and counsellors? . . .

Are you not ashamed before your slave Váska Shibánov, who preserved his piety and, having attached himself to you with a kiss of the cross, did not reject you before the Tsar and the whole people, though standing at the gate of death, but praised you and was all too ready to die for you? But you did not emulate his devotion: on account of a single angry word of mine, have you lost not only your own soul, but the souls of all your ancestors: for, by God's will, had they been given as servants to our grandfather, the great Tsar, and they gave their souls to him and served him up to their death, and ordered you, their children, to serve the children and grandchildren of our grandfather. But you have forgotten everything and traitorously, like a dog, have you transgressed the oath and have gone over to the enemies of Christianity, and, not considering your wrath, you utter stupid words, hurling, as it were, stones at the sky. . . .

We have never spilled blood in the churches. As for the victorious, saintly blood,—there has none appeared in our land, as far as we know. *The thresholds of the churches :* as far as our means and intelligence permit and our subjects are eager to serve us, the churches of the Lord are resplendent with all kinds of adornments, and through the gifts which we have offered since your satanic domination, not only the thresholds and pavements, but even the antechambers shine with ornaments, so that all the strangers may see them. We do not stain the thresholds of the churches with any blood, and there are no martyrs of faith with us now-a-days. . . . Tortures and persecutions and deaths in many forms we have devised against no one. As to treasons and magic, it is true, such dogs everywhere suffer capital punishment. . . .

It had pleased God to take away our mother, the pious Tsarítsa Helen, from the earthly kingdom to the kingdom of heaven. My brother George, who now rests in heaven, and I were left orphans and, as we received no care from any one, we laid our trust in the Holy Virgin, and in the prayers of all the saints, and in the blessing of our parents. When I was in my eighth year, our subjects acted according to their will, for they found the empire without a ruler, and did not deign to bestow their voluntary attention upon us, their master, but were bent on acquiring wealth and glory, and were quarrelling with each other. And what have they not done! How many boyárs, how many friends of our father and generals they have killed! And they seized the farms and villages and possessions of our uncles, and established themselves therein. The treasure of our mother they trod under foot and pierced with sharp sticks, and transferred it to the great treasure, but some of it they grabbed themselves; and that was done by your grandfather Mikháylo Tuchkóv. The Princes Vasíli and Iván Shúyski took it upon themselves to have me in their keeping, and those who had been the chief traitors of our father and mother they let out of prison, and they made friends with them. Prince Vasíli Shúyski with a Judas crowd fell in the court belonging to our uncle upon our father confessor Fedór Mishúrin, and insulted him, and killed him; and they imprisoned Prince Iván Fedórovich Byélski and many others in various places, and armed themselves against the realm; they ousted metropolitan Daniel from the metropolitan see and banished him: and thus they improved their opportunity, and began to rule themselves.

Me and my brother George, of blessed memory, they brought up like vagrants and children of the poorest. What have I not suffered for want of garments and food! And all that against my will and as did not become my extreme youth. I shall mention just one thing: once in my childhood we were playing, and Prince Iván Vasílevich Shúyski was sitting on a bench, leaning with his elbow against our father's bed, and even putting his foot upon it; he treated us not as a parent, but as a master . . . who could bear such presumption? How can I recount all the miseries which I have suffered in my youth? Often did I dine late, against my will. What had become of the treasure left me by my father? They had carried everything away, under the cunning pretext that they had to pay the boyár children from it, but, in reality, they had kept it back from them, to their own advantage, and had not paid them off according to their deserts; and they had also held back an immense treasure of my grandfather and father, and made it into gold and silver vessels, inscribing thereupon the names of their parents, as if they had been their inheritance. . . . It is hardly necessary to mention what became of the treasure of our uncles: they appropriated it all to themselves! Then they attacked towns and villages, tortured the people most cruelly, brought much misery upon them, and mercilessly pillaged the possessions of the inhabitants. . . .

When we reached the age of fifteen, we, inspired by God, undertook to rule our own realm and, with the aid of almighty God, we ruled our realm in peace and undisturbed, according to our will. But it happened then that, on account of our sins, a fire having spread, by God's will, the royal city of Moscow was consumed. Our boyárs, the traitors whom you call martyrs, whose names I shall purposely pass over in silence, made use of the favourable opportunity for their mean treachery, whispered into the ears of a stupid crowd that the mother of my mother, Princess Anna Glínski, with all her children and household, was in the habit of extracting men's hearts, and that by a similar sorcery she had put Moscow on fire, and that we knew of her doings. By the instigation of these our traitors, a mass of insensate people, crying in the manner of the Jews, came to the apostolic cathedral of the holy martyr Dimítri of Selún, dragged out of it our boyár Yúri Vasílevich Glínski, pulled him inhumanly into the cathedral of the Assumption, and killed the innocent man in the church, opposite the metropolitan's place; they stained the floor of the church with his blood, dragged his body through the front door, and exposed him on the market-place as a criminal,—everybody knows about this murder in the church. We were then living in the village of Vorobévo; the same traitors instigated the populace to kill us under the pretext (and you, dog, repeat the lie) that we were keeping from them Prince Yúri's mother, Princess Anna, and his brother, Prince Mikhaíl. How is one not to laugh at such stupidity? Why should we be incendiaries in our own empire? . . .

You say that your blood has been spilled in wars with foreigners, and you add, in your foolishness, that it cries to God against us. That is ridiculous! It has been spilled by one, and it cries out against another. If it is true that your blood has been spilled by the enemy, then you have done your duty to your country; if you had not done so, you would not have been a Christian but a barbarian:—but that is not our affair. How much more ours, that has been spilled by you, cries out to the Lord against you! Not with wounds, nor drops of blood, but with much sweating and toiling have I been burdened by you unnecessarily and above my strength! Your many meannesses and persecutions have caused me, instead of blood, to shed many tears, and to utter sobs and have anguish of my soul. . . .

You say you want to put your letter in your grave: that

shows that you have completely renounced your Christianity! For God has ordered not to resist evil, but you renounce the final pardon which is granted to the ignorant; therefore it is not even proper that any mass shall be sung after you. In our patrimony, in the country of Lifland, you name the city of Volmir as belonging to our enemy, King Sigismund: by this you only complete the treachery of a vicious dog! . . .

Written in our great Russia, in the famous, royal, capital city of Moscow, on the steps of our imperial threshold, in the year from the creation of the world 7072, the fifth day of July.

The Domostróy. (XVI. century.)

The *Domostróy, i. e.*, House-government, is an important document of the sixteenth century, as it throws a light on the inner life of the Russians in the time of Iván the Terrible. Its authorship is ascribed in the extant manuscripts to Sylvester, the adviser of Iván the Terrible, but it is assumed that he was only the last compiler of various codes of conduct that were known in Russia before his day. At least, the whole production bears the stamp of being a composite work. Two distinct groups are discerned in it: the first has continual references to the Tsar and the honours due him; the other deals with a society whose chief interest is purely commercial, and appeals to the judgment of the people, instead of to that of the Tsar. From this the inference is drawn that the first had its origin in Moscow, the second in Nóvgorod. The morality of the *Domostróy* is one of external formalism. To preserve appearances before God and men is, according to this code, the chief aim in life.

HOW TO EDUCATE CHILDREN AND BRING THEM UP IN THE FEAR OF GOD

If God send children, sons or daughters, father and mother must take care of these their children. Provide for them and bring them up in good instruction. Teach them the fear of God and politeness and propriety, and teach them some handicraft, according to the time and age of the children: the mother instructing her daughters, and the father his sons, as best he knows and God counsels him. Love them and watch them and save them through fear. Teach-

ing and instructing them and reasoning with them, punish
them. Teach your children in their youth, and you will
have a quiet old age. Look after their bodily cleanliness,
and keep them from all sin, like the apple of your eye and
your own souls. If the children transgress through the
neglect of their parents, the parents will answer for these
sins on the day of the terrible judgment. If the children are
not taken care of and transgress through lack of the parents'
instruction, or do some evil, there will be both to the parents
and children a sin before God, scorn and ridicule before men,
a loss to the house, grief to oneself, and cost and shame from
the judges. If by God-fearing, wise and sensible people
the children be brought up in the fear of God, and in good
instruction and sensible teaching, in wisdom and politeness
and work and handicraft, such children and their parents are
loved by God, blessed by the clerical vocation, and praised
by good people; and when they are of the proper age, good
people will gladly and thankfully marry off their sons, according to their possessions and the will of God, and will
give their daughters in marriage to their sons. And if God
take away one of their children, after the confession and
extreme unction, the parents bring a pure offering to God,
to take up an abode in the eternal mansion; and the child is
bold to beg for God's mercy and forgiveness of his parents'
sins.

HOW TO TEACH CHILDREN AND SAVE THEM THROUGH FEAR

Punish your son in his youth, and he will give you a quiet
old age, and restfulness to your soul. Weaken not beating
the boy, for he will not die from your striking him with the
rod, but will be in better health: for while you strike his
body, you save his soul from death. If you love your son,
punish him frequently, that you may rejoice later. Chide
your son in his childhood, and you will be glad in his manhood, and you will boast among evil persons, and your
enemies will be envious. Bring up your child with much
prohibition, and you will have peace and blessing from him.

Do not smile at him, or play with him, for though that will diminish your grief while he is a child, it will increase it when he is older, and you will cause much bitterness to your soul. Give him no power in his youth, but crush his ribs while he is growing and does not in his wilfulness obey you, lest there be an aggravation and suffering to your soul, a loss to your house, destruction to your property, scorn from your neighbours and ridicule from your enemies, and cost and worriment from the authorities.

HOW CHRISTIANS ARE TO CURE DISEASES AND ALL KINDS OF AILMENTS

If God send any disease or ailment down upon a person, let him cure himself through the grace of God, through tears, prayer, fasting, charity to the poor, and true repentance. Let him thank the Lord and beg His forgiveness, and show mercy and undisguised charity to everybody. Have the clergy pray to the Lord for you, and sing the mass. Sanctify the water with the holy crosses and holy relics and miracle-working images, and be anointed with the holy oil. Frequent the miracle-working and holy places, and pray there with a pure conscience. In that way you will receive from God a cure for all your ailments. But you must henceforth abstain from sin, and in the future do no wrong, and keep the commands of the spiritual fathers, and do penance. Thus you will be purified from sin, and your spiritual and bodily ailment will be cured, and God will be gracious to you.

THE WIFE IS ALWAYS AND IN ALL THINGS TO TAKE COUNSEL WITH HER HUSBAND

In all affairs of every-day life, the wife is to take counsel with her husband, and to ask him, if she needs anything. Let her be sure that her husband wants her to keep company with the guests she invites, or the people she calls upon. Let her put on the best garment, if she receives a

guest, or herself is invited somewhere to dinner. By all
means let her abstain from drinking liquor, for a drunk man
is bad enough, but a drunk woman has no place in the world.
A woman ought to talk with her lady-friends of handwork
and housekeeping. She must pay attention to any good
word that is said in her own house, or in that of her friend:
how good women live, how they keep house, manage their
household, instruct their children and servants, obey their
husbands, and ask their advice in everything, and submit to
them. And if there be aught she does not know, let her
politely inquire about it. . . . It is good to meet such
good women, not for the sake of eating and drinking with
them, but for the sake of good converse and information, for
it is profitable to listen to them. Let not a woman rail at
anyone, or gossip about others. If she should be asked
something about a person, let her answer: "I know nothing
about it, and have heard nothing of it; I do not inquire
about things that do not concern me; nor do I sit in judgment over the wives of princes, boyárs, or my neighbours."

HOW TO INSTRUCT SERVANTS

Enjoin your servants not to talk about other people. If
they have been among strangers, and have noticed anything
bad there, let them not repeat it at home; nor should they
bruit about what is going on at home. A servant must remember what he has been sent for, and he must not know,
nor answer any other questions that are put to him. The
moment he has carried out his commission, he should return
home and report to his master in regard to the matter he
has been sent for; let him not gossip of things he has not
been ordered to report, lest he cause quarrel and coldness
between the masters.

If you send your servant, or son, to tell, or do something,
or buy a thing, ask him twice: "What have I ordered you
to do? What are you to say, or do, or buy?" If he repeats to you as you have ordered him, all is well. . . .
If you send anywhere some eatables or liquids, send full
measures, so that they cannot lie about them. Send your

wares after having measured or weighed them, and count the money, before you send it out. Best of all, dispatch under seal. Carefully instruct the servant whether he is to leave the things at the house, if the master be absent, or if he is to bring them back home. . . .

When a servant is sent to genteel people, let him knock at the door softly. If anyone should ask him, as he passes through the courtyard: " What business brings you here ? " let him not give him any satisfaction, but say: " I have not been sent to you; I shall tell to him to whom I have been sent." Let him clean his dirty feet before the antechamber, or house, or cell, wipe his nose, clear his throat, and correctly say his prayer; and if he does not receive an " amen " in response, he should repeat the prayer in a louder voice, twice or three times. If he still receives no answer, he must softly knock at the door. When he is admitted, he should bow before the holy images, give his master's respects, and tell his message. While doing so, let him not put his finger in his nose, nor cough, nor clean his nose, nor clear his throat, nor spit. If he absolutely must do so, let him step aside. He must stand straight and not look to either side when reporting the message; nor should he relate any matter not relevant to the message. Having done his duty, he should forthwith return home, to report to his master.

Songs Collected by Richard James. (1619-1620.)

Richard James, a graduate of Oxford, had been sent to Russia to look after the spiritual welfare of the young Englishmen who were connected with the Merchant Company. He arrived in Moscow on January 19, 1619, and started back by the way of Arkhángelsk on August 20 of the same year. Having been shipwrecked, he was compelled to pass the winter in Kholmogóry, from which place he left for England the next spring. He took with him a copy of six songs that some Russian had written out for him: they are now deposited in the Bodleian Library. These songs are interesting as being the oldest folksongs collected in Russia, and as having been composed immediately after the events which they describe.

The Song of the Princess Ksêniya Borísovna is given in W. R. Morfill's *Story of Russia*, New York and London, 1890.

INCURSION OF THE CRIMEAN TARTARS[1]

Not a mighty cloud has covered the sky,
Nor mighty thunders have thundered:
Whither travels the dog, Crimea's tsar?—
To the mighty tsarate of Muscovy.
"To-day we will go against stone-built Moscow,
But coming back, we will take Ryazán."
And when they were at the river Oká,
They began their white tents to pitch.
"Now think a thought with all your minds:
Who is to sit in stone-built Moscow,
And who is to sit in Vladímir,
And who is to sit in Súzdal,
And who will hold old Ryazán,
And who will sit in Zvenígorod,
And who will sit in Nóvgorod?"
There stepped forward Diví Murza, son of Ulán:
"Listen, our lord, Crimea's tsar!
You, our lord, shall sit in stone-built Moscow,
And your son in Vladímir,
And your nephew in Súzdal,
And your relative in Zvenígorod,
And let the equerry hold old Ryazán,
But to me, O lord, grant Nóvgorod:
There, in Nóvgorod, lies my luck."
The voice of the Lord called out from heaven:
"Listen, you dog, Crimea's tsar!
Know you not the tsarate of Muscovy?
There are in Moscow seventy Apostles,[2]
Besides the three Sanctified;

---

[1] Having destroyed almost the whole of Moscow by fire in 1572, Devlét-Giréy made again an incursion the next year. He was so sure of an easy victory, that the streets of Moscow, so Kúrbski tells, were allotted in advance to the Murzas. He came with an army of 120,000 men, and left on the field of battle 100,000.

[2] Either churches or images of the apostles; a similar interpretation holds for the next line.

And there is in Moscow still an orthodox Tsar.''
And you fled, you dog, Crimea's tsar,
Not over the highways, nor the main road,
Nor following the black standard.

THE SONG OF THE PRINCESS KSÉNIYA BORÍSOVNA [1]

There weepeth a little bird,
A little white quail:
"Alas, that I so young must grieve !
They wish to burn the green oak,
To destroy my little nest,
To kill my little ones,
To catch me, quail.''
In Moscow the Princess weepeth:
"Alas that I so young must grieve !
For there comes to Moscow the traitor,
Gríshka Otrépev Rozstríga, [2]
Who wants to take me captive,
And having captured make me a nun,
To send me into the monastery.
But I do not wish to become a nun,
To go into a monastery:
I shall keep my dark cell open,
To look at the fine fellows.
O our beautiful corridors !
Who will walk over you
After our tsarian life
And after Borís Godunóv ?
O our beautiful palace halls !
Who will be sitting in you
After our tsarian life
And after Borís Godunóv ? ''
And in Moscow the Princess weepeth,

[1] She was shorn a nun by order of the False Demetrius, and was
sent to a distant monastery.

[2] *Rozstríga* means ''he who has abandoned his tonsure.''

The daughter of Borís Godunóv:
" O God, our merciful Saviour !
Wherefore is our tsardom perished,—
Is it for father's sinning,
Or for mother's not praying ?
And you beloved palace halls!
Who will rule in you,
After our tsarian life ?
Fine stuffs of drawn lace !—
Shall we wind you around the birches ?
Fine gold-worked towels !
Shall we throw you into the woods ?
Fine earrings of hyacinth
Shall we hang you on branches,
After our tsarian life,
After the reign of our father,
Glorious Borís Godunóv ?
Wherefore comes to Moscow Rozstríga,
And wants to break down the palaces,
And to take me, princess, captive,
And to send me to Ustyúzhna Zheléznaya,
To make me, princess, a nun,
To place me behind a walled garden ?
Why must I grieve,
As they take me to the dark cell,
And the abbess gives me her blessing ? ''

THE RETURN OF PATRIARCH FILARÉT TO MOSCOW [1]

The tsarate of Muscovy was happy
And all the holy Russian land.
Happy was the sovereign, the orthodox Tsar,
The Grand Duke Mikhaíl Fedórovich,
For he was told that his father had arrived,
His father Filarét Nikítich,

[1] Filarét Nikítich, the father of Mikhaíl Feódorovich, returned
from his Lithuanian captivity in 1619 and was at once proclaimed
Patriarch.

From the land of the infidel, from Lithuania.
He had brought back with him many princes and boyárs,
He had also brought the boyár of the Tsar,
Prince Mikhaíl Borísovich Sheyn.
There had come together many princes, boyárs, and digni-
     taries,
In the mighty tsarate of Muscovy:
They wished to meet Filarét Nikítich
Outside the famous stone-built Moscow.
'T is not the red sun in its course,—
'T is the orthodox Tsar that has gone out,
To meet his father dear,
Lord Filarét Nikítich.
With the Tsar went his uncle,
Iván Nikítich the boyár.—
'' The Lord grant my father be well,
My father, lord Filarét Nikítich.''
They went not into the palace of the Tsar,
They went into the cathedral of the Most Holy Virgin,
To sing an honourable mass.
And he blessed his beloved child:
'' God grant the orthodox Tsar be well,
Grand Duke Mikhaíl Fedórovich!
And for him to rule the tsarate of Muscovy
And the holy Russian land.

Yúri Krizhánich.   (1617–about 1677.)

Krizhánich was a Croatian who had studied at the Croatian Seminary at Vienna, at the university of Bologna, and at the Greek College of St. Athanasius at Rome, where he came in contact with
some Russians. He early dreamed of a union of all the Slavic nations under the rule of Russia, and in 1657 he went to Southern
Russia, where he began a propaganda among the Cossacks in favour
of a union with that country. Two years later he appeared in
Moscow, where his Catholic religion and his efforts at introducing a
Western culture brought him into disrepute, and he was at once
banished to Siberia, where he lived until the year 1676. He composed a large number of works on an Universal Slavic language, on
the Russian empire in the seventeenth century, and on the union
of the Churches, writing not in Russian, but in a strange mixture of

several Slavic languages, of his own invention. In these he developed a strong Panslavism, full of hatred of everything foreign, except foreign culture, and expressed high hopes for Russia's future greatness. His works are said to have been used by Peter the Great, but they were not published until 1860.

POLITICAL REASONS FOR THE UNION OF THE CHURCHES

The sixth reason for my contention is of a political nature, and refers to the nation's weal. For this discord of the Churches is even now the cause of Doroshénko's rebellion and the Turkish invasion, and continuation of the present war, and has from the beginning been the cause of much evil. The Poles have an ancient adage: Aut Moscovia Polonizat, aut Polonia Moscovizat, *i. e.*, Either Moscow shall become Polish, or Poland shall be a part of the Russian empire. It is written in the histories of other nations, and the advisers of the Tsar know it, that in the days of Feódor Ivánovich and later there have been many congresses held and embassies sent for the purpose of securing a Russian ruler for Poland and Lithuania. There is no doubt but that Poland and Lithuania would have become possessions of the Russian Tsars, if it were not for the division of the Churches. And there would not have been many old and new wars, nor bloodshed, in which so many hundreds of thousands of innocent people have perished by the sword, and have been led into Mussulman captivity. And the Russian nation would have long ago been far advanced in profane and political sciences that are so necessary for all well-educated persons, and would not be scorned and ridiculed and hated by the European nations for its barbarism. Nor would it suffer such unbearable disgrace and losses in war and commerce from the Germans and Crimeans, as it is suffering now. Book knowledge and political wisdom is a leaven of the mind, and a fast friendship with the Poles and Lithuanians would have made the Russian nation more renowned and more feared by the surrounding peoples, and richer in all earthly possessions.

ON KNOWLEDGE

Kings must instruct their subjects, parents their children, how to obtain knowledge. The time has come for our nation to be instructed in various branches, for God has in His mercy and kindness uplifted through Russia a Slavic kingdom to glory, power and majesty, such as for splendour has never existed before among us. We observe with other nations that as soon as a kingdom rises to higher import- ance, the sciences and arts at once begin to flourish among them. We, too, must learn, for under the honoured rule of the Righteous Tsar and Great King Alexis Mikháylovich we have an opportunity to wipe off the mould of our ancient barbarism, to acquire various sciences, to adopt a better organisation of society, and to reach a higher well-being.

ON FOREIGNERS

We are not possessed of an innate vivacity, nor praise- worthy national characteristics, nor sincerity of heart. For people who have such pride do not allow foreigners to com- mand them, except by force, whereas our nation of its own free will invites foreigners to come to its country. Not one people under the sun has since the beginning of the world been so abused and disgraced by foreigners as we Slavs have been by the Germans. Our whole Slavic nation has been subject to this kind of treatment; everywhere we have upon our shoulders Germans, Jews, Scotchmen, Gyp- sies, Armenians, Greeks and merchants of other nationali- ties, who suck our blood. In Russia you will see nowhere any wealth, except in the Tsar's treasury; everywhere there is dire, bare poverty.

Grigóri Kotoshíkhin. (1630–1667.)

Grigóri Kotoshíkhin was a clerk, and later a scribe (*podyáchi*) in the Department of Legations, a kind of Foreign Office. He had been frequently employed as an ambassador in connection with various treaties between Russia and Sweden and Poland. While at Moscow, he had been guilty of some dishonesty to his own country by giving certain secrets of State to the Swedish ambassador; but that was an offence not uncommon at Moscow, where patriotism was seldom of a disinterested character. In 1664 he was sent out with the Russian army that was then operating against Poland. Shortly after, its two generals, Cherkásski and Prozoróvski, were recalled, and Dolgorúki was sent in their place. The latter tried to get Kotoshíkhin's aid in denouncing his two predecessors for traitorous actions, but Kotosh-íkhin refused. Fearing the wrath of Dolgorúki, he fled, first to Poland, and then, through Prussia and Lubeck, to Sweden. He settled in Stockholm, where he was employed in a semi-official capacity in the Foreign Office. In a fit of intoxication he killed his host, who was the official Russian translator of Sweden, and for this crime he was beheaded.

Kotoshíkhin had evidently formed the plan of writing about Russian customs before his arrival in Stockholm, but he was also encouraged by distinguished Swedish statesmen, who hoped to find important information about Russia in his work. In his capacity of Legation scribe Kotoshíkhin had an excellent opportunity to become intimately acquainted with the immediate surroundings of the Tsar ; but he supplemented his knowledge by a clear insight, which he had gained in his intercourse with other nations. There is no other work of Old Russia that gives so detailed an account of contemporary society. Kotoshíkhin's work was first discovered in 1840, though several manuscript translations in Swedish were known to be extant in various libraries.

THE EDUCATION OF THE PRINCES
FROM CHAP. I.

For the bringing up of the Tsarévich or Tsarévna they select from among the women of all ranks a good, pure, sweet-tempered and healthy woman, and that woman resides for a year in the Upper Palace, in the apartments of the Tsarítsa. At the expiration of the year, the husband of that woman, if she be of noble origin, is made governor of a city, or receives some lands in perpetuity; if she be a scribe's, or some other serving-man's wife, he is promoted and granted a goodly salary; if he be a countryman, he is given a good sum, and both are freed from the taxes and other imposts of the Tsar during their whole lives. The Tsarévich and Tsarévna have also a chief-nurse to look after them, a distinguished boyár's wife, — an old widow, and a nurse and other servants. When the Tsarévich reaches the

age of five, he is put in the keeping of a renowned boyár, a
quiet and wise man, and the latter has for a companion
a man from the lower ranks; they also choose from among
the children of the boyárs a few of the same age as the
Tsarévich, to be his servants and butlers. When the time
arrives to teach the Tsarévich to read and write, they select
teachers from the instructed people, who are of a quiet disposition and not given to drinking; the teacher of writing is
chosen from among the Legation scribes; they receive instruction in Russia in no other language, neither Latin,
Greek, German nor any other, except Russian.

The Tsaréviches and Tsarévnas have each separate apartments and servants to look after them. No one is permitted
to see the Tsarévich before his fifteenth year, except those
people who serve him, and the boyárs and Near People [1];
but after fifteen years he is shown to all people, as his father
goes with him to church or to entertainments. When the
people find out that he has been presented, they come on
purpose from many cities to get a look at him. As the
Tsaréviches, when they are young, and the elder and
younger Tsarévnas go to church, there are borne cloth
screens all around them, so that they cannot be seen; likewise, they cannot be seen when they stand in church, except by the clergy, for they are surrounded in church with
taffeta, and there are few people in church during that time
but boyárs and Near People. Similarly, when they travel
to the monasteries to pray, their carriages are covered with
taffeta. For their winter rides, the Tsarítsa and Tsarévnas
use kaptánas, that is, sleighs in the shape of small huts that
are covered with velvet or red cloth, with doors at both
sides, with mica windows and taffeta curtains; for their summer rides they use kolymágas that are also covered with
cloth; these are entered by steps and are made like simple
carts on wheels, and not like carriages that hang down on
leather straps. These kolymágas and kaptánas have two
shafts, and are without an axle; only one horse is hitched
in them, with other horses in tandem.

[1] A division of nobility below the boyárs.

THE PRIVATE LIFE OF THE BOYÁRS AND OF OTHER RANKS (CHAP. 13)

Boyárs and Near People live in their houses, both of stone and wood, that are not well arranged; their wives and children live all in separate rooms. Only a few of the greater boyárs have their own churches in their courts; and those of the high and middle boyárs who have no churches of their own, but who are permitted to have priests at their houses, have the matins and vespers and other prayers said in their own apartments, but they attend mass in any church they may choose; they never have the mass in their own houses. The boyárs and Near People pay their priests a yearly salary, according to agreement; if the priests are married people, they receive a monthly allowance of food and drink, but the widowed priests eat at the same table with their boyárs.

On church holidays, and on other celebrations, such as name days, birthdays and christenings, they frequently celebrate together.

It is their custom to prepare simple dishes, without seasoning, without berries, or sugar, without pepper, ginger or other spices, and they are little salted and without vinegar. They place on the table one dish at a time; the other dishes are brought from the kitchen and are held in the hands by the servants. The dishes that have little vinegar, salt and pepper are seasoned at the table; there are in all fifty to one hundred such dishes.

The table manners are as follows: before dinner the hosts order their wives to come out and greet their guests. When the women come, they place themselves in the hall, or room, where the guests are dining, at the place of honour,[1] and the guests stand at the door; the women greet the guests with the small salute,[2] but the guests bow to the ground. Then the host makes a low obeisance to his guests and bids them kiss his wife. At the request of his guests, the host kisses

[1] In the front corner, under the holy images.
[2] Bending as far as the girdle.

his wife first; then the guests make individual bows and, stepping forward, kiss his wife and, walking back again, bow to her once more; she makes the small salute each time she kisses a guest. Then the hostess brings each guest a glass of double- or treble-spiced brandy, the size of the glass being a fourth, or a little more, of a quart. The host makes as many low obeisances as there are guests, asking each one in particular to partake of the brandy which his wife is offering them. By the request of the guests, the host bids his wife to drink first, then he drinks himself, and then the guests are served; the guests make a low obeisance before drinking, and also after they have drunk and as they return the glass. To those that do not drink brandy, a cup of Rumney or Rhine wine, or some other liquor, is offered.

After this drinking the hostess makes a bow to the guests and retires to her apartments to meet her guests, the wives of the boyárs. The hostess and the wives of the guests never dine with the men, except at weddings; an exception is also made when the guests are near relatives and there are no outsiders present at the dinner. During the dinner, the host and guests drink after every course a cup of brandy, or Rumney or Rhine wine, and spiced and pure beer, and various kinds of meads. When they bring the round cakes to the table, the host's daughters-in-law, or married daughters, or the wives of near relatives come into the room, and the guests rise and, leaving the table, go to the door and salute the women; then the husbands of the women salute them, and beg the guests to kiss their wives and drink the wine they offer. The guests comply with their request and return to the table, while the women go back to their apartments. After dinner the host and guests drink more freely each other's healths, and drive home again. The boyárs' wives dine and drink in the same manner in their own apartments, where there are no men present.

When a boyár or Near Man is about to marry off his son, or himself, or a brother, or nephew, or daughter, or sister, or niece, he, having found out where there is a marriageable girl, sends his friends, men or women, to the father of that girl, to say that such and such a one had sent them to inquire whether he would be willing to give his daughter or relative to him or his relative, and what the girl's dowry would be in the trousseau, money, patrimony and serfs. If the person addressed is willing to give him his daughter, or relative, he replies to the inquiry that he intends to marry off the girl, only he has to consider the matter with his wife and family, and that he will give a definite answer on a certain day; but if he does not wish to give him the girl, knowing that he is a drunkard, or fast, or has some other bad habit, he will say at once that he will not give him the girl, or he will find some excuse for refusing the request.

Having taken counsel with his wife and family, and having decided to give him the girl, he makes a detailed list of her dowry, in money, silver and other ware, dresses, patrimony and serfs, and sends it to the people who had come to him from the prospective bridegroom, and they, in their turn, take it to the bridegroom. Nothing is told of the matter to the prospective bride, who remains in ignorance thereof.

The dowry of the bride appearing satisfactory, the groom sends his people to the bride's parents, to ask them to present the girl. The bride's parents reply that they are willing to show their daughter, only not to the prospective groom, but to his father, mother, sister or near female relative, in whom the groom may have special confidence. On the appointed day the groom sends his mother or sister to inspect the bride; the bride's parents make preparations for that day, attire their daughter in a fine garment, invite their relatives to dinner, and seat their daughter at the table.

When the inspectress arrives, she is met with the honour due her, and is placed at the table near the bride. Sitting at the table, the inspectress converses with the girl on all kinds of subjects, in order to try her mind and manner of speech, and closely watches her face, eyes and special marks, in order to bring a correct report to the bridegroom; having stayed a short time, she returns to the bridegroom. If the inspectress takes no liking to the bride, having discovered that she is silly, or homely, or has imperfect eyes, or is lame, or a poor talker, and so reports to the groom, he gives her up, and that is the last of it.   But if the bride has found favour in the inspectress's eyes, and she tells the groom that the girl is good and clever, and perfect in speech and all things, the groom sends his former friends again to the girl's parents, telling them that he likes their daughter, and that he wishes to come to a parley to write the marriage contract, in order to marry her on a certain date.   The bride's parents send word to the groom through his trusted people that he should come to the parley with a few of his friends in whom he has most confidence on a certain day, in the forenoon or afternoon.

On the appointed day the groom puts on his best clothes, and drives with his father, or near relatives, or friends whom he loves best to the bride's parents.   Upon arrival, the bride's parents and her near relatives meet them with due honour, after which they go into the house and seat themselves according to rank.   Having sat a while, the groom's father or other relative remarks that they have come for the good work, as he has bid them; the host answers that he is glad to see them, and that he is ready to take up the matter.   Then both sides begin to discuss all kinds of marriage articles and to set the day for the wedding according to how soon they can get ready for it, in a week, a month, half a year, a year, or even more.   Then they enter their names and the bride's name and the names of witnesses in the marriage contract, and it is agreed that he is to take the girl on a certain date, without fail, and that the girl is to be turned over to him on that date, without fail; and it is provided in that contract that if the groom does not take the girl on the appointed day, or the father will not give him his daughter on that day, the offending party has to pay 1000, or 5000, or 10,000 roubles, as the agreement may be.   Having stayed a while, and having eaten and drunk, they return home, without having seen the bride, and without the bride having seen the groom; but the mother, or married sister, or wife of some relative comes out to present the groom with some embroidery from the bride.

If after that parley the groom finds out something prejudicial to the bride, or someone interested in the groom tells him that she is deaf, or mute, or maimed, or has some other bad characteristic, and the groom does not want to take her, —and the parents of the bride complain about it to the Patriarch that he has not taken the girl according to the marriage articles, and does not want to take her, and thus has dishonoured her; or the bride's parents, having found out about the groom that he is a drunkard, or diceplayer, or maimed, or has done something bad, will not give him their daughter, and the groom complains to the Patriarch,—the Patriarch institutes an inquiry, and the fine is collected from the guilty party according to the contract, and is given to the groom or bride, as the case may be; and then both may marry whom they please.

But if both parties carry out their agreement, and get ready for the wedding on the appointed day, then the groom invites to the wedding his relatives and such other people as he likes, to be his ceremonial guests, in the same manner as I described before about the Tsar's wedding [1]; on the part of the bride the guests are invited in the same way. On the

---

[1] "The wedding ceremony is as follows: on the Tsar's side the first order is the father and mother, or those who are in place of his parents; the second order, the *travellers*,—the chief priest with the cross, the *thousand-man*, who is a great personage in that procession, and then the Tsar: eight boyárs. The duties of the *travellers* are as follows: they stay with the Tsar and Tsarítsa at the crowning in church, and at the table occupy higher places than the others; the *friends* (drúzhka), whose duty it is to call the guests to the wedding, to make speeches at the wedding in the name of the thousand-man and Tsar, and to carry presents; the *bride'smaids* (svákha) whose duty it is to watch the Tsarítsa, to dress her and undress her; the *candleholder*, who holds the candle when they get the Tsarítsa ready for the crowning; the *breadholders*, who carry the bread on litters to and from church (these litters are covered with gold velvet and embroidered cloth and sable furs; the *equerry* with his suite. The third order is the *sitting* boyárs, twelve men and twelve women, who sit as guests at the tables, with the Tsar's parents, but do not go to church with the Tsar. The fourth order is *of the court*, who attend to the food and drink."

day of the wedding tables are set at the houses of the groom and bride, and the word being given the groom that it is time to fetch the bride, they all set out according to the ceremonial rank: First the bread-men carry bread on a tray, then, if it be summer, the priest with the cross rides on horseback, but in winter in a sleigh; then follow the boyárs, the thousand-man, and the groom.

Having reached the court of the bride's house, they enter the hall in ceremonial order, and the bride's father and his guests meet them with due honour, and the order of the wedding is the same as described in the Tsar's wedding. When the time arrives to drive to church to perform the marriage, the bride'smaids ask her parents to give the groom and bride their blessing for the marriage. They bless them with words, but before leaving bless them with a holy image, and, taking their daughter's hand, give her to the groom.

Then the ceremonial guests, the priest, and the groom with his bride, whose hand he is holding, go out of the hall, and her parents and their guests accompany them to the court; the groom places the bride in a kolymága or kaptána, mounts a horse, or seats himself in a sleigh; the ceremonial guests do likewise, and all drive to the church where they are to be married. The bride's parents and their guests return to the hall, where they eat and drink until news is brought from the groom; the bride is accompanied only by her own and the bridegroom's go-betweens. The two having been united, the whole troop drives to the groom's house, and news is sent to the bride's father that they have been propitiously married. When they arrive at the groom's court, the groom's parents and their guests meet them, and the parents, or those who are in their stead, bless them with the images, and offer them bread and salt, and then all seat themselves at the table and begin to eat, according to the ceremony; and then the bride is unveiled.

The next morning the groom drives out with the bride's-maid to call the guests, those of his and the bride's, to dinner. When he comes to the bride's parents, he thanks them for their having well brought up their daughter, and for having given her to him in perfect health; after having made the round to all the guests, he returns home. When all the guests have arrived, the bride offers gifts to all the ceremonial guests. Before dinner the groom goes with all the company to the palace to make his obeisance to the Tsar. Having arrived in the presence of the Tsar, all make a low obeisance, and the Tsar, without taking off his cap, asks the married couple's health. The groom bows to the ground, and then the Tsar congratulates those who are united in legitimate wedlock, and blesses the married pair with images, and he presents them with forty sables, and for their garments a bolt of velvet, and atlas, and gold-coloured silk, and calamanco, and simple taffeta, and a silver vessel, a pound and a half to two pounds in weight, to each of them; but the bride is not present at the audience. Then the Tsar offers the thousand-man, and bridegroom, and the ceremonial guests a cup of Rumney wine, and then a pitcher of cherry wine, and after they have emptied their wine the Tsar dismisses them.

After arriving home, they begin to eat and drink, and after the dinner the parents and guests bless the married couple with images and make them all kinds of presents, and after dinner the guests drive home. On the third day, the bride and groom and the guests go to dinner to the bride's parents, with all their guests, and after the dinner the bride's parents and their guests make presents to the married couple, and they drive home; and that is the end of the festivity.

During the time that the groom is in the presence of the Tsar, the bride sends in her name presents to the Tsarítsa and Tsarévnas, tidies of taffeta, worked with gold and silver and pearls; the Tsarítsa and Tsarévnas accept these gifts, and send to inquire about the bride's health.

During all the wedding festivities, no women are present, and there is no music, except blowing of horns and beating of drums.

The proceeding is the same when a widowed daughter, or

sister, or niece is married off : the ceremonial and the festivity are the same.

In the beginning of the festivity, the priest who is to marry the pair receives from the Patriarch and the authorities a permit, with the seal attached to it, to marry them, having first ascertained that the bride and groom are not related by sponsorship, nor by the ties of consanguinity in the sixth and seventh generation, nor that he is the husband of a fourth wife, nor she the wife of a fourth husband; but if he discover that they are related by sponsorship, and so forth, he is not allowed to marry them. Should the priest permit such an unlawful marriage to take place, with his knowledge or without his knowledge, he would be discharged from his priesthood and, if he was knowingly guilty, he has to pay a big fine, and the authorities lock him up for a year; but the married pair is divorced, without being fined, except the sin which they have incurred, and if they have not been previously married three times, they may marry again.

If a widower wants to marry a maiden, the ceremonial at the wedding is the same, but during the wreathing in church the wreath is placed on the groom's right shoulder, whereas the bride wears her wreath upon her head; if a widower for the third time marries a maiden, the ceremonial is the same, but the wreath is placed on the groom's left shoulder, and the bride wears hers upon her head. The same is done when a widow marries for the second or third time. But when a widower marries for the second or third time a widow, then there is no wreathing, and only a prayer is said instead of the wreathing, and the wedding ceremonial is different from the one mentioned above.

The manner of the parley, marriage and ceremonial wedding is the same with the lower orders of the nobility as described above, and the wedding is as sumptuous as they can afford to make it, but they do not call upon the Tsar, except those of his retinue.

Among the merchants and peasants the parley and the ceremonial are exactly the same, but they differ in their acts and dresses from the nobility, each according to his means.

It sometimes happens that a father or mother has two or three daughters, where the eldest daughter is maimed, being blind, or lame, or deaf, or mute, while the other sisters are perfect in shape and beauty and speech. When a man begins to sue for their daughter, and he sends his mother, or sister, or someone else in whom he has confidence to inspect her, the parents sometimes substitute the second or third daughter for their maimed sister, giving her the name of the latter, so that the inspectress, not knowing the deceit, takes a liking to the girl and reports to the groom that she is a proper person to marry. Then the groom, depending upon her words, has a parley with the girl's parents, that he is to marry her upon an appointed day, and that the parents are to give her to him upon the appointed day, and the fine is set so high that the guilty party is not able to pay it. When the wedding takes place, the parents turn over to him the maimed daughter, whose name is given in the articles of marriage, but who is not the one the inspectresses had seen. But the groom cannot discover on the wedding day that she is blind, or disfigured, or has some other defect, or that she is deaf or mute, for at the wedding she is veiled and does not say a word, nor can he know whether she is lame, because her bride'smaids lead her under her arms.

But in that case the man who has been deceived complains to the Patriarch and authorities, and these take the articles of marriage and institute an inquiry among the neighbours and housefolk, each one individually, whether the person he had married is the one indicated by name in the marriage articles. If so, the articles are valid, and no faith is to be put in his contention, on the ground that it was his business to be sure whom he was going to marry. But if the neighbours and housefolk depose that the bride is not the same as mentioned by name in the articles, the married pair is divorced, and the parents have to pay a large fine and damages to the groom, and besides the father is beaten with the knout, or his punishment is even more severe, according to the Tsar's will.

The same punishment is meted out to the man who presents his serving maid or a widow in place of his unmarried daughter, by giving her another name and dressing her up so as to look like his daughter, or when his daughter is of short stature and they place her on a high chair in such a way that her defect is not noticeable.

When parents have maimed or old daughters, and no one wants to marry them, they are sent to a monastery to be shorn nuns.

When a man wants to inspect the bride himself, and the parents grant the request, knowing that she is fair and that they need not be ashamed of her, but the groom, having taken no liking to her, decries her with damaging and injurious words, and thus keeps other suitors away from her, —and the bride's parents complain to the Patriarch or authorities: these institute an inquiry, and having found the man guilty, marry him to the girl by force; but if he has married another girl before the complaint has been entered, the girl's disgrace is taken from her by an ukase.

When a man marries off his daughter or sister, and gives her a large dowry in serfs and patrimony, and that daughter or sister, having borne no children, or having borne some who have all died, dies herself,— the dowry is all taken from her husband and is turned over to those who had married her off.   But if she leaves a son or daughter, the dowry is, for the sake of her child, not taken from her husband.

Gentle reader! Wonder not, it is nothing but the truth when I say that nowhere in the whole world is there such deception practised with marriageable girls as in the kingdom of Muscovy; there does not exist there the custom, as in other countries, for the suitor to see and sue for the bride himself.

The boyárs and Near People have in their houses 100, or 200, or 300, or 500, or 1000 servants, male and female, according to their dignity and possessions. These servants receive a yearly salary, if they are married, 2, 3, 5 or 10 roubles, according to their services, and their wearing apparel, and a monthly allowance of bread and victuals; they live in their own rooms in the court of the boyár's house. The best of these married servants are sent out by the boyárs every year, by rotation, to their estates and villages, with the order to collect from their peasants the taxes and rents. The unmarried older servants receive some small wages, but the younger ones receive nothing; all the unmarried servants get their wearing apparel, hats, shirts and boots; the older of these servants live in the farther lower apartments, and receive their food and drink from the kitchen; on holidays they receive two cups of brandy each. The female servants who are widows remain living in the houses of their husbands, and they receive a yearly wage and a monthly allowance of food; other widows and girls stay in the rooms of the boyárs' wives and daughters, and they receive their wearing apparel, and their food from the boyár's kitchen.

When these girls are grown up, the boyárs marry them, and also the widows, to some one of their servants to whom they have taken a liking, but sometimes by force. The wedding takes place in the boyár's hall, according to the rank of the marrying parties; the food and festive dresses are furnished by the boyár. The girls are never married to any person outside the boyár's court, because both male and female servants are his perpetual serfs. In the boyár's house there is an office for all domestic affairs, where an account is kept of income and expenses, and all the affairs of the servants and peasants are investigated and settled.

Simeón Pólotski. (1629–1680.)

Simeón, whose father's name was Emelyán Petróvski-Sitniánovich, studied at Kíev, where the Western scholasticism had found entrance through the Polish, and where the Orthodox Church stood in less violent opposition to the Catholic and Protestant Churches and the sacred and profane learning which they disseminated. Simeón took the tonsure as a monk in Pólotsk, and developed there his early pedagogical activity,—hence his name Pólotski. When Pólotsk was occupied by the Poles, Simeón went to Moscow, where he attracted the attention of Alexis Mikháylovich by his verses upon the birth of the Tsarévich Feódor. He became the first Court poet, was employed as instructor of Alexis, Feódor, and, later, Peter himself, and had great influence on the education of their sister Sophia. He was also appointed a teacher of Latin in the School of the Redeemer, where his first pupils were scribes of the Secret Department, and where later a new generation of men, among them Lomonósov, received their earliest instruction in Western culture. Simeón developed an untiring activity in literature, standing alone in his efforts to engraft an antiquated scholasticism on the Russian orthodoxy. He was a very learned man, but, like his spiritual peer Tredyakóvski of the next century, devoid of poetic genius. His poetry, collected in two large works, *The Flowery Pleasaunce* and the *Rhythmologion*, is merely a paraphrase of foreign models in forced rhymes and a syllabic versification which is entirely unsuited to the Russian language. He wrote two plays, in the manner of the old Mysteries, which were among the first to be given at the newly established Court theatre. He translated much from the Latin, and composed more than two hundred sermons. In spite of the mediocrity of his literary efforts, his influence on the next generation was great ; Lomonósov received his first impulse for writing verses from a perusal of Pólotski's works.

ON THE BIRTH OF PETER THE GREAT

A great gladness the month of May has brought us, for the Tsarévich Peter was born in it. But yesterday the famous Constantinople was captured by the Turks;—to-day the most glorious salvation has appeared. The conqueror has come, and he will avenge the insult, and will free the ruling city. O Constantine's city, mightily rejoice! And you, holy church of Sophia, rejoice! An orthodox Tsarévich was born to us to-day, a Grand Prince of Moscow, Peter Aleksyéevich: he will endeavour to adorn you in honour, and to subdue the Moslem abomination. And you, ruling city of Moscow, rejoice! For a great joy has taken up its abode within you. He strengthened your stone-walls that surround you, porphyrogenite, God-sent son of the Tsar! Peter is his name,—a firm rock,[1] and being born to strengthen the gates he will be brave and terrible to the enemy that opposes him. By a wondrous name a rock of faith, an adornment and joy to the Tsar is born, and an eternal glory to his parents.

The younger Joseph was beloved by his father, and thus

---

[1] That is, deriving *Peter* from Greek πέτρα, rock.

is the younger Tsarévich beloved by his father. The
youngest Benjamin was loved by his brothers; even thus the
youngest Peter is beloved by his two brothers. Peter is a
rock of fortune and a precious stone, endowed by God for the
confirmation of the Church. You, planet Ares and Zeus, rejoice, for the Tsarévich was born under your lustre! The
Tsarévich was born in the quadrant aspect, and he has come
to rule in his house. He announces the four-cornered token,
as if to rule the four corners of the earth. From God this
being was given to this planet, for this planet was found to
be the best for his achievements: bravery, wealth and
glory reside upon it, to place a wreath upon the head of the
Tsar.

Rejoice to-day, orthodox Tsar! A glorious son has been
born to you! May your years and the years of the Tsarítsa
be many, and may you and your children prosper, and the
new-born Tsarévich, Peter Aleksyéevich, even now glorious!
May you vanquish all foreign mights, and unite all lands
and kingdoms under your rule! May God grant you to see
the third and fourth generation, and your throne for ever
unshaken !

AN EVIL THOUGHT

A man found a snake stiff with cold and cast upon the
path into the snow; he took pity on it, and placed it in his
bosom. When it was revived, it began to creep, then bit
the senseless man that had warmed it. Even thus it happens
to him who harbours evil thoughts: they soon come to life,
and give mortal stings to the thinker.

THE MAGNET

Iron with a magnet rubbed assumes the power of a magnet: it then attracts needles, one after another, as long as its
power lasts, which God has placed in the ore. Even so the
righteous do in this world: the wisdom which is given
them they give to others, that having been made wise they
may turn from the world, and may turn their hearts to the
living God, and may lead each other into the heavenly region prepared by God for those who serve Him faithfully.

The Story of Misery Luckless-Plight, How That Misery Luckless-Plight Caused a Youth to Turn Monk. (XVII. or XVIII. century.)

This beautiful story was found in a manuscript collection of the seventeenth and eighteenth centuries. It consists of two parts: the first is an apocryphal account of the fall of man, with the customary substitution of the grapevine for the apple-tree, in order to inculcate abstinence from the bowl; the second part, relating the pursuit of the young man by the demon Misery Luckless-Plight, bears every evidence of popular origin. The dramatic element of the story, the symbolic account of the pursuit in the shape of animals, the parallel-ism of phrases, are all devices which recur in the popular tales, from the *Word of Igor's Armament* to the present time.

By the will of the Lord our God and Saviour, Jesus Christ, who encompasses all, from the beginning of the human race.

In the beginning of this perishable world, God created heaven and earth, God created Adam and Eve. He ordered them to live in holy paradise, and gave them this divine command: He told them not to eat the fruit of the grapevine, from the great tree of Eden. But the human heart is un-thinking and irresistible, and Adam and Eve were tempted. They forgot God's command, ate of the fruit of the grape-vine, from the great and wonderful tree, and for that great transgression of theirs God was wroth with Adam and Eve and drove them out of the holy Edenic paradise. He settled them upon the low earth, blessed them to grow and multiply, and told them to appease their hunger through their own labour from the fruits upon earth. . . . God gave them this commandment: there should be marriages, for the propagation of the race of men and for beloved children.

But the human race was evil: from the very start it was not submissive, looked with disdain at the father's instruc-tion, did not obey the mother, was untrue to the advice of friends. Then there came a weak and wretched race that turned to reckless deeds, and began to live in turmoil and wrong, and discarded humility of spirit. And God grew wroth with them, and sent great calamities down upon them, and great misery, and immeasurable shame, evil plight, fiendish visitations, a wretched nakedness, and endless poverty and extreme want, in order to humble us, to punish us, to lead us on the path of salvation. Such is the race of man from its father and mother.

The youth had reached the age of discretion and absence of wantonness. His father and mother loved him much, and they began to teach and instruct him, to prepare him for good deeds:

"Dear child of ours, listen to your parents' words of instruction, listen to their saws, the good and cunning and wise, and you will not be in want, you will not be in great poverty. Go not, child, to feasts and celebrations; do not seat yourself on a high place; drink not two beakers at once; be not tempted by good, fair maidens, fathers' daughters. Lie not down in the wilderness. Fear not the wise man, fear the fool, lest the fools lay hands on you and take off your costly garments, and cause you great shame and aggravation, and expose you to the scorn and empty prattle of men. Go not, my child, to the dice-players and innkeepers, and keep no company with the frequenters of the tavern. Make no friends with the foolish and simple. Steal not, rob not, nor deceive, nor tell a lie, nor do wrong. Be not tempted by gold and silver; collect not unrighteous wealth. Be not a witness to false swearing, and think no evil of father and mother, or any other man,—that God may protect you from all evil. Dishonour not, child, the rich and the poor, but regard them all alike. Keep company with the wise and sensible, and make friends with friends you may rely upon, who will not deliver you to evil."

The youth was then young and foolish, not in his full senses and imperfect in mind: he was ashamed to submit to his father and bow before his mother, but wanted to live as he listed. If the youth earned fifty roubles, he found easily fifty friends, and his honour flowed like a river: the youth gained many friends for himself, and they accounted themselves of his race.

And the youth had a trusted friend: he named himself his plighted brother, and he tempted him with tempting words; he called him to the tavern yard, led him into the hall of the inn, brought him a cup of green wine, handed him a beaker of heady beer, and spoke to him the following words:

"Drink, plighted brother of mine, to your joy, and happiness, and health. Empty the cup of green wine, and follow it by a glass of sweet mead. And if you drink, brother, until you be drunk, lie down to sleep where you have drunk, —depend upon me, your plighted brother. I shall sit down and keep watch over you: at your head, dear friend, I shall place a beaker of sweet Ishem wine, by your side I shall place green wine, and near you I shall place heady beer. I shall watch well over you, dear friend, and shall take you back to your father and mother."

At that time the youth depended on his plighted brother; he did not wish to disobey him. He settled himself near the heady drinks, and emptied a cup of green wine, followed it by a glass of sweet mead, and he drank also the heady beer. He drank until he lost his senses, and where he had drunk, there he fell asleep: he depended upon his plighted brother.

The day was inclining towards night, and the sun was in the west, when the youth awoke from his sleep. The youth looked all around him: all the costly garments had been taken away from him, his shoes and stockings were all gone, his shirt even was taken from him, and all his property was stolen. A brick was lying under his unruly head; he was covered with a tavern sackcloth, and at his feet lay ragged sandals; at his head his dear friend was no more. And the youth stood up on his bare feet, and began to clothe himself: he put on the ragged sandals, covered himself with the tavern sackcloth, covered his white body, and washed his white face. Sorrow entered the youth's heart, and he spoke the following words:

" Though God has granted me a good life, I have now nothing to eat or drink! Since my money is gone, even the last half-farthing, I have not a friend, not even half a friend.

They no longer account themselves of my race, all my friends have disappeared!''

The youth felt ashamed to show himself before father and mother, and his race and family, and to his former friends. He went into a strange, distant, unknown land. He found a court, a town in size, and a house in that court, a palace in height. In that house was given a splendid feast: the guests drank, ate and made merry. The youth came to the splendid feast, made the sign of the cross over his white face, bowed before the wonderful images, made his obeisance to the good people on all four sides. And when the good people saw the youth, how well he made the sign of the cross, how he acted according to the written rule, they took him by the hands, seated him at the oaken table, not in a great place, nor in a small, they seated him in a middle place, where the younger guests are seated. And the feast was a merry one, and all the guests at the feast were drunk and merry and boastful; but the youth sat, not merry at all, gloomy, sorrowful, joyless, and neither ate, nor drank, nor made merry, nor boasted of anything at the feast. Said the good people to the youth:

''Wherefore, O good youth, do you sit, not merry at the feast, gloomy, sorrowful, joyless; you neither drink, nor make merry, nor boast of anything at the feast? Or has the cup of green wine not reached you, or is not your seat according to your father's worth? Or have small children insulted you? Or foolish and unwise people made light of you, youth? Or are our children not kind to you?''

But the good youth remained sitting and said:

''Gentlemen and good people! I will tell you of my great misfortune, of my disobedience to my parents, of my drinking at the inn the cup of mead, the tempting drinking of heady wine. When I took to drinking the heady wine, I disobeyed both father and mother: their blessing departed from me; the Lord grew wroth with me, and to my poverty were added many great and incurable sorrows and sadness without comfort, want, and misery, and extreme wretchedness. Want has tamed my flowery speech; sadness has dried up

my white body. For this my heart is not merry, and my
white face is sad, and my eyes dim. I have lost my paternal
honour, and my youthful valour has left me. Gentlemen
and good people! Tell me and teach me how to live in a
strange land, among strange people, and how to find dear
friends!''

Said the good people to the youth:

'' You are a sensible youth! Be not haughty in a strange
land: submit to friend and foe, bow to old and young, tell
not of the affairs of others, neither what you hear, nor see.
Flatter not friends nor enemies; have no tortuous fits, nor
bend as a cunning snake; be humble before all, but withal
keep to truth and right,—and you will have great honour and
glory. When people will find you out, they will respect and
honour you for your great truth, your humility and wisdom;
—and you will have dear friends, who will call themselves
your plighted brothers.''

And the youth went hence into a strange land, and began
to live wisely, and through his great wisdom acquired greater
wealth than before. He looked out for a bride according to
custom, for he wished to marry. The youth prepared a
splendid feast, according to his father's worth and as best he
knew, and invited the honoured guests and friends. But
through his own sin, by God's will and the devil's temptation, he boasted before his honoured guests and friends and
plighted brothers. A boastful word is always rotten, and
self-praise brings the destruction of man: '' I, the youth,
have gained more possessions than ever!''

Misery Luckless-Plight heard the young man's boasting,
and spoke the following words:

'' Young man, boast not of your fortune, praise not your
wealth! I, Misery, have known people who were wiser and
richer than you, but I, Misery, have outwitted them. When
a great misfortune befell them, they struggled with me unto
their death; they were worsted by their luckless plight,—could
not get away from me, Misery, until they took their abode in
the grave, and I covered them for ever with the earth. Only
then they were rid of nakedness, and I, Misery, left them,

though luckless plight remained upon their grave!" And
again it cawed ominously: " I, Misery, attached myself to
others, for I, Misery Luckless-Plight, cannot live empty-
handed: I, Misery, wish to live among people, from whom
I cannot be driven away with a whip; but my chief seat and
paternal home is among the carousers!"

Spoke grey Misery the miserable:

" How am I to get at the youth?" and evil Misery devised cunningly to appear to the youth in his dream:

"Young man, renounce your beloved bride, for you
will be poisoned by your bride; you will be strangled by
that woman; you will be killed for your gold and silver!
Go, young man, to the Tsar's tavern: save nothing, but
spend all your wealth in drink; doff your costly dress, put
on the tavern sackcloth.   In the tavern Misery will remain,
and evil Luckless-Plight will stay,—for Misery will not
gallop after a naked one, nor will anyone annoy a naked
man, nor has assault any terrors for a bare-footed man.'"

The young man did not believe his dream, but evil Misery
again devised a plan, and stuck once more to the youth for
a new luckless plight:

"Are you not, youth, acquainted with immeasurable
nakedness, and its great lightness and inexpensiveness?
What you buy for yourself is money spent, but you are a
brave fellow, and can live without expense! They do not
beat, nor torture naked people, nor drive them out of paradise, nor drag them down from the other world; nor will
anyone annoy a naked man, nor has assault any terrors for
a naked man!"

The young man believed that dream: he went and spent
all his wealth in drink; he doffed his costly dress, put on
the tavern sackcloth, covered his white body. The youth
felt ashamed to show himself to his dear friends. He went
into a strange, distant, unknown land. On his way he came
to a swift river. On the other side were the ferrymen, and
they asked for money to ferry him across; but the youth had
none to give, and without money they would not take him
across. The youth sat a whole day, until evening, and all

that day the youth had nothing to eat, not even half a piece of bread. The young man arose on his swift feet, and standing he fell to grieving, and he spoke the following words:

"Woe to me, miserable Luckless-Plight! It has overtaken me, young man, has starved me, young man, with a hungry death. Three unlucky days have I passed, for I, young man, have not eaten half a piece of bread! I, young man, will jump into the swift river: swallow my body, swift river! And eat, O fish, my white body! ,And that will be better than my shameful life, for I have fallen into the hands of Misery Luckless-Plight."

At that hour Misery leaped from behind a rock near the swift river: Misery was bare-footed and naked, and there was not a thread upon it, and it was girded with a bast thong, and it called out with a mighty voice:

"Wait, young man, you will not escape from me, Misery! Jump not into the swift river, nor be in your misery doleful! Though you live in misery, you need not be doleful, but let your dolefulness die in misery! Remember, young man, your former life: how your father spoke to you, and your mother instructed you! Why did you not then obey them? You would not submit to them, and were ashamed to bow to them, but wanted to live as you listed! But he who will not listen to the good teaching of his parents will learn from me, Misery Luckless-Plight!"

Luckless-Plight spoke the following words:

"Submit to me, impure Misery; bow before me, Misery, to the damp earth, for there is no one wiser in the whole world than I, Misery; and you will be ferried across the swift river, and the good people will give you to eat and drink."

The young man saw his inevitable calamity, and he submitted to impure Misery, bowed before Misery to the damp earth!

The good fellow went ahead with a light step over the beautiful fair bank, over the yellow sand. He went happy, not at all doleful, for he had appeased Misery Luckless-Plight. And as he went, he thought a thought: Since I have nothing, I need not worry about anything! And as the youth was not sorrowful, he started a fair song, a mighty, sensible song it was:

"Sorrowless mother has borne me; with a comb she combed my little locks, dressed me in costly garments, and stepping aside shaded her eyes and looked at me: 'Does my child look well in costly garments? In costly garments my child is a priceless child!' Thus my mother always spoke of me! And then I learned and know it well that a scarlet gown cannot be made without a master, nor a child be comforted without a mother, nor a drunkard ever become rich, nor a dice-player be in good renown; and I was taught by my parents to be a well-dressed boy, who was born devoid of everything."

The ferrymen heard the good fellow's song, took the young man across the swift river, and took nothing from him for the ferrying. The good people gave him to drink and to eat, took off his tavern sackcloth, gave him peasant's clothes, and spoke to him:

"You are a good fellow, so go to your home, to your beloved, respected parents, to your father and mother dear, greet your parents, father and mother, and receive from them the parental blessing!"

From there the youth went to his home. When he was in the open field, evil Misery had gone before him; it met the youth in the open field, and began to caw above the youth, like an ill-omened crow above a falcon. Misery spoke the following words:

"Wait! you have not gone away from me, good fellow! Not merely for a time have I, Misery Luckless-Plight, attached myself to you; I shall labour with you to your very death! And not I, Misery, alone, but all my family, and there is a goodly race of them: we are all gentle and insinuating, and he who joins our family will end his days among us! Such is the fate that awaits you with us. Even if you were to be a bird of the air, or if you went into the blue sea as a fish, I would follow you at your right hand."

The youth flew as a clear falcon, and Misery after him as

a white gerfalcon; the youth flew as a steel-blue dove, and Misery after him as a grey hawk; the youth went into the field as a grey wolf, and Misery after him with hounds; the youth became the steppe-grass in the field, and Misery came with a sharp scythe, and Luckless-Plight railed at him:

" You, little grass, will be cut down; you, little grass, will lie on the ground, and the boisterous winds will scatter you!"

The youth went as a fish into the sea, and Misery after him with close-meshed nets, and Misery Luckless-Plight railed at him:

" You, little fish, will be caught at the shore, and you will be eaten up and die a useless death!"

The youth went on foot along the road, and Misery at his right hand. It taught the youth to live as a rich man, by killing and robbing, so that they might hang the young man for it, or might put him with a stone in the water. The youth bethought himself of the road of salvation, and at once the youth went to a monastery to be shorn a monk, and Misery stopped at the holy gates,— no longer clung to the youth.

And this is the end of the story: Lord, preserve us from eternal torment, and give us, O Lord, the light of paradise! For ever and ever, amen!

THE FOLKLORE

THE FOLKLORE

Epic Songs.

The first collection of epic songs was published in 1804, based on the collection made some years before by the Siberian Cossack Kirshá Danílov. Since the fifties of the eighteenth century large numbers of these songs have been gathered in the extreme north-east, by Kiryéevski, Rýbnikov, Gílferding, and others. They are generally divided into the cycle of Kíev, with Vladímir and his druzhína, who defend the country against external enemies, and the cycle of Nóvgorod, in which is described the wealth and luxury of the once famous commercial emporium. There is also a division into the older heroes, of which Volkh Vseslávevich is one, and the younger heroes, of which Ilyá of Múrom is the most noted.

Good accounts of the epic songs may be found in most of the general works on Russian literature mentioned in the Preface. The only work which gives a large number of these epics, with notes, is *The Epic Songs of Russia*, by Isabel Florence Hapgood, with an introductory note by Prof. Francis J. Child, New York, 1886.

VOLKH VSESLÁVEVICH

IN the heavens the bright moon did shine,
But in Kíev a mighty hero was born,
The young hero Volkh Vseslávevich:
The damp earth trembled,
Trembled the famous Indian realm,
And the blue sea also trembled
On account of the birth of the hero,
The young Volkh Vseslávevich:
The fish went into the depth of the sea,
The birds flew high into the clouds,
The aurochses and stags went beyond the mountains,
The hares and foxes into the woods,

The wolves and bears into the pine-forests,
The sables and martens upon the isles.
Volkh was old an hour and a half,
And Volkh spoke, like peals of thunder:
" Hail to thee, lady mother,
Young Márfa Vseslávevna!
Swathe me not in swaddling-clothes of bast,
Gird me not with bands of silk,—
Swathe me, my dear mother,
In strong mail of tempered steel;
On my grim head place a helmet of gold,
Into my right hand put a club,
A heavy club of lead,
In weight that club of thirty puds."
Volkh was seven years old:
His mother gave him to be instructed;
As soon as he had learned to read,
She put him down to write with pen,
And he learned swiftly how to write.
When Volkh was ten years old:
Then Volkh learned all cunning arts:
The first of these cunning arts was
To change himself into a falcon clear;
The second cunning art that Volkh had learned
Was to change himself into a grey wolf;
The third cunning art that Volkh had learned
Was to change himself into a dun aurochs with horns of
    gold.
When Volkh was twelve years old,
He began to collect a druzhína for himself.
He got together a druzhína within three years,
His druzhína was seven thousand strong.
Volkh himself was fifteen years old,
And all his druzhína were fifteen years old.
All that famous host started out
For the capital, for Kíev town:
The Tsar of India was arming himself,
He was boasting and bragging to all

That he would take Kíev town by assault,
Would let God's churches go up in smoke,
Would destroy the worshipful monasteries.
As soon as Volkh had found that out,
He started out with his druzhína brave
For the famous kingdom of India,
With his druzhína he at once started out.
The druzhína sleeps, but Volkh sleeps not:
He turns himself into a grey wolf,
Runs, races over dark forests and wolds,
And strikes down the antlered beasts;
Nor does he give quarter to wolf or bear,
And sables and panthers are his favourite morsel,
Nor does he disdain hares and foxes.
Volkh gave his brave druzhína to eat and drink,
Gave apparel and footwear to his valiant men:
His men all wore black sable furs,
And other coats of panthers.
The druzhína sleeps, but Volkh sleeps not:
He turns himself into a clear falcon,
And flies far away, beyond the blue sea,
And strikes down the geese, the white swans,
Nor does he give quarter to the grey-white ducks;
And he gave his druzhína to eat and drink:
And his viands were of many a kind,
Of many a kind, and sweetmeats too.

ILYÁ OF MÚROM AND NIGHTINGALE THE ROBBER

Young Ilyá of Múrom, Iván's son, went to matins on Easter morn. And as he stood there in the church, he vowed a great vow: " To sing a high mass that same Easter day in Kíev town, and go thither by the straight way." And yet another vow he took: "As he fared to that royal town by the straight way, not to stain his hand with blood, nor yet his sharp sword with the blood of the accursed Tartars."

His third vow he swore upon his mace of steel: "That though he should go the straight way, he would not shoot his fiery darts."

Then he departed from the cathedral church, entered the spacious courtyard and began to saddle good Cloudfall, his shaggy bay steed, to arm himself and prepare for his journey to the famous town of Kíev, to the worshipful feast and the Fair Sun Prince Vladímir of royal Kíev. Good Cloudfall's mane was three ells in length, his tail three fathoms, and his hair of three colours. Ilyá put on him first the plaited bridle, next twelve saddle-cloths, twelve felts, and upon them a metal-bound Circassian saddle. The silken girths were twelve in number — not for youthful vanity but for heroic strength; the stirrups were of damascened steel from beyond the seas, the buckles of bronze which rusteth not, weareth not, the silk from Samarcand which chafeth not, teareth not.

They saw the good youth as he mounted, — as he rode they saw him not; so swift was his flight there seemed but a smoke-wreath on the open plain, as when wild winds of winter whirl about the snow. Good Cloudfall skimmed over the grass and above the waters; high over the standing trees he soared, the primeval oaks, yet lower than the drifting clouds. From mountain to mountain he sprang, from hill to hill he galloped; little rivers and lakes dropped between his feet; where his hoofs fell, founts of water gushed forth; in the open plain smoke eddied and rose aloft in a pillar. At each leap Cloudfall compassed a verst and a half.

In the open steppe young Ilyá hewed down a forest, and raised a godly cross, and wrote thereon:

"Ilyá of Múrom, the Old Cossack, rideth to royal Kíev town on his first heroic quest."

When he drew near to Chernígov, there stood a great host of Tartars, — three Tsaréviches, each with forty thousand men. The cloud of steam from the horses was so great that the fair red sun was not yet seen by day, nor the bright moon by night. The grey hare could not course, nor the clear falcon fly about that host, so vast was it.

When Ilyá saw that, he dismounted; flying down before good Cloudfall's right foot, he entreated him:

"Help me, my shaggy bay!" So Cloudfall soared like a falcon clear, and Ilyá plucked up a damp, ringbarked oak from the damp earth, from amid the stones and roots, and bound it to his left stirrup, grasped another in his right hand, and began to brandish it: "Every man may take a vow," quoth he, "but not every man can fulfill it."

Where he waved the damp oak a street appeared; where he drew it back, a lane. Great as was the number that he slew, yet twice that number did his good steed trample under foot. Not one was spared to continue their race.

The gates of Chernígov were strongly barred, a great watch was kept, and the stout and mighty hero stood in counsel. Therefore Ilyá flew on his good steed over the city wall (the height of the wall was twelve fathoms) and entered the church where all the people were assembled, praying God, repenting and receiving the sacrament against sure and approaching death. Ilyá crossed himself as prescribed, did reverence as enjoined, and cried:

"Hail, ye merchants of Chernígov, warrior maidens, and mighty heroes all! Why repent ye now and receive the sacrament? Why do ye bid farewell thus to the white world?"

Then they told him how they were deceived by the accursed Tartars, and Ilyá said: "Go ye upon the famous wall of your city, and look towards the open plain."

They did as he commanded, and lo! where had stood the many, very many foreign standards, like a dark, dry forest, the accursed Tartars were now cut down and heaped up like a field of grain which hath been reaped.

Then the men of Chernígov did slowly reverence to the good youth, and besought him that he would reveal his name and abide in Chernígov to serve them as their Tsar, King, Voevóda,—what he would; and that he would likewise accept at their hand a bowl of pure red gold, a bowl of fair silver and one of fine seed pearls.

"These I will not take," Ilyá made answer, "though I

have earned them: neither will I dwell with you either as Tsar or peasant. Live ye as of old, my brothers, and show me the straight road to Kíev town."

Then they told him: " By the straight road it is five hundred versts, and by the way about, a thousand. Yet take not the straight road, for therein lie three great barriers: the grey wolf trotteth not that way, the black raven flieth not overhead. The first barrier is a lofty mountain; the second is the Smoródina River, six versts in width, and the Black Morass; and beside that river, the third barrier is Nightingale the Robber.

" He hath built his nest on seven oaks, that magic bird. When he whistleth like a nightingale, the dark forest boweth to the earth, the green leaves wither, horse and rider fall as dead. For that cause the road is lost, and no man hath travelled it for thirty years."

When Ilyá, the Old Cossack, heard that, he mounted his good steed, and rode forthwith that way. When he came to the lofty mountain, his good steed rose from the damp earth, and soared as a bright falcon over them and the tall, dreaming forest. When he came to the Black Morass, he plucked the great oaks with one hand, and flung them across the shaking bog for thirty versts, while he led good Cloudfall with the other. When he came to Mother Smoródina, he beat his steed's fat sides, so that the horse cleared the river at a bound.

There sat Nightingale the Robber (surnamed the Magic Bird), and thrust his turbulent head out from his nest upon the seven oaks; sparks and flame poured from his mouth and nostrils. Then he began to pipe like a nightingale, to roar like an aurochs, and to hiss like a dragon. Thereat good Cloudfall, that heroic steed, fell upon his knees, and Ilyá began to beat him upon his flanks and between his ears.

" Thou wolf's food!" cried Ilyá, " thou grass bag! Hast never been in the gloomy forest, nor heard the song of the nightingale, the roar of wild beast, nor serpent's hiss ? "

Then Ilyá brake a twig from a willow that grew nearby, that he might keep his vow not to stain his weapons with blood, fitted it to his stout bow, and conjured it: " Fly, little dart! Enter the Nightingale's left eye; come out at his right ear!"

The good heroic steed rose to his feet, and the Robber Nightingale fell to the damp earth like a rick of grain.

Then the Old Cossack raised up that mighty Robber, bound him to his stirrup by his yellow curls, and went his way. Ere long they came to the Nightingale's house, built upon seven pillars over seven versts of ground. About the courtyard there was an iron paling, upon each stake thereof a spike, and on each spike the head of a hero. In the centre was the strangers' court, and there stood three towers with golden crests, spire joined to spire, beam merged in beam, roof wedded to roof. Green gardens were planted round about, all blossoming and blooming with azure flowers, and the fair orchards encircled all.

When the Magic Bird's children looked from the latticed casements and beheld the hero riding with one at his stirrup, they cried: "Ay, lady mother! Our father cometh, and leadeth a man at his stirrup for us to eat."

But Eléna, the One-Eyed, Nightingale's witch daughter, looked forth and said: " Nay, it is the Old Cossack, Ilyá of Múrom, who rideth and leadeth our father in bond."

Then spoke Nightingale's nine sons: " We will transform ourselves into ravens, and rend that peasant with our iron beaks, and scatter his white body over the plains." But their father shouted to them that they should not harm the hero.

Nevertheless Eléna the witch ran into the wide court-yard, tore a steel beam of a hundred and fifty puds' weight from the threshold, and hurled it at Ilyá. The good youth wavered in his saddle, yet, being nimble, he escaped the full force of the blow. Then he leaped from his horse, took the witch on his foot: higher flew the witch then than God's temple, higher than the life-giving cross thereon, and fell against the rear wall of the court, where her skin burst.

" Foolish are ye, my children!" cried the Nightingale. " Fetch from the vaults a cartload of fair gold, another of pure silver, and a third of fine seed pearls, and give to the Old Cossack, Ilyá of Múrom, that he may set me free."

Quoth Ilyá: "If I should plant my sharp spear in the earth, and thou shouldst heap treasures about it until it was covered, yet would I not release thee, Nightingale, lest thou shouldst resume thy thieving. But follow me now to glorious Kíev town, that thou mayest receive forgiveness there."

Then his good steed Cloudfall began to prance, and the Magic Bird at his stirrup to dance, and in this wise came the good youth, the Old Cossack to Kíev, to glorious Prince Vladímir.

Now, fair Prince Vladímir of royal Kíev was not at home; he had gone to God's temple. Therefore Ilyá entered the court without leave or announcement, bound his horse to the golden ring in the carven pillars, and laid his commands upon that good heroic steed: "Guard thou the Nightingale, my charger, that he depart not from stirrup of steel!"

And to Nightingale he said: "Look to it, Nightingale, that thou depart not from my good steed, for there is no place in all the white world where thou mayest securely hide thyself from me!"

Then he betook himself to Easter mass. There he crossed himself and did reverence, as prescribed, on all four sides, and to the Fair Sun, Prince Vladímir, in particular. And after the mass was over, Prince Vladímir sent to bid the strange hero to the feast, and there inquired of him from what horde and land he came, and what was his parentage. So Ilyá told him that he was the only son of honourable parents. "I stood at my home in Múrom, at matins," quoth he, "and mass was but just ended when I came hither by the straight way."

When the heroes that sat at the Prince's table heard that, they looked askance at him.

"Nay, good youth, liest thou not? boastest thou not?" said Fair Sun Vladímir. "That way hath been lost these thirty years, for there stand great barriers therein; accursed Tartars in the fields, black morasses; and beside the famed Smoródina, amid the bending birches, is the nest of the

Nightingale on seven oaks; and that Magic Bird hath nine sons and eight daughters, and one is a witch. He hath permitted neither horse nor man to pass him these many years.''

'' Nay, thou Fair Sun Prince Vladímir,'' Ilyá answered: '' I did come the straight way, and the Nightingale Robber now sitteth bound within thy court.''

Then all left the tables of white oak, and each outran the other to view the Nightingale, as he sat bound to the steel stirrup, with one eye fixed on Kíev town and the other on Chernígov from force of habit. And Princess Apráksiya came forth upon the railed balcony to look.

Prince Vladímir spoke: '' Whistle, thou Nightingale, roar like an aurochs, hiss like a dragon.''

But the Nightingale replied: '' Not thy captive am I, Vladímir. 'T is not thy bread I eat. But give me wine.''

'' Give him a cup of green wine,'' spake Ilyá, '' a cup of a bucket and a half, in weight a pud and a half, and a cake of fine wheat flour, for his mouth is now filled with blood from my dart.''

Vladímir fetched a cup of green wine, and one of the liquor of drunkenness, and yet a third of sweet mead; and the Nightingale drained each at a draught. Then the Old Cossack commanded the Magic Bird to whistle, roar and hiss, but under his breath, lest harm might come to any.

But the Nightingale, out of malice, did all with his full strength. And at that cry, all the ancient palaces in Kíev fell in ruins, the new castles rocked, the roofs through all the city fell to the ground, damp mother earth quivered, the heroic steed fled from the court, the young damsels hid themselves, the good youths dispersed through the streets, and as many as remained to listen died. Ilyá caught up Prince Vladímir under one arm, and his Princess under the other, to shield them; yet was Vladímir as though dead for the space of three hours.

'' For this deed of thine thou shalt die,'' spake Ilyá in his wrath, and Vladímir prayed that at least a remnant of his people might be spared.

The Nightingale began to entreat forgiveness, and that he might be allowed to build a great monastery with his ill-gotten gold. "Nay," said Ilyá, "this kind buildeth never, but destroyeth alway."

With that he took Nightingale the Robber by his white hands, led him far out upon the open plain, fitted a burning arrow to his stout bow and shot it into the black breast of that Magic Bird. Then he struck off his turbulent head, and scattered his bones to the winds, and, mounting his good Cloudfall, came again to good Vladímir.

Again they sat at the oaken board, eating savoury viands and white swans, and quaffing sweet mead. Great gifts and much worship did Ilyá receive, and Vladímir gave command that he should be called evermore Ilyá of Múrom, the Old Cossack, after his native town.— From I. F. Hapgood's *The Epic Songs of Russia.*

Historical Songs.

The historical songs are composed in the same manner as the epic songs, of which they are an organic continuation. The oldest historical songs treat of the Tartar invasion. A large number are centred about Iván the Terrible, and those that describe Yermák's exploits and conquests in Siberia are probably the most interesting of that period. Some of those referring to the time of the Borís Godunóv have been given on pp. 130-4, having been collected by Richard James, the English divine. There are also songs dealing with Sténka Rázin, the robber, who was executed in 1671, and Peter the Great, of which that on the taking of Ázov in 1696 is given below.

There are few collections of these songs in English : W. R. Morfill's *Slavonic Literature* and Talvi's *Historical View* are the only ones that give extracts of any consequence. Accounts of these songs may be found in most of the Histories of Russian Literature mentioned in the Preface.

YERMÁK

On the glorious steppes of Sarátov,
Below the city of Sarátov,
And above the city of Kamýshin,
The Cossacks, the free people, assembled;
They collected, the brothers, in a ring;

The Cossacks of the Don, the Grebén, and the Yaík,
Their Hetman was Yermák, the son of Timoféy;
Their captain was Asbáshka, the son of Lavrénti.
They planned a little plan.
" The summer, the warm summer is going,
And the cold winter approaches, my brothers.
Where, brothers, shall we spend the winter?
If we go to the Yaík, it is a terrible passage;
If we go to the Vólga, we shall be considered robbers;
If we go to the city of Kazán, there is the Tsar—
The Tsar Iván Vasílevich, the Terrible.
There he has great forces."
" There, Yermák, thou wilt be hanged,
And we Cossacks shall be captured
And shut up in strong prisons."
Yermák, the son of Timoféy, takes up his speech:—
" Pay attention, brothers, pay attention,
And listen to me—Yermák!
Let us spend the winter in Astrakhán;
And when the fair Spring reveals herself,
Then, brothers, let us go on a foray;
Let us earn our wine before the terrible Tsar!"

  .   .   .   .

" Ha, brothers, my brave Hetmans!
Make for yourselves boats,
Make the rowlocks of fir,
Make the oars of pine!
By the help of God we will go, brothers;
Let us pass the steep mountains,
Let us reach the infidel kingdom,
Let us conquer the Siberian kingdom,—
That will please our Tsar, our master.
I will myself go to the White Tsar,
I shall put on a sable cloak,
I shall make my submission to the White Tsar."
" Oh! thou art our hope, orthodox Tsar;
Do not order me to be executed, but bid me say my say,
Since I am Yermák, the son of Timoféy!

I am the robber Hetman of the Don;
'T was I went over the blue sea,
Over the blue sea, the Caspian;
And I it was who destroyed the ships;
And now, our hope, our orthodox Tsar,
I bring you my traitorous head,
And with it I bring the empire of Siberia."
And the orthodox Tsar spoke;
He spoke—the terrible Iván Vasílevich:
" Ha! thou art Yermák, the son of Timoféy,
Thou art the Hetman of the warriors of the Don.
I pardon you and your band,
I pardon you for your trusty service,
And I give you the glorious gentle Don as an inheritance."
                    —From W. R. Morfill's *Slavonic Literature*.

THE BOYÁR'S EXECUTION

" Thou, my head, alas! my head,
Long hast served me, and well, my head;
Full three-and-thirty summers long;
Ever astride of my gallant steed,
Never my foot from its stirrup drawn.
But alas! thou hast gained, my head,
Nothing of joy or other good;
Nothing of honours or even thanks."

Yonder along the Butcher's street,
Out to the field through the Butcher's gate,
They are leading a prince and peer.
Priests and deacons are walking before,
In their hands a great book open;
Then there follows a soldier troop,
With their drawn sabres flashing bright.
At his right the headsman goes,
Holds in his hand the keen-edged sword;
At his left goes his sister dear,
And she weeps as the torrent pours,
And she sobs as the fountains gush.

Comforting speaks her brother to her:
" Weep not, weep not, my sister dear!
Weep not away thy eyes so clear,
Dim not, O dim not thy face so fair,
Make not heavy thy joyous heart!
Say, for what is it thou weepest so?
Is 't for my goods, my inheritance?
Is 't for my lands, so rich and wide?
Is 't for my silver, or is 't for my gold,
Or dost thou weep for my life alone?"

" Ah, thou, my light, my brother dear!
Not for thy goods or inheritance,
Not for thy lands, so rich and wide,
Is 't that my eyes are weeping so;
Not for thy silver and not for thy gold,
'T is for thy life I am weeping so."

"Ah, thou, my light, my sister sweet!
Thou mayest weep, but it won't avail;
Thou mayest beg, but 't is all in vain;
Pray to the Tsar, but he will not yield.
Merciful truly was God to me,
Truly gracious to me the Tsar,
So he commanded my traitor head
Off should be hewn from my shoulders strong."

Now the scaffold the prince ascends,
Calmly mounts to the place of death;
Prays to his Great Redeemer there,
Humbly salutes the crowd around:
" Farewell, world, and thou people of God!
Pray for my sins that burden me sore!"
Scarce had the people ventured then
On him to look, when his traitor head
Off was hewn from his shoulders strong.

—From Talvi's Historical View.

THE STORMING OF ÁZOV

The poor soldiers have no rest,
    Neither night nor day!
Late at evening the word was given
    To the soldiers gay;
All night long their weapons cleaning,
    Were the soldiers good;
Ready in the morning dawn,
    All in ranks they stood.

Not a golden trumpet is it,
    That now sounds so clear;
Nor the silver flute's tone is it,
    That thou now dost hear.
'T is the great White Tsar who speaketh,
    'T is our father dear.
" Come, my princes, my boyárs,
    Nobles, great and small!
Now consider and invent
    Good advice, ye all,
How the soonest, how the quickest,
    Fort Azov may fall!"

The boyárs, they stood in silence,—
    And our father dear,
He again began to speak,
    In his eye a tear:
"Come, my children, good dragoons,
    And my soldiers all,
Now consider and invent
    Brave advice, ye all,
How the soonest, how the quickest,
    Fort Azov may fall!"

Like a humming swarm of bees,
    So the soldiers spake,
With one voice at once they spake:
    " Father dear, great Tsar!

Fall it must! and all our lives
   Thereon we gladly stake."
Set already was the moon,
   Nearly past the night;
To the storming on they marched,
   With the morning light;
To the fort with bulwarked towers
   And walls so strong and white.

Not great rocks they were, which rolled
   From the mountains steep;
From the high, high walls there rolled
   Foes into the deep.
No white snow shines on the fields,
   All so white and bright;
But the corpses of our foes
   Shine so bright and white.
Not upswollen by heavy rains
   Left the sea its bed;
No! In rills and rivers streams
   Turkish blood so red!

          —From Talvi's *Historical View.*

Folksongs.

Pagan Russia was rich in ceremonies in honour of the various divinities representing the powers of nature. Christianity has not entirely obliterated the memory of these ancient rites: they are preserved in the ceremonial songs that are recited, now of course without a knowledge of their meaning, upon all church holidays, to which the old festivities have been adapted. Thus, the feast of the winter solstice now coincides with Christmas, while the old holiday of the summer solstice has been transferred to St. John's Day, on June 24th.

The *kolyádas* are sung at Christmas, and seem to have been originally in honour of the sun. The name appears to be related to the Latin " calenda," but it is generally supposed that this is only accidental, and that *Kolyáda* was one of the appellations of the sun. Young boys and girls march through the village or town and exact contributions of eatables by reciting the kolyádas. In other places they sing, instead, songs to a mythical being, Ovsén, on the eve of the New Year. This Ovsén is some other representation of the sun.

During the Christmas festivity fortunes are told over a bowl of water which is placed on the table, while in it are put rings, earrings, salt, bread, pieces of coal. During the fortune-telling they sing the *bowl-songs*, after each of which a ring, or the like, is removed. After the fortune-telling follow the games and the songs connected with these.

Spring songs are recited in the week after Easter. Soon after, and lasting until the end of June, the round dance, the *khorovód*, is danced upon some eminence, and the khorovód songs, referring to love and marriage, are sung. There are still other reminiscences of heathen festivals, of which the most important is that to Kupála, on the night from the 23rd to the 24th of June, when the peasants jump over fires and bathe in the river.

The *wedding-songs*, of which there is a large number in the long ceremony of the wedding (*cf.* Kotoshíkhin's account of the seventeenth century wedding, p. 143 *et seq.*), contain reminiscences of the ancient custom of the stealing of the bride, and, later, of the purchase of the bride. Most of the love songs that are not part of the khorovód are detached songs of the wedding ceremonial.

The *beggar-songs* are more properly apocryphal songs of book origin, handed down from great antiquity, but not preceding the introduction of Christianity. There are also *lamentations*, *charms*, and other similar incantations, in which both pagan and Christian ideas are mingled.

An account of the folksong will be found in Talvi's *Historical View of the Languages and Literatures of the Slavic Nations*, New York, 1850; W. R. S. Ralston's *The Songs of the Russian People*, London, 1872; *Russian Folk-Songs as Sung by the People, and Peasant Wedding Ceremonies*, translated by E. Lineff, with preface by H. E. Krehbiel, Chicago, 1893. Also in the following periodical articles: *The Popular Songs of Russia*, in Hogg's Instructor, 1855, and the same article, in Eclectic Magazine, vol. xxxvi; *Russian Songs and Folktales*, in Quarterly Review, 1874 (vol. cxxxvi). A number of popular songs have been translated by Sir John Bowring in his *Specimens of the Russian Poets*, both parts.

KOLYÁDKA

Beyond the river, the swift river,
    Oy Kolyádka!
There stand dense forests:
In those forests fires are burning,
    Great fires are burning.
Around the fires stand benches,
    Stand oaken benches,

On these benches the good youths,
The good youths, the fair maidens,
  Sing Kolyáda songs,
  Kolyáda, Kolyáda!
In their midst sits an old man;
He sharpens his steel knife.
A cauldron boils hotly.
Near the cauldron stands a goat.
They are going to kill the goat.
" Brother Ivánushko,
Come forth, spring out!"
" Gladly would I have sprung out,
But the bright stone
Drags me down to the cauldron:
The yellow sands
Have sucked dry my heart."
    Oy Kolyádka! Oy Kolyádka!
—From W. R. S. Ralston's *The Songs of the Russian People.*

BOWL-SONG

A grain adown the velvet strolled — Glory!
No purer pearl could be — Glory!
The pearl against a ruby rolled — Glory!
Most beautiful to see — Glory!
Big is the pearl by ruby's side — Glory!
Well for the bridegroom with his bride — Glory!
    —From John Pollen's *Rhymes from the Russian.*

A PARTING SCENE

" Sit not up, my love, late at evening hour,
Burn the light no more, light of virgin wax,
Wake no more for me till the midnight hour;
Ah, gone by, gone by is the happy time!
Ah, the wind has blown all our joys away,
And has scattered them o'er the empty field.
For my father dear, he will have it so,
And my mother dear has commanded it,

That I now must wed with another wife,
With another wife, with an unloved one!
But on heaven high two suns never burn,
Two moons never shine in the stilly night,
And an honest lad never loveth twice!
But my father shall be obeyed by me,
And my mother dear I will now obey;
To another wife I 'll be wedded soon,
To another wife, to an early death,
To an early death, to a forcèd one."

Wept the lovely maid many bitter tears,
Many bitter tears, and did speak these words:
" O belovèd one, never seen enough,
Longer will I not live in this white world,
Never without thee, thou my star of hope!
Never has the dove more than one fond mate,
And the female swan ne'er two husbands has,
Neither can I have two belovèd friends."

No more sits she now late at evening hour,
But the light still burns, light of virgin wax;
On the table stands the coffin newly made;
In the coffin new lies the lovely maid.

　　　　　　　—From Talvi's *Historical View*.

THE DOVE

On an oak-tree sat,
Sat a pair of doves;
And they billed and cooed
And they, heart to heart,
Tenderly embraced
With their little wings;
On them, suddenly,
Darted down a hawk.

One he seized and tore,
Tore the little dove,

With his feathered feet,
Soft blue little dove;
And he poured his blood
Streaming down the tree.
Feathers, too, were strewed
Widely o'er the field;
High away the down
Floated in the air.

Ah! how wept and wept,—
Ah! how sobbed and sobbed
The poor doveling then
For her little dove.

" Weep not, weep not so,
Tender little bird! "
Spake the light young hawk
To the little dove.

" O'er the sea away,
O'er the far blue sea,
I will drive to thee
Flocks of other doves.
From them choose thee then,
Choose a soft and blue,
With his feathered feet,
Better little dove."

" Fly, thou villain, not
O'er the far blue sea!
Drive not here to me
Flocks of other doves.
Ah! of all thy doves
None can comfort me;
Only he, the father
Of my little ones."

    —From Talvi's *Historical View*.

THE FAITHLESS LOVER

Nightingale, O nightingale,
Nightingale so full of song!
Tell me, tell me, where thou fliest,
Where to sing now in the night?
Will another maiden hear thee,
Like to me, poor me, all night
Sleepless, restless, comfortless,
Ever full of tears her eyes?
Fly, O fly, dear nightingale,
Over hundred countries fly,
Over the blue sea so far!
Spy the distant countries through,
Town and village, hill and dell,
Whether thou find'st anyone,
Who so sad is as I am?

Oh, I bore a necklace once,
All of pearls like morning dew;
And I bore a finger-ring,
With a precious stone thereon;
And I bore deep in my heart
Love, a love so warm and true.
When the sad, sad autumn came,
Were the pearls no longer clear;
And in winter burst my ring,
On my finger, of itself!
Ah! and when the spring came on,
Had forgotten me my love.

—From Talvi's *Historical View.*

ELEGY

O thou field! thou clean and level field!
O thou plain, so far and wide around!
Level field, dressed up with everything,
Everything; with sky-blue flowerets small,
Fresh green grass, and bushes thick with leaves;
But defaced by one thing, but by one!

For in thy very middle stands a broom,
On the broom a young grey eagle sits,
And he butchers wild a raven black,
Sucks the raven's heart-blood glowing hot,
Drenches with it, too, the moistened earth.
Ah, black raven, youth so good and brave!
Thy destroyer is the eagle grey.
Not a swallow 't is, that hovering clings,
Hovering clings to her warm little nest:
To the murdered son the mother clings.
And her tears fall like the rushing stream,
And his sister's like the flowing rill;
Like the dew her tears fall of his love:
When the sun shines, it dries up the dew.

—From Talvi's *Historical View*.

THE FAREWELL

Brightly shining sank the waning moon,
And the sun all beautiful arose;
Not a falcon floated through the air,
Strayed a youth along the river's brim.
Slowly strayed he on and dreamingly,
Sighing looked unto the garden green,
Heart all filled with sorrow mused he so:
"All the little birds are now awake,
All, embracing with their little wings,
Greeting, all have sung their morning songs.
But, alas! that sweetest doveling mine,
She who was my youth's first dawning love,
In her chamber slumbers fast and deep.
Ah, not even her friend is in her dreams,
Ah! no thought of me bedims her soul,
While my heart is torn with wildest grief,
That she comes to meet me here no more."

Stepped the maiden from her chamber then;
Wet, oh, wet with tears her lovely face!

All with sadness dimmed her eyes so clear,
Feebly drooping hung her snowy arms.
'T was no arrow that had pierced her heart,
'T was no adder that had stung her so;
Weeping, thus the lovely maid began:
" Fare thee well, belovèd, fare thee well,
Dearest soul, thy father's dearest son!
I have been betrothed since yesterday;
Come, to-morrow, troops of wedding guests;
To the altar I, perforce, must go!
I shall be another's then; and yet
Thine, thine only, thine alone till death."
                 —From Talvi's *Historical View.*

Sing, O sing again, lovely lark of mine,
Sitting there alone amidst the green of May!

In the prison-tower the lad sits mournfully;
To his father writes, to his mother writes:
Thus he wrote, and these, these were the very words:
" O good father mine, thou belovèd sir!
O good mother mine, thou belovèd dame!
Ransom me, I pray, ransom the good lad,—
He is your beloved, is your only son!"
Father, mother,—both,—both refused to hear,
Cursed their hapless race, cursed their hapless seed:
" Never did a thief our honest name disgrace,—
Highwayman or thief never stained the name!"

Sing, O sing again, lovely lark of mine,
Sitting there alone in the green of May!

From the prison-tower thus the prisoner wrote,
Thus the prisoner wrote to his belovèd maid:
" O thou soul of mine! O thou lovely maid!
Truest love of mine, sweetest love of mine!
Save, O save, I pray, save the prisoned lad!"
Swiftly then exclaimed that belovèd maid:
" Come, attendant! Come! Come, my faithful nurse!

Servant faithful, you that long have faithful been,
Bring the golden key, bring the key with speed!
Ope the treasure chests, open them in haste;
Golden treasures bring, bring them straight to me:
Ransom him, I say, ransom the good lad,
He is my beloved, of my heart beloved."

Sing, O sing again, lovely lark of mine,
Sitting there alone amidst the green of May!
> —From Sir John Bowring's *Specimens of the
> Russian Poets*, Part II.

WEDDING GEAR

The blacksmith from the forge comes he—Glory!
And carries with him hammers three—Glory!
O blacksmith, blacksmith, forge for me—Glory!
A wedding crown of gold, bran-new!—Glory!
A golden ring, oh, make me, do!—Glory!
With what is left a gold pin too!—Glory!
The crown on wedding day I 'll wear—Glory!
On golden ring my troth I 'll swear—Glory!
The pin will bind my veil to hair—Glory!
> —From John Pollen's *Rhymes from the Russian.*

THE SALE OF THE BRAID

It was not a horn that in the early morning sounded;
It was a maiden her ruddy braid lamenting:
" Last night they twined my braid together,
And interweaved my braid with pearls.
Luká Ivánovich—Heaven requite him!—
Has sent a pitiless svákha hither.
My braid has she begun to rend.
Tearing out the gold from my braid,
Shaking my pearls from my ruddy braids."
—From W. R. S. Ralston's *The Songs of the Russian People.*

MARRIAGE SONG

Her mother has counselled Máryushka,
Has given counsel to her dear Efímovna.
    " Go not, my child,
    Go not, my darling,
Into thy father's garden for apples,
    Nor catch the mottled butterflies,
    Nor frighten the little birds,
Nor interrupt the clear-voiced nightingale.
    For shouldst thou pluck the apples
    The tree will wither away;
    Or seize the mottled butterfly,
    The butterfly will die.
And shouldst thou frighten a little bird,
    That bird will fly away;
Or interrupt the clear-voiced nightingale,
    The nightingale will be mute:
    But catch, my child,
    My dear one, catch
The falcon bright in the open field,
    The green, the open field."

    Máryushka has caught,
    Caught has the dear Efímovna,
The falcon bright in the open field,
    The green, the open field.
    She has perched him on her hand,
    She has brought him to her mother.
    " Mother mine, Gosudárynya,
    I have caught the falcon bright."
—From W. R. S. Ralston's *The Songs of the Russian People*.

BEGGARS' SONG

" Whither art Thou fleeing?" they spoke in tears to
Christ. " For whom art Thou leaving us? Who will
without Thee give us to drink and eat, will clothe us and
protect us against dark night?"

"Weep not, poor people," replied Christ: "Weep not, mendicants and homeless and small orphans! I will leave you a golden mountain, will give you a honeyed river, will give you vineyards, will give you heavenly manna. Only know how to manage that golden mountain, and to divide it among yourselves: and you will be fed and given drink; you will be clothed and covered up in dark nights."

Then John the Theologue retorted: "Hail to Thee, real Christ, King of heaven! Permit me to tell Thee a few words, and take not ill my words! Give them not a golden mountain, nor a honeyed river and vineyards, give them not heavenly manna! They will not know how to manage that mountain; it will be beyond their strength, and they will not be able to divide up: they will not harvest the grapes, will not taste the manna. Princes and noblemen, pastors, officials and merchants will hear of that mountain, and they will take away from them the golden mountain and honeyed river, the vineyards and heavenly manna: they will divide up the golden mountain among themselves according to their ranks, but the poor people will not be admitted, and there will be much murder, and much spilling of blood. The poor will have nothing to live on, nothing to wear, and nothing to protect themselves with against dark night: the poor will die of starvation, will freeze to death in cold winter. Give them rather Thy holy name and Word of Christ; and the poor will go all over the earth, will glorify Thee, and the orthodox will give them alms; the poor will be fed and given drink, will be clothed and protected against cold night."

"Thank you, John the Theologue!" replied Christ the heavenly King. "You have said a sensible word, and have discussed well,—you have taken good care of the poor."

AN ORPHAN'S WAILING

O mother dear that bare me, O with sadness longed-for one! To whom hast thou left us, on whom are we orphans to rest our hopes? From no quarter do warm breezes breathe on us, we hear no words of kindness. Great folks turn away from us, our kinsfolk renounce us; rust eats into our orphaned hearts. The red sun burns in the midst of a hot summer, but us it keeps not: scarcely does it warm us, O green mother-grave! Have a care for us, mother dear, give us a word of kindness! No, thou hast hardened thy heart harder than stone, and hast folded thy uncaressing hand over thy heart.

O white cygnet! For what journey hast thou prepared and equipped thyself; from which side may we expect thee?

Arise, O ye wild winds, from all sides! Be borne, O winds, into the Church of God! Sweep open the moist earth! Strike, O wild winds, on the great bell! Will not its sounds and mine awaken words of kindness?—From Ralston's *The Songs of the Russian People.*

CONJURATION OF A MOTHER SEPARATED FROM HER CHILD

I, poor mother, weep in the high chamber of my house; from the dawn I look afar over the fields, even until the sun goes to rest. There I sit until night, till the damp dew falls; there I sit in grief, until, weary of this torment, I resolve to conjure my cruel sorrow. I go into the field; I have taken the nuptial cup, the taper of betrothal and the handkerchief of marriage. I have drawn water from the mountain spring, I have gone into the dark forest, and tracing around me a magic circle, I have said aloud these words:—

" I conjure my dearest child by that nuptial cup, by that fresh water and by that marriage handkerchief. With that water I lave his fair face, with that handkerchief I wipe his honeyed lips, his sparkling eyes, his rosy cheeks, his thoughtful brow; with that waxen taper I light up his splendid garments, his sable bonnet, his belt of divers colours, his embroidered boots, his chestnut locks, his noble figure and manly limbs, that thou mayest be, my child, more brilliant than the brightest sunbeams, sweeter to look upon than a sweet spring day, fresher than water from the fountain, whiter than the wax, stronger than the magic stone. Far be from thee the demon of sorrow, the impetuous hurricane, the one-eyed spirit of the woods, the domestic demon of strange houses, the spirit of the waters, the sorcery of Kíev, the woman of the twinkling billows, the cursed Baba-yagá, the winged and fiery serpent, the crow of evil omen. I put myself between thee and the ogre, the false magician, the sorcerer, the evil magic, the seeing blind and the old of double sight. By my words of power, may thou be, my child, by night and by day, from hour to moment, in the market-place, and asleep or in watching, safe against the power of the evil spirits, against death, grief and calamity; upon the water, against shipwreck; in fire, against burning.

"When thy last hour shall come, recall, my child, our tender love, our bread and salt. Turn thyself towards thy glorious country, salute it seven times—seven times with thy face to the earth, bid farewell to thy family, throw thyself upon the damp ground and lull thyself to a calm sleep.

"May my word be stronger than water, higher than the mountain, weightier than gold, harder than rock, stronger than an armed horseman, and if any dare to bewitch my child, may he be swallowed by Mount Ararat, in bottomless precipices, in burning tar and crackling fire; that sorceries and magic may for ever be powerless against thee."—From *The Popular Songs of Russia*, in Hogg's Instructor, 1855.

Fairy Tales.

For an account of the fairy tales see the chapter on Folklore. The following works, of which Ralston's is still the best, give a large number of such stories: *Russian Popular Tales*, from the German version of Anton Dietrich, London, 1857 ; W. R. S. Ralston, *Russian Folk-Tales*, London, 1873 ; J. T. Naake, *Slavonic Fairy Tales*, London, 1874 ; E. M. S. Hodgetts, *Tales and Legends from the Land of the Tzar*, London, 1890; Jeremiah Curtin, *Myths and Folk Tales of the Russians, Western Slavs and Magyars*, Boston, 1890; A. Gerber, *Great Russian Animal Tales* (vol. vi, No. 2 of the Publications of the Modern Language Association), Baltimore, 1891 ; R. Nisbet Bain, *Russian Fairy Tales from the Skazki of Polevoi*, Chicago, 1895. There are also some articles in periodicals: *Household Tales of the Sclavonians and Hungarians*, and *The Household Fictions of Esthonia and Russia*, in Dublin University Magazine, 1867 (vol. lxx); *Russian Popular Legends* (by Ralston), in Fortnightly Review, 1869 ; *Russian Songs and Folktales*, in Quarterly Review, 1874 (vol. cxxxvi).

FROST

There was once an old man who had a wife and three daughters. The wife had no love for the eldest of the three, who was a step-daughter, but was always scolding her. Moreover, she used to make her get up ever so early in the morning, and gave her all the work of the house to do. Before daybreak the girl would feed the cattle and give them to drink, fetch wood and water indoors, light the fire in the stove, give the room a wash, mend the dress and set everything in order. Even then her step-mother was never satisfied, but grumbled away at Márfa, exclaiming:

"What a lazybones! What a slut! Why, here is a brush not in its place, and there is something put wrong, and she has left the muck inside the house!"

The girl held her peace, and wept; she tried in every way to accommodate herself to her step-mother, and to be of service to her step-sisters. But they, taking pattern by their mother, were always insulting Márfa, quarrelling with her, and making her cry: that was even a pleasure to them! As for them, they lay in bed late, washed themselves in water got ready for them, dried themselves with a clean towel and did not sit down to work till after dinner.

Well, our girls grew and grew, until they grew up and were old enough to be married. The old man felt sorry for his eldest daughter, whom he loved because she was industrious and obedient, never was obstinate, always did as she was bid and never uttered a word of contradiction. But he did not know how to help her in her trouble. He was feeble, his wife was a scold and his daughters were as obstinate as they were indolent.

Well, the old folks set to work to consider—the husband how he could get his daughter settled, the wife how she could get rid of the eldest one. One day she says to him:

"I say, old man! Let 's get Márfa married."

"Gladly," says he, slinking off (to the sleeping-place) above the stove. But his wife called after him:

"Get up early to-morrow, old man, harness the mare to

the sledge and drive away with Márfa. And, Márfa, get your things together in a basket, and put on a clean shift; you are going away to-morrow on a visit."

Poor Márfa was delighted to hear of such a piece of good luck as being invited on a visit, and she slept comfortably all night. Early next morning she got up, washed herself, prayed to God, got all her things together, packed them away in proper order, dressed herself (in her best things) and looked something like a lass! a bride fit for any place whatsoever!

Now it was winter-time, and out of doors there was a rattling frost. Early in the morning, between daybreak and sunrise, the old man harnessed the mare to the sledge, and led it up to the steps, then he went indoors, sat down in the window-sill, and said:

"Now then! I have got everything ready."

"Sit down to table and swallow your victuals!" replied the old woman.

The old man sat down to table, and made his daughter sit by his side. On the table stood a pannier; he took out a loaf, and cut bread for himself and his daughter. Meantime his wife served up a dish of old cabbage soup and said:

"There, my pigeon, eat and be off; I have looked at you quite enough! Drive Márfa to her bridegroom, old man. And look here, old greybeard! drive straight along the road at first, and then turn off from the road to the right, you know, into the forest—right up to the big pine that stands on the hill, and there hand Márfa to Morózko (Frost)."

The old man opened his eyes wide, also his mouth, and stopped eating, and the girl began lamenting.

"Now then, what are you hanging your chaps and squealing about?" said her step-mother. "Surely your bridegroom is a beauty, and he is that rich! Why, just see what a lot of things belong to him: the firs, the pine-tops and the birches, all in their robes of down—ways and means anyone might envy; and he himself a bogatýr!"

The old man silently placed the things on the sledge, made his daughter put on her warm pelisse and set off on the journey. After a time, he reached the forest, turned off the road and drove across the frozen snow. When he got into the depths of the forest, he stopped, made his daughter get out, laid her basket under the tall pine and said:

"Sit here, and await the bridegroom. And mind you receive him as pleasantly as you can!"

Then he turned his horse round and drove off homewards.

The girl sat and shivered. The cold pierced her through. She would fain have cried aloud, but she had not strength enough; only her teeth chattered. Suddenly she heard a sound. Not far off, Frost was cracking away on a fir. From fir to fir was he leaping and snapping his fingers. Presently he appeared on that very pine under which the maiden was sitting, and from above her head he cried:

"Art thou warm, maiden?"

"Warm, warm am I, dear father Frost," she replied.

Frost began to descend lower, all the more cracking and snapping his fingers. To the maiden said Frost:

"Art thou warm, maiden? Art thou warm, fair one?"

The girl could scarcely draw her breath, but still she replied:

"Warm am I, Frost dear; warm am I, father dear!"

Frost began cracking more than ever, and more loudly did he snap his fingers, and to the maiden he said:

"Art thou warm, maiden? Art thou warm, pretty one? Art thou warm, my darling?"

The girl was by this time numbed with cold, and she could scarcely make herself heard as she replied:

"Oh! Quite warm, Frost dearest!"

Then Frost took pity on the girl, wrapped her up in furs and warmed her with blankets.

Next morning the old woman said to her husband:

"Drive out, old greybeard, and wake the young people!"

The old man harnessed his horse and drove off. When he came to where his daughter was, he found she was alive and had got a good pelisse, a costly bridal veil and a pannier with rich gifts. He stowed everything away on the sledge without saying a word, took a seat on it with his daughter, and drove back. They reached home, and the daughter fell at her step-mother's feet. The old woman was thunderstruck when she saw the girl alive, and the new pelisse and the basket of linen.

"Ah, you wretch!" she cries.' 'But you sha'n't trick me!"

Well, a little later the old woman says to her husband:

"Take my daughters, too, to their bridegroom. The presents he's made are nothing to what he'll give them."

Well, early next morning the old woman gave her girls their breakfast, dressed them as befitted brides and sent them off on their journey. In the same way as before the old man left the girls under the pine.

There the girls sat, and kept laughing and saying:

" Whatever is mother thinking of? All of a sudden to marry both of us off! As if there were no lads in our village, forsooth! Some rubbishy fellow may come, and goodness knows who he may be!"

The girls were wrapped up in pelisses, but for all that they felt the cold.

"I say, Praskóvya! The Frost's skinning me alive. Well, if our bridegroom does n't come quick, we shall be frozen to death here!"

" Don't go talking nonsense, Máshka; as if suitors turned up in the forenoon! Why, it's hardly dinner-time yet!"

" But I say, Praskóvya! If only one comes, which of us will he take?"

" Not you, you stupid goose!"

" Then it will be you, I suppose!"

" Of course, it will be me!"

" You, indeed! There now, have done talking stuff and treating people like fools!"

Meanwhile, Frost had numbed the girls' hands, so our damsels folded them under their dresses, and then went on quarrelling as before.

" What, you fright! You sleepy face! You abominable shrew! Why, you don't know so much as how to begin weaving; and as to going on with it, you have n't an idea!"

"Aha, boaster! And what is it you know? Why, nothing

at all except to go out merrymaking and lick your lips there. We 'll soon see which he 'll take first!'"

While the girls went on scolding like that, they began to freeze in downright earnest. Suddenly they both cried out at once:

"Whyever is he so long coming? You know, you have turned quite blue!"

Now, a good way off, Frost had begun cracking, snapping his fingers and leaping from fir to fir. To the girls it sounded as if someone were coming.

"Listen, Praskóvya! He 's coming at last, with bells, too!"

"Get along with you! I won't listen; my skin is pealing with cold."

"And yet you 're still expecting to get married!"

Then they began blowing their fingers.

Nearer and nearer came Frost. At length he appeared on the pine, above the heads of the girls, and said to them:

"Are ye warm, maidens? Are ye warm, pretty ones? Are ye warm, my darlings?".

"Oh, Frost, it 's awfully cold! We are utterly perished! We 're expecting a bridegroom, but the confounded fellow has disappeared."

Frost slid lower down the tree, cracked away more, snapped his fingers oftener than before.

"Are ye warm, maidens? Are ye warm, pretty ones?"

"Get along with you! Are you blind, that you can't see our hands and feet are quite dead?"

Still lower descended Frost, still more put forth his might and said:

"Are ye warm, maidens?"

"Into the bottomless pit with you! Out of my sight, accursed one!" cried the girls—and became lifeless forms.

Next morning the old woman said to her husband:

"Old man, go and get the sledge harnessed; put an armful of hay in it, and take some sheepskin wraps. I dare say the girls are half dead with cold. There is a terrible frost outside! And, mind you, old greybeard, do it quickly!"

Before the old man could manage to get a bite, he was out of doors and on his way. When he came to where his daughters were, he found them dead. So he lifted the girls on the sledge, wrapped a blanket round them and covered them up with a bark mat. The old woman saw him from afar, ran out to meet him and called out ever so loud:

" Where are my girls ? "

" In the sledge."

The old woman lifted the mat, undid the blanket and found the girls both dead.

Then, like a thunder-storm, she broke out against her husband, abusing him and saying:

" What have you done, you old wretch ? You have destroyed my daughters, the children of my own flesh, my never-to-be-gazed-on seedlings, my beautiful berries! I will thrash you with the tongs; I will give it you with the stove-rake."

" That 's enough, you old goose! You flattered yourself you were going to get riches, but your daughters were too stiff-necked. How was I to blame? It was you yourself would have it."

The old woman was in a rage at first, and used bad language; but afterwards she made it up with her step-daughter, and they all lived together peaceably, and thrived, and bore no malice. A neighbour made an offer of marriage, the wedding was celebrated and Márfa is now living happily. The old man frightens his grandchildren with (stories about) Frost, and does not let them have their own way.—From W. R. S Ralston's *Russian Folk-Tales*.

THE CAT, THE GOAT AND THE RAM

Once upon a time there lived in a yard a Goat and a Ram, and they lived in great friendship with each other: say there was but a bunch of hay—even that they divided in two equal halves. If there was anyone to be punched in his sides, it was only Tom-Cat Váska; he was such a thief and robber,—always on the lookout for prey, and let there be anything not under lock, his stomach immediately growled for it.

The Goat and the Ram were once lying quietly and having a friendly chat, when who should turn up but grey-browed, Purring Váska, and he was whining pitifully. So the Goat and Ram asked him:

" Kitty-Cat, grey-browed Cat, why are you whining so, and why do you hop about on three legs ? "

" How can I help crying ? The old woman has beaten me; she struck me hard, almost pulled my ears out, nearly broke my legs, and came very near choking my life out of me."

" What have you been guilty of, to deserve such a fate ? "

"All the trouble was, I was hungry, and lapped up the cream." And the Purring Cat once more began to whine.

" Kitty-Cat, grey-browed Cat! What are you whining about ? "

" How can I help crying ? As the old woman was beating me, she kept on saying: ' Where shall I get the cream when my son-in-law will come to-morrow ? I 'll have to butcher the Goat and the Ram!'"

The Goat and the Ram howled loud: " O you grey Cat, senseless head! Why have you ruined us ? We 'll butt you to death!"

Then Purring Váska humbly confessed his guilt and begged forgiveness. They forgave him, and the three held a council of how matters stood and what was to be done.

" Well, middle brother Ram," asked Purring Cat, " have you a tough head ? Just try it against the gate!"

The Ram took a run and hit the gate with his head: the gate shook, but did not open. Then rose the elder brother Billy-Goat, took a run, hit the gate and it flew open.

The dust rose in a cloud, the grass bent to the ground, while the Goat and Ram were running, and the grey-browed Cat was hopping after them on three legs. He grew tired, and he begged his plighted brothers: " Elder brother and middle brother! Don't abandon your younger brother a prey to the wild beasts!"

So the Goat stopped and took him on his back, and again they raced over hills, and vales, and drifting sands. And they came to a steep hill and a standstill. Under that steep hill was a mowed meadow, and on that meadow there was a whole town of haystacks. The Goat, and Ram, and Cat stopped to take a rest; it was a cold autumn night. Where were they to get some fire? The Goat and the Ram were still thinking about it, when the Purring Cat got some twigs with which he tied the Goat's horns, and he told the Goat and the Ram to strike each other's heads. They hit each other with such a might that sparks flew from their eyes: the twigs crackled.

"That 'll do," said the grey Cat. "Now we will warm ourselves." No sooner said than he put a haystack on fire.

They had not yet gotten warm, when lo! there was an un-called guest, a Peasant-in-gabardine, Mikháylo Ivánovich. "Let me," he said, "warm myself and take a rest; I don't feel well."

"You are welcome, Peasant-in-gabardine, Ant-eater! Good fellow, where do you come from?"

"I went to the beehives and had a fight with the peasants; so I am sick now, and I am on my way to the Fox to get cured."

They passed the dark night together: the Bear under a haystack, Purring Váska on the haystack, and the Goat and the Ram by the fire.

"Ugh, ugh!" said the White Wolf, "it is not Russian flesh I smell. What manner of people may they be? I must find out!"

The Goat and the Ram bleated with fright, and Purring Váska held such discourse: "Listen, White Wolf, Prince of all the wolves! Don't anger our eldest one, for if he should get at you, it will be your end. Don't you see his beard? that 's where his strength lies. With his beard he strikes down the animals, but with his horns he only flays them. You had better ask him with due respect to let you have your fun with your younger brother that is lying under the haystack."

So the wolves bowed to the Goat, and surrounded Míshka, and began to tease him. He got up, waxed angry and just grabbed a wolf with each paw; they howled their "Lazarus," but somehow managed to get away with drooping tails, and they raced as fast as their feet would carry them.

In the meanwhile the Goat and the Ram seized the Cat, and ran into the woods, where they once more met some grey wolves. The Cat crawled up to the top of a pine-tree, and the Goat and the Ram got hold of a branch of the pine-tree with their fore legs, and hung down from it. The wolves stood under the tree, grinned and howled, watching the Goat and the Ram. The grey-browed Cat saw that things were very bad, so he began to throw down pine cones upon the wolves, and kept saying: "One wolf! Two wolves! Three wolves! Just a wolf apiece. It is not so long ago I, Purring Váska, ate up two wolves with all their bones, so I am not hungry yet; but you, big brother, have been out a-hunting bears, and you did not get any, so you may have my share!"

Just as he said that, the Goat could not hold on any longer, and dropped with his horns straight down on a wolf. But Purring Váska yelled out: "Hold him, catch him!" The wolves were so frightened that they started on a run, and did not dare look back. That was the last of them.

THE FOX AND THE PEASANT

Once upon an evening the Fox, feeling grieved, took a walk to divert herself and breathe the fresh air. Though she had not expected it, there presented itself an opportunity to have her revenge, for whom should she see but Vúkol in his cart! As she scented some fish, she decided to steal them. The question now was how to steal them out of Vúkol's cart. Of course, it was too risky to crawl in, for Vúkol would lay on his whip, or, catching her by her tail, would kill her altogether. So Lísa Patrikyéevna softly ran all around the Peasant, who was hastening home, lay down on the ground and barely breathed. The rogue lay there as if she really were dead: her mouth open, her teeth grinning, her snout turned upwards, her nose flabby; she neither moved, nor heaved, nor wagged her tail.

Vúkol was travelling at a slow pace, when suddenly his nag neighed. "What's the matter?" spoke Vúkol, rose and looked down the road. "Oh, I see! God has sent me a nice gift. I 'll pick it up; it will be a fine thing for my wife, for its fur is as soft as a shawl." Having very wisely discussed thus, Vúkol took the Fox by the tail and put her on the fish, and went over the bridge. But Lísa Patrikyéevna was very happy and, to carry out the first part of her program, quietly devoured a good-sized tench; then she started dropping one fish after another on the road, until she had emptied the whole cart. Then she stealthily dropped down from the cart herself and started on a run without turning back, so that the dust flew up.

It grew dark, and murky night was near; Vúkol Sílych pulled his reins, and the horse raced faster. He reached his house, without discovering the theft, and, smiling to his wife, he said with a merry voice to her: "Woman, just look into the cart and see what I have brought you! I found it in the road, near the bridge, by the pines and birches."

His wife Dárya rummaged in the hay, tossed it to and fro, hoping to find her present. "Where is it? What a shame!" She turned everything upside down, shook the fish bag, but she only got her hands dirty,—the present she did not find. Put 'out about such a deception, she said to her husband, Vúkol: "What a stupid you are!"

In the meantime Patrikyéevna carried all the fish to her lair, and she had an easy time of it all autumn, and even winter. But this revenge is insignificant: her greater revenge is still ahead. Things are bad for you, Vúkol Sílych! Be prepared for the worst.

Proverbs.

The first collection of Russian proverbs was made by the poet Bogdanóvich, at Catherine's command. The most extensive collection of the present time is the one by Dal. In the English language there are but two small accounts of these proverbs: one, in R.

Pinkerton's *Russia ; or, Miscellaneous Observations on the Past and Present of the Country and its Inhabitants*, London, 1833, and *Russian Proverbs*, in Quarterly Review, vol. cxxxix.

The heart has ears.

Home is a full cup.

A maiden's heart is a dark forest.

Calumny is like a coal: if it does not burn it will soil.

Good luck disappears like our curls; bad luck lasts like our nails.

Sorrow kills not, but it blights.

The pine stands afar, but whispers to its own forest.

Blame not my bast shoes, my boots are in the sledge.

The poor man has a sheepskin coat, but a human soul too.

Behind the orphan God Himself bears a purse.

Poverty is not a sin, but twice as bad.

Seven nurses cost the child an eye.

May God make me fleshy: rosiness I can get for myself.

A dog is wiser than a woman: it does not bark at its master.

Seven axes will lie together, but two spindles asunder.

Let a woman into Paradise, she 'll be for bringing her cow with her.

The Holy Russian land is large, but everywhere the dear sun shines.

Our stove is our own mother.

Not corners but pies make a room fair.

Even bad kvas is better than water.

By that which wounded may your wound be cured.

Black may be toil, but white is its price.

God waits long, but hits hard.

Terrible are dreams, but God is merciful.

God is high, and the Tsar far off.

Pray to God, but row to shore.

The wolf catches the destined sheep.

Be born neither wise nor fair, but lucky.

Moustaches for honour, but even a goat has a beard.

An old crow croaks not for nothing.

Love your wife like your soul, and beat her like your fur coat.

Not long hurt the bumps from a loved one's thumps.

A wife is not a guitar; when your playing is done, you can't hang her up on the wall.

It 's a bore to go alone, even to get drowned.

A parent's blessing can neither be drowned in water nor consumed in fire.

A visible girl is of copper, but an invisible one of silver.

Hold out, Cossack; thou wilt become Hetman.

He who sweats afield, and prays to God at home, will never starve.

Boldness drinks mead and chafes fetters.

A bad peace is better than a good quarrel.

If the thunder rolls not, the muzhík will not cross himself.

Don't beat the muzhík with a cudgel, but beat him with a rouble.

To rotten wares the seller is blind.

A snipe is small, but, for all that, a bird.

Fear not the threats of the rich but the tears of the poor.

Drink at table, not behind a pillar.

Who can withstand God and Nóvgorod the Great ?

Where there is an oath, there is also a crime.

God's will and the Tsar's decree.

The Tsar's wrath is the messenger of death.

God loves the just, but judges love the pettifogger.

I bailed him out: he taught me a lesson.

The knout is not the devil, but it will seek out the truth.

Wide is the gateway leading into a boyár's court, but narrow—out of it.

Slavery drinks mead, and freedom water.

—From Quarterly Review, vol. cxxxix.

THE EIGHTEENTH CENTURY

THE EIGHTEENTH CENTURY

Iván Tikhónovich Pososhkóv. (1670–1726.)

An interesting figure that belongs both to the old and the new régime is Pososhkóv. He was the son of a peasant and had received no other education than what he could pick up from the reading of church books. He also acquired a knowledge of arithmetic, a rare science for the men of the older generation, and of grammar, and much practical experience in his wanderings through Russia. Being a good business man and a close observer of current events, he became very rich, owned several factories, and carried on commerce on a large scale. He had brought from his peasant home the religious piety of the old order of things, but at the same time was shrewd enough to see the advantages of reform, which he favoured to the best of his ability. His son was among the first Russians who were sent abroad to be instructed. He provided him with ample means and a written *Father's Testament to his Son, with a Moral, in Confirmation of Holy Writ.* This *Testament* belongs in the same category as the *Domostróy* (see p. 126), but the spirit of reform has softened many of the ancient crudities. Of his other works the most interesting is his *The Book on Poverty and Wealth, That is, An Exposition of what Causes Dire Poverty and Abundantly Increases Wealth*, which is characteristic of the transitional stage of Russia. In this work, Pososhkóv combines shrewd guesses on economic problems with crude conceptions of their solution.

"THE BOOK ON POVERTY AND WEALTH"

FROM THE CHAPTER "ON MERCHANTS"

THE merchant guild must not be disregarded, for without merchants no country, neither large nor small, can exist. The merchant is the companion of the military: the soldier fights, and the merchant aids him by furnishing him with all the necessaries. For this reason an unstinted care should be bestowed upon them, for as the soul cannot exist without a body, even so the soldier cannot get along without the merchant; nor can the merchant get along without the soldier. A country expands through the profession of war, and is beautified through commerce. Consequently the merchants must be protected against offenders, so that they receive not the least insult from government officials. Many unthinking people disdain the merchants, loathe them and offend them without provocation, and yet there is no condition of life which can get along without the merchant.

But the merchants must be guarded not only against outside offenders : they must not interfere with each other as well, and men from other ranks must not enter the merchant guild and thus cause them no end of disturbance. Commerce should be free, so that they themselves may be benefited and the interests of his Imperial Highness be guarded.

If commerce were free for the Russian merchants, and neither men from other ranks nor foreigners would in the least impair the commerce of Russians, the revenue would be increased. I am of the opinion that without changing the duties, the revenue would be doubled or trebled, whereas now the greater half is lost through the traders from the other ranks.

If a person belonging to some other rank, whether he be senator, or officer, or nobleman, or government official, or clerical, or peasant, should wish to carry on commerce, let him leave his former rank and join the merchant guild, and trade in a straightforward manner, and not by stealth, and pay his duties and other merchant taxes, and let him never again do anything by stealth, as before, without consent of the Merchant Commander, and escape the paying of imposts.

Every rank must behave in such a manner as not to sin before God and do wrong before the Tsar; and they should live as is their profession: if one be a soldier, let him be a soldier, and if he have another vocation, let him devote himself entirely to that vocation.

Our Lord Himself has said: No man can serve two masters. So let the soldier, or man of another rank, stay in his profession, and let him not enter into another rank, for if he devote himself to commerce, he will curtail his military duties. The Lord Himself has said: Where your treasure is, there will be your heart also. And St. Paul the apostle has said that no soldier can find favour with his captain who meddles with commerce. There is a popular saw which says, Choose one or the other, war or commerce.

For these reasons it does not behoove the soldier or man of another rank to trade. If, however, he have a desire to become a merchant, let him join the guild.

If there be no prohibition for external merchants, from the ranks of the nobles, officers or peasants, the merchants will not be able to become enriched, and it will not be possible for the revenue to be increased.

. . . At the present time boyárs, noblemen and their people, soldiers and peasants carry on commerce, without paying any tax, and many merchants carry on trade in their names, and pay no tax. Not half the revenue is collected, nor ever can be collected, if commerce is not to be made free from the nobles and officials, since many mighty people have taken to trade, and some who are not themselves powerful but are not subject to the magistrate.

I know, for example, one case in a Nóvgorod county where there are a hundred or two of merchant-peasants, and who do not pay a farthing's worth of taxes. And if a collector, seeing them, tries to collect the revenue, the gentry take the peasant's part and send the collector away more dead than alive, and the government officers look on, and dare not interfere. And there are some wealthy men, who have some five or six hundred peasants carrying on such illicit trade, and pay not a farthing to the Great Tsar. If all be arranged as I have proposed, commerce will awaken as if from a dream.

It is a very bad custom the merchant people have, to do each other wrong by cheating each other. Both foreigners and Russians are in the habit of showing good-looking wares that are badly made within or filled up with bad stuff; or bad wares are mixed with wares of a good quality and are sold as if of good quality, taking for them an unfair price, and greatly deceiving inexperienced people. They give wrong weights and measures, deceive in price, and do not think all that to be a sin, although they cause so much injustice to the inexperienced. Yet those who deceive are in the end ruined through their own iniquity, and become impoverished.

. . . In order to establish justice in the Merchant Rows, let there be appointed hundred-men and fifty-men and ten-men, and over the shop where there is an hundred-man let there be nailed a round board, painted white, so that it can be easily seen, and on that board let there be written " hundred-man." Do the same with the shop of the fifty-man and ten-man, so that those who purchase any goods may know where to show their wares, if they should want to find out whether they have received the right weight, or measure, or whether the wares are good or bad, and whether they have paid the correct price for them.

If a merchant have received more than the worth of the wares, let him be fined a dime or two for every unfair kopek, and let him be beaten with rods or a whip, that he may not do so again in the future; and if he repeat his offence, let the fine and punishment be increased.

But if one give wrong measure and weight, or sell different goods from what the buyer demanded, and give him inferior goods, let his punishment be much more severe, and the fine be ten times the price of the goods.

And if an hundred-man, or fifty-man, or ten-man be guilty of such a transgression, let the fine for the ten-man be tenfold, for the fifty-man fiftyfold, and for the hundred-man hundredfold, and let the punishment be with the knout, as many strokes as may be decided upon. The hundred-men and fifty-men should receive very stringent instructions to watch without relenting the ten-men and not to be indulgent to them, but to fear the law like fire, lest their transgressions reach the ears of high personages. And the ten-men should watch all the shops under their charge, and see to it that no inferior wares are adulterated by the admixture of better material, but that they are sold such as they are, the good wares as good wares, the mediocre as mediocre, and the poor as poor, and that right weights and measures be given, and that the prices be not raised on the goods, and that there be no adulterations. Let only the right price be asked, and let them measure foreign stuffs, brocade, calamanco and silks from the first end, and not from the last. And no matter what buyer there come, whether rich or poor, whether experienced or inexperienced, let them all be treated in the same fair manner, and let there not a kopek be added to the price of one rouble or ten roubles.

Whatever fine is to be collected should be collected by the hundred-men, without delay, on the day the offence has been committed. All the fines ought to be entered in a ledger which should be reported every month in the proper office. No transaction, neither great nor small, should take place with the foreigners who frequent the fairs, without the permission of the Chief Commander of the Merchant Guild. Whoever dares to sell even a rouble's worth of goods to these foreigners without the permission of the Chief Commander shall be fined a hundredfold, a hundred roubles for every rouble sold, and the punishment shall be administered with the knout, as many strokes as may be decreed, that they should remember them and never do so again.

FROM THE CHAPTER "ON THE PEASANTRY"

Much might be added to the protection of the peasantry if their houses were rebuilt so that they could live more freely and peacefully; for much damage is done to them through overcrowding: if one man's house take fire, the whole village is threatened, and frequently not a single house is left. This leads to endless poverty. If they had not been so much crowded in their settlements, they would not be so easily ruined. It is against this ruin that they ought to be protected. Let them build their houses farther from each other, nor join yard to yard, but with intervals, a few houses

in a lot; the streets ought to be wide, where there is sufficient space, not less than two hundred feet in width; where
the space is crowded, not less than one hundred feet in
width. In this way, if there should be a fire, all the neighbours would run to put it out: there being intervals between
the houses, it would be easy to reach them from all sides,
and as there would be little danger for the neighbouring
houses, the peasants would not rush, as before, to save their
own possessions, but would aid their unfortunate neighbour.
As the settlements are now arranged, it is utterly impossible
for the neighbours to bring aid; they rush for their own,
which they cannot all save, but generally lose everything
they have. Thus they are ruined and become impoverished.

Not a small degree of annoyance is caused the peasants
from not having literate people among them. There are
many villages of twenty or thirty houses that have not a
single man that can read; if any come to them with an
ukase, or without an ukase, pretending to have one, they
believe him, and suffer damages; for they are all blind,—
they see nothing and understand nothing. They are not
able to dispute with the people that pretend having ukases,
and they frequently pay unwarranted taxes to them. To
guard the peasants from such losses, it seems to me, they
ought to be compelled to send their children of ten years and
less to some subdeacon to be instructed how to read and
write. I think it would not be a bad thing if the smallest
village were not without a literate man, so there ought to
be a strict law compelling the peasants to have their children
instructed for three or four years. And there ought to be a
severe punishment for those who do not have their children
taught anything for four years, or who do not have them
instructed at all as they grow up.

Having learned to read and write, they will not only conduct more intelligently the affairs of their masters, but they
will be also useful in the Government, being eligible as
hundred-men and fifty-men, and no one would abuse them
and mulct them for nothing.

Feofán (in private life Eleázar) Prokopóvich.
(1681–1763.)

Peter the Great's reforms were not so much the beginning of a new movement, as the accomplishment of a mental ferment which was taking place in Russia towards the end of the seventeenth century, and they were successful and permanent in the degree that he made use of persons who were already in sympathy with Western culture. The most important of these was Feofán Prokopóvich. Prokopóvich studied in the schools of Kíev, then became a Uniat and continued his studies in Poland, then went to Rome and entered the College of St. Athanasius, which had been established for the purpose of a Catholic propaganda among the Greeks and Slavs of the Eastern Church. There he distinguished himself for his brilliant learning, which included a thorough knowledge of the classics. He returned to Russia in 1702, renounced his Uniat affiliations and became a teacher in the Kíev Academy. Here he composed a text-book on the art of poetry and a tragi-comedy, *Vladímir*, which was played by the students of the Academy. Peter I. met Feofán in 1709, after the victory at Poltáva, when the latter received him in Kíev with a panegyric. In 1716 he was called to St. Petersburg, where, during the absence of Peter, he employed his oratorical powers to advocate the Emperor's reforms. The following year he was made bishop of Nóvgorod. The following year he was entrusted with reforming the government of the Church, which he did by his famous *Spiritual Reglement*, a work that breathes the most enlightened liberalism. One of the chief changes introduced by this *Reglement* was the abandonment of the all-powerful Patriarchate, and the substitution for it of the Holy Synod, of which he became the ruling spirit. After the death of Peter the Great, his enemies swooped down upon him, but, having passed the school of the Jesuits, he was an adept at diplomacy and intrigue, and paid them back in their own coin. However, Prokopóvich is remembered for the enormous good he did, for his prodigious learning, to which many foreigners who visited Russia are witnesses, but especially for encouraging scholarship and literature. Tatíshchev and Kantemír were his friends, and upon the appearance of Kantemír's first satire (see p. 223), he was the first to hail his promising talent.

There is a translation of Prokopóvich's Catechism under the title, *The Russian Catechism*, composed and published by order of the Czar [Peter I. Translated from the Russian by J. T. Philipps], London [1723], second edition 1725.

FROM "THE SPIRITUAL REGLEMENT"

OF INSTRUCTION

It is known to the whole world how weak and impotent the Russian army was when it had no regular instruction, and how incomparably its strength was increased and became great and terrible when our august monarch, his Imperial Highness Peter the First, instructed it in a proper manner. The same is true of architecture, medicine, political government, and all other affairs.

But, most of all, that is true of the government of the Church: when there is not the light of instruction, the Church cannot have any good conduct, and impossibly can there be avoided disorder and superstitions that deserve a great deal of ridicule, as well as strife, and most foolish heresies.

Many foolishly assert that instruction is the cause of heresy. But the heretics of ancient days, the Valentinians, Manichæans, Catharists, Euchites, Donatists and others, whose stupid acts are described by Irenæus, Epiphanius, Augustine, Theodoret and others, raved, not through instruction, but through arrogant foolishness. And did not our own dissenters rave so deliriously through their lack of culture, and ignorance? Though there are some heresiarchs, such as were Arius, Nestorius and a few others, yet their heresies arose not through instruction, but from an imperfect understanding of the Holy Writ, and they grew and were strengthened through malice and false pride which did not permit them to change their wrong opinion after they had discovered the truth, and against their conscience. And though their instruction gave them the power to use sophisms, that is, cunning proofs of their elucubrations, yet he who would want to ascribe this evil simply to instruction would be compelled to say that where a physician poisons a patient, his knowledge of medicine was the cause thereof, and where a soldier valiantly and cunningly strikes down the enemy, military art is the cause of killing. And when we look through history, as through a telescope, at

the past ages, we shall discover more evil in the Dark Ages
than in those that were enlightened through culture. The
bishops were not so arrogant before the fifth century as
they were afterwards, especially the bishops of Rome and
Constantinople, because before there was learning, and afterwards it grew less. If learning were dangerous to the
Church and State, the best Christians would not study themselves, and would forbid others to study; but we see that
all our ancient teachers studied not only the Holy Writ,
but also profane philosophy. Besides many others, the
most famous pillars of the Church have advocated profane
learning, namely: Basil the Great in his instruction to the
studying youths, Chrysostom in his books on monastic
life, Gregory the Theologue in his sermon on Julian the
Apostate. I should have a great deal to say, if I were to
dwell on this alone.

Good and thorough instruction is the root and seed and
foundation of all usefulness, both for the fatherland and the
Church. There is, however, a kind of instruction which
does not deserve that name, though it is deemed by certain
clever but not well-informed men to be the real instruction.

Many are in the habit of asking in what schools such and
such an one has been educated? When they hear that he has
been in rhetoric, philosophy and theology, they are prone
to place him very high, for the sake of those names, but in
that they frequently err, for not all get good instruction
from good teachers, one on account of his dulness, another
on account of his laziness; how much is that the case when
the teacher is little, or not at all, proficient in his subject!

It is important to know that from the sixth to the fifteenth
century, that is, for nine hundred years, all learning in
Europe was of a very meagre and imperfect character, so that
we see in the authors who wrote at that time great sharp-
ness of wit, but small enlightenment. With the fifteenth
century there began to appear better-informed and more
skilful teachers, and by degrees many academies acquired a
greater importance than in those ancient Augustan times;
many other schools, on the contrary, stuck fast in their

ancient slime, preserving, indeed, the names of rhetoric, philosophy and other sciences, but in reality having none of them.   Different causes have led to this, but space does not permit their mention here.

People who have received, so to say, an empty and fantastic education in these institutions are generally more stupid than those who have received none at all.   Being themselves in the dark, they deem themselves to be perfect, and imagining that they have learned all that there is to be learned, neither have the desire, nor think it worth while to read books and study more.   On the other hand, a man who has received the proper schooling is never satisfied with his knowledge, and never stops learning, even though he has passed the age of Methuselah.

But this is the greatest misfortune: the above-mentioned imperfectly instructed people are not only useless, but also very harmful to society, State and Church.   They humble themselves beyond necessity before the authorities, attempting through cunning to appropriate to themselves favours, and crawl into higher places.   They hate people of the same standing as themselves, and if anyone is praised for his learning, they use their utmost endeavour to depreciate and denounce him before the people and authorities.   They are prone to take part in rebellions, hoping to gain advantages for themselves through them.   When they take to theological discussions, they cannot help falling into heresies, for, being ignorant, they easily fall into error, after which they will not change the opinion they have uttered, for fear of appearing not to have known all.   But wise men have this proverb: '' It is the property of a wise man to change his opinion.''

FUNERAL SERMON ON PETER THE GREAT

What is this, and what have we lived to see, O Russians? What are we doing now?   We are burying Peter the Great! Is it not a dream?   Not a vision of the night?   Oh, what a real sorrow!   Oh, what certain bitter reality!   Contrary to all expectations and hopes he has ended his life who has been the cause of our innumerable benefactions and joys, who has resuscitated Russia as if from the dead, and has raised it to great power and glory, nay, has begot it and brought it up, he the true father of his country, whom for his deserts all the good sons of Russia wished to be immortal, and whom, on account of his youth and bodily strength, they had hoped to see many years alive. O dire calamity! He has ended his life just as he was beginning to live after his labours, unrest, sorrows, calamities, after so many and varied deaths.

We see well how we have angered Thee, O Lord, and how long we have tempted Thy long-suffering! O we unfortunate and unworthy people! O the infinitude of our sins! He who does not see that is blind. He who sees it and does not confess is turned to stone in his heartlessness. But why should we increase our woes and heart-pain, which we ought rather attempt to allay? But if we are to mention his great talents, acts and works we shall only be stung more severely by the loss of our good man, and we shall sob aloud. Only in a lethargy, or some deathlike sleep, could we at all forget our so sad loss. What a great and what a good man we have lost!

O Russia, this Samson of yours came to you when no one in the world had expected him, and when he appeared the whole world marvelled. He found you weak in power, and to conform with his name he made you of stone and adamant. He found an army dangerous at home, weak in the field and scorned by the foe, and he gave his country a useful army that is terrible to the enemy, and everywhere renowned and glorious. He defended his country, and at the same time returned to it the lands that had been taken away from it, and increased it by the acquisition of new provinces. When he crushed those who rose against us, he at the same time broke the strength of our ill-wishers and subdued their spirits, and, closing up the lips of envy, compelled the whole world to proclaim glorious things of himself.

O Russia, he was your first Japheth, who had accomplished

a deed unheard of in your annals, having introduced the
building and sailing of ships. He gave you a new fleet that,
to the wonderment of the world and surpassing all expecta-
tion, was in no way inferior to much older fleets, and he
opened for you a path to all the ends of the earth, and spread
your power and glory to the extreme corners of the ocean,
to the limits of your usefulness, to the limits which justice
had placed; and the might of your dominion, which heretofore was firm on land, he has now made strong and permanent upon the sea.

O Russia, he is your Moses! Are not his laws like a firm
protection of truth, and like unbreakable fetters of wrong-
doing? And are not his statutes clear, a light upon your
path? And are not the high ruling Senate and the many
special institutions of his so many lights in the search of
advantage, the warding off of harm, the safety of the peaceful, and the unmasking of the wrongdoers? He has verily
left us in doubt whether he is more to be praised for being
loved and cherished by the good and simple-hearted, or for
being hated by unrepenting flatterers and rascals.

O Russia, he is your Solomon, who has received from the
Lord his very great reason and wisdom. Have we not sufficient testimony thereof in the many philosophic arts, which
he himself practised and many subjects introduced under his
supervision, and in the many cunning industrial arts which
have never before been heard of among us? And he also
introduced the chins [1] and degrees, and civil order, and decent manners in daily intercourse, and the rules of acceptable habits and customs, and now we see and admire the
external appearance and internal worth of our country, which
from within and without is far superior to what it was in
former years.

He is also, O Russian Church, your David and Constantine. The synodal government is his creation, and its written and oral instructions were his care. Oh, how often
his heart was heavy when he saw the ignorance in the path

[1] There are fourteen rank distinctions, called "chins," in Russia;
they are acquired through service only, independently of birth.

of salvation! How great his zeal was against superstition and deceptive simulations, and the senseless, hostile and destructive heresy amongst us! How great was his desire and endeavour to see more learning among the clergy, and a greater godliness and more decent worship in the people!

But, O renowned man! Can we in a short sermon mention all his glory? The present sorrow and grief which compels us to shed tears and sigh does not allow of an extended speech. Perhaps in time this thorn that stings our hearts will be dulled, and then we will speak at greater length of his deeds and virtues, though we shall never be able sufficiently to praise him according to his worth. To-day, though we are only making a short mention of him and, as it were, are only touching the hems of his garments, we, poor unfortunate people, see, O hearers, who has left us and whom we have lost.

Let us not, O Russians, faint with sorrow and grief, for the great monarch and our father has not left us in a bad plight. He has left us, but not poor and necessitous: the immeasurable wealth of his power and glory, which has been realised by his above-mentioned deeds, is with us. Russia will be such as he has made it; he has made it an object of love to the good, and it will be loved; he has made it terrible to the enemy, and terrible it will remain; he has made it glorious throughout the whole world, and it will not cease to be glorious. He has left us religious, civil and military institutions. He has left us, and his body will decay, but his spirit will stay.

Above all, in leaving this temporal world, he has not left us orphaned. How could we, indeed, call ourselves orphaned when we see his legacy to the throne, his real helpmate in life, a ruler like him after his demise, you, most gracious and autocrat Empress, great heroine and monarch, and mother of all the Russias? The whole world is a witness that your sex does not prevent your being like Peter the Great. Who does not know your wisdom as a ruler, and your motherly womanliness, and your natural God-given talents? And all this took place and was confirmed in you

not merely through your association with so great a monarch, but also in your communion with his wisdom, labours
and various calamities. He, having tried you during a series
of years, like gold in the crucible, deemed it insufficient to
have you as a cohabiter of his bed, but made you also the
heir to his crown, and power, and throne. How can we
help hoping that you will confirm what he has done, will
create anew what he has left undone and will keep all in
good condition? Only, O valiant soul, try to overcome this
unendurable calamity which has been intensified by the loss
of your most beloved daughter, and which, like a severe
wound, has been torn beyond measure by this new sting.
And as you have been seen by all ever present with Peter
of glorious deeds, an incessant companion in all his labours
and troubles, so try even now to be such in this your very
bitter loss.

And you, noble assembly, of all ranks and degrees, sons
of Russia, with your faithfulness and obedience console your
Empress and mother. Console yourselves also, seeing the
undoubted signs of Peter's spirit in your Empress, and that
not all of Peter has passed away. Then let us bow before
our Lord who has thus visited us, praying Him, the God of
mercy and father of all consolation, to wipe the unrestrained
tears of her Highness, our most autocratic Empress, and her
precious blood, her daughters, grandchildren, nieces and
all the high family, and to soothe the grief of their hearts
with His gracious care, and to console us all in His mercy.

O Russia, seeing what a great man has left you, see also
how great he has left you. Amen!

Vasili Nikitich Tatíshchev. (1686–1750.)

Tatíshchev was one of the most distinguished and intelligent
friends of the reforms of Peter the Great. Having studied first at
Moscow and then in Germany, he was attached to the Berg-und-
Manufaktur-Kolleg (Department of Mining and Manufactures). The
president of the institution pointed out to Peter the Great the necessity for a geography of the empire, and this task was entrusted to
Tatíshchev. In the course of his work, the latter was induced to
make a thorough study of old historical documents, of which he

discovered a large number. Several of the chronicles he mentions and had access to have not been preserved, and later historians have to rely on the statements made by Tatíshchev for some important historical information. In 1720 he was sent to Siberia for the purpose of prospecting for copper and silver and establishing various plants. Then began a laborious career, in a large variety of capacities, among them that of Governor of Astrakhán. The years 1724-26 he passed in Sweden, where he cultivated the acquaintance of Swedish scholars and made a study of foreign sources of Russian history. Thus Tatíshchev had ample opportunities for becoming the first historiographer of Russia. His *History of Russia*, which was published in the reign of Catherine the Great, shows an intimate knowledge of the philosophical systems of Descartes and Tomasius, and the political systems of Christian Wolff, Puffendorf and Hugo Grotius, as well as Machiavelli and Locke. He was opposed to a political supremacy of the Church even more decidedly than Prokopóvich, the author of the *Spiritual Reglement* (see p. 211). It is an interesting fact that when Tatíshchev found no sympathy for his *History* in St. Petersburg, he corresponded with a friend in England for the purpose of having it published in English by the Royal Society at London, but there could not be found an Englishman who was competent to undertake the translation. Of his other works, his *Spiritual Testament and Instruction to my Son Evgráf*, though replete with liberal views, is the last in the long chain of *Instructions* in which the older period abounds, such as the *Instruction* of Vladímir Monomákh (p. 50), and the *Domostróy* of Sylvester (p. 126). It has been translated into English: *The Testament of B. Tatischef*, translated from the Russian manuscript by J. Martinof, Paris, 1860.

FROM THE "RUSSIAN HISTORY"

One ought not to discuss the usefulness of history, for everybody can see and feel it; but as some are not accustomed to see things clearly and discuss them in detail, and often through their perverted understanding make the useful to appear as harmful and the harmful as useful, and consequently transgress in their acts and deeds (as indeed I have heard such people, to my disgust, talk loud of the uselessness of history), I deemed it proper to give a short review of it.

To begin with, history is nothing else than the recounting of past acts and occurrences, good and bad; for all that we have experienced in recent or long-passed days through our senses of hearing, seeing and feeling, or that we reproduce by our memory, is really history, and it teaches us, whether through our acts or those of others, to emulate the good and beware of the evil. For example, when I recollect that I saw yesterday a fisherman who had been catching fish and had had a certain success in it, I naturally receive in my mind an impulse to do likewise; or if I saw yesterday a thief or some other criminal, who had been sentenced to a severe punishment or death, terror will naturally keep me from committing such an act as would cause my utter ruin. All the histories we read act upon us in the same manner: the deeds of ancient days are represented to us so vividly that we seem to have seen and felt them ourselves.

For this reason we may say that no man, no condition of life, no profession, science, nor government, much less a single individual, can be perfect, wise and useful without a knowledge of the same. For example, let us take the sciences. The first and greatest of them all is theology, that is, the science of God, His all-wisdom, almightiness, which alone leads us to future bliss, and so forth. Now, no theologian can be called wise who does not know the ancient divine acts which have been revealed to us in the Holy Scriptures, and when, with whom and why there have been disputes about certain dogmas and articles of faith, or when and why this has been established and that discarded; why certain statutes and orders of the ancient Church have been changed, discontinued, and new ones introduced; consequently he must know divine and church history, as well as civil history, as Huet, the famous French theologian, has sufficiently pointed out.

The second science is jurisprudence, which teaches proper conduct and our duties to God, ourselves and our neighbours, in order to acquire peace of body and soul. No jurist can be called wise who does not know former interpretations and discussions of natural and civil laws. And how can a judge pass right judgment if he does not know the origin and application of old and new laws? Indeed, he must know the history of the laws.

The third is medicine, or leechcraft, which science consists in the art of preserving health, and bringing back the
lost health, or in preventing the disease from spreading.
All this depends on history, for the physician must gain his
knowledge from the ancients, must know what is the cause
of diseases, what medicine and treatment to give, what the
property and strength of each medicine is, all of which no
man could find out in a hundred years through his own
experience and investigation. But to experiment on the
sick is a dangerous matter, from which they could easily be
ruined, though this is not infrequently the case with certain
ignoramuses.   I shall not mention many other parts of philosophy, but I may summarise by saying that all philosophy
is based on history and supported by it, for all the right and
wrong and faulty opinions which we find with the ancients
are history as regards our knowledge, and form the basis for
our corrections.

Statesmanship is composed of three different parts: of the
internal government, or economy, external relations, and
military affairs. All three demand not less history than
the other sciences, and without it cannot be perfect. Thus,
in political economy it is necessary to know what has caused
ruin in former days; how it has been warded off or minimised;
what have been the favourable influences; how obtained and
preserved, so that the present and future may be wisely
judged in the light of that knowledge. On account of this
wisdom, the ancient Romans represented their god Janus
with two faces, for he knew perfectly the past, and from its
examples wisely judged the future.

For the administration of foreign affairs it is necessary to
know not only one's own country, but also other govern-
ments: what conditions they have formerly been in; what
has brought about changes in them; what states they are in
now; with whom they have had disputes and wars, and for
what; what treaties have been made and confirmed with
them, in order to proceed intelligently in the acts at hand.

For military leaders it is very important to know by what
device and cunning great forces of the enemy have been

vanquished, or kept from victory, and so forth, as we see Alexander the Great having held Homer's books on the Trojan war in great respect, and having been instructed by them. For this reason many great generals have described their own acts and those of others. Of these the most illustrious example is Julius Cæsar, who has described his wars, that future generals might after him use his acts for their own examples, and many famous generals on land and on the sea have followed in his footsteps by writing of their exploits. Many great rulers have either themselves written of their acts, or have ordered expert people to write of them, not only that their memory should live in glory, but that their descendants should have examples to follow.

As regards the usefulness of Russian history it must be remarked, that, as is the case with all other histories, the knowledge of one's own history and geography is more important for any nation or region than that of foreign histories; at the same time it must be kept in mind that without the knowledge of foreign histories, one's own is not clear and sufficient: 1. That the writer of contemporary history cannot know all the external influences for good and bad; 2. That the writers are frequently compelled, out of fear, to suppress, or change, or modify some very important circumstances of contemporary history; 3. That from passion, love, or hatred, they describe quite differently from what were the actual occurrences, and that the facts are frequently related more correctly and in detail by outsiders. Thus, in my present work, the first part, dealing with the Russian antiquity, has mainly been drawn from foreign sources for lack of native writers, and in the other parts many errors and lacunæ have been corrected and filled out from foreign sources. European historians accuse us of having no old history, and of knowing nothing of our antiquity, simply because they do not know what historians we possess, and though some have made a few extracts, or have translated from them a passage here and there, others, thinking that we have no better ones than those quoted, despise them. Some of our own ignorant writers agree with them, while

those who do not wish to trouble themselves by looking into
the ancient sources or who do not understand the text, have,
ostensibly to give a better explanation, but in reality to hide
the truth, invented fables of their own and thus have obscured
the real facts as told by the ancients, as, for example, in the
case of the foundation of Kíev, and that of Nóvgorod by
Slavén, and so forth.

I wish to say here emphatically that all the famous European historians will not be able to know or tell anything
correctly of many of our antiquities, no matter what their
efforts in Russian history may be, if they do not read our
sources,—for example, of the many nations who have existed
here in ancient days, as the Amazons, Alans, Huns, Avars,
Cimbrians and Cimmerians; nor do they know anything of
the Scythians, Sarmatians and Slavs, their tribes, origin,
habitations and migrations, or of the anciently famous large
cities of the Essedonians, Archipeans, Cumanians, etc.,
where they have lived, and what their present names are;
but all this they could find out through a study of Russian
history.   This history is not only of use to us Russians, but
also to the whole learned world, in order that by it the fables
and lies invented by our enemies, the Poles and others, for
the sake of disparaging our ancestors, may be laid bare and
contradicted.

Such is the usefulness of history.   But everybody ought
to know, and this is easily perceived, that history describes
not only customs, deeds and occurrences, but also the con-
sequences resulting from them, namely, that the wise, just,
kind, brave, constant and faithful are rewarded with honour,
glory and well-being, while the vicious, foolish, evildoers,
avaricious, cowardly, perverse and faithless will gain eternal
dishonour, shame and insult: from which all may learn how
desirable it is to obtain the first and avoid the second.

Prince Antiókh (Antiochus) Kantemír.   (1708–1744.)

Antiókh Kantemír was not a Russian by birth.   His father,
Demetrius, had for a number of years been hospodar of Moldavia.
Harassed by the intrigues of a rival at Constantinople, he emigrated

with four thousand of his Moldavians to Russia, where he arrived after the unfortunate Prut expedition, in 1711. Himself one of the most accomplished scholars and linguists of Europe, he with the aid of his cultivated Greek wife bestowed the minutest care on the education of his six children.

Having arrived in Russia in his third year, Antiókh acquired Russian as his mother tongue, though he also spoke fluently six or seven other languages, and was well versed in Latin and ancient Greek. By education, however, he was anything but a Russian, and his sympathies were naturally directed towards the most extreme reformatory tendencies which Peter the Great advocated for the State and Feofán Prokopóvich for the Church; both of them were not slow in recognising his unusual talents. In 1732 Empress Anna appointed him ambassador to the Court of St. James, and in 1738 he was transferred to Paris, where he passed his short life in communion with Maupertuis, Montesquieu, Abbé Guasco, and others. Besides a few shorter poems and imitations and translations of Anacreon, and an unfinished ode on the death of Peter the Great, Kantemír composed ten satires, of which the one below is the first. It is on these satires that his reputation mainly rests. In style, they are imitations of Boileau and Horace, though never slavish. His language is not always free from Gallicisms, but otherwise it represents the first successful attempt to introduce colloquial Russian into poetry. The chief value of the satires, independently of their literary perfection, lay in their powerful attack on all the contemporary elements of Russian society that were antagonistic to the Western reform.

Specimens from several of Kantemír's satires are given in C. E. Turner's *Studies in Russian Literature*, London, 1882, and the same article, in Fraser's Magazine, 1877.

Parts of the First Satire, in article on *Russian Literature*, in Foreign Quarterly Review, vol. i.

TO MY MIND

Immature Mind, fruit of recent study! Be quiet, urge not the pen into my hands: even without writing one may pass the fleeting days of life and gain honours, though one be not a poet. Many easy paths lead in our days to honours, and bold feet need not stumble upon them: the least acceptable is the one the nine barefooted sisters have laid out. Many a man has lost his strength thereon, without reaching a goal. You have to toil and moil there, and while you labour, people avoid you like the plague, rail at you, loathe you. He who bends over the table, fixing his eyes upon books, will gain no magnificent palaces, nor gardens adorned with marbles; will add no sheep to his paternal flock.

'T is true, in our young monarch[1] a mighty hope has risen for the Muses, and the ignorant flee in shame from him. Apollo has found in him a strong defender of his glory, and has seen him honouring his suite and steadily intent upon increasing the dwellers on Parnassus.[2] The trouble is, many loudly praise in the Tsar what in the subject they haughtily condemn.

"Schisms and heresies are begot by science.[3] He lies most who knows most; who pores over books becomes an atheist." Thus Crito grumbles, his rosary in his hands, and sighs, and with bitter tears the saintly soul bids us see how dangerous is the seed of learning that is cast among us : our children, who heretofore gently and meekly walked in the path of their forefathers, eagerly attending divine service and listening in fear to what they did not understand, now, to the horror of the Church, have begun to read the Bible; they discuss all, want to know the cause of all, and put little faith in the clerical profession; they have lost their good habits, have forgotten how to drink kvas, and will not be driven with a stick to partake of salt meat. They place no candles before the images, observe no feasts. They regard the worldly power misplaced in clerical hands, and whisper that worldly possessions ill become those who have renounced a worldly life.

Sylvan finds another fault with science: "Education," he says, "brings famine in its track. We managed to get along before this without knowing Latin much better than we live now. We used to harvest more grain in our ignorance, but now that we have learned a foreign language, we lose our corn. What of it if my argument be weak and

---

[1] Peter II., born 1715; ascended the throne in 1729, the year the satire was written in.

[2] Immediately upon arriving in Moscow, Peter II. confirmed the privileges of the Academy of Sciences.

[3] Compare Feofán Prokopóvich's *Spiritual Reglement*, p. 212.

without sense and connection,—what matters that to a nobleman? Proof, order of words, is the affair of low-born men;
for aristocrats it suffices boldly to assent, or contradict.
Insane is he who examines the force and limitations of his
soul; who toils whole days in his sweat, in order to learn
the structure of the world and the change or cause of things:
't is like making pease to stick to the wall. Will all that
add one day to my life, or one penny to my coffers? Can I
by means of it find out how much my clerk and superintendent steal a year or how to add water to my pond, or to increase the number of barrels in my still?

" Nor is he wise who, full of unrest, dims his eyes over a
smoking fire, in order to learn the properties of ores. We
have passed our A B C, and we can tell without all that the
difference between gold, silver and copper. The science of
herbs and diseases is idle talk. You have a headache, and
the physician looks for signs of it in your hand! The blood
is the cause of all, if we are to put faith in them. When we
feel weak, it is because our blood flows too slowly; if it
moves fast, there is a fever, he says boldly, though no one
has ever seen the inside of a living body. And while he
passes his time in such fables, the contents of our money-bags
go into his. Of what use is it to calculate the course of the
stars, and without rhyme or reason pass sleepless nights,
gazing at one spot : for mere curiosity's sake to lose your
rest, trying to ascertain whether the sun moves, or we with
the earth? We can read in the almanac, for every day in
the year, the date of the month and the hour of sunrise.
We can manage to divide the land in quarters without
Euclid, and we know without algebra how many kopeks
there are in a rouble." Sylvan praises but one science to
the skies,—the one that teaches how to increase his income
and to save expenses. To labour in that from which your
pocket does not swell at once, he deems a very dangerous
occupation for a citizen.

Red-faced Lucas, belching thrice, speaks in a chanting
voice: " Study kills the companionship of men. We have
been created by God as social beings, and we have been

given intelligence not for our own sakes alone. What good does it do anybody, if I shut myself up in my cabinet, and for my dead friends lose the living—when all my comrade-ship, all my good fellows, will be ink, pen, sand and paper? In merriment, in banquets we must pass our lives. Life is short, why should we curtail it further, worry over books, and harm our eyes? Is it not better to pass your days and nights over the winecup? Wine is a divine gift, there is much good in it: it befriends people, gives cause for con-versation, makes glad, dispels heavy thoughts, eases misery, gives courage to the weak, mollifies the cruel, checks sullen-ness, and leads the lover more readily to his goal. When they will begin to make furrows in the sky, and the stars will shine through the surface of the earth; when swift rivers will run to their sources, and past ages will return; when at Lent the monk will eat nothing but dried sturgeon, then will I abandon my cup and take to books."

Medor is worried because too much paper is used for letters and for printed books, and because he will soon be left with-out paper to curl his locks with. He would not change for Seneca a pound of good face-powder; in comparison with Egór,[1] Vergil is not worth two farthings to him, and he showers his praises on Rex,[2] not Cicero.

This is a part of the speeches that daily ring in my ears, and for this, O Mind, I advise you to be dumber than a dumpling. Where there is no profit, praise encourages to work, and without it the heart grows faint. But it is much worse, when instead of praises you earn insults! It is harder than for a tippler not to get his wine, or for a priest not to celebrate on Holy Week, or for a merchant to forego heady liquor.

I know, O Mind, that you will boldly answer me that it is not easy for an evil-minded man to praise virtue; that the dandy, miser, hypocrite, and the like, must perforce scorn science, and that their malevolent discourse concerns no men of culture.

[1] A famous shoemaker in Moscow ; died in 1729.
[2] A German tailor of Moscow.

Your judgment is excellent, correct; and thus it ought to be, but in our days the words of the ill-disposed control the wise. Besides, the sciences have other ill-wishers than those whom, for shortness' sake, I merely mentioned or, to tell the truth, dared to mention. There are many more. The holy keepers of the keys of heaven and those to whom Themis has entrusted the golden scales little love, nearly all of them, the true adornment of the mind.

You want to be an archbishop? Don a surplice, above it let a gorgeous chasuble adorn your body, put a golden chain[1] around your neck, cover your head with a high hat, your belly with a beard, order the crosier to be carried in pomp before you; place yourself comfortably in your carriage and, as your heart bursts with anger, cast your benedictions to the right and left. By these signs you will easily be recognised as the archpriest, and they will reverently call you " Father." But science? What has the Church to gain from it? Some priest might forget a part, if he wrote out his sermon, and thus there would be a loss of the Church's revenues, and these are the Church's main privileges and greatest glory.

Do you wish to become a judge? Don a wig full of locks, scold him who comes with a complaint but with empty hands, let your heart firmly ignore the tears of the poor, and sleep in your arm-chair when the clerk reads the brief. When someone mentions to you the civil code, or the law of nature, or the people's rights, spit in his face; say that he lies at random and tries to impose an intolerable burden on the judges; that it is the clerk's business to rummage through mountains of documents, but that it suffices for a judge to announce his sentence.

The time has not come down to us when Wisdom presided over everything and distributed wreaths, and was the only means for advancement. The golden age has not come down to our generation. Pride, indolence, wealth, have

[1] With the image of the Holy Virgin or the Saviour,—the so-called panagia.

vanquished wisdom; ignorance has taken the place of wisdom: it glorifies itself under the mitre, walks in embroidered
gowns, sits in judgment behind the red cloth, boldly leads
armies.   Science trudges along in rags and patches, and is
driven from nearly all houses with contumely; they do not
want to know her and evade her friendship, just as those
who have suffered upon the sea avoid service on a ship.   All
cry: '' We see no good in science; the heads of learned men
are full, but their hands are empty.''

If one knows how to shuffle cards, to tell the flavours of
various wines, can dance, plays three pieces on the flute,
cleverly matches the colours in his apparel, for him, even in
his tender years, all high honours are but a small reward,
and he regards himself to be the equal of the Seven
Sages.

'' There is no justice in the world!'' cries the brainless
subdeacon.   '' They have not yet made me a bishop, though
I read fluently the Book of the Hours,[1] the Psalter and the
Epistles, and even Chrysostom without stumbling, although I do not understand him.''

The warrior grumbles because he has not yet charge of his
regiment, though he knows how to sign his name.   The
scribe is angry because he is not yet seated behind the red
cloth, though he is able to make a copy in a clear hand.
He thinks it an insult to grow old in obscurity, though he
counts seven boyárs in his family and is possessed of two
thousand village houses, even though he can neither read
nor write.

Hearing such words, and seeing such examples, be silent,
Mind, complain not of your obscurity.   His life has no terrors, though he may deem it hard, who silently retires to his
quiet nook.   If gracious Wisdom has taught you anything,
rejoice in secret, meditating by yourself over the advantages
of learning.   Explain it not to others, lest, instead of
praises which you expect, you be roundly scolded.

---

[1] Prayer-book containing the prayers for every hour ; it was com-
monly used as a text-book for reading.

Vasíli Kiríllovich Tredyakóvski. (1703–1769.)

Like Lomonósov, Tredyakóvski was of humble origin, his father having been a priest in the city of Astrakhán ; also, like his more illustrious colleague a few years later, he walked to Moscow and there entered the School of the Redeemer. He later passed a few years abroad, where he became acquainted with French literature. Upon his return to St. Petersburg in 1730, he translated a French book ; in this translation the spoken Russian is for the first time used, free from Slavic influence. Even before this, Tredyakóvski had written verses in the syllabic versification, but in 1735 he discovered that the tonic versification was the only one adapted to the Russian language, and at once set out to write in that measure. His chief deserts do not lie in poetry, for his verses show an absolute absence of talent, and he later became a byword for insipidity. He was the first man to point out the necessity of using the Russian language for literary purposes, and to indicate the line in which Russian poetry must develop. By his enormous industry in translating from foreign languages he became an important factor in the dissemination of learning. The following ode is really an imitation of Boileau's *Sur la prise de Namur.*

ODE ON THE SURRENDER OF DANTZIG

What strange intoxication emboldens my voice to singing ? Muses, dwellers of Parnassus, does not my mind perceive you ? I hear your sweet-sounding strings, your beautiful measure and moods, and a fire arises in my thoughts. O nations, listen all! Stormy winds, do not blow: my verse sings of Anna.

Pindar, and after him Flaccus, have in high-flowing diction risen from the mist to the bright stars, like swift eagles. But if my song to-day were to equal my sincere and eternal zeal for Anna, Orpheus of Thrace and Amphion of Thebes would be in ecstasy from it.

Now I strike the dulcet lyre to celebrate the magnificent victory to the greater downfall of the enemy. Oh, what victorious might has adorned our joy, for the might of the adversary was equal to ours. There is no limit to our pure joy that surpasses all example, that has given balm to our hearts.

Has Neptune himself built the walls, those that stand by the sea ? Do they not resemble the Trojan walls, for they would not let in the innumerable Russian army, mightily opposing it? Do not all call the Vistula Skamander? Do they not all regard Stoltzenberg as Mount Ida?

That is not Troy, the mother of fables: there is not one Achilles here; everyone of the rank and file is in bravery a Hercules. What might is that that hurls lightning? Is it not Minerva gleaming in her helmet? 'T is evident from her looks, from her whole appearance, that she is a goddess: without her ægis she is terrible,—'t is Anna, chief of all empresses.

That also is a Russian army that has closely invested Dantzig, the city of the foe. Each warrior, hastening to the battle, it behooves to call a Mars. Each is ready boldly to shed his blood, or to crown the undertaking for Anna's sake. Each one is strong with Anna's fortune: Anna is their strong hope; and, knowing that Anna is gracious to them, they are faithful and not undecided.

Golden beam of the European and Asian Sun! O Russian monarch, the key to your happiness is the kindness to your subjects and your benign rule! The whole world honours your name, and the universe will not hold your glory seeing that, O beautiful flower of virtues!

What do I see? Does not my eye deceive me? A youth has opposed himself to Hercules, lifting high his brows behind ramparts, beyond the river! 'T is Dantzig, having taken foolish counsel, as if drunk with heady wine, that dares to oppose the great autocrat! In its blindness it does not see the abysses, nor all death-bearing valleys.

It receives Stanislaus in its midst, who seeks twice a crown, and hopes to be defended to the end through nearby Neptune: fearing the Russian thunder it invokes the aid of a distant people from the banks of the Seine: but they beat the drums at the waters of Wechselmünde for a retreat.

Dantzig is proud of its fire and steel, and its regiments of soldiers, and directs its engines of war against the Russians on the hills. Being rich in stores it calls to Stanislaus; it in vain implores its soldiers that have no brave hearts, but think only of this, how to save their lives, and run.

O Dantzig, oh! What are you daring! Come to your senses, collect yourself, for you are hurling yourself to destruction. Why have you stopped? You are hesitating! Surrender! Wherefore have you such boldness and do not tremble before Anna? Many tribes of their own free will and without strife submit to her: China bows down before her twice, in order not to pay her tribute.

Nowhere has there been the like of Anna in kindness, nor is there anywhere in the world one so able to wage war with the unyielding. Her sword wound with the olive branch is only ominous in war. Abandon, Dantzig, your evil purpose: you see, the Alcidæ are ready with cruel miseries for your inhabitants. You hear Anna's angry voice: save yourself!

You are closely pressed by thousands of athletes; you are mightily struck by the flash of angry lightnings. You cannot withstand: the thunder is ready not in jest. Your ramparts are without defence; the earth opens up abysses; roofs fly into the air; your walls are emptied of men.

If all the powers combined were to aid you, O Dantzig; if the elements defended you; if from all the ends of the world soldiers came to spill their blood for you,—yet nothing would be able to save you from suffering and to stop your misery, and wring you out of Anna's hands.

Your adversaries see to-day the bravery of Russian soldiers: neither fire nor water harms them, and they advance with open breasts. How readily they advance! How forgetful they are of their lives! The cannon's thunder frightens them not! They make the assault, as if going to a wedding feast! Only through smoky darkness one may see that their brows are facing the forts.

Within the walls of the wretched city all are struck down with fear: everything falls and flies to dust,—the besiegers are on the walls! The last magistrates, seeing from their tower their vain hope in the distant armies and Stanislaus who had taken refuge within their walls, besides themselves, exclaim: " We are fated to fall!"

What I have prophesied is about to happen,—Dantzig

begins to tremble: all think of surrendering, as before they all decided to fight, and of saving themselves from the engines of war, from flying bombs and from all the pests the city is oppressed by. All cry, for the burden was too heavy to carry, "It is time now to open the gates to Anna's army."

So it is done: the sign for surrender is given, and Dantzig is at our feet! Our soldiers are happy in their success; the fires have gone out; there is an end to misery. Immediately Glory took its flight and announced with its thundering trumpet : "Anna is fortunate ! Anna is unconquerable; Anna, exalted by all, is their common glory and honour."

Lyre! abate your song: it is not possible for me properly to praise diadem-bearing Anna and her great goodness, any more than I can fly. It is Anna's good fortune that she is loved by God. He always watches over her, and through Him she is victorious. Who would dare to oppose her? May Anna live many years!

Princess Natálya Borísovna Dolgorúki. (1714–1771.)

The Princess Dolgorúki was the daughter of Count Sheremétev, who was intimately connected with the reforms of Peter the Great. In 1729 she was betrothed to Prince Iván Aleksyéevich Dolgorúki, the favourite of Peter II.; Feofán Prokopóvich performed the ceremony of the betrothal, and the whole Imperial family and the most distinguished people of the capital were present. A few days later Peter II. died, and Anna Ioánnovna ascended the throne. Dolgorúki was banished to Siberia, and she married him in order to follow him into exile. They passed eight years in the Government of Tobólsk, when her husband was taken to Nóvgorod and executed. For three years she remained in ignorance of his fate, when the Empress Elizabeth permitted her to return to St. Petersburg. In 1758 Princess Dolgorúki entered a monastery at Kíev, and ten years later she wrote her *Memoirs*, at the request of her son Michael. In 1810 her grandson, the poet Dolgorúki (see p. 422), had these *Memoirs* printed. The Princess Dolgorúki has become a synonym for a devoted Russian woman, and she has frequently been celebrated in poetry, especially by Rylyéev, Kozlóv and Nekrásov. There is also an English book treating of her life: *The Life and Times of Nathalia Borissovna, Princess Dolgorookov*, by J. A. Heard, London, 1857.

FROM HER "MEMOIRS"

My mind totters when I recall all that has befallen me after my happiness which at that time appeared to me to be eternal. I did not have a friend to teach me that I ought to walk more warily on the slippery road of pleasure. My Lord! What a threatening storm arose against me, and what calamities from the whole world befell me! Lord! Give me strength to tell of my sufferings, that I may describe them for the information of the curious and the consolation of the afflicted who, thinking of me, might be consoled. I have passed all the days of my life in misery, and have experienced all: persecution, exile, want, separation from my beloved one,—everything that one can think of. I do not boast of my endurance, but will boast of the mercy of the Lord who has given me so much strength to bear all that I have borne up to now. It would be impossible for a man to endure such strokes, if the power of the Lord did not strengthen him from on high. Consider my bringing up, and my present state!

Here is the beginning of my misery that I had never expected. Our Emperor had departed from this life, and before I had expected it, there was a change of the crown. It evidently had pleased God to chastise the people for their sins: a merciful Tsar was taken away from them, and great was the weeping in the nation. All my relatives came together, were sorrowing and weeping, and wondering how to announce to me the calamity. I generally slept late, until nine o'clock; as soon as I awoke, I noticed that the eyes of all were in tears; though they were careful to hide it, yet it was quite obvious they had been weeping. I knew that the Tsar was sick, and even very sick, but I had great hope the Lord would not abandon His orphans. They were of necessity compelled to tell me the truth. As soon as this news reached my ears, I lost my consciousness; when I regained it, I kept on repeating: "I am lost, lost!" No other words left my lips but "lost." However they tried to console me, they could not stop my weeping, nor keep me quiet. I knew too well the custom of my country, that all the favourites perish with the death of their Emperors: what could I, then, expect? Yet, I did not think that the end would be as bad as it actually was, for though my fiancé was beloved by the Tsar, and had many distinctions, and all kinds of affairs of State had been entrusted to him, yet I placed some hope in his honest acts. Knowing his innocence, and that he had not been tainted by any improper conduct, it appeared to me that a man would not be accused without a proper judicial trial, or be subject to disfavour, and be deprived of his honours and possessions; I learned only later that truth is not helpful in misfortune.

So I wept unconsolably. My relatives, in their search for means of consoling me, pointed out to me that I was yet a young person, and had no reason to grieve so senselessly; that I could reject my fiancé if things went badly with him, and that there were other suitors who were not of less worth than he, even if they had not his high honours. And indeed there was a suitor who was very anxious to have me, but I did not like him, though all my relatives wanted me to marry him. That proposition weighed so heavily upon me, that I was not able to answer them. Consider yourself, what kind of a consolation that could be to me, and how dishonourable such an act would have been,—to be ready to marry him when he was great, but to refuse him the moment he was cast into misfortune. I could not agree to any such unscrupulous advice; I resolved at once to live and die together with him to whom I had given my heart, and not to allow anyone else to share my love. It was not my habit to love one to-day and another to-morrow; such is the fashion in the world, but I proved to the world that I was faithful in love. I have been a companion to my husband in all his troubles, and I am telling the truth when I assert that in all my misery I never repented having married him, and did not murmur against the Lord for it. He is my witness: I bore everything while loving him, and as much as was in my power, I kept up his courage. My relatives were evidently of a different opinion, and therefore advised me otherwise, or maybe they simply pitied me.

Towards evening my fiancé came to my house, and complained to me of his misfortune. He told me of the pitiable death of the Emperor, who did not lose consciousness to the last, and bid him good-bye. While he told me all this, we both wept, and swore to each other that nothing should separate us but death; I was ready to go with him through all the terrestrial misfortunes. Thus it grew worse from hour to hour. Where were those who formerly had sought our protection and friendship? They had all hid themselves, and my relatives stood aloof from me; they all left me for the new favourites, and all were afraid to meet me, lest they should suffer through the suspicion under which I was. It were better for a person not to be born in this world, if he is to be great for a while, and then will fall into disgrace: all will soon despise him, and no one will speak to him.

.   .   .   .

Here we remained about a week, while a vessel was being fitted out to take us down the river. All that was terrible to me, and I ought to pass it in silence. My governess, to whose care I had been entrusted by my mother, did not wish to leave me, and had come with me to the village. She thought that we would pass all the days of our misfortune there; but things turned out differently, and she was compelled to leave me. She was a foreigner, and could not endure all the hardships; yet, as much as she could she did for me in those days: went on the ill-starred vessel that was to take us away, fixed everything there, hung the walls with tapestry to keep out the dampness, that I might not catch a cold; she placed a pavilion on board, partitioned off a room, in which we were to live, and wept for me all the time.

At last there arrived the bitter day when we must depart. We were given ten people to attend on us, and a woman for each person, in all, five. I had intended to take my maid with me, but my sisters-in-law dissuaded me: they gave me theirs to take her place, and gave me another maid for an assistant to the laundresses, who could do nothing else but wash clothes; I was compelled to agree to their arrangement.

My maid wept, and did not want to part from me. I asked her not to importune me with her tears, and to take things as fate had decreed. Such was my equipment: I had not even my own serf, and not a penny of money. My governess gave me every kopek she had; it was not a great sum, only sixty roubles, and with that I departed. I do not remember whether we went on foot to the vessel, or whether we drove to it in a carriage. The river was not far from our house; there I bid good-bye to my family, for they had been permitted to see us off.

I stepped into the cabin, and saw how it was fixed up: my governess had done all she could to help me in my evil plight. I had to thank her here for the love she had shown to me, and for the education she had given me; I also bid her farewell, not expecting ever to see her again: we grasped each other's necks, and my hands grew stiff with cold, and I do not remember how we were torn from each other. I regained consciousness in the place that served as a cabin. I was lying in the bed, and my husband was standing over me, holding me by my hand, and making me smell some salts. I jumped down from my bed, ran upstairs, thinking that I would still catch a glimpse of it all, but those were all unfamiliar scenes,—we had sailed away a long distance. Then I noticed that I had lost a pearl that I wore on my finger; I evidently dropped it in the water as I bade my family farewell; I was not even sorry for it,— other thoughts were occupying me: life was lost, and I was left alone, had lost all for the sake of one man. And thus we sailed all night long.

The next day there was a stiff breeze; there was a storm on the river, and the thunder sounded more terrible on the water than on land, and I am naturally very much afraid of thunder. The vessel rolled from side to side, and every time it thundered people fell down. My younger sister-in-law was very much frightened, and wept and cried aloud. I thought the world had come to an end; we were compelled to make for the shore, where we passed a sleepless night in terror. As soon as it dawned, the storm subsided; we continued our voyage, which lasted three weeks. Whenever the weather was quiet, I sat near the window in the cabin; I wept or washed my kerchiefs, while the water was nearby. At times I bought a sturgeon, and, tying him to a rope, let him swim by my side, so that I was not the only captive, but the sturgeon with me. Whenever the wind began to rock the boat, my head began to ache, and I felt nauseated; then they took me out on deck, where I lay unconscious until the wind subsided, being covered with a fur coat: on the water the winds are piercing. Often he sat by my side, to keep me company. When the storm was over, I rested; but I could not eat much from nausea.

Here is what once happened to us: There was a frightful storm, and there was not a person on board who knew where there were the deep places and the shallows, or where we could land. The sailors were merely peasants that had been taken from the plough, and who were sailing where the wind bore them. It was getting dark, the night was near, and the wind did not permit us to make a landing. They threw out an anchor in the middle of the stream, where it was deepest, and the anchor was carried away. The companion of my misfortunes would not let me go on deck, for he was afraid that I would be crushed in the turmoil. The people were running all about the boat: some were pumping out the water, others were tying up the anchor; all were at work. While nothing was being done successfully, the boat was suddenly drawn into an eddy. I heard a terrible noise, and did not know what had happened. I arose to look out: our boat was standing as if in a box, between two shores. I asked where we were, but nobody could tell me, for they did not know themselves. On one shore there was nothing but a birch wood, but it was not a very thick forest. The earth on that shore began to settle, and the forest slid several fathoms into the river, or eddy, where we were standing. The forest rustled terribly under our very boat, and then we were lifted up, and again drawn into the eddy. Thus it lasted for a long time. All thought that we would perish, and the sailors were ready to save their lives in boats, and

to leave us to death.   Finally, so much of the land was torn
loose that only a small strip was left, and beyond it we could
see some water, supposedly a lake.   If that strip were carried away, we would be in that lake.   The wind was awful,
and our end would certainly have come, if God's mercy had
not saved us.   The wind calmed down, and no more land was
being carried away, and we were saved; at daylight we rode
out of the eddy into the river, and continued our voyage.
That eddy had carried part of my life away; yet I endured
it all, all the terrors, for the end of my sufferings was not
yet to be: I was preparing myself for greater woes, and God
gave me strength for them.

.   .   .   .

We reached the provincial town of the island where we
were to reside.   We were told that the way to that island
was by water, and that a change would be made here: the
officer of the guard was to return, and we were to be turned
over to an officer of the local garrison, with a detachment of
twenty-four soldiers.   We stayed here a week, while they
were fixing the boat that was to take us there, and we were
transferred from hand to hand, like prisoners.   It was such
a pitiable sight that even a heart of stone would be softened.
At this departure, the officer wept, and said: '' Now you will
suffer all kinds of insult.   These are not ordinary men: they
will treat you like common people, and will show you no
indulgence.''   We all wept, as if we were parting from a
relative.   We had at least gotten used to him.   However
badly we were off, yet he had known us in our fortune, and
he felt ashamed to treat us harshly.

When they had fixed the boat, a new commander took us
to it.   It was quite a procession.   A crowd of soldiers followed us, as if we were robbers.   I walked with downcast
eyes, and did not look around: there was a great number
of curious people along the road on which they led us.   We
arrived at the boat.   I was frightened when I saw it, for it
was quite different from the former one: out of disrespect to
us, they gave us a worthless one.   The boat was in accord-

ance with the designation which we bore, and they did not
care, if we were to perish the next day: we were simply
prisoners,—there was no other name for us. Oh, what can
there be worse than that appellation? The honour we received was in conformity with it! The boards on the boat
were all warped, and you could see daylight through them;
the moment a breeze began to blow, it creaked. It was
black with age and soot: labourers had been making fires in
it, and no one would have thought to travel in it. It had
been abandoned, and was intended for kindling wood. As
they were in a hurry with us, they did not dare keep us back
long, and gave us the first boat they could find. But maybe
they had express orders to drown us. God having willed
otherwise, we arrived safely at the appointed place.

We were compelled to obey a new commander. We tried
all means to gain his favour, but in vain. How could we
have found any means? God grant us to suffer with a
clever man! But he was a stupid officer. He had risen
from a common peasant to be a captain. He thought he
was a great man, and that we must be kept as severely as
possible, since we were criminals. He regarded it below his
dignity to speak to us; yet in spite of all his arrogance, he
came to dine with us. Consider for yourself whether the
man had any sense from the way he was dressed: he wore
his uniform right over his shirt, and slippers on his bare
feet; and thus he sat down to dinner with us! I was younger
than the rest, and uncontrollable: I could not help laughing
as I looked at his ridiculous get-up. He noticed that I was
laughing at him, and said, himself smiling: "Lucky for
you that my books have burnt, or I should have a talk with
you!" However bitter I felt, I tried to get him to talk
more; but he never uttered another word. Just think what
a commander we were given to watch us in all we did!
What were they afraid of? That we would run away?
Not their watch kept us back, but our innocence: we were
sure that in time they would see their error, and would
return us to our former possessions. Besides, we were re-
strained by the fact that we had a large family. And thus

we sailed with the stupid commander a whole month until we arrived at the town where we were to reside.

Mikhaíl Vasílevich Lomonósov. (1711-1765.)

Lomonósov was born in the village of Denísovka, in the Government of Arkhángelsk, not far from the spot where, one hundred and fifty years before, the English had rediscovered Russia. In his letters to Shuválov, Lomónosov tells us of the difficulties with which he had to contend at home and at the School of the Redeemer at Moscow. His brilliant progress caused him to be chosen among the first men to be sent abroad at Government expense to study mining, and to get acquainted with mining methods in Holland, England and France. In spite of insufficient support from the Government and a roving life at German universities, Lomonósov made excellent progress in philosophy, under Christian Wolff at Marburg, and in the sciences at Freiburg. After marrying a German woman, wandering about and starving, Lomónosov returned to St. Petersburg. Before reaching home, he had sent to St. Petersburg his *Ode on the Occasion of the Capture of Khotín*. It was the first time the tonic versification was successfully applied to the language, and though the diction of the ode is turgid and the enthusiasm forced, yet it became the model for a vast family of odes and eulogies, generally written to order, until Derzhávin introduced a new style with his *Felítsa*.

Upon his return, Lomonósov became attached to the University, which was mainly filled with German professors. His own unamiable temper, combined with the not more amiable characters of German colleagues, was the cause of endless quarrels and exasperations. Under the most depressing difficulties, Lomonósov, the first learned Russian, developed a prodigious activity. He perfected the Russian literary language, lectured on rhetoric and the sciences and wrote text-books, odes and dramas. For a century he passed in Russia as a great poet, and his deserts in other directions were disregarded. But a more sober criticism sees now in Lomonósov a great scientist who has increased knowledge by several discoveries, and only a second-rate poet. Only where he described phenomena of nature or scientific facts, did he become really inspired, and write poems that have survived him. His services to the Russian language and literature are many. He did for them what Peter the Great did for the State: by his own mighty personality and example he put them on the road which they have never abandoned, and though lacking originality, the school of Lomonósov itself survived in Russian literature to the end of the eighteenth century.

But few of Lomonósov's poems have been translated into English.

Ode from Job, Morning Meditations, Evening Meditations, are given in Sir John Bowring's *Specimens of the Russian Poets,* Part II.; the *Evening Meditations,* in another version, is also given by him in Part I.

Ode in Honour of the Empress Anna, in F. R. Grahame's *The Progress of Science, Art and Literature in Russia.*

Morning Meditation, and part of the *Ode on the Accession of Catherine II.,* in C. E. Turner's *Studies in Russian Literature,* and, the same article, in Fraser's Magazine, 1877.

A Chronological Abridgement of Russian History; translated from the original Russian . . . and continued to the present by the translator (J. G. A. F.), London, 1767.

LETTERS TO I. I. SHUVÁLOV [1]

I

Dear Sir, Iván Ivánovich:—Your Excellency's kind consideration in honouring me with a letter assures me, to my great joy, of your unchanged feelings to me, and this I have for many years regarded as one of my great fortunes. How could the august generosity of our incomparable Empress, which I enjoy through your fatherly intercession, divert me from my love and zeal to the sciences, when extreme poverty, which I have endured voluntarily for the sake of science, has not been able to distract me from it? Let not your Excellency think it self-praise in me, if I am bold to present to you my defence.

When I was studying in the School of the Redeemer, I was surrounded on all sides with powerful obstacles that made against science, and in those years the influence of these tendencies was almost insurmountable. On the one hand, my father, who had never had any other children but me, said that in leaving him I, being his only son, had left all his possessions (such as they were in those parts), which he had acquired for me in the sweat of his brow, and which strangers would carry away after his death. On the other

[1] To his patron, upon his having expressed his fear that Lomonósov would lose his zeal for the sciences when he received the gift of an estate from the Empress.

hand, I was confronted with unspeakable poverty: as I received but three kopeks a day, all I dared spend a day for food was half a kopek for bread and half a kopek for kvas, while the rest went for paper, shoes and other necessities. In this way I passed five years, and did not abandon study. On the one hand, they wrote to me that, knowing the well-being of my father, well-to-do people of my village would give me their daughters in marriage, and in fact they proposed them to me, when I was there; on the other hand, the small schoolboys pointed their fingers at me, and cried: "Look at the clodhopper who has come to study Latin at the age of twenty!" Soon after that I was taken to St. Petersburg, and was sent abroad, receiving an allowance forty times as large as before. But that did not divert my attention from study, but proportionately increased my eagerness, though there is a limit to my strength. I most humbly beg your Excellency to feel sure that I will do all in my power to cause all those who ask me to be wary in my zeal to have no anxiety about me, and that those who judge me with malicious envy should be put to shame in their unjust opinion, and should learn that they must not measure others with their yardstick, and should also remember that the Muses love whom they list.

If there is anyone who persists in the opinion that a learned man must be poor, I shall quote on his side Diogenes, who lived in a barrel with dogs, and left his countrymen a few witticisms for the increase of their pride; on the other side I shall mention Newton, the rich Lord Boyle, who had acquired all his glory in the sciences through the use of a large sum of money; Wolff, who with his lectures and presents had accumulated more than five hundred thousand, and had earned, besides, a baronetcy; Sloane, in England, who had left such a library that no private individual was able to purchase it, and for which Parliament gave twenty thousand pounds. I shall not fail to carry out your commands, and remain with deep respect your Excellency's most humble servant, Mikháylo Lomonósov. St. Petersburg, May 10, 1753.

II

Dear Sir, Iván Ivánovich:—I received yesterday your Excellency's letter of May 24th, in which I see an unchangeable token of your distinguished favour to me, and which has greatly pleased me, especially because you have deigned to express your assurance that I would never abandon the sciences. I do not at all wonder at the judgment of the others, for they really have had the example in certain people who, having barely opened for themselves the road to fortune, have at once set out on other paths and have sought out other means for their farther advancement than the sciences, which they have entirely abandoned; their patrons ask little or nothing of them, and are satisfied with their mere names, not like your Excellency who ask for my works in order to judge me. In these above-mentioned men, who in their fortune have abandoned science, all can easily perceive that all they know is what they have acquired in their infancy under the rod, and that they have added no new knowledge since they have had control of themselves. But it has been quite different with me (permit me, dear sir, to proclaim the truth not for the sake of vainglory, but in order to justify myself): my father was a good-hearted man, but he was brought up in extreme ignorance; my step-mother was an evil and envious woman, and she tried with all her might and main to rouse my father's anger by representing to him that I eternally wasted my time with books; so I was frequently compelled to read and study anything that fell into my hands, in lonely and deserted places, and to suffer cold and hunger, until I went to the School of the Redeemer.

Now that I have, through your fatherly intercession, a complete sufficiency from her august Imperial Highness, and your approbation of my labours, and that of other experts and lovers of the sciences, and almost their universal delight in them, and finally no longer a childish reasoning of an imperfect age,—how could I in my manhood disgrace my early life ? But I shall stop troubling your patience with these considerations, knowing your just opinion of me. So I shall report to your Excellency that which your praiseworthy zeal wishes to know of the sciences.

First, as to electricity: There have lately been made here two important experiments, one by Mr. Richmann by means of the apparatus, the other by me in the clouds. By the first it was proved that Musschenbroek's experiment with a strong discharge can be transferred from place to place, separating it from the apparatus for a considerable distance, even as much as half a mile. The second experiment was made on my lightning apparatus, when, without any perceptible thunder or lightning, on the 25th of April, the thread was repelled from the iron rod and followed my hand; and on the 28th of the same month, during the passage of a rain-cloud without any perceptible thunder or lightning, there were loud discharges from the lightning apparatus, with bright sparks and a crackling that could be heard from a great distance. This has never been noticed before, and it agrees completely with my former theory of heat and my present one of the electric power, and this will serve me well at the next public lecture. This lecture I shall deliver in conjunction with Professor Richmann: he will present his experiments, and I shall illustrate the theory and usefulness arising from them; I am now preparing for this lecture.

As to the second part of the text-book on eloquence, it is well on its way, and I hope to have it printed by the end of October. I shall use all my endeavour to have it out soon; I do not send your Excellency any manuscript of it, as you have asked for printed sheets. As I have promised, I am also using all my endeavour in regard to the first volume of the *Russian History*, so as to have it ready in manuscript by the new year. From him who delivers lectures in his subject, who makes new experiments, delivers public lectures and dissertations, and besides composes all kinds of verses and projects for solemn expressions of joy; who writes out the rules of eloquence for his native language and a history of his country, which, at that, he has to furnish for a certain date,—I cannot demand anything more, and I am ready to be patient with him, provided something sensible will result in the end.

Having again and again convinced myself that your Excellency likes to converse about science, I eagerly await a pleasant meeting with you, in order to satisfy you with my latest endeavours, for it is not possible to communicate them all to you at a distance. I cannot see when I shall be able to arrange, as I had promised, the optical apparatus in your Excellency's house, for there are no floors, nor ceilings, nor staircases in it yet, and I lately walked around in it with no small degree of danger to myself. The electric balls I shall send you, as you wish, without delay, as soon as possible. I must inform your Excellency that there is here a great scarcity in mechanics, so that I have not been able to get anywhere, not even at your estate, a joiner for any money, to build me an electric apparatus, so that up to the present I have been making use, instead of a terrestrial machine, of the clouds, to which I have had a pole erected from the roof. Whatever instruments your Excellency may need, I beg you to permit me to report in the office of the Academy in your name that the orders for them should be given to the mechanics, or else the business will be endlessly prolonged. In fine, I remain, with the expression of deep respect, your most humble and faithful servant, Mikháylo Lomonósov. St. Petersburg, May 31, 1753.

ODE IN HONOUR OF THE EMPRESS ANNA, ON THE OCCASION OF THE CAPTURE OF KHOTÍN FROM THE TURKS, BY THE RUSSIAN ARMIES, IN 1739

A sudden ecstasy has seized my soul; it transports me to the summit of a lofty mountain, where the wind has ceased to howl, and all is hushed in the deep valleys below. Silent are the listening streams, to which it is natural to murmur, or with loud rush to roll down the mountains; crowns of laurel are weaving; thither rumour is seen to hasten; afar off the blue smoke rises in the fields.

Is not Pindus beneath my feet? I hear the sweet music of the pure sisters. Parnassian fire burns within me. I hasten to the sacred band. They offer me to taste of the healing stream. " Drink, and forget thy troubles; bathe thine eyes in Castilian dew; stretch them forth over the deserts and hills, and fix them on the spot where the bright light of day is seen rising out of the dark shadows of night."

As a ship, amidst the angry waves which seek to over-whelm her, sails on triumphantly, and appears to threaten should they dare to impede her course; grey froth foams around her, her track is imprinted in the deep; thus crowds of Tartars rush towards and surround the Russian forces, but in vain; powerless and breathless they fall.

The love of their country nerves the souls and arms of Russia's sons; eager are all to shed their blood; the raging tumult but inspires them with fresh courage; as the lion, by the fearful glare of his eyes, drives before him whole herds of wolves, their sharp teeth vainly showing; the woods and shores tremble at his roar; with his tail he lashes the sand and dust; with his strength he beats down every opposing force.

Hear I not the deafening din of Ætna's forges? Roars not the brass within, bubbling with boiling sulphur? Is not Hell striving to burst its chains, and ope its jaws? The posterity of the rejected deity have filled the mountain track with fire, and hurl down flame and liquid metal; but neither foe nor nature can withstand the burning ardour of our people.

Send away thy hordes, Stamboul, beyond these mount-ains, where the fiery elements vomit forth smoke, ashes, flame and death; beyond the Tigris, whose strong waves drag after them the huge stones from the shores, but the world holds no impediment to arrest the eagle in his flight. To him the waters, the woods, the mountains, the preci-pices and the silent deserts are but as level paths; wherever the wind can blow, thither he can wing his way.

Let the earth be all motion like the sea; let myriads

oppose; let thickest smoke darken the universe; let the Moldavian mountains swim in blood; such cannot harm you, O Russians! whose safety Fate itself has decreed for the sake of the blessed Anna. Already in her course your zeal has led you in triumph against the Tartars, and wide is the prospect before you.

The parting ray of daylight falls gently into the waters, and leaves the fight to the night fires; Murza has fallen on his long shadow; in him the light and soul of the infidels pass from them. A wolf issues from the thick forest and rushes on the pale carcass, even in the Turkish camp. A dying Tartar, raising his eyes towards the evening star for the last time, " Hide," he feebly cries, " thy purple light, and with it the shame of Mahomet; descend quickly with the sun into the sea."

Why is my soul thus oppressed with terror? My veins grow stiff, my heart aches. Strange tones meet mine ear; a howling noise seems passing through the desert, the woods and the air. The wild beast has taken refuge in its cavern; the gates of heaven are opened; a cloud has spread itself over the army; suddenly a countenance of fire shines forth: a hero appears chasing his enemies before him, his sword all red with blood.

Is it not he who, near the rapid waters of the Don, destroyed the walls raised to check the Russians' progress? And the Persians in their arid deserts, was it not by his arms they fell? Thus looked he on his foes when he approached the Gothic shores; thus lifted he his powerful arm; thus swiftly his proud horse galloped over those fields where we see the morning star arise.

Loud thunder rattles around him; the plains and the forests tremble at the approach of Peter, who by his side so sternly looks towards the south, girt round with dreadful thunder! Is it not the conqueror of Kazán? It is he, ye Caspian waters, who humbled the proud Selim, and strewed the desert with the dead bodies of his enemies.

Thus the heroes addressed each other: " Not in vain we toiled; not fruitless our united efforts, that the whole world should stand in awe of Russia. By the aid of our arms, our boundaries have been widened on the north, on the west, and on the east. Anna now triumphs in the south; she has crowned her troops with victory.'' The cloud has passed, and the heroes within it: the eye no longer sees, the ear no longer hears them.

The blood of the Tartar has purpled the river; he dares not again venture to the fight; he seeks refuge in the desert; and, forgetful alike of the sword, the camp, his own shame, he pictures to himself his friends weltering in their blood; the waving of the light leaf startles him like whizzing balls as they fly through the air.

The shouts of the victors echo through the woods and valleys; but the wretch who abandons the fight dreads his own shadow. The moon, a witness to her children's flight, shares in their shame, and, deeply reddening, hides her face in darkness. Fame flies through the gloom of the night; her trumpet proclaims to the universe the terrible might of Russia.

The Danube rushes into the sea, and, roaring in echo to the acclamations of the conquerors, dashes its furious waves against the Turk, who seeks to hide his shame behind its waters. To and fro he runs like a wild beast wounded, and, despairing, he thinks that for the last time he moves his steps; the earth disdains to support the wretch who could not guard her; darkness and fear confuse his path.

Where is now the boasting Stamboul?—thy courage, thy obstinacy in the fight, thy malice against the nations of the North, thy contempt of our strength? No sooner hadst thou commanded thy hordes to advance than thou thoughtest to conquer; cruelly thy janissary vented his rage; like a tiger he rushed upon the Muscovite troop. Soon the boaster fell; he weltered in his own blood.

Water with your tears, children of Hagar, the foot which has trampled you down! Kiss ye that hand whose bloody sword brought fear before your eyes. Anna's stern glance is quick to grant relief to those who seek it; it shines forth, for the storm has passed away. She sees you prostrate before her; fervent in affection towards her own subjects, to her enemies she proffers punishment or pardon.

Already has the golden finger of the morning star withdrawn the starry curtain of night; a horse fleet as the wind, his rider Phœbus in the full blaze of his glory, issues from the east, his nostrils breathing sparks of radiant light. Phœbus shakes his fiery head, dwells in wonder on the glorious work and exclaims: " Few such victories have I witnessed, long as I have continued to give light to the world, long as the circle of ages has revolved."

Like as the serpent rolls itself up, hissing and hiding its sting under a rock, when the eagle, soaring into those regions where the winds blow not, above lightnings, snow and tempests, looks down upon the beasts, the fishes and the reptiles beneath him, thus Khotín trembles before the eagle of Russia; thus its inhabitants crouch within its walls.

What led your Tartar race, Kalchák,[1] to bend so promptly beneath the Russian power? to deliver up the keys of your town in token of submission, evading thus disgrace more deep? The clemency of Anna, of her who is ever ready to raise the suppliant. Where flows the Vistula, and where the glorious Rhine, even there her olive-trees have flourished; there have the proud hearts of her defeated foes yielded up their lives.

Joyful are the lands which have thrown off the cruel yoke; the burden the Turks had laid on them is thrown back upon themselves! The barbarian hands which held them in restraint now wear their chains in captivity; and the feet are shackled which trampled down the field of the stranger, and drove away his flocks.

Not thus alone must thou be humbled; not all thy punishment this, O Turkey! A far greater hast thou merited, for thou didst refuse to let us live in peace. Still does the rage of your haughty souls forbid you to bend before Anna? Where would ye hide yourselves from her? Damascus, Cairo, Aleppo, shall flame! Crete shall be surrounded with her fleets; Euphrates shall be dyed with your blood.

[1] Kalchák-pasha was the commander of Khotín.

A sudden and universal change! A dazzling vision passes before my eyes, and with heaven's purest beams outshines the brightness of the day! The voices of heroes strike upon my ear. Anna's joyous band, in glory clad, bear up eternity beyond the starry orbs, and Truth with her golden pen traces her glorious deeds in that book which is not reached by corruption.

Russia thrives like a young lily under Anna's care; within China's distant walls she is honoured, and every corner of the earth is filled with her subjects' glory. Happy art thou, O my country, under the rule of thy Empress! Bright the laurels thou hast gained by this triumph. Fear not the ills of war; they fly from the land where Anna is glorified by her people. Malicious envy may pour forth her poison, she may gnaw her tongue in rage. Our joy heeds it not.

The robbers who, from beyond the Dniester, came to plunder the fields of the Cossacks, are driven back, scattered like dust; no longer dare they venture on that soil where the fruits of the earth and the blessings of peace together flourish. In safety the merchant pursues his traffic, and the mariner sees a boundary to the waves; no obstacles impede his course. The old and the young are happy; he who wished for the hour of death now prays for lengthened life; his heart is gladdened by his country's triumphs.

The shepherd drives his flocks into the meadow, and enters the forest without fear; there, with his friend who tends his sheep, he sings the song of joy, his theme the bravery of the soldier; he blesses the passing moments of his life, and implores endless peace on the spot where he sleeps in quiet. Thus, in the simple sincerity of his heart, he glorifies her who shields him from his enemies.

O thou great Empress! The love of Russia, the dread of thy foes, the heroine of the northern world, the hope, the joy, the goddess of the shores of seven wide seas, thou shinest in the cloudless lights of goodness and beneficence. Forgive thy slave that he has chosen thy glory for his lay, and that his rugged verse, in token of submission to thy rule, has thus dared to attempt to magnify thy power.—Given in F.

R. Grahame's *The Progress of Science, Art and Literature in Russia.*

MORNING MEDITATIONS

O'er the wide earth yon torch of heavenly light
Its splendour spreads and God's proud works unveils;
My soul, enraptured at the marvellous sight,
Unwonted peace, and joy, and wonder feels,
And with uplifted thoughts of ecstasy
Exclaims, " How great must their Creator be!"

Or, if a mortal's power could stretch so high—
If mortal sight could reach that glorious sun,
And look undazzled at its majesty,
'T would seem a fiery ocean burning on
From time's first birth, whose ever-flaming ray
Could ne'er extinguished be by time's decay.

There waves of fire 'gainst waves of fire are dashing,
And know no bounds; there hurricanes of flame,
As if in everlasting combat flashing,
Roar with a fury which no time can tame:
There molten mountains boil like ocean-waves,
And rain in burning streams the welkin laves.

But in Thy presence all is but a spark,
A little spark: that wondrous orb was lighted
By Thy own hand, the dreary and the dark
Pathway of man to cheer—of man benighted;
To guide the march of seasons in their way,
And place us in a paradise of day.

Dull Night her sceptre sways o'er plains and hills,
O'er the dark forest and the foaming sea;
Thy wondrous energy all nature fills,
And leads our thoughts, and leads our hopes to Thee.
" How great is God!" a million tongues repeat,
And million tongues re-echo, " God, how great!"

But now again the day star bursts the gloom,
Scattering its sunshine o'er the opening sky;
Thy eye, that pierces even through the tomb,
Has chased the clouds, has bid the vapours fly;
And smiles of light, descending from above,
Bathe all the universe with joy and love.
—From Sir John Bowring's *Specimens of the Russian Poets.*

EVENING MEDITATIONS

ON SEEING THE AURORA BOREALIS

The day retires, the mists of night are spread
Slowly o'er nature, darkening as they rise;
The gloomy clouds are gathering round our heads,
And twilight's latest glimmering gently dies:'
The stars awake in heaven's abyss of blue;
Say, who can count them?—Who can sound it?—Who?

Even as a sand in the majestic sea,
A diamond-atom on a hill of snow,
A spark amidst a Hecla's majesty,
An unseen mote where maddened whirlwinds blow,
And I midst scenes like these—the mighty thought
O'erwhelms me—I am nought, or less than nought.

And science tells me that each twinkling star
That smiles above us is a peopled sphere,
Or central sun, diffusing light afar;
A link of nature's chain:—and there, even there,
The Godhead shines displayed—in love and light,
Creating wisdom—all-directing might.

Where are thy secret laws, O Nature, where?
In wintry realms thy dazzling torches blaze,
And from thy icebergs streams of glory there
Are poured, while other suns their splendent race
In glory run: from frozen seas what ray
Of brightness?—From yon realms of night what day?

Philosopher, whose penetrating eye
Reads nature's deepest secrets, open now
This all-inexplicable mystery:
Why do earth's darkest, coldest regions glow
With lights like these?—Oh, tell us, knowing one,
For thou dost count the stars, and weigh the sun!

Whence are these varied lamps all lighted round?—
Whence all the horizon's glowing fire?—The heaven
Is splendent as with lightning—but no sound
Of thunder—all as calm as gentlest even ;
And winter's midnight is as bright, as gay,
As the fair noontide of a summer's day.

What stores of fire are these, what magazine,
Whence God from grossest darkness light supplies?
What wondrous fabric which the mountains screen,
Whose bursting flames above those mountains rise;
Where rattling winds disturb the mighty ocean,
And the proud waves roll with eternal motion?

Vain is the inquiry—all is darkness, doubt:
This earth is one vast mystery to man.
First find the secrets of this planet out,
Then other planets, other systems scan!
Nature is veiled from thee, presuming clod!
And what canst thou conceive of Nature's God?
—From Sir John Bowring's *Specimens of the Russian Poets*.

Alexander Petróvich Sumarókov. (1718–1777.)

Sumarókov is the first littérateur of Russia, that is, the first man to regard literature as a profession, independently of an official position. After graduating from the military school, in 1740, he served for a while under some military commanders, but devoted all his leisure time to writing poetry according to the rules laid down by Tredyakóv-ski. There was no species of poetical literature in which he did not try himself and did not produce prolifically. He has left odes, eulogies, fables, satires and dramas. In many of these he broke virgin soil in Russia, and in his unexampled conceit he was not slow to proclaim his highest deserts : " What Athens has seen and Paris now sees, after a long period of transition, that you, O Russia, have perceived at once by my efforts." In spite of his mediocrity and acquaintance with only the pseudo-classic French style (for he disdained all serious study of antiquity), Sumarókov was highly valued in his day, and his example has done much to advance Russian literature. In 1756 the Russian Theatre was created by a decree of the Senate, and Sumarókov was chosen as its first director. To fill his repertoire, he was compelled to write plays himself, and he produced them with astounding facility. His best drama is probably *The False Demetrius*, though there is little historical truth in it. In 1761 he issued the first independent journal, *The Industrious Bee*, which, however, was filled mainly with his own writings. Sumarókov's influence on Russian letters lasted up to the time of Púshkin, though Karamzín was the first to doubt his greatness.

Sumarókov's *The False Demetrius* has been translated into English: *Demetrius the Impostor;* a tragedy [in five acts and in prose], translated from the Russian, London, 1806.

Act II., Scene 7, is also given in C. E. Turner's *Studies in Russian Literature*, and, the same, in Fraser's Magazine, 1877.

THE FALSE DEMETRIUS

ACT II., SCENE I.   GEORGE AND XENIA

Xenia. Blessed in the world is that purple-bearing man who does not suppress the freedom of our souls, who elevates himself for society's good, and with leniency adorns his royal dignity, who gives his subjects auspicious days, and whom evildoers alone have cause to fear.

George. O thou sad Kremlin! Thou art this day a witness how that virtue was cast down from the throne. Languishing Moscow trembles in despair; happiness flees its walls in sorrow; the bright days seem darker than dense night; the fair groves about Moscow are clad in sombreness. When the solemn bell rings in the city, it seems to us that it repeats the city's general groan and that it proclaims our Church's fall through the machinations of the pope. O Lord, remove that terror from the Russians! Already the report flies through the square that Clement has promised reward in heaven to the rebels, the foes of our country's city, and that he in advance forgives them all their sins. Moscow will suffer as suffers the New World! There the papists have

stained with blood the earth, have slaughtered its inhabitants, have plundered the surviving, have burnt the innocent
in their own land, holding the cross in one hand, in the other
—the bloody sword. What has happened to them in their
dire fate will now, O Russia, be done to you!

Xenia. All powers of evil,—Demetrius, Clement, Hell,—
will not efface you from my heart! O Heaven, remove the
fury of the papal power, and with it Xenia's unbearable
distress, that Russia might raise its head, and I might be
my sweetheart's wife! Grant us to see the monarch on the
throne, subject to truth, not arbitrary will! All truth has
withered; the tyrant's law is only what he wants; but on the
happiness of their subjects are based the laws of righteous
kings, for their immortal glory. God's vicar is to be the
Tsar. Strike me, destroy me, merciless Tsar! Megæra has
swept you from Tartarus, the Caucasus has borne you, Hyr-
cania has nurtured you. The heretic, with his crowd of
slaves, will, cursing, oust the bodies of saintly men from their
graves. Their names will in Russia for ever perish, and the
houses of God will in Moscow be deserted. Nation, tear the
crown from the creator of dire torments; hasten, wrest
the sceptre from the barbarian's hands!

SCENE 7

Demetrius (alone). My crown lies not firmly upon my head,
and the end of my greatness is at hand. Each moment I
expect a sudden change. O Kremlin's walls that frighten
me! Meseems each hour you announce to me: "Villain,
you are a foe, a foe to us and the whole land!" The citizens
proclaim: "You have ruined us!" And the temples weep:
"We are stained with blood!" The fair places about Moscow are deserted, and Hell from its abyss has oped its jaws
at me; I see the sombre steps that lead to the infernal regions, and the tormented shades of Tartarus: I am already
in Gehenna, and burn in the flame; I cast my glance to
heaven, and see the celestial regions: there are good kings
in all the beauty of their natures, and angels besprinkle them
with dew of paradise; but what hope have I to-day in my

despair? I shall be tormented in eternity even as I suffer now. I am not a crowned potentate in a magnificent city, but an evil malefactor, in hell tormented. I perish, dragging a multitude of the people to destruction. Flee, tyrant, flee! From whom?—From myself, for I see no one else before me. Run! But whither? Your hell is ever with you! The assassin is here, run! But I am that assassin! I tremble before myself, and before my shade. I shall avenge myself! On whom? Myself. Do I hate myself? I love myself! For what? I see it not. All cry against me: rapine, unfair justice, all terrible things,—they cry together against me. I live to the misfortune, shall die to the fortune of my nearest. The fate of men, the lowliest, I envy: even the mendicant is sometimes happy in his poverty. But I rule here,—and am always tormented. Endure and perish, having ascended the throne by deceit! Drive, and be driven! Live and die a tyrant!

INSTRUCTION TO A SON

Perceiving his tearful end near at hand, a father thus instructed his beloved, only begotten son:

" My son, beloved son! I am old to-day; my mind grows dull, my fervour is all gone; I am preparing to go before the Judge, and shall soon pass to eternity, the immeasurable abode of mortals. So I wish to tell you how you may live, and to show you the road to happiness. You will travel over a slippery path: though all in the world is vanity, yet why should one disdain happiness in life? Our whole mind ought to be bent upon obtaining it, and our endeavour should be to get all we need.

" Give up that chimera which men call honour; of what good is it when you have nothing to eat? It is impossible to get along in commerce without cheating, and in poverty without dishonesty and theft. By hook and by crook I have scraped together a fortune for you; now, if you should squander it all, I shall have sold my soul in vain. Whenever I think of that, my rest is gone.

17

" Increase your income, keep indolence from your heart, and keep your money against an evil day. Steal, if you can steal, but do it secretly,—by all means increase your income every year! The eye is not satisfied with mere looking on. If you can cheat, cheat artfully, for 't is a shame to be caught in the act, and it often leads to the gallows. Make no acquaintances for the mere sake of knowing them, but put your spoon there where the jam is thickest! Revere the rich, to get your tribute from them. Never tire praising them with condescension ; but if they be distinguished people, subdue them by creeping!

" Be humble with all men, and simulate! If a mighty person chides anyone, together with the mighty chide him! Praise those whom the powerful praise, and belittle those they belittle! Keep your eyes wide open and watch whom great boyárs are angry with.

" If you walk upon the straight road, you will find no fortune. Swim there where favourable winds carry you! Against men whom the people honour speak not a word; and let your soul be ever ready to thank them, though you receive nothing from them! Endeavour to speak like them. Whatever the puissant man says are sacred words; never contradict him, for you are a small man! If he say red of that which is black, say too: ' 'T is rather red!' Before low-born men rave like a devil; for if you do not, they will forget who you are, and will not respect you: the common people honour those who are haughty. But before the high-born leap like a frog, and remember that a farthing is as nothing in comparison with a rouble. Big souls have they, but we, my beloved son, have only little souls! Be profuse in thanks, if you expect some favour from your benefactor; spare your thanks where you have nothing to gain, for your grateful spirit will be lost.

" Do yourself no injury, and remain honest to yourself, loving yourself most sincerely! Do no injury to yourself, but for others have only appearances, and remember how little wisdom there is in the world, and how many fools. Satisfy them with empty words: honour yourself with your heart, but others with your lips, for you will have to pay no toll for fondling them. Let others think that you place yourself much lower than them, and that you have little regard for yourself; but do not forget that your shirt is nearer to your body than your caftan!

" I will allow you to play cards, provided you know how to handle them. A game without cunning has no interest, and playing you must not sacrifice yourself to others. Whatever game you play, my son, remember not to be always honest!—Have contempt for peasants, seeing them below your feet, but let your lips proclaim the puissant as gods, and speak no surly word to them. But love none of them, no matter what their worth, though their deeds be trumpeted through the subsolar world! Give bribes, and yourself accept them! When there are no witnesses, steal and cheat as much as you please, but be wary with your misdoings in presence of witnesses! Change the good that there is in people into evil, and never say a good word of another! For what are you to gain from praising them? Indeed, their virtues put you only in a bad light. Go not out of the way to serve another, where there is no gain for you.

" Hate the learned, and despise the ignorant, and ever keep your thoughts fresh for your own advantage! Above all, beware of getting into the satire of impudent scribblers! Disturb and break the ties of families, friendship and marriage, for 't is more convenient to fish in muddy waters. Know no love, family nor friends, for ever holding yourself alone in mind! Deceive your friends, and let them suffer through you sorrow and misfortune, if you are the winner thereby! Garner your fruits wherever you can! There are some who foolishly call it dishonest to bring woes to your friends, but they do not see that duty teaches me only to love myself, and that it is not at all dishonourable when necessity demands that others perish: it is contrary to nature not to love yourself best. Let misfortune befall my country, let it go to the nethermost regions; let everything that is not mine be ruined,—provided I have peace.

"Forget not my rules! I have left you my fortune and my wisdom. Live, my son, live as your father has lived!"

He had barely uttered these words, when he was struck by lightning, and he departed from his child and home; and the soul that had for so long been disseminating poison flew out of the body and took its flight to hell.

TO THE CORRUPTERS OF LANGUAGE

In a strange land there lived a dog in a thick forest. He deemed his citizens to be uncultured, so passed his days in the country of the wolves and bears. The dog no longer barked, but growled like a bear, and sang the songs of wolves. When he returned to the dogs, he out of reason adorned his native tongue. He mixed the growl of bears and howl of wolves into his bark, and began to speak unintelligibly to dogs. The dogs said: "We need not your new-fangled music—you only spoil our language with it"; and they began to bite him, until they killed him.

I have read the tombstone of that dog: "Never disdain your native speech, and introduce into it nothing foreign, but adorn yourself with your own beauty."

THE HELPFUL GNAT

Six fine horses were pulling an immense carriage. The carriage would have been a heavy one without any people in it; but this enormous carriage was filled with people, and was in size a haystack. It slowly moved along, travelling not over boards, but carrying the master and his wife through heavy sand, in which it finally stuck fast. The horses' strength gave out; the lackeys on the footboard, to save the horses and wheels, stepped down; but yet the rick did not move. The driver called to the horses: "Get up, get up!" and struck them with the whip, as if it was their guilt. He struck them hard and yelled and yelled, until he grew hoarse, while the horses were covered with foam, and steam rose from them.

A gnat flew by, perceived the plight of the carriage, and

was anxious to do it a good turn, and help it out. So it began to goad the horses and the driver, to make the driver on his box more agile, and that the horses might draw with more vim. Now it stung the driver, now the horses; it perspired, worked with might and main, but all in vain; it buzzed and buzzed, but all its songs were useless; there was not the slightest sign that the carriage would move; so after having laboured hard, it flew away. In the meanwhile, the horses had rested themselves, and dragged the huge mass out of the sand. The gnat saw the carriage from afar, and said: " How foolish it all was of me to abandon the carriage just as it was to move! 'T is true I have worked hard in the sand, but at least I have moved the carriage."

FOUR ANSWERS

You ask me, my friend, what I would do: (1) if I were a small man and a small gentleman; (2) if I were a great man and a small gentleman; (3) if I were a great man and a great gentleman; (4) if I were a small man and a great gentleman. To the first question I answer: I should use all my endeavour to become acquainted in the houses of distinguished people and men of power; I would not allow a single holiday to pass, without making the round of the city, in order to give the compliments of the season; I would walk on tiptoes in the antechambers of the mighty, and would treat their valets to tobacco; I would learn to play all kinds of games, for when you play cards you can sit down shoulder to shoulder with the most distinguished people, and then bend over to them and say in a low tone: " I have the honour to report to your Excellency such and such an affair," or again become bolder and exclaim: " You have thirteen and I fourteen." I would not dispute anything, but would only say: "Just so; certainly so; most certainly so; absolutely so." I would tell the whole world that such and such a distinguished gentleman had condescended to speak to me, and if I could not say so truthfully, I would lie about it, for nothing so adorns speech as a lie, to which poets are witnesses.

Finally, I would obtain by humility and flattery a profitable place, but above all I would strive to become a governor, for that place is profitable, honourable and easy. It is profitable, because everybody brings gifts; it is honourable, because everybody bows before a governor; it is easy, because there is very little work to do, and that is done by a secretary or scribe, and, they being sworn people, one may entirely rely upon them. A scribe has been created by God by whom man has been created, and that opinion is foolish which assumes that a scribe's soul is devoid of virtue. I believe there is little difference between a man and a scribe, much less difference than between a scribe and any other creature.

If I were a great man and a small gentleman, I would, in my constant attempt to be useful to my country and the world at large, never become burdensome to anyone, and would put all my reliance upon my worth and my deserts to my country; and if I should find myself deceived in this, I should become insane from so much patience, and should be a man who not only does nothing, but even thinks nothing.

If I were a great man and a great gentleman, I would without cessation think of the welfare of my country, of incitements to virtue and dignity, the reward of merit, the suppression of vice and lawlessness, the increase of learning, the cheapening of the necessaries of life, the preservation of justice, the punishment for taking bribes, for grasping, robbery and theft, the diminution of lying, flattery, hypocrisy and drunkenness, the expulsion of superstition, the abatement of unnecessary luxury, the limitation of games at cards which rob people of their valuable time, the education, the founding and maintenance of schools, the maintenance of a well-organised army, the scorn of rudeness, and the eradication of parasitism.

But if I were a small man and a great gentleman, I would live in great magnificence, for such magnificence is rarely to be found in a great soul; but I will not say what else I would do.

Vasíli Ivánovich Máykov. (1728–1778.)

Máykov was the son of a landed proprietor. He entered military service, in 1766 was made Associate Governor of Moscow, and occupied other high offices. He began to write early and, being an admirer of Sumarókov,—like all the other writers of his day,—he wrote odes, eulogies, fables, tragedies, all of them in the pseudo-classic style. He knew no foreign languages, and his imitations are at second hand. This, however, gave him a great advantage over his contemporaries, in that he was better acquainted with Russian reality than with foreign models. His mock-heroic poem *Eliséy, or Excited Bacchus*, from which "The Battle of the Zimogórans and Valdáyans," given below, is an extract, is far superior for real humour, Russian environment and good popular diction to anything else produced by the Russian writers of the eighteenth century ; and the undisputed popularity of the *Eliséy*, which was not dimmed even by Bogdanóvich's *Pysche*, was well merited.

THE BATTLE OF THE ZIMOGÓRANS AND VAL-DÁYANS

The field was all ploughed and sowed in oats, and after these labours all the cattle and we were resting. Already had the grain sprouted a quarter of an inch, and our time had come to cut the hay. Our meadow, as all know well, bordered on the meadow of the Valdáyans; no one could tell where the line between them was but a surveyor, so the strongest hand mowed the grass there, and the meadows were always a cause of quarrels; even then they were the cause of our terrible battle.

The day had come, and we went into the meadow, taking with us milk, eggs and whey-cheese, loading ourselves with kvas, beets, dumplings, brandy and buckwheat cakes. No sooner had we appeared with our provender in the meadow, than we espied the host before us: the proud Valdáyans were standing there with arms of war. We became frightened and ran away like rabbits, and running we looked for weapons resembling theirs: withes, pales, poles, cudgels and clubs. We vied with each other to arm ourselves with sticks and to prepare ourselves for the fray. The chief of our village, foreseeing a terrible calamity, seated himself on his horse

and gathered us all together; having gotten us together, he
took a pen and began to scribble.   Though he was not a
Frenchman nor a Greek, but a Russian, yet he was a government official and wore a crimson uniform.   God forfend
that a scribe should be a military commander!   He took out
his pen, and began to write down the names, while our
backs were already smarting from the descent of a hail of
stones upon them.   Is it possible Pallas was with the scribe?
For he was still writing down names, while the Valdáyans
were drubbing us.   Old women in the huts were lamenting
to heaven; small children, all the girls and women, and
chickens hid behind the stove and underneath it.

Seeing that there was to be no end to his writing, we no
longer listened to the scribe, but like a whirlwind swept
down from all sides and, pressing forward in a mass, hastened
to the fight.   Neither fences nor water could keep us back,
and the only salvation for the Valdáyans was in flight; but
they stood out stubbornly against us, and with agility swung
their wooden arms at us.   We could not break asunder the
order of their ranks, and from both sides there flew upon us
stones and mud, the implements of war of furious men.   We
were bespattering and striking each other down without
mercy, but ours stood like a firm wall.

Forgive me for mentioning names which it would not be
otherwise proper to utter here, except that without them we
would not have been victorious.   Even if our scribe had been
much wiser, he would not have broken that wall with his
skull, which we barely smashed with our clubs.   We had for
some time been striking each other mightily with stones,
when our Stépka the intrepid (he was not very clever, but a
powerful man) rushed with grim rage into the thickest fight
among the Valdáyans: he struck them down with a cudgel,
and they raised a cry, but Stépka hacked among them like a
butcher.   Then his nephew, too, took a club, flew at them,
but lost courage and showed them his back, whereupon a
frisky Valdáyan jumped upon it and was on top of our hero.
In the very midst of the sanguinary fray he had jumped upon
the hero's shoulder, and boasted before his whole horde that

he had begun with a battle and had ended with leapfrog. But the jest ended badly for him, for the Valdáyan had not yet thanked us for the ride, when Stépka's nephew grabbed the Valdáyan by the girdle and so hurled him to the ground that he broke his nose and so flattened it that he now has to wear a plaster upon it.

Then, lo, we all suddenly noticed in the distance a rider all covered with dust: that was the proud leader of the Valdáyans; that beast was a worthy likeness of our own manager. Raging with an internal fire against us, he galloped upon his steed towards our hero. All thought that they would end the terrible battle by a duel; we all stood in quiet expectancy, and terror seized us all. Already the heroes approached each other on their horses, but suddenly, it seemed, they changed their minds: they did not fight, they only cursed each other, leaving us alone to finish the battle, while their horses took them back to their homes.

In the meantime, if you wish to know it, the sun shone so that it was time for us to dine; if the accursed battle had not taken place, I, no doubt, would have swallowed two or three bites by that time; but, under the circumstances, I thought neither of beet soup nor buckwheat mush.

When the horses had taken away the commanders, we carried on a real war: all order was suddenly gone, and at the same time all distinction of great and small disappeared; we were all mixed up, and all were equal. Suddenly my brother swooped down like a hawk, to aid us, and he mixed up the battle, like wheat mush in a vat. Accuse me not of lying in what I am going to tell of my brother: holding a heavy club in his hand, he carried terror to all our enemies: wherever he passed there was a street, and where he turned about, there was a square. He had been vanquishing the Valdáyans for an hour, and they had all been running away from him, when all at once there appeared his adversary. My brother's exploit was stopped, for that Valdáyan hung upon his neck, and bit off my brother's right ear. And thus my beloved brother Ilyúkha, who had come to the battle with ears, went away with but one. He dragged himself along, bleeding like a pig, maimed, torn, but above all, disgraced.

Think of my loss! He lost an ear, and I a brother! Since then I no longer recognise him as my brother. Do not imagine that I have spoken this in vain: when he was possessed of both ears, he was easily moved by the words of the unfortunate; but now that door is entirely locked, and he hears only when one says: "Here, take this!" but he no longer hears the word "give," and with his left ear accepts nobody's prayers. In an empty well it is not likely you will find a treasure, and without it I do not care even for my brother.

Having lost such a hero, we were bereft of all means of victory; the Valdáyans henceforth got the better of us, struck us down, pressed hard upon us and drove us from the field. We should have been that day entirely undone, had not Stépka saved us from our dire distress: like a bolt of lightning he suddenly rushed upon us from behind, and stopped us, who were then in full flight. "Stand still, good fellows!" he yelled, "stand still! Come together in close array, and begin anew the battle!" All was changed. O most happy hour! At Stépka's voice crowds of men came together, came, bore down the adversary, defeated them, and wrung the victory they held from their hands. They rushed together, correcting their disorder, and hotter than before the battle was renewed.

Already we were driving our enemy back to their village, and depriving them of their cudgels and sticks, and our battle would have been at an end, if a monk had not appeared to their aid. This new Balaam was urging on his beast and beating it with a stick for its sluggishness; but all his beating of his dobbin moved her not a step ahead. He somehow managed to reach the top of the hill, and there his holy lips uttered curses against us. But neither these, nor the wooden arms, kept us back, and we flew against our enemy, and did our work among them. That worthy man, seeing our stubbornness, leaped from his horse, and showed the swiftness of his feet, which was greater than when he first had come, and, showing us his back, fled to his house.

Dark night had already put out its veil, when all were worn out with fighting. The Valdáyans being vanquished, we all went from the field, and reached home, though hungry, yet alive.

THE COOK AND THE TAILOR

'T is easier for a cook to roast and stew than for a tailor to talk of cookery. It was, I know not where, in Lithuania or Poland,—he knows of it who knows more than I; all I know is that a lord was travelling, and as he was returning from a visit he was, naturally, drunk. A man came from the opposite direction, and he met the lord, phiz to phiz. The lord was blown up with conceit and liquor, and two servants led his horse for him. The horse strutted proudly along, and the lord was steeped in arrogance like a cock. The man that met him was poorly clad. The lord interrogated him, like a man of sense:

"What handicraft have you?"

"A cook, my lord, stands before you."

"If so, then answer me, before I spit into your face: you are a cook, so you know what dainties are; what then is the greatest dainty?"

"A roast pig's hide," the cook answered without hesitation.

"You, cook, are not a fool," the lord said to him, "and gave me readily an answer, from which I conclude that you know your business."

With these words, the lord gave him a generous reward, just like a father, though he had begot no children. My cook, for joy, tripped lightly along and was soon out of sight. Whom should he meet but a tailor, an old acquaintance, nay, a friend,—not to the grave, yet a friend.

"Whither do you hurry so fast, friend Ilyá?"

The other replied: "Now, my friend, I can boldly assure you that the cook's profession is better than yours. You, drunken Petrúshka, do not even guess that Ilyá is going to have a big celebration! Look at my pocket. I

and my wife will be satisfied with what we now have; we
cannot unto our deaths spend all the lord, who just passed
me drunk upon the road, has given me.''

And he pulled out his purse that was filled with gold coins:
'' That 's what I got for a pig!''

And he showed his money in his bag, and told his friend
all that had happened. The tailor was melting with envy,
as he tried to count the money, and he thought: '' Of course
the lord is a fool for having given a bag full of money for a
pig; I will run after him, and overtake him, and if all the
wisdom is only in a pig's hide, I 'll shave him clean, like a
scribe.''

Having said this, the senseless man started on the road.
The lord was riding leisurely along, and as the tailor was
running fast, he soon overtook him. He cried to him:

'' Wait, lord! I am not a Tartar, and I will not cut you
down; I have no sword, and I will not injure you. I am all
worn out with running; I am a cook, and not a thief.''

The lord heard the words and, looking back, saw that it
was not a robber with a club, so he reined in his horse. The
tailor ran up to him, panting like a dog, and barely breathing, having lost his strength in running. The lord asked
him:

'' Why, beast, have you been running so senselessly after
me? You have only frightened me: I thought it was a
robber with a club that was after me.''

The tailor said: '' I am not a thief, my lord!''

To which the lord: '' What manner of creature are you,
then?''

'' I am a cook by trade, and know how to stew and roast
well.''

The lord asked him at once: '' What is the sweetest part
of the ox?''

The rash man said: '' The hide.''

No sooner said than the cook's sides and face, and belly
and back were swollen, being struck with a whip. The
tailor walked slowly off, weeping disconsolately, and cursing
the lord and the trade of a cook.

Mikhaíl Vasílevich Danílov. (1722-1790.)

The *Memoirs* of Danílov are interesting for the reason that they indicate the sources from real life from which Catherine II., Fon-Vízin and others drew the characters for their comedies. Thus, Matréna Petróvna of Danílov's *Memoirs* is the prototype of Mávra's mistress in *O Tempora* (p. 272) and of Mrs. Uncouth in *The Minor*, p. 342.

FROM HIS "MEMOIRS"

I was my father's favourite son. When I was about seven years old, or more, I was turned over, in the village of Kharín where my father lived, to the sexton Philip, named Brudásty, for instruction. The sexton was of low stature, broad in his shoulders; a large round beard covered his chest, his head of thick hair came down to his shoulders, and gave the appearance of having no neck. There studied with him at the same time two of my cousins, Eliséy and Borís. Our teacher Brudásty lived alone with his wife in a very small hut; I used to come to Brudásty for my lessons early in the morning, and I never dared to open his door, until I had said aloud my prayer, and he answered "Amen." I remember to the present day the instruction I received from Brudásty, probably for the reason that he often whipped me with a switch. I cannot in all faithfulness say that I was then guilty of indolence or stubbornness; on the contrary I studied very well for my years, and my teacher gave me lessons of moderate length and not above my strength, so that I readily memorised them. But we were not allowed to leave Brudásty for a moment, except for dinner; we had to sit uninterruptedly on the bench, and during the long summer days I suffered greatly from this continuous sitting, and grew so faint that my memory left me, and when it came to reciting my lesson in the evening, I had forgotten all I knew, and could not read half of it, for which the final resolve was that I was to be whipped for my stupidity. I grew to believe that punishment was an indispensable accompaniment of study. Brudásty's wife kept on inciting us, during the absence of her husband, that we should yell

louder, even if it was not our lesson. We felt some relief in
our tedious sitting when Brudásty was away in the field
working. Whenever Brudásty returned I recited my lessons correctly and without breaking down, just as I did in
the morning when my thoughts were not yet tired out.
From this I conclude that compulsory study is useless to the
child, because the mental powers weaken from bodily labour
and become languid. This truth becomes apparent when
we compel a child to play beyond its pleasure: both the game
and toys become wearisome to the child from mere ennui,
and it will rarely play with them, if not altogether hate
them. . . . Such is the fruit of senseless and worthless
teachers, like Brudásty: from mere weary sitting, I got into
the habit of inventing all kinds of accidents and diseases,
which, in reality, I never had.

Having learned the A B C from Brudásty, my father took
me near the city of Túla to a widow, Matréna Petróvna, who
had married a relative of ours, Afanási Denísovich Danílov.
Matréna Petróvna had at her house a nephew of hers and
heir to her property, Epishkóv. It was for his sake that she
had asked my father to bring me to her house to study, that
her nephew might have a companion. As the widow loved
her nephew very much and fondled him, we were never compelled to study; but being left to my choice in the matter,
and fearing no punishment, I soon finished my oral instruction, which consisted only of the two books: the Book of the
Hours and the Psalter.

The widow was a very pious woman: hardly a day passed
without having divine services in her house, either with a
priest, or sometimes a servant acted in his capacity. I was
employed to read the prayers during these services, and as
the widow's favourite cousin had not yet learned to read, he,
from great envy and anger, used to come to the table where
I was reading the psalms, and kick me so painfully with his
boots that I could not repress my tears. Though the widow
saw her nephew's naughtiness, she never said anything
more than in a drawling voice, as if against her will: " Ványa, you have had enough fun!" as though she did not see

that Ványa's fun had caused tears to flow from my eyes. She could not read; but she used to open every day a large book on her table, and pretended to read loudly the prayer of the Holy Virgin to her people. The widow was very fond of cabbage soup with mutton at dinner, and I must confess that as long as I lived at her house I do not remember a single day that passed without a drubbing. The moment she seated herself at the table to eat her favourite soup, some of the servants dragged the cook that had cooked the soup into the dining-room, put her on the floor and mercilessly beat her with rods, and the widow never stopped eating as long as they beat the cook and she cried with pain; that had become a regular custom and evidently served to heighten her appetite. The widow was so stout that her width was only a trifle less than her height.

One day her nephew and I took a walk, and there was with us a young servant of hers who taught us to read and was at the same time studying himself. Her nephew and prospective heir led us to an apple-tree that grew outside the enclosure, and he began to knock down some apples, without having first asked his aunt's permission. This crime was reported to his aunt. She ordered all three of us to be brought into her presence for a just punishment. She ordered in great anger to take up at once our innocent servant and teacher and to place him on a wooden horse, and he was unmercifully whipped for a long time, while they kept on repeating: "Don't knock the apples off the tree!" Then came my turn: the widow ordered to have me put on the horse, and I received three blows on my back, though I, like the teacher, had not knocked down any apples. Her nephew was frightened, and he thought that his turn would now come to be punished, but his fear was groundless; all the widow did was to reprimand him as follows: "It is wrong, it is not proper, sir, to knock down apples without having received my permission," and then she kissed him and said: "I suppose, Ványa, you were frightened as they whipped your companions; don't be afraid, my darling! I'll not have you whipped."

Catherine the Great. (1729–1796.)

The French culture, which had held sway in Russia before Catherine II., became even more pronounced when she ascended the throne. She corresponded with Voltaire, offered d'Alembert the place of tutor to her son, paid Diderot a salary as keeper of his own library, which she had purchased from him, and, in the first part of her reign, laboured, at least platonically, for the introduction of new laws in the spirit of Rousseau and Montesquieu. She planned to build schools and academies, encouraged the establishment of printing presses, by making them free from government control, and by her own example did much to foster literature.   One of her earliest ventures is her famous *Instruction* for the commission that had been called to present a project for a new code of laws. She composed a large number of comedies, tragedies and operas, wrote a work on Russian proverbs and a number of fairy tales. Of the latter her *Prince Khlor* gave Derzhávin an occasion to immortalise her as *Felítsa*, and to inaugurate a new style of ode. Catherine was the first to found a satirical journal, the *All Kinds of Things* (see p. 326), the prototype of a number of similar periodical publications. The latter part of her reign is characterised by a reactionary tendency, due to her general distrust of the Masons, who had taken a firm foothold in Russia and whom she suspected of favouring the French Revolution. She then put literature under a ban, and caused much annoyance to men like Nóvikov and Radíshchev.

Her *Prince Khlor* has been translated into English under the title : *Ivan Czarovitz; or, The Rose Without Prickles That Stings Not*, A Tale, written by her Imperial Majesty, translated from the Russian Language, London, 1793. It had previously appeared in a periodical paper, *The Bee*, published at Edinburgh. It is reproduced here.

Act I., Scene 4, of *Mrs. Grumble's Birthday*, in C. E. Turner's *Studies in Russian Literature*, and the same, in Fraser's Magazine, 1877.

There is also a translation of Catherine's *Memoirs*, originally written by her in French, under the title : *Memoirs of the Empress Catherine II., Written by Herself*, with a Preface by A. Herzen, translated from the French, London and New York, 1859.

O TEMPORA

ACT I., SCENE I.   MR. SENSIBLE, MÁVRA

Mávra. Believe me, I am telling you the truth. You cannot see her. She is praying now, and I dare not go into her room myself.

Sensible. Does she really pray all day long ? No matter

at what time I come, I am told I cannot see her: she was this morning at matins, and now she is praying again.

Mávra. That is the way our time is passed.

Sensible. It is good to pray. But there are also duties in our life, which we are obliged to carry out. Do you mean to tell me that she prays day and night?

Mávra. No. Our exercises are often changed, yet all goes in a certain order. Sometimes we have simple services; at others they read the Monthly Readings; at others again the reading is omitted, and our lady gives us a sermon on prayer, abstinence and fasting.

Sensible. I have heard it said that your lady is very sanctimonious, but I have not heard much about her virtues.

Mávra. To tell the truth, I cannot say much about that either. She very often speaks to her servants on abstinence and fasting, especially when she distributes the monthly allowances. She never shows so much earnestness in praying as when creditors come and ask to be paid for goods taken on credit. She once hurled the prayer-book so violently at my head that she hurt me and I was compelled to lie in bed for nearly a week. And why? Because I came during vesper service to report that the merchant had come to ask for his money which he had loaned to her at six per cent., and which she had loaned out again at sixteen. "Accursed one," she cried to me, " is this a time to disturb me? You have come, like Satan, to tempt me with worldly affairs at a time when all my thoughts are given to repentance and are removed from all cares of this world." After having uttered this in great anger, she hurled her prayer-book at my temple. Look, there is still a mark there, but I have covered it with a beauty-spot. It is very hard to please her, for she is a very strange person: sometimes she does not want to be spoken to; and then again she prattles in church without stopping. She says that it is sinful to judge your neighbour, and yet she herself passes judgment on all, and talks about everybody. She especially cannot bear young ladies, and she is always of the opinion that they never do as they ought to do.

Sensible. I am glad to find out about her habits. This

knowledge will help me a great deal in the matter of Mr. Milksop's marriage. But, to tell the truth, it will be a hard thing for him to get along with such a woman: she will either drive him out of the house or into his grave. She demanded herself that I should come to Moscow to talk over her grandchild's marriage. So I took a leave of absence for twenty-nine days, and came down here from St. Petersburg. It is now three weeks that I have been here, and that I have attempted to see her, and she is all the time finding new excuses. My time will soon be up, and I shall have to return. What is it going to be to-day? She has promised to give a decisive answer, though I do not yet see the beginning of it.

Mávra. Have a little patience, sir. Maybe you will be able to see her after vespers; before that time she does not like to receive guests.

Sensible. But I have a great deal to talk to her about, so please tell her that I am here. Maybe she will let me in this time.

Mávra. No, sir, for nothing in the world will I report to her, for I shall be beaten, or at least roundly scolded. She grumbles at me as it is and calls me a heathen because I sometimes read the Monthly Essays, or Cleveland.

Sensible. But you may tell her that I am very anxious to see her.

Mávra. As soon as vespers are over, I shall go to her, but not sooner. Yet, I do not advise you to stay longer than six o'clock. At that time she receives the visits of ladies like her who amuse her with bits of news that they have gathered in all the corners of the city. They talk about all their acquaintances, and malign them, and in their Christian love pass them over in review. They inform her of all the news of St. Petersburg, adding to them their own lying inventions: some say less, others more. No one in that assembly is responsible for the truth,—that we do not care for,—provided all they have heard and have invented has been told.

Sensible. Will she at least invite me to supper? What do you think about that?

Mávra. I doubt it. What suppers do you expect of fasters?

Sensible. What? Do you fast out of stinginess? To-day is not a fast-day.

Mávra. I did not mean exactly that, only,—only—we do not like extra guests.

Sensible. Speak more openly with me, Mávra, for you certainly must know your mistress. Tell me the truth. It seems to me that she is full of superstitions and hypocrisy, and that she is at that a mean woman.

Mávra. He who looks for virtues in long prayers and in external forms and observances will not leave my lady without praise. She strictly observes all holidays; goes every day to mass; always places a taper before the images on a holiday; never eats meat on a fast-day; wears woollen dresses,—do not imagine that she does so from niggardliness,—and despises all who do not follow her example. She cannot bear the customs of the day and luxury, but likes to boast of the past and of those days when she was fifteen years old, since when, the Lord be blessed! there have passed fifty years or more.

Sensible. As regards external luxury, I myself do not like it, and I gladly agree with her in that, just as I respect the sincerity of ancient days. Praiseworthy, most praiseworthy is the ancient faithfulness of friendship, and the stern observance of a promise, for fear that the non-observance of the same might redound to one's dishonour. In all that I am of the same opinion with her. It is a pity, a real pity, that now-a-days people are ashamed of nothing, and many young people no longer blush when they utter a lie or cheat their creditors, nor young women when they deceive their husbands.

Mávra. Let us leave that alone. In her dress and headgear, you will find the representation of the fashion of her ancestors, and in this she discovers a certain virtue and purity of morals.

Sensible. But why ancestral morals? Those are nothing else but meaningless customs which she does not distinguish or cannot distinguish from morals.

Mávra. Yet, according to the opinion of my lady, the older a dress, the more venerable it is.

Sensible. Tell me, then, what she does during the whole day.

Mávra. But how can I remember it all? And then, I can hardly tell it all, for you will only laugh. Well, I do not care; I 'll tell you a little about it. She rises in the morning at six o'clock and, following a good old custom, gets out of bed bare-footed; then she fixes the lamp before the images; then reads her morning prayers and the Book of the Saints; then she combs her cat and picks the fleas off of her, and sings the verse: " Blessed is he who is kind to the beasts!" During this singing she does not forget to think of us also: she favours one with a box on her ears, another with a beating, and another with scolding and cursing. Then begins the morning mass, during which she alternately scolds the servant and mumbles prayers; she now sends the people that had been guilty of some transgression on the previous day to the stable to be beaten with rods, and now again she hands the censer to the priest; now she scolds her grandchild for being so young, and now again she makes her obeisances as she counts the beads on the rosary; now she passes in review the young men into whose hands she could rid herself of her grandchild without a dowry, and now . . . ah! wait a minute, sir, I hear a noise, and it is time for me to get away from here. It is, no doubt, my lady, and I am afraid she might find us together: there is no telling what she might think of it. (*Exit.*)

PRINCE KHLOR

Before the times of Ki, Kuyaz of Kíev, a Tsar lived in Russia, a good man who loved truth, and wished well to everybody. He often travelled through his dominions, that he might know how the people lived, and everywhere informed himself if they acted fairly.

The Tsar had a Tsarítsa. The Tsar and the Tsarítsa lived harmoniously. The Tsarítsa travelled with the Tsar, and did not like to be absent from him.

The Tsar and Tsarítsa arrived at a certain town built on a high hill in the middle of a wood, where a son was born to the Tsar; and they gave him the name Khlor. But in the midst of this joy, and of a three-days' festivity, the Tsar received the disagreeable intelligence that his neighbours do not live quietly,—make inroads into his territories, and do many injuries to the inhabitants of the borders. The Tsar took the armies that were encamped in the neighbourhood, and went with his troops to protect the borders. The Tsarítsa went with the Tsar; the Tsarévich remained in the same town and house in which he was born. The Tsar appointed to him seven prudent matrons, well experienced in the education of children. The Tsar ordered the town to be fortified with a stone wall, having towers at the corners; but they placed no cannon on the towers, because in those days they had no cannon. The house in which the Tsarévich remained was built of Siberian marble and porphyry, and was very neat and conveniently laid out. Behind the palace were planted gardens with fruit trees, near which fish-ponds beautified the situation; summer-houses made in the taste of various nations, from which the view extended to the neighbouring fields and plains, added agreeableness to the dwelling.

As the Tsarévich grew up, his female guardians began to remark that he was no less prudent and sprightly than handsome. The fame of the beauty, wisdom and fine accomplishments of the Tsarévich was spread abroad on all sides. A certain Khan of the Kirgíz Tartars, wandering in the deserts with his kibítkas,[1] heard of this and was anxious to see so extraordinary an infant; and having seen him, he formed a wish to carry him away into the desert. He began by endeavouring to persuade the guardians to travel with the Tsarévich and him into the desert. The matrons told him with all politeness that it was impossible to do this without the Tsar's permission; that they had not the honour of knowing my lord Khan, and that they never pay any visits

[1] A sort of tents made of mats; also a kind of covered waggon used for travelling in Russia.

with the Tsarévich to strangers. The Khan was not contented with this polite answer, and stuck to them closer than formerly, just like a hungry person to a piece of paste, and insisted that the nurses should go with the child into the desert. Having at last received a flat denial, he was convinced he could not succeed in his intentions by entreaties, and sent them a present. They returned him thanks,—sent his present back, and ordered to tell him that they were in want of nothing.

The Khan, obstinate and fixed in his resolution, considered what was to be done. It came into his head to dress himself in tattered clothes; and he sat down at the gate of the garden, as if he were a sick old man; and he begged alms of the passengers. The Tsarévich happened to take that day a walk in the garden; and, observing that a certain old man sat at the gate, sent to ask who the old man was. They returned with answer that he was a sick beggar; Khlor, like a boy possessed of much curiosity, asked leave to look at the sick beggar. The matrons, to pacify Khlor, told him that there was nothing to be seen; and that he might send the beggar alms. Khlor wished to give the money himself, and ran off. The attendants ran after him; but the faster they ran, the faster the child set out, and got without the gate. Having run up to the faint beggar, his foot catched a stone, and he fell upon his face. The beggar sprang up, took the child under his arm, and set a-running down the hill. A gilded rospúski (a kind of cart with four wheels) trimmed with velvet, stood there: he got on the rospúski, and galloped away with the Tsarévich into the desert.

When the guardians had run up to the gate, they found neither beggar nor child; nor did they see any traces of them. Indeed there was no road at the place where the Khan went down the hill. Sitting on the rospúski, he held the Tsarévich before him with one hand, like a chicken by the wing; and with the other he waved his cap round his head, and cried three times, "Hurrah!" On hearing his voice, the guardians ran to the slope of the hill, but it was too late: they could not overtake them.

The Khan carried Khlor in safety to his camp, and went into his kibítka, where the grandees met the Khan. The Khan appointed to Khlor his best starshiná.[1] This starshiná took him in his arms, and carried him into a richly ornamented kibítka, covered with Chinese stuffs and Persian carpets. He set the child on a cushion of cloth, and tried to pacify him; but Khlor cried and repented he had run away from his guardians. He was continually asking whither they were carrying him, for what reason, to what purpose, and where he was. The starshiná and the Kirgíz that were with him told him many stories. One said that it was so ordained by the course of the stars; another that it was better living than at home. They told him all but the truth. Seeing that nothing could pacify him, they tried to frighten him with nonsense; they told him they would turn him into a bat or a hawk,—that they would give him to the wolf or frog to be eaten. The Tsarévich was not fearful, and amid his tears laughed at such nonsense. The starshiná, seeing that the child had left off crying, ordered the table to be covered. They covered the table and served the supper. The Tsarévich ate a little: they then presented preserves and such fruit as they had. After supper they undressed him and put him to sleep.

Next morning before daybreak, the Khan gathered his grandees, and spoke to them as follows: " Let it be known unto you that I yesterday carried off the Tsarévich Khlor, a child of uncommon beauty and prudence. I wish to know perfectly whether all is true that is said of him; and I am determined to employ every means of trying his qualifications." The grandees having heard the Khan's words bowed themselves to the girdle. The flatterers among them praised the Khan's conduct, that he had carried off a child, nay, the child of a neighbouring Tsar. The mean-spirited approved, saying: "Right lord Khan, our hope, whatever you do must be right." A few of them who really loved the Khan shook their heads, and when the Khan asked why they held their tongues, they told him frankly: " You have

[1] An elder.

done wrong in carrying off the son of a neighbouring Tsar; and you cannot escape misfortune, unless you compensate for this step." The Khan answered: "Just so,—you are always discontented!" and passed by them. He ordered the Tsarévich to be brought to him as soon as he should awake. The child, seeing that they wished to carry him, said: "Do not trouble yourselves, I can walk. I will go myself." Having come into the Khan's kibítka, he bowed to them all, first to the Khan, and then to the rest on the right and left. He then placed himself before the Khan with such a respectful, polite and prudent mien, that he filled all the Kirgíz and the Khan himself with wonder. The Khan, however, recollecting himself, spoke as follows: "Tsarévich Khlor! They say of you that you are a wise child, pray seek me a flower,—a rose without prickles that stings not. Your tutor will show you a wide field. I give you a term of three days." The child bowing again to the Khan said: "I hear," and went out of the kibítka to his home.

In the way he met the Khan's daughter, who was married to the Sultan Bryúzga.[1] This man never laughed himself, and could not bear that another should smile. The Sultana, on the contrary, was of a sprightly temper and very agreeable. She, seeing Khlor, said to him: "Welcome, Khlor, how do you do? Where are you going?" The Tsarévich answered: "By order of your father the Khan, I am going to seek the rose without prickles that stings not." The Sultana Felítsa (that was her name) wondered that they should send a child to seek such a rarity, and, taking a sincere liking to the boy, she said to him: "Tsarévich, stay a little, I will go with you to seek the rose without prickles that stings not, if my father will give me leave." Khlor went into his kibítka to dine, for it was dinner-time, and the Sultana went to the Khan to ask leave to go with the Tsarévich to seek the rose without prickles that stings not. He did not only not give her leave, but strictly forbade her to go with the child to seek the rose without prickles that stings not.

[1] From a word meaning choleric.

Felítsa, having left the Khan, persuaded her husband, Sultan Bryúzga, to stay with her father the Khan, and went herself to the Tsarévich. He was very happy to see her, and begged her to sit down beside him, which she did, and said: " The Khan has forbid me to go with you, Tsarévich, to seek the rose without prickles that stings not; but I will give you good advice: pray do not forget,—do you hear—do not forget what I tell you." The Tsarévich promised to remember. "At some distance from hence," continued she, " as you go to seek the rose without prickles that stings not, you will meet with people of very agreeable manners who will endeavour to persuade you to go with them. They will tell you a great many entertainments, and that they spend their time in innumerable pleasures. Do not believe them: they lie. Their pleasures are false, and attended with much weariness. After them you will see others who will still more earnestly press you on the same subject. Refuse them with firmness, and they will leave you. You will then get into a wood. There you will find flatterers who by agreeable conversation, and every other means, will endeavour to draw you out of your proper way. But do not forget that you have nothing to do but to seek one flower, a rose without prickles that stings not. I love you, and will send my son to meet you, who will help you to find the rose without prickles that stings not." Khlor, having heard the words of Felítsa, asked her: " Is it so difficult to find the rose without prickles that stings not ? " " No," answered the Sultana, " it is not so very difficult to an upright person who perseveres firmly in his intention." Khlor asked if ever anybody had found that flower. " I have seen," said Felítsa, " peasants and tradesmen who have as happily succeeded in this pursuit as nobles, kings or queens." The Sultana having said this, took leave of the Tsarévich. The starshiná, his tutor, led him to seek the rose without prickles that stings not; and for this purpose let him out at a wicket into a large game park.

On entering the park, Khlor saw a vast number of roads. Some were straight, some crooked, and some full of intricate windings. The child did not know which way to go, but on seeing a youth coming towards him, he made haste to meet him and ask who he was. The youth answered: "I am Razsúdok (Reason), the son of Felítsa. My mother sent me to accompany you in your search for the rose without prickles that stings not."

The Tsarévich thanked Felítsa with heart and lips and, having taken the youth by the hand, informed himself of the way he should go. Razsúdok said with a cheerful and assured look: "Fear naught, Tsarévich, let us go on the straight road, where few walk though it is more agreeable than the others." "Why do not all keep the straight road?" said the Tsarévich. "Because," replied the youth, "they lose themselves and get bewildered in the others." In going along, the youth showed Khlor a very beautiful little path, and said: "Look, Tsarévich! This is called the Path of the Nonage of Well-Disposed Souls. It is very pretty but very short."

They pursued their way through a wood into an agreeable plain, through which ran a rivulet of clear water. On the banks they saw troops of young people. Some were sitting on the grass, and others were lying under the trees. As soon as they saw the Tsarévich, they got up and came to him. One of them with great politeness and insinuation of manner addressed him. "Give me leave," said he, "to ask you, sir, where you are going? Did you come here by chance? Can we have the pleasure of serving you in anything? Your appearance fills us with respect and friendship, and we are ravished with the number of your brilliant accomplishments." The Tsarévich, recollecting the words of Felítsa, replied: "I have not the honour to know you, and you also are unacquainted with me. I therefore attribute your compliments to your politeness, and not to my own merits. I am going to seek the rose without prickles that stings not." Another of the company joined the conversation, and said: "Your intention is a proof of your talents. But oblige us so far as to favour us with your company a few days, and to take a share in the inimitable pleasures which we enjoy." Khlor told him that he was restricted to a time, and that he could not delay lest he should incur the Khan's displeasure. They endeavoured to persuade him that rest was necessary for his health, and that he could not find a place for this purpose more convenient, nor people more inclined to serve him. It is impossible to conceive how they begged and persuaded him. At length the men and women took each other by the hand, and formed a ring about Khlor and his conductor, and began to leap and dance, and hinder them from going farther; but while they were whirling themselves about, Razsúdok snatched Khlor under his arm and ran out of the ring with such speed that the dancers could not catch hold of them.

Having proceeded farther, they came to Lentyág [1] Murza (the sluggard chief), the chief governor of the place, who was taking a walk with his household. He received Khlor and his conductor very civilly, and asked them into his lodging. As they were a little tired, they went in with him. He desired them to sit down on the divan, and laid himself by them on down pillows covered with old-fashioned cloth of gold. His domestic friends sat down round the walls of the chamber. Lentyág Murza then ordered pipes, tobacco and coffee to be served. Having understood that they did not smoke nor drink coffee, he ordered the carpets to be sprinkled with perfumes, and asked Khlor the reason for his excursion into the game park. The Tsarévich answered that by the order of the Khan he was in quest of the rose without prickles that stings not. Lentyág Murza was amazed that he could undertake such an arduous attempt at so early an age. Addressing himself to Khlor: "Older than you," said he, "are scarce equal to such a business. Rest a little, don't proceed farther. I have many people here who have endeavoured to find out this flower, but have all got tired and have deserted the pursuit." One of them that were present then got up and said: "I myself more than once tried to find it, but I tired of it, and instead of it I have found my benefactor Lentyág Murza, who supplies me with meat and drink."

[1] From a word meaning indolent.

In the midst of this conversation Lentyág Murza's head sunk into a pillow, and he fell asleep. As soon as those that were seated about the walls of the room heard that Lentyág Murza began to snore, they got up softly. Some of them went to dress themselves, some to sleep. Some took to idle conversation, and some to cards and dice. During these employments some flew into a passion, others were well pleased, and upon the faces of all were marked the various situations of their souls. When Lentyág Murza awoke, they again gathered around them, and a table covered with fruit was brought into the room. Lentyág Murza remained among his pillows, and from thence asked the Tsarévich, who very earnestly observed all that passed, to eat. Khlor was just going to taste what was offered by Lentyág Murza, when his conductor pulled him gently by the sleeve, and a bunch of fine grapes which he had laid hold of fell out of his hand and was scattered upon the pavement. Recollecting himself immediately he got up, and they left Lentyág Murza.

Not far from this they spied the house of a peasant, surrounded by several acres of well-cultivated ground, on which were growing several kinds of corn, as rye, oats, barley, buckwheat, etc. Some of this corn was ripening, and some only springing up. A little farther they saw a meadow on which horses, cows and sheep were grazing. They found the landlord with a watering-pan in his hand, with which he was watering the cucumbers and cabbage set by his wife. The children were employed in clearing away the useless weeds from among the garden stuffs. Razsúdok addressed them: "God be with you, good people!" They answered; "Thank you, young gentlemen," and they made a distant bow to the Tsarévich as to a stranger; but in a friendly manner they addressed Razsúdok: "Be so kind as to go into our dwelling: your mother the Sultana loves us, visits us and does not neglect us." Razsúdok consented and with Khlor went into the yard. In the middle of the yard there stood an old and lofty oak, under which was a broad and clean-scraped bench, with a table before it. The landlady and her daughter-in-law spread a table-cloth, and placed on the table a bowl of buttermilk, and another with poached eggs. They set down also a dish of hot pancakes, soft-boiled eggs, and in the middle a good bacon ham. They brought brown bread, and set down to everyone a can of sweet milk, and by way of dessert presented fresh cucumbers and cranberries with honey.

The landlord pressed them to eat. The travellers, who were hungry, found everything excellent, and during supper talked with the landlord and landlady, who told them how healthily, happily and quietly they lived, and in all abundance suitable to their condition, passing their time in country work, and overcoming every want and difficulty by industry. After supper they spread on the same bench mats, and Razsúdok and Khlor put their cloaks on the mats. The landlady gave to each a pillow with a clean pillow-slip; so they lay down, and being tired they soon fell asleep.

In the morning they got up at daybreak, and having thanked their landlord, who would have nothing for their lodging, they pursued their journey. Having got about half a mile, they heard the sound of the bagpipe. Khlor wanted to go nearer, but Razsúdok hinted that the bagpipe would lead them out of their way. Curiosity got the better of Khlor, and he went up to the bagpipe, but when he saw the mad pranks of disfigured drunkards staggering about the piper, he was terrified, and threw himself into the arms of Razsúdok, who carried him back to the road.

Having passed through a grove, they saw a steep hill. Razsúdok told Khlor that the rose without prickles that stings not grew there. Khlor, oppressed with the heat of the sun, grew tired. He began to fret, said there was no end to that road, how far it is, and asked if they could not find a nearer way. Razsúdok answered that he was carrying him the nearest way, and that difficulties are only to be overcome by patience. The Tsarévich in ill-humour cried out, "Perhaps I shall find the way myself !" waved his hand, doubled his pace, and separated himself from his guide.

Razsúdok remained behind and followed slowly in silence. The child entered a market town where there were few who took notice of him, for it was a market-day, and everybody was engaged in business in the market-place. The Tsarévich, wandering among carts and traders, began to cry. One person who did not know him passed by, and seeing him crying said to him: "Have done crying, you little whelp; without you we have noise enough here." At that very moment Razsúdok had overtaken him. The Tsarévich complained that they had called him whelp. Razsúdok said not a word, but conducted him out of the crowd. When Khlor asked him why he did not talk with him as formerly, Razsúdok answered: "You did not ask my advice, but went to an improper place, and so don't be offended if you did not find the people to your mind." Razsúdok wished to prolong his speech when they met a man, not overyoung, but of an agreeable appearance, surrounded with a great many boys. As Khlor was curious to know everything, he called one of the boys, and asked who the man was. "This man is our master," said the boy; "we have got our lesson and are going to take a walk,—but pray where are you going?" The Tsarévich told him that they were seeking the rose without prickles that stings not. "I have heard," said the boy, "from our master an explanation of the rose without prickles that stings not. This flower signifies nothing more than virtue. Some people think to find it by going byways, but nobody can get it unless he follows the straight road; and happy is he that by an honest firmness can overcome all the difficulties of that road. You see before you that hill on which grows the rose without prickles that stings not; but the road is steep and full of rocks." Having said this, he took his leave and went after his master.

Khlor and his guide went straight to the hill, and found a narrow and rocky track on which they walked with difficulty. They there met an old man and woman in white, both of a respectable appearance, who stretched out their staffs to them and said: "Support yourselves on our staffs and you will not stumble." The people thereabouts told them that the name of the first was Honesty, and of the other Truth.

Having got to the foot of the hill, leaning on the staffs, they were obliged to scramble from the track by the branches, and so from branch to branch they got at length to the top of the hill, where they found the rose without prickles that stings not. He made haste to the Khan with the flower, and the Khan dismissed him to the Tsar. The Tsar was so well pleased with the arrival of the Tsarévich and his success that he forgot all his anxiety and grief. The Tsar, the Tsarítsa and all the people became daily more fond of the Tsarévich, because he daily advanced in virtue. Here the tale ends, and who knows better, let him tell another.

Prince Mikháylo Mikháylovich Shcherbátov.
(1733–1790.)

Prince Shcherbátov derived his origin from St. Vladímir, and united in his person a love of the ancient order of things and the prerogatives of the nobility with a refined liberalism, the result of an education according to Western ideas. In the sixties, Catherine II. entrusted Prince Shcherbátov with the arrangement of the archives of Peter the Great, and the result of his labours in this direction was the publication of a number of chronicles and documents referring to various periods of Russian history. Then he wrote a *History of Russia* from the most ancient times to the election of Mikhaíl Feódorovich, in seven volumes. Though not distinguished for elegance of style, it deserves especial mention as the first native history in which not only native sources were thoroughly ransacked, but the facts were properly co-ordinated in a philosophical system. His sympathies for the old régime led him to emphasise the dark side of the period following the reform of Peter the Great, and he elaborated his theory in a work *On the Corruption of Manners in Russia*, which was so bold in laying bare the immorality of the Court at his time that he did not dare to publish it. It first saw the light in London in 1858, where it was issued by Herzen. In another work, *Journey to the Land of Ophir, by Mr. S., a Swedish Nobleman*, he developed his ideas of what a monarchy ought to be, in the manner of Sir Thomas More's *Utopia*. This work was first published a few years ago.

ON THE CORRUPTION OF MANNERS IN RUSSIA

Ancient families were no longer respected, but "chins" and deserts and long service. Everybody was anxious to

get some " chin," and as it is not given to everybody to distinguish himself through some meritorious act, many tried
through flattery and subserviency to the Emperor and the
dignitaries to gain that which merit gave to others. By the
regulations of the military service, which Peter the Great
had newly introduced, the peasants began with their masters
at the same stage as soldiers of the rank and file: it was not
uncommon for the peasants, by the law of seniority, to reach
the grade of officer long before their masters, whom, as their
inferiors, they frequently beat with sticks. Noble families
were so scattered in the service that often one did not come
again in contact with his relatives during his whole lifetime.

How could there remain any manliness and firmness in
those who in their youth trembled before the rod of their
superiors; who could not obtain any honours except by ser-
vility; and who, being left without the active support of their
relatives, without union and protection, were left alone, at
any time liable to fall into the hands of the mighty ?

I must praise Peter the Great for his attempts to eradicate
superstition in the observances of the divine Law, for indeed
superstition is not a worship of God and the Law, but rather
a desecration; to ascribe to God improper acts is nothing
but blasphemy.

In Russia they regarded the beard as a physical attribute
of God, for which reason they thought it a sin to shave it
off, thus falling into the heresy of anthropomorphism. They
proclaimed everywhere miracles, needlessly performed, and
holy images, whose properties were rarely attested; they encouraged superstitious worship, and increased the revenues
of corrupt servants of the Lord. All that Peter the Great
endeavoured to abolish: he promulgated ukases for the
shaving off of beards, and by means of the *Spiritual Reglement* put a stop to false miracles and visions, as well as improper gatherings near the holy images on the crossroads.
Being convinced that the divine Law demands the preservation of the human race, and not its uncalled-for destruction,
he by a decision of the Synod and all the Patriarchs granted
a dispensation to eat meat during the fast, in case of neces-

sity, particularly in the service on the seas, where people are subject to scurvy; he ordered that those who, by such abstinence, of their own free will sacrificed their lives and became subject to diseases resulting therefrom, should be cast into the water. All that is very good, only the latter thing is a little too severe.

But when did he enact that? When the people were not yet enlightened, and by thus abating the superstition of the unenlightened, he at the same time deprived them of their faith in the divine Law. This act of Peter the Great is to be likened to the act of the unskilled gardener who lops the watery branches of a weak tree, that absorb its sap. If the tree were well rooted, this lopping would cause it to bring forth good and fruitful branches; but, being weak and sickly, the cutting off of the branches that imbibed the external moisture through its leaves and fed the weak tree causes no healthy and abundant growth of new branches, nor does the wound heal up, but there are formed cavities that threaten the destruction of the tree. Similarly the lopping off of the superstitions has been injurious to the fundamental parts of faith itself: superstition has decreased, but so has also faith; there has disappeared the slavish terror of hell, but also the love of God and His divine Law; and the manners that were formerly corrected by faith have lost this corrective and, lacking any other enlightenment, soon began to be corrupted.

With all the reverence that I have in my heart for this great monarch and great man, with all my conviction that the weal of the Empire demanded that he should have other legitimate children than Alexis Petróvich as heirs of his throne,—I cannot but censure his divorce from his first wife, née Lopúkhin, and his second marriage to the captive Catherine Aleksyéevna, after his first wife had been sent to a monastery. This example of the debasement of the sacred mystery of marriage has shown that these bonds may be broken without fear of punishment. Granted that the monarch had sufficient cause for his action, though I do no see it, except her leaning for the Monses, and opposition to his new regulations; but what reasons of State led his imitators to do likewise? Did Paul Ivánovich Eguzínski, who sent his first wife into a monastery and married another, *née* Galóvkin, have any reasons of State for getting heirs by breaking the divine Laws? Not only many high dignitaries, but those of lower ranks, like Prince Borís Sóntsev-Zasyékin, have also imitated him.

Although Russia, through the labours and care of this Emperor, has become known to Europe and has now weight in affairs, and her armies are properly organised, and her fleets have covered the White and Baltic seas, so that she has been able to conquer her old enemies and former victors, the Poles and Swedes, and has gained fine districts and good harbours; although the sciences, arts and industries began to flourish in Russia, and commerce to enrich her, and the Russians were transformed from bearded men into clean-shaven ones, and exchanged their long cloaks for short coats, and became more sociable and accustomed to refinement; yet at the same time the true attachment to the faith began to disappear, the mysteries fell into disrepute, firmness was weakened and gave way to impudent, insinuating flattery; luxury and voluptuousness laid the foundation for their domination, and with it selfishness began to penetrate the high judicial places, to the destruction of the laws and the detriment of the citizens. Such is the condition of morals in which Russia was left after the death of the great Emperor, in spite of all his attempts, in his own person and through his example, to ward off the encroachment of vice.

Now let us see what progress vice has made during the reign of Catherine I. and Peter II., and how it has established itself in Russia.

The feminine sex is generally more prone to luxury than the male, and so we see the Empress Catherine I. having her own court even during the life of her husband, Peter the Great. Her chamberlain was Mons, whose unbounded luxury was his first quality that brought him to a shameful death; her pages were Peter and Jacob Fedórovich Balkóv, his nephews, who during his misfortune were driven from the Court. She was exceedingly fond of ornaments, and carried her vanity to such an excess that other women were not permitted to wear similar ornaments, as, for example, to wear diamonds on both sides of the head, but only on the left side; no one was allowed to wear ermine furs with the tails, which she wore, and this custom, which was confirmed by no ukase or statute, became almost a law; this adornment was appropriated to the Imperial family, though in Germany it is also worn by the wives of burghers. Does not this vanity seem to indicate that when her age began to impair her beauty, she was trying to enhance it by distinctive adornments? I do not know whether this opinion was just, and whether it was proper for the Emperor to appear every hour of the day before his subjects in a masquerade dress, as if he lacked other distinguishing adornments.

Vasíli Petróvich Petróv. (1736-1799.)

Petróv was the son of a poor clergyman. He studied in the Theological Academy at Moscow, where he was made a teacher in 1760. Through Potémkin, his friend, he was presented to the Empress, who, in 1768, appointed him her private translator and reader. In 1772 he was sent to England, where he soon acquired the language. In London he translated Milton's *Paradise Lost* and made a careful study of Addison, especially of his *Cato*. Petróv wrote a large number of adulatory odes, now long forgotten ; he showed more talent in his satires, which he wrote in England, and in which the influence of the English writers whom he studied may be perceived. The following ode, probably his best, is from Sir John Bowring's *Specimens of the Russian Poets*, Part II.

ON THE VICTORY OF THE RUSSIAN OVER THE TURKISH FLEET [1]

O triumph! O delight! O time so rich in fame
Unclouded, bright and pure as the sun's midday flame!
Ruthenia's strength goes forth—see from the sea emerge
The Typhons of the north!—The lightning, in its might,
      Flashes in dazzling light,—
      And subject is the surge.

[1] At Chesma, where, on July 26, 1770, the Turkish fleet was destroyed.

They wander o'er the waves,—their eye impatiently
Seeks where the Moslem's flag flaunts proudly o'er the sea:—
"'T is there! 'T is there!" exclaim the brave, impatient
    crowd,—
The sails unfurled,—each soul with rage and courage
    burns,—
       Each to the combat turns:
       They meet,— it thunders loud!

I see from Ætna's rocks a floating army throng:
A hero,[1] yet unsung, wafts the proud choir along,—
The masts, a fir-tree wood,—the sails, like outspread wings.
List to the shoutings! See the flash! They thunder near.
       Earthquakes and night are there,—
       With storm the welkin rings.

There January speeds,—there Svyatosláv moves on,
And waves and smoke alike are in the tempest thrown;
And there the ship that bears the three-times hallowed[2]
    name,
And Rostisláv and Europe, there triumphant ride;
       While the agitated tide
       Is startled with the flame.

Evstáf, in fire concealed, scatters the deathlike brand,
And earth and heaven are moved, and tremble sea and land;
And there, a mountain pile, sends round the deeds of death,
As if Vesuvius' self in combat were engaged,—
       While other mountains raged,
       And poured their flaming breath.

The roar, the whiz, the hum, in one commingling sound,
The clouds of smoke that rise, and spread and roll around;
The waves attack the sky in wild and frenzied dance;
The sails are white as snow; and now the sun looks on,
       Now shrouds him on his throne,
       And the swift lightnings glance.

[1] Count Orlóv, commander of the fleet.
[2] Ship named *The Three Saints*.

Hard proof of valour this,—the spirit's fiery test:
Fierce combat, grown more fierce,—bear high the burning
    breast!
See on the waves there ride two mountains, fiery-bound,
Ætna and Hecla, loose on ocean's heaving bed,—
       The burning torches spread,
       And ruin stalks around.

Ocean, and shore, and air, rush backward at the sight,
The Greek and Turk stand still, and groan in wild affright;
Calm as a rock the Russ is welcoming death with death;
But ah! destruction now blazes its fiery links,
       And even victory sinks
       Its heavy weight beneath.

O frightful tragedy!   A furnace is the sea,—
The triumph ours,— the flames have reached the enemy:
He burns, he dies in smoke, beneath the struggle rude
The Northern heroes sink, with weariness oppressed,
       And ask a moment's rest,
       As if they were subdued.

And whence that threatening cloud that hangs upon their
    head?
That threatens now to burst? What? Is their leader dead?
And is he borne away, who all our bosoms warmed?
He fell,—there lies his sword,—there lie his shield and helm.
       What sorrows overwhelm
       The conqueror disarmed!

Oh, no! He wakes again from night,—he waves his hand,
Beckoning to the brave ranks that mourning round him
    stand:
" My brother! " cried he —" Heaven! And is my brother
    gone?
Their sails unfurl! My friends, oh, see! oh, see! They fly,—
       On,—' Death or vengeance! ' cry,
       On, on to Stamboul's throne! "

He fled. O hero! Peace! There is no cause for grief,—
He lives,—thy brother lives, and Spiridóv, his chief!
No dolphin saved them there,—it was the Almighty God,
The God who sees thy deed, thy valour who approves,
     And tries the men He loves
     With His afflictive rod.

The dreadful dream is passed,—passed like a mist away,
And dawns, serene and bright, a cloudless victory day:
The trump of shadeless joy,—the trump of triumph speaks;
The hero and his friend are met, and fled their fears;
     They kiss each other's cheeks,
     They water them with tears.

They cried, "And is our fame, and is our glory stained?
God is our shield,—revenge and victory shall be gained!
We live,—and Mahmud's might a hundred times shall fall;
We live,—the astonished world our hero-deeds shall see,
     And every victory
     A burning fleet recall."

Whence this unusual glare o'er midnight's ocean spread?
At what unwonted hour has Phœbus left his bed?
No, they are Russian crowds who struggle with the foe,
'T is their accordant torch that flashes through the night.
     Sequana, see the might
     Of Stamboul sink below!

The harbour teems with life, an amphitheatre
Of sulphurous pitch and smoke, and awful noises there.
The fiends of hell are loose, the sea has oped its caves,
Fate rides upon the deep, and laughs amidst the fray,
     Which feeds with human prey
     The monsters of the waves.

See, like a furnace boils and steams the burning flood,
'T is filled with mortal flesh, 't is red with mortal blood;

Devoured by raging flames, drunk by the thirsty wave,
The clouds seem palpable,— a thick and solid mass,—
    They sink like stone or brass
    Into their water-grave.

Thou ruler of the tomb! Dread hour of suffering,
When all the elements,— drop, Muse, thy feeble wing!—
Hell, with its fiends, and all the fiends that man e'er drew
There mingled,—Silence, veil that awful memory o'er!
    I see the hero pour
    The tears of pity too!

O Peter! Great in song, as great in glory once,
Look from thy throne sublime upon thy Russia's sons!
See, how thy fleets have won the palm of victory,
And hear the triumph sound, even to the gate of heaven,—
    The Turkish strength is riven
    Even in the Turkish sea.

Thee Copenhagen saw, the Neptune of the Belt;
Now Chesma's humbled sons before thy flag have knelt.
The helpless Greeks have fled,—thy banner sees their shore,
Trembling they look around, while thy dread thunder swells,
    And shakes the Dardanelles,
    And Smyrna hears its roar.

Ye Frenchmen![1] Fear ye not the now advancing flame,
Recording, as it flies, your own, your country's shame?
In the dark days of old, your valiant fathers trod
In the brave steps of Rome, towards lands of Southern glow;
    Ye fight with Russians now,
    Beneath the Moslems' rod.

Where innocence is found, there, there protection wakes;
Where Catherine's voice is heard,— there truth, there justice
    speaks:

[1] An agent of the French Government had fortified the Dardanelles.

A ruler's virtues are the strength and pride of states,
And surely ours shall bloom where Catherine's virtues stand.
    O enviable land!
    Glory is at our gates.

Soar, eagle, soar again, spring upward to the flight!
For yet the Turkish flag is flaunting in the light:
In Chesma's port it still erects its insolent head,
And thou must pour again thy foes' blood o'er the sea,
    And crush their treachery,
    And wide destruction spread!

But fame now summons thee from death to life again,
The people's comfort now, their glory to maintain;
The hero's palm is won.—Now turn thee and enhance
The hero's triumphs with the patriot's milder fame.
    O Romans! Without shame
    On Duil's spoils we glance.

We 'll consecrate to thee a towering marble dome!
From yonder Southern sea, oh, bring thy trophies home,
Bring Scio's trophies home,—those trophies still shall be
Thy glory, Orlóv! Thine the records of thy deeds,
    When future valour reads
    Astrea's victory!

Oh, could my wakened Muse a worthy offering bring!
Oh, could my grateful lyre a song of glory sing!
Oh, could I steal from thee the high and towering thought,
With thy proud name the world, the listening world I 'd fill!
    And Camoens' harp be still,
    And Gama be forgot!

Thine was a nobler far than Jason's enterprise,
Whose name shines like a star in history's glorious skies:
He bore in triumph home the rich, the golden fleece;
But with thy valour thou, and with thy conquering band,
    Hast saved thy fatherland,
    And given to Hellas peace.

But oh! My tongue is weak to celebrate thy glory,
Thy valiant deeds shall live in everlasting story,
For public gratitude thy name will e'er enshrine,—
Who loves his country, who his Empress loves, will throw
      His garland on thy brow,
      And watch that fame of thine.

But when thou humbledst low the Moslem's pride and scorn,
And bad'st her crescent sink, her vain and feeble horn,
And pass'dst the Belt again, with songs and hymns of joy,
Who that perceived thy flag, in all its mightiness,—
      What Russian could repress
      The tears that dimmed his eye?

I see the people rush to welcome thee again,
Thy ships, with trophies deep, upon the swelling main;
I see the maidens haste, the aged and the young;
The children wave their hands, and to their father turn,
      And thousand questions burn
      On their inquiring tongue.

" Is this the eagle proud of whom we have been told,
Who led against the Turks the Russian heroes bold,
And with their warriors' blood the azure ocean dyed?
Is this our Orlóv,—this with eagle's heart and name,
      His foe's reproach and shame,
      And Russia's strength and pride?"

Oh, yes! Oh, yes, 't is he! The eagle there appears,
And ocean bears him on, as proud of him she bears:
And see his brother too, who led to victory, there—
And Spirídov, whose praise all ages shall renew,
      And Greyg and Ilín too,—
      The heroes, without fear.

But wherefore do I rest,— what fancies led me on?
The glorious eagle now to Asia's coast is flown,

O'er streams, and hills, and vales, he takes his course sub-
    lime,
My eye in vain pursues his all-subduing flight.
        O vision of delight!
        O victory-girded time!

And heaven, and earth, and sea have seen our victories won,
And echo with the deeds that Catherine has done;
The Baltic coasts in vain oppose the march of Paul,
Not the vast North alone, but all th' Ægean Sea
        Shall own his sovereignty,
        And the whole earthly ball!

Mikhaíl Matvyéevich Kheráskov. (1733-1807.)

The son of a Wallachian emigrant, Kheráskov served in succession
in the army, the Kommerz-Kolleg (Ministry of Finances) and the
Moscow University, where he was first Director and later Curator.
He began to write early, and for half a century produced a very large
number of poems in every imaginable field of the pseudo-classic
school.   They now appall us with their inane voluminousness, but in
his day he was regarded as a great poet, a veritable Russian Homer.
His best heroic epics are his *Rossiad* and *Vladímir Regenerated*.
The first, containing some ten thousand verses, celebrates the conquest of Kazán by Iván the Terrible; the second, of even more imposing length, tells of the introduction of Christianity into Russia.
Though containing some fine passages, these epics reveal too much
the influence of Vergil and Tasso, and make rather dreary reading.

FROM THE "ROSSIAD"

I sing Russia delivered from the barbarians, the trampled
power of the Tartars, and their pride subdued, the stir of
ancient mights, their labours, bloody strife, Russia's victory,
Kazán destroyed! How from the circle of those times, the
beginning of peaceful years, a bright dawn has shone forth
in Russia!

Oh, thou gleamest above the radiant stars, spirit of poetry!
Come from thy heights, and shed over my weak and dim
creation thy light, thy art and illumination! Open, O
eternity, to me the gates of those habitations where all

earthly care is cast away, where the souls of the righteous
receive their rewards, where fame and crowns are deemed a
vanity, where before the star-sprinkled altar the lowest
slave stands in a row with a king, where the poor man forgets his misery, the unfortunate his grief, where every man
will be equal to every other.   Eternity, reveal thyself to me,
that with my lyre I may attract the attention of the nations
and their kings!

In the grottoes within the Caucasian icy mountains, which
the bold glance of mortal has never spied, where the frost
creates an eternal translucent vault and dulls the fall of the
sun's rays, where lightning is dead, where thunder is fettered, there stands, cut into ice, a mighty mansion.   There
are the storms, there are the cold, blizzards, tempests; there
Winter reigns, devouring years. This austere sister of other
days, though hoary, is swift and agile.   Rival of Spring,
Autumn and Summer, she is clad in the purple woven of
snow; stark-frozen steam serves her as veil.   Her throne
has the form of a diamond mountain.   Great pillars, of ice
constructed, cast a silvery sheen, illumined by the sun; over
the heavenly vault glides the solar splendour, and then it
seems a mass of ice is on fire.

The elements have no motion: the air dares not move, nor
the fire glow.   There are no coloured fields; among the
fields of ice gleam only frozen flowery vapours; the waters in
the heavens, melted by the rays, hang, petrified, in wavy
layers; there in the air you may discern the words of
prophecy, but all is stark, and nature dead.   Only tremor,
chill and frost have life: hoar frosts move about, while
zephyrs grow dumb; snowstorms whirl about in flight,
frosts reign in the place of summer luxury.   There the ice
represents the ruins of cities, one look at which congeals
your blood.   Pressed by the frosts, the snows there form
silvery mounds and fields of diamonds.   From there Winter
spreads her dominion over us, devouring the grass in the
fields, the flowers in the vales, and sucking up the living
sap of trees, and on cold pinions bears frosts to us, driving

day away, prolonging gloomy nights, and compelling the sun to turn aside his beaming eyes: with trembling, forests and rivers await her, and chills weave her shrouds from the white billows.

Platón (in civil life Peter Geórgevich) Levshín. (1737–1812.)

What Feofán Prokopóvich had been to the reign of Peter the Great, Platón was to Catherine II. After having studied in the Moscow Theological Academy, where he became a teacher even before ending his course, he took the tonsure at twenty-two; at twenty-five he was made rector of the Seminary. In the same year he attracted Catherine's attention by an eloquent speech *On the Usefulness of Piety*, and he was at once called to St. Petersburg to be her son's spiritual teacher (see p. 326). Platón rose rapidly, and in 1787 he was made metropolitan of Moscow. His liberal and enlightened views on theology were valued not only at home, but his *Brief Theology*, originally published in 1755, has been translated into most European languages, and three times into English. A Russian source informs us that his book on theology was made a text-book at Oxford and Cambridge. Several Englishmen who had visited him, and Dr. Stanley, spoke in the highest terms of this Russian divine.

The translation of his *Brief Theology* in English bears the following titles: *The Present State of the Greek Church in Russia; or, A Summary of Christian Divinity*, by Platon, Late Metropolitan of Moscow, translated from the Slavonian . . . by Robert Pinkerton, Edinburgh, 1814, and New York, 1815; *The Orthodox Doctrine of the Apostolic Eastern Church; or, A Compendium of Christian Theology*, translated from the Greek . . . to which is appended a *Treatise on Melchisedec*, London, Manchester [printed], 1857; Κατηχησις— *The Great Catechism of the Holy Catholic Apostolic and Orthodox Church*, translated from the Greek by J. T. S., London, 1867. *A Sermon preached by order of Her Imperial Majesty, on the Tomb of Peter the Great, in the Cathedral Church of St. Petersburg*, London, 1770.

WHAT ARE IDOLATERS?

The second commandment forbiddeth idolatry, and every unlawful mode of worshipping God.

At one time, almost all nations were in such a state of error (and even now there are many in the same situation), that they worshipped the creatures as gods, such as the sun, the moon, fire, also the lower animals, as bulls, cats, crocodiles; and some even worshipped herbs, such as onion and garlic; and to all these they offered sacrifices, and paid other divine honours, or they made statues in the likeness of men and other animals, and bowed down before them as if they were divinities. But from these shocking and awful errors, the grace of Jesus Christ has delivered us (1 Peter iv. 3).

Such persons also resemble those idolaters as labour for Mammon and their belly; that is, whose thoughts are all taken up about amassing riches, which they either do not make use of, or only sacrifice to their fleshly lusts. With such people, Mammon and the belly are the idols, to whom they devote all their services; and on this account the Holy Scriptures call the love of riches, idolatry (Col. iii. 5); and those also idolaters who make their belly their God (Phil. iii. 19).

This commandment also forbids the use of all unlawful means in the worship of God; that is, when anyone thinks of pleasing God by that which is not acceptable to Him, and which is not commanded in His Word. Such, for instance, were those Israelites who presented to God costly sacrifices while they led ungodly lives. And therefore God, through His prophet Isaiah, declared sacrifices presented from such hands to be hateful in His eyes; that is, their oblations were vain, their incense was an abomination and their fatted calves like dogs in His sight (chap. i. 11). Those persons consequently transgress against this commandment:

1. Who offer hypocritical worship.—Who utter long prayers, which of itself is pious, but suppose that they shall be heard for their much speaking, though at the same time they feel no contrition of spirit. Of a similar character, also, are those hypocrites who on every occasion show themselves zealous for the name of God, zealous for the faith, the glory and the interests of the Church, and who introduce all their speeches with spiritual observations (which in themselves are praiseworthy), but who with all this have nothing in

view but the indulgence of a spirit of ostentation, or promoting their own interest in all that they do, and whose zeal consists only in words with which their conduct does not in the least agree.

2. Hypocritical observances of the fasts.—Who fast, that is, abstain from certain kind of food, and on that account hope for divine acceptance, though at the same time they live in every kind of iniquity.   By them the real fast, which does not consist merely in abstinence from food, but in restraining the corrupt passions, is evil spoken of.   Such, also, are those who adorn the churches, or cover the pictures of the saints with gold and silver, yet at the same time oppress the innocent, who are the Church of the living God, or leave the poor without food.   It is in vain, however, for them to declare that they have done all that they should have done in order to be saved; for, according to the words of Christ " these ought they to have done, and not to leave the other undone " (Matt. xxiii. 23).

3. The superstitious.— Who invent certain miraculous kinds of appearances, for the sake of filthy lucre, or from some sort of extravagant ideas about the salvation of their souls, or who attach an unknown kind of sanctity to some particular places, believing that God will hear prayers sooner in one place than in another.   In a word, all those who transgress against this commandment, who, according to the testimony of Christ, place their hope of salvation in externals, and " omit the weightier matters of law, judgment, mercy and faith."   Therefore, respecting such characters, divine truth declares " This people draweth nigh unto me with their mouth, and honoureth me with their lips; but their heart is far from me.   But in vain they do worship me, teaching for doctrines the commandments of men " (Matt. xv. 8, 9).

Reverencing the pictures is not contrary to this commandment.

We do not act contrary to this commandment, when, according to the ancient custom of Christians, we adorn our temples with the holy pictures. For, in the first place, we do not attempt to draw upon the canvas a representation of the unseen and incomprehensible God, whom we never can represent; but we represent our Saviour in the fashion of a man which He took upon Himself, or His favourites. Secondly, the pictures are made and placed in our churches, not for deification, but to commemorate the acts of God and of His chosen servants, that we, in beholding them (as, for instance, in looking on the picture of our crucified Saviour), may stir up our soul to piety and to the imitation of them in many acts of their lives. Thirdly, the obeisance which we make before the pictures we do not render to the pictures themselves, that is, to the boards, colours, ornaments or skill of the artist, but we render this to the person whom they represent, and to the pictures only an affectionate salutation. Thus, for example, I bow before the picture of my Saviour, but the devotion of my spirit, my faith, supplication and hope, and the obeisance which I pay, are all rendered to my Saviour alone, who is in heaven, and everywhere present, and the picture is only a kind of sensible incitement of my devotion. Moreover, it is necessary to be known that the obeisance performed before the picture of our Saviour, and that before the picture of any of the saints, though to appearances the same, yet in reality are very different indeed. For the worship which I perform before the picture of the Saviour consists in the deepest humility of soul before Him as Lord and Creator of all; but that which I perform before the pictures of the saints is a reverence which I render to them out of a loving heart as His favourites, and as of the same nature, and of the same Church, and members of the same body with myself.

Of such as err in reverencing the pictures.

But notwithstanding all that has been said, this lawful and holy reverencing of the pictures may be turned into the most abominable sin of idolatry. This is the case when anyone hopes in, or attaches all his respect to the holy pictures, and trusts in their material substance; when, for instance, anyone finds greater sanctity in one picture than in another, or places in them any hope of salvation. They, too, are chargeable with this guilt who bring their own particular picture into the church along with them, and only worship before it, or who respect those pictures more which are adorned than the unadorned, the old more than the new, or decline praying at all when they have not a picture before them. All these, and such like, are great transgressors, and prove a great disgrace to the real profession of the Christian faith.

In order to avoid the above-named errors, it is necessary to remember, 1st, That the worship of God can never be sincere, unless it proceed from a contrite and unfeigned spirit. For all external rites of worship are only marks testifying our internal piety and sincerity towards God, without which they signify nothing. And therefore the gospel requires that the worshippers of God should worship Him in spirit (not externally alone), and in truth, or not in hypocrisy. 2d, We must hold to the divine Word alone, and rest assured that it only contains the true rules by which we ought to please God. And therefore Christ said concerning the Holy Scriptures that in them is contained eternal life.—From *The Present State of the Greek Church in Russia*, translated by R. Pinkerton.

FROM THE ADDRESS UPON THE ACCESSION OF ALEXANDER I.

Thus has the Lord granted to us the privilege of seeing our Emperor crowned and exalted above men. But we, sons of Russia, what is our part in this solemnity? Do not our thanksgivings resound in gratitude to the King of kings for the grace He has bestowed on our monarch and upon us? Yes, they resound with heartfelt fervour, warmed with hopes of a future reign of national glory and happiness! . . .

This crown, Sire, on your head, is a pledge to us of honour, fame and renown, but imposes upon you duties and labours which can only cease with your life; this sceptre in your

right hand, a guarantee to us of repose, demands of you incessant vigilance for our protection; this emblem of empire
in your left hand, a promise to us of security, exacts of you
little but anxiety and care; this purple, for us a shield and
defence from our enemies, challenges you to war and con-
tests; finally, this whole Imperial attire, to us a source of
consolation and confidence, is for you a burden wrought
with danger and toil—yes, a burden and a labour. For see,
to your eyes there will appear an empire the largest upon
which the sun has ever shone; from your wisdom it looks for
the harmonious connection of its parts, the regulation of the
whole. You will see flocking to your feet widows, orphans,
the most destitute, the victims of the abuse of power, of
favour, of corruption and of crime. . . .

But, alas! that near the angels of light the eye should discover the fiendish spirits of darkness. Flattery, calumny
and cunning, with all their wretched brood, will surround
your throne, and foolishly imagine that their hypocrisy will
beguile you. Bribery and partiality will raise their glossy
heads and labour to lower the scale of justice. Luxury,
adorned with every voluptuous charm, presents the intoxicat-
ing draughts of perilous joys to lead astray from the path
of virtue the pure spirit, and engulf it in the slough of indolence and sensuality. Besieged by this riotous band, you
will undoubtedly turn to truth, justice, wisdom and religion,
and, united with you, they will raise their voice to God that
He may rise again in you, and scatter your enemies.

Monarch of Russia! This struggle awaits you. For this
contest gird on your sword! Draw it with valour, young
hero! Fight, conquer and govern! The omnipotent arm
of the Almighty will wonderfully protect you. We say
rightly " wonderfully "; for here not to fall, here to conquer,
here to maintain order and peace, truly! for this is more
than human strength required; and, though the decree of
the Eternal Being has appointed for you an exalted rank
among men, you are nevertheless a man like any of us.—
Given in Grahame's *The Progress of Science, Art and Literature in Russia.*

Iván Ivánovich Khémnitser. (1745-1784.)

Khémnitser was the son of a German physician who had emigrated to Russia. At thirteen years of age he left his home and entered military service, which he left in 1769 as a lieutenant; he then served in the Department of Mines, and died in Smyrna, where he was Russian consul. Khémnitser translated La Fontaine's and Gellert's fables, but two-thirds of all the fables he wrote are his own. He forms the transitional stage between Sumarókov and Krylóv, and is distinguished for extreme simplicity of language and a certain elegiac tone.

Sir John Bowring has translated his *The House-Builder*, *The Rich and the Poor Man*, *The Lion's Council of State*, and *The Waggons*. Sutherland Edwards, in his *The Russians at Home*, gives a version of *The Metaphysician*, which is also reprinted in F. R. Grahame's *The Progress of Science, Art and Literature in Russia*.

THE LION'S COUNCIL OF STATE

A lion held a court for state affairs:
Why? That is not your business, sir, 't was theirs!
He called the elephants for counsellors—still
The council-board was incomplete;
And the king deemed it fit
With asses all the vacancies to fill.
Heaven help the state—for lo! the bench of asses
The bench of elephants by far surpasses.

He was a fool, the foresaid king, you 'll say:
Better have kept those places vacant surely,
Than fill them up so poorly.
O no! that 's not the royal way;
Things have been done for ages thus,—and we
Have a deep reverence for antiquity:
Naught worse, sir, than to be, or to appear
Wiser and better than our fathers were.
The list must be complete, even though you make it
Complete with asses; for the lion saw
Such had for ages been the law,—
He was no radical to break it!

" Besides," he said, " my elephants' good sense
Will soon my asses' ignorance diminish,
For wisdom has a mighty influence."
They made a pretty finish!
The asses' folly soon obtained the sway:
The elephants became as dull as they!

> —From Sir John Bowring's *Specimens of
> the Russian Poets*, Part I.

THE METAPHYSICIAN

A father had heard that children were sent beyond the sea
to study, and that those who had been abroad are invariably
preferred to those who had never been there, and that such
people are respected as being possessed of wisdom. Seeing
this, he decided to send his son also beyond the sea, for he
was rich and did not wish to fall behind the others.

His son learned something, but, being stupid, returned
more stupid yet. He had fallen into the hands of scholastic
prevaricators who more than once have deprived people of
their senses by giving explanations of inexplicable things;
they taught him no whit, and sent him home a fool for ever.
Formerly he used to utter simply stupid things, but now he
gave them a scientific turn. Formerly fools only could not
understand him, but now even wise men could not grasp
him: his home, the city, the whole world, was tired of his
chattering.

Once, raving in a metaphysical meditation over an old
proposition to find the first cause of all things,—while he
was soaring in the clouds in thought,—he walked off the road
and fell into a ditch. His father, who happened to be with
him, hastened to bring a rope, in order to save the precious
wisdom of his house. In the meantime his wise offspring
sat in the ditch and meditated: " What can be the cause of
my fall? The cause of my stumbling," the wiseacre con-
cluded, " is an earthquake. And the precipitous tendency
towards the ditch may have been produced by an aërial
pressure, and a coactive interrelation of the seven planets
and the earth and ditch."   .   .   .

His father arrived with the rope: " Here," he said, " is a rope for you! Take hold of it, and I will pull you out. Hold on to it and do not let it slip!" " No, don't pull yet: tell me first what kind of a thing is a rope?"

His father was not a learned man, but he had his wits about him, so, leaving his foolish question alone, he said: "A rope is a thing with which to pull people out of ditches into which they have fallen." " Why have they not invented a machine for that? A rope is too simple a thing." " 'T would take time for that," his father replied, " whereas your salvation is now at hand." " Time? What kind of a thing is time?" " Time is a thing that I am not going to waste with a fool. Stay there," his father said, " until I shall return!"

How would it be if all the other verbose talkers were collected and put in the ditch to serve him as companions? Well, it would take a much larger ditch for that.

Yákov Borísovich Knyazhnín. (1742–1791.)

Knyazhnín was born in Pskov, where he received his early education ; in St. Petersburg he acquired German, French and Italian, and began to write verses. He served in civil and military government offices. In 1769 he wrote his first tragedy, *Dido*, which attracted Catherine's attention to him. He then married Sumarókov's daughter and devoted himself more especially to literature. Knyazhnín wrote a number of tragedies and comedies : the subject of all of these is taken from Italian and French, thus his *Vadím of Nóvgorod* is based on Metastasio's *Clemenza di Tito*, and the original of *Odd People* is Destouches's *L'homme singulier*. The *Vadím of Nóvgorod* had a peculiar history. Knyazhnín had great admiration for Catherine and her autocratic rule. In his *Vadím* he tried to depict the struggle between republican Nóvgorod and the monarchic Rúrik, in which the latter comes out victorious, to the advantage of unruly Nóvgorod. He had written it in 1789, but did not stage it on account of the disturbed condition of Europe under the incipient French Revolution. Two years after his death, in 1793, Princess Dáshkov, the President of the Academy, inadvertently ordered it to be published. The book appeared most inopportunely, at the very time the Revolution had broken forth. The tendency of the tragedy was overlooked, and only the republican utterances of Vadím were taken notice of. The book was ordered to be burnt by the executioner, but as only a few copies could be found in the storeroom of the Academy, the rest having been sold in the meanwhile, they were privately destroyed.

VADÍM OF NÓVGOROĎ

ACT I., SCENE 2. VADÍM, PRENÉST AND VÍGOR

Vadím. Could Rúrik so transform your spirit that you only weep where your duty is to strike?

Prenést. We burn to follow you, to be glorified for ever, to crush the haughty throne, to resuscitate our land; but though the zeal already burns within our hearts, it sees as yet no means of its fulfilment. Disdaining harsh and laborious days, if needs we must die, we are ready; but that our death be not in vain and could save our beloved land from evil, and that, intent to break the fetters, we tighten them not more in servitude,—we must expect the aid of the immortals, for the gods can give us a favourable opportunity.

Vadím. So we must depend alone upon the gods and ingloriously remain the slaves we are? The gods have given us the opportunity to wrest back freedom, and hearts to dare, and hands to strike! Their aid is within us: what else do you wish? Go, creep, await in vain their thunder, but I alone, boiling with anger, will move to die for you, for I can brook no master! O fate! For three years absent from my country, enticed by victory for its glory I left liberty and happiness within these walls against us erected, and have been hurling pride into the dust. I bear the fruit of my exploits a gift to my nation: but what do I see? Lords who have lost their liberty bent in loathsome slavery before the king, and kissing their yoke under the sceptre. Tell me, how could you, seeing your country's fall, for a moment prolong your life in shame? And if you could not preserve your liberty,—how could you bear the light and want to live?

Vígor. As before, we burn with love for our fatherland!

Vadím. Prove it not with words, but with your blood! From your speech reject that sacred word. Or can slaves have a fatherland?

Vígor. Your spirit justly is with grief embittered, but in

vain you, bedimmed by anger, accuse us, who are innocent,
of such an evil crime. No sooner did you before the army
bid our land good-bye, than many lords, seeing a means
for evildoing, they, the mighty, let into the city, for the
country's doom, arrogance, envy, hatred, riot. The home
of peace was transformed into a hell; the holy truth henceforth passed away; liberty, flurried, tottered to its fall; civil
strife with brazen brow erected a house of death upon the
bodies of its citizens. The people seeing itself a prey of
hungry ravens fought with madness for the election of a
tyrant. The whole Vólkhov boiled with reeking blood.
Pitiful Nóvgorod, you saw no salvation! The venerable
Gostomýsl, with grey hair adorned, had lost all his sons
under these our walls, and, weeping not for them but the
calamity of the citizens, was alone given to us a consolation
by the immortals. He invited Rúrik to our aid, and with
his sword returned happiness to us. Just then, worn out
from years and woes, Gostomýsl ended his days, beaming
with joy for having brought back peace to his country; but
departing to the gods and honouring Rúrik's heroism, he
enjoined the nation to leave to him the power which had put
a stop to its groans and sorrows. Our people, touched by
so great deserts, placed the saviour over itself as ruler.

Vadím. Ruler! Rúrik! What nation has he saved?
Having come to our aid, what has he done for us? He has
paid a debt! However his benefactions may have seemed to
you to deserve repayment, were you compelled to pay with
your liberty, and make your enslavement a gift to merit?
O low souls that fall down before fate and are inveigled by
the stream of chance,— oh, if you had known how to respect
yourselves! Blessed would Rúrik be, if he had been able,
though clad in porphyry, to become equal to our citizens.
Renowned by his high title among all kings, he would have
been sufficiently rewarded by this distinction. Tell me: did
Gostomýsl, aware of his heroic deeds, enjoin fetters to you,
to end your woes, or was his will the freedom of the citizens?
Or did he turn you over to him, like those beasts whom
anyone who lists may bridle?

ODD PEOPLE

ACT II., SCENE 2.   MRS. INDOLENT, ÚLINKA, WEATHERVANE

Weathervane. Ma charmante Úlinka! Oh, how beautiful you are! Tous ces gens, how stupid, how dishonest, and they will not see in your eyes what I see.

Úlinka. And what do you see?

Weathervane. Friponne! As if you did not know yourself that it is not possible to hate you, that you are fairer than heaven! (*Úlinka courtesies.*) You courtesy! How elegant! What a consolation to have such a daughter! (*To Mrs. Indolent.*) Is it not so, Maman?

Mrs. Indolent. I must confess that her education is what her birth demands, and as she has all liberty in her movements, as behooves a daughter born of me, she is, sir, removed from all coarseness; and keeping herself aloof from everything, as our dignity demands, she knows neither how to sew nor weave, leaving such occupations to common people; she dances like a peacock, sings like a nightingale, and, knowing French like a Frenchwoman, she would like to forget her Russian; she retires at three o'clock, rises at twelve, and passes two hours at her toilet.

Weathervane. Bravo, madam! That's the way it ought to be before the world and men,—ah, how do you call it? pour les gens du haut ton. You must pardon me a little, madam, if I too, duly cautious of my honour, regard our language to be nothing but a jargon, in which it is not possible properly to express your thoughts, and where you have to wear yourself out mercilessly in the attempt of finding your ideas. Only out of compulsion do I speak that language to my lackey, coachman and with all common people, where there is no need to exert yourself in thinking. But with our distinguished people it would be to appear a fool, not to speak French to them. Pray tell me, how could I fall in love? Je brûle, je languis! How could I express that in Russian to charming Úlinka: I faint, I burn,—

fi donc! I must assume that you speak French, and so does your époux. . . .

Mrs. Indolent (perplexed). Of course, of course! Comment vous portez-vous?

Weathervane. Bravo, madam!

Mrs. Indolent. I am now a little out of practice, but formerly I never prattled in Russian.

Weathervane. You will hardly believe how poor I am in Russian! In Russian my intelligence is so narrow, so small! But in French: o, que le diable m'emporte! My intelligence at once walks in by the grande porte. I 'll tell you what once happened to me. I was once sitting with a young lady who did not know two words of French, and that caused ma tête horriblement to ache, so that I had to pass a whole day at home in undress.

Mrs. Indolent. I should not think the harm could be so great. The pain, no doubt, was caused through nagimation.

Weathervane. Imagination you meant to say?

Mrs. Indolent. That 's it. You see, though I am a little out of practice, I am still able to adorn our coarse tongue, which I despise, with French morsels. My époux has always seemed such an odd fellow to me because, though he knows French like a Frenchman, he does not care to amuse himself with that charming language.

Weathervane. That, madam, I cannot understand. A nobleman . . .

Mrs. Indolent. Oh! His race is as distinguished as the ace of trumps, and nobody can compare with him in antiquity of origin: he can recount his ancestors a thousand years back.

Weathervane. And so there is not the least obstacle, ma charmante Úlinka, for regarding you as my own! (*Úlinka makes a courtesy.*) Everything is equal in us: the graces, and pleasures, and intelligence, je m'en flatte, and even our families. (*Úlinka courtesies.*) How delicate your courtesying at the mention of family! Courtesying takes the place of redundant language, de discours frivoles, superfluous babbling. She knows how to say everything in a charming manner, and with modesty to express an immodest wish, who knows how to courtesy like Úlinka. (*Noticing Mrs. Indolent's husband.*) Please tell me who is that bear that is walking towards us?

Mrs. Indolent. My husband.

Weathervane. You are joking! Is it not rather his ancestor who a thousand years ago began his race?

Mrs. Indolent. The exterior, you know, does not tell much. In this world, sir, it is not rare for hidden nobility to deceive the eye: though the diamond does not shine in the bark, yet it is a diamond. He is, I assure you, a nobleman of ancient race, and, forgive me, a bit of a philosopher.

Weathervane. Is it not a shame to rank yourself with asses? Is it an occupation for a nobleman to philosophise?

Mrs. Indolent (*to Úlinka*). Now, Úlinka, you cannot stay here; we have to talk with father about you. (*Úlinka courtesies. Exit.*)

SCENE 3. INDOLENT, MRS. INDOLENT, WEATHERVANE

Mrs. Indolent (*aside*). O Heaven! Help me to end all successfully. I tremble, I am afraid my husband will give me away, for he cannot speak a word of French, and it is but recently that he was made a nobleman. How unfortunate I am! How am I to bear it all? (*To her husband.*) You see here that distinguished cavalier who is doing us the extreme honour.

Weathervane (*bending, greets him foppishly*). I wish to be a son-in-law. . . .

Indolent (*seating himself*). He who wants to sit down, let him sit down. I have no use for your manners, according to which one has to be urged to sit down. Well, distinguished cavalier . . . (*Weathervane bows again foppishly*) please quit your monograms which you are making with your feet. By bowing in flourishes, between us be it said, you will find little favour with me. With all these goatlike leaps a person appears to me to be full of wind and without a soul. Sir, make a mental note of it, if you wish to be my son-in-law.

Weathervane. If I wish? O ciel! Those are tous mes vœux! Agnes Sorel was not so loved by the French king, as your daughter by me. Je jurerai toujours, I may say without making any court to her, she is a divinité!

Indolent (to his wife in amazement). From where, dear wife, has God sent you such a cavalier?

Weathervane. Beaucoup d'honneur, monsieur! So I have found favour in your eyes? I knew I would. You will not find another one like me, monsieur!

Indolent. Mosyo, give me a chance to regain my senses! I beg you. . . .

Weathervane. But you put me to shame: you flatter me by saying that you are stunned by me.

Indolent. Proceed, tormentor!

Weathervane. 'T is true I have merite; without boasting, j'ose vous dire that; but I do not know whether it will cause any delire,—only the world says that it would take a pretty good man to beat me for talent; qu'un homme tel que moi . . .

Indolent. Don't believe it, the world often rants.

Weathervane. Comment?

Indolent. Tell me, are you a Russian or a Frenchman?

Weathervane. Hélas! I am not a Frenchman!

Indolent. What makes you groan so?

Weathervane (sorrowfully). I am a Russian, and that is a burden on my heart.

Indolent. And so you regard it an insult to be a Russian? A fine distinguished nobleman!

Weathervane. I am very, very glad, on ne peut plus, that I have pleased you, monsieur; que vous avez the same thoughts as I. How can we best prove our nobility? By not knowing Russian, despising all that is ours,— those are the veritable signs of our descent.

Indolent. Though I cannot understand everything you say, since I do not know any foreign words, yet by the marks . . .

Weathervane. Vous vous moquez, monsieur. You do know French.

Indolent (*angrily*). No, no, no!

Weathervane. At your age, monsieur, it is not proper for you to deceive me. You speak French like a Frenchman, or like myself.

Indolent (*impatiently*). Wife, assure him of it, and put a stop to this nonsense.

Weathervane (*angrily*). Je ne le croirai point! How stubborn you are!

Indolent (*excitedly*). The devil . . .

Mrs. Indolent (*rapidly*). My darling, please do not get angry.

Indolent (*excitedly*). Both of you go to! I have not seen the like of him in all my life.

Mrs. Indolent. You are a philosopher, and does Seneca, sir, teach you that?

Indolent (*coolly*). I am ready to constrain myself, if only he will talk Russian with me.

Weathervane. What! you are of a very noble origin, and you are piqued?

Indolent (*beside himself*). Who told you so? I am of burgher origin, but of a good family.

Weathervane. You, monsieur, have been a nobleman these thousand years.

Indolent. Believe me, I am a new-baked dumpling; but I am more juicy than those that have grown tough.

Mrs. Indolent. Stop that . . .

Indolent. That we may understand each other, I shall tell you plainly: my father, all remember that, was an honest smith.

Weathervane. Qu'entends-je! (*He walks away, singing a French song.*)

Indolent. Good-bye!

Mrs. Indolent (*fainting away*). I am undone! Oh, I am sick!

Indolent. What nonsense! To feel sick because I cannot speak French, and because my father is a smith! You ought not to have treated me that way, by lying about me. No, my Úlinka shall not mary him.

Princess Ekaterína Románovna Dáshkov.
(1743–1810.)

Princess Dáshkov was educated in the house of her uncle, Vice-Chancellor Vorontsóv. She knew a number of foreign languages and took an interest in politics, rummaging through the documents in her uncle's archives. She travelled much abroad, where she cultivated the acquaintance of Diderot and Voltaire; during a visit in England, when her son was graduating from the Edinburgh University, she met also Robertson and Adam Smith. Upon her return to Russia, Catherine II., partly from a sincere respect for her talents, and partly to reward her for her efforts in obtaining the throne for the Empress, made her the President of the Russian Academy which Princess Dáshkov had herself founded. Her labours for the Academy were both thorough and far-reaching. She encouraged young writers, sent men abroad to be educated, published the first dictionary of the Russian language, caused others to translate from foreign tongues, and herself translated, especially from English; she established several periodicals and did much for the advancement of science. In 1795, Princess Dáshkov incurred the Empress's disfavour for permitting Knyazhnín's drama, *Vadím of Nóvgorod*, to be published in the *Russian Theatre* (see p. 308). Paul, who ascended the throne the next year, removed her from her post, but at the accession of Alexander I., the Academy unanimously voted to reinstate her as its President, but she declined the offer.

Her *Memoirs* were originally written in French, but they first saw the light in English, under the title: *Memoirs of Princess Dashkaw, Written by Herself*, edited by Mrs. W. Bradford, London, 1840, 2 vols.

THE ESTABLISHMENT OF A RUSSIAN ACADEMY

One day, whilst I was walking with the Empress in the gardens of Tsárskoe Seló, our conversation turned on the beauty and richness of the Russian language, which led me to express a sort of surprise that her Majesty, who could well appreciate its value, and was herself an author, had never thought of establishing a Russian Academy.

I observed that nothing was wanting but rules, and a good dictionary, to render our language wholly independent of those foreign terms and phrases, so very inferior to our own in expression and energy, which had been so absurdly introduced into it.

"I really know not," replied her Majesty, "how it happens that such an idea has not been already carried into effect; the usefulness of an establishment for the improvement of our own language has often occupied my thoughts, and I have even given directions about it."

"That is very surprising, madam," said I, "for surely nothing can well be easier than the execution of such a project. There is a great variety of models to be found, and you have only to make choice of the best."

"Do you, Princess, I beg," returned her Majesty, "give me a sketch of one."

"It would be better, madam," replied I, "were you to order one of your secretaries to present you with a plan of the French Academy, the Academy at Berlin, and a few others, with remarks on such particulars as might be better adapted to the genius and habits of your own people."

"I entreat of you, I must beg to repeat it," said the Empress, "that you will take upon yourself this trouble, for then I can confidently look forward, through your zeal and activity, to the accomplishment of an object which, with shame I confess it, has been too long delayed."

"The trouble, madam," I said, "will be very trifling, and I will obey you as expeditiously as possible; but I have not the books I wish to refer to at hand, and I must be allowed the liberty of again assuring your Majesty that any of the secretaries in the ante-chamber would execute the commission better than myself."

Her Majesty, however, continuing to express herself of a different opinion, I found it useless to offer objections.

When I returned home in the evening, I set myself, therefore, to consider how I might best execute her orders, and before I went to bed I drew up a sort of plan, which I thought might furnish some ideas for the formation of the establishment in view, and sent it off to the Empress, more, indeed, for the purpose of complying with her wishes than from any serious thought of furnishing a design worthy of her choice and adoption. My astonishment may therefore be imagined, when I received back, from the hands of her

Majesty, this imperfect outline of a scheme hastily conceived and informally drawn up, with all the ceremonial of an official instrument, confirmed by the sanction of her Imperial signature, and accompanied with an ukase which conferred on me the presidentship of the embryo academy. A copy of this ukase, I at the same time learned, had been transmitted to the Senate.

Though this had the air of the Empress's being in earnest, and resolute in her intentions with regard to me, I nevertheless went to Tsárskoe Seló two days afterwards, still hoping to prevail on her Majesty to make choice of some other president. Finding my efforts unavailing, I told her Majesty that as Director of the Academy of Arts and Sciences I had already at my disposal sufficient funds for the maintenance of the new establishment, and that she need be at no other expense, at present, than the purchase of a house for it. These funds, I observed, in explanation, would arise out of the five thousand roubles which she gave annually, from her private purse, for translations of the classics. The Empress evinced her surprise and satisfaction, but expressed her hopes that the translations should be continued.

" Most assuredly, madam," said I, " the translations shall be carried on, and I trust more extensively than hitherto, by the students of the Academy of Sciences, subject to the revision and correction of the professors; and thus the five thousand roubles, of which the directors have never rendered any account, and which, to judge from the very few translations that have appeared, they seem to have put into their own pockets, may now be turned to a very useful purpose. I will have the honour, madam," added I, " of presenting you soon with an estimate of all the necessary expenses of the proposed establishment; and considering the sum I have stated as the extent of its means, we shall then see if anything remains for the less absolute requisites, such as medals and casts,—a few of which may be deemed, indeed, almost indispensable, in order to reward and distinguish the most deserving of its students."

In the estimate, which I accordingly made, I fixed the

salary of two secretaries at 900 roubles, and of two translators at 450 roubles each. It was necessary, also, to have a
treasurer, and four persons, invalid soldiers, to heat the
stove and take care of the house. These appointments
together I estimated at 3300 roubles, which left the 1700 for
fuel, paper and the occasional purchase of books, but no
surplus whatever for casts and medals.

Her Majesty, who had been accustomed to a very different
scale of expenditure, was, I think, more surprised than
pleased at this estimate; but signified her desire to add
whatever was wanted for the purposes not provided for in it,
and this I fixed at 1250 roubles. The salary of the president,
and contingent perquisites of office, were not usually forgotten in estimates of this nature, but in the present I had not
assigned myself a single rouble; and thus was a most useful
establishment, answering every object of its institution,
founded and supported at no greater expense to her Majesty
than the price of a few honorary badges.

To sum up all that may be said on the subject of the Russian Academy, I may be allowed to state the following particulars: viz., in the first place, that with three years' arrears
of her Majesty's bounty, originally granted for the translation
of the classics, which had not been paid to Mr. Domáshuev,
—that is to say, with 15,000 roubles, in addition to what sums
I could spare from the economic fund,—I built two houses in
the court of the house given by the Empress for the Academy,
which added a rent of 1950 roubles to its revenue; I furnished the house of the Academy, and by degrees purchased
a very considerable library, having, in the meantime, lent
my own for its use; I left 4900 roubles as a fund, placed in
the Foundling Hospital; I began, finished and published a
dictionary; and all this I had accomplished at the end of
eleven years. I say nothing of the new building for the
Academy, the elevation of which has been so much admired,
executed, indeed, under my directions, but at the expense of
the Crown, and therefore not to be enumerated among those
labours which were more especially my own. Besides, had
it been, strictly speaking, a work of mine, I could never

have considered it as one of my labours; for with so decided a taste, or rather passion, as I had for architecture, such a work would have formed one of my highest gratifications.

I ought to observe, before I dismiss the subject, that many things occurred at Court relative to the concerns of my office both to vex and disgust me. The enlightened part of the public, indeed, rendered me more than justice in the tribute of praise they bestowed on my zeal and public-spiritedness, to which they were pleased to refer all the merit of the institution of a Russian Academy, as well as the astonishing rapidity with which the first dictionary of our native language was completed.

This latter work was the subject of a very clamorous criticism, particularly as to the method of its verbal arrangement, which was not according to an alphabetical, but an etymological order. This was objected to, as rendering the dictionary confused, and ill adapted for popular use; an objection very loudly echoed by the courtiers as soon as it was known to have been made by the Empress, who asked me more than once why we had adopted so inconvenient an arrangement. It was, I informed her Majesty, no unusual one in the first dictionary of any language, on account of the greater facility it afforded in showing and even discovering the roots of words; but that the Academy would publish, in about three years, a second edition, arranged alphabetically, and much more perfect in every respect.

I know not how it was that the Empress, whose perception could embrace every object, even those the most profound, appeared not to comprehend me, but this I know, that I experienced in consequence much annoyance, and notwithstanding my repugnance to declare the opinion which her Majesty had pronounced against our dictionary, at a sitting of the Academy, I determined to bring forward the question again at our first meeting, without entering into some other matters connected with it for which I had often been made accountable.

All the members, as I expected, gave their judgment that it was impossible to arrange otherwise the first dictionary of our language, but that the second would be more complete, and disposed in aphabetical order.

I repeated to the Empress, the next time I saw her, the unanimous opinion of the academicians, and the reason for it. Her Majesty, however, continued to retain her own, and was, in fact, at that time much interested in a work dignified by the name of a dictionary, of which Mr. Pallas was the compiler. It was a sort of vocabulary, in nearly a hundred languages, some of which presented the reader with about a score of words only, such as *earth, air, water, father, mother* and so forth. Its learned author, celebrated for the publication of his travels in Russia, and for his attainments in natural history, had dared to run up the expense of printing this work, called a dictionary, to flatter a little prejudice of her Majesty, to a sum exceeding 20,000 roubles, not to mention the very considerable cost it brought on the Cabinet in dispatching couriers into Siberia, Kamchatka and so forth, to pick up a few words in different languages, meagre and of little utility.

Paltry and imperfect as was this singular performance, it was extolled as an admirable dictionary, and was to me at that time an occasion of much disgust and vexation.

Semén Andréevich Poroshín. (1741–1769.)

Poroshín studied in the military school, where he distinguished himself for his knowledge of foreign languages and mathematics. Even as a student, he became a contributor to literary magazines. After leaving school, he was attached as adjutant to Peter III. From 1762 he was teacher of mathematics to Paul, whom he tried to impress with a sense of duty and love of country. In 1764 and 1765 he kept a diary of his relations to the young Grand Duke, hoping some day to use it as material for a history of his reign. In 1769 he died during an expedition against Turkey, being then commander of a regiment of infantry.

FROM HIS "DIARY"

October 29, 1764.—Having dressed himself, his Highness sat down to study. Then he went incognito to his drawing-room to get a look at the Turkish ambassador, who was having an audience with his Excellency Nikíta Ivánovich. He was received in the same manner as the first time. But when I arrived, his Highness did not receive me so kindly as to make me satisfied with him. I do not wish now to enter into any especial discussion of the cause of it, but will only remark that his Highness is frequently greatly influenced by the remarks made in regard to absent persons which he happens to overhear. I have repeatedly noticed that if anything favourable or laudatory is said in his hearing of someone, his Highness later shows himself kindly disposed to him; if, on the contrary, something unfavourable and deprecatory is said of anyone, especially when the remark is not made directly to his Highness, but as if by accident, he, seeing him, appears to be cold to him.

We seated ourselves at the table. His Excellency Nikíta Ivánovich did not dine with us. Of outsiders there was only Count Alexander Sergyéich Stroganóv. I have suffered terrible anguish to-day at table. How could one help suffering, considering what had taken place? We were talking about Peter the Great. Someone, passing in silence all the great qualities of that monarch, deemed it proper to dwell only on the fact that the Tsar used often to get drunk, and that he beat his ministers with his cane. Another person, incautiously emulating this conversation, which ought in no way be tolerated in the presence of his Highness, added that when the Tsar was at one time beating with his cane one of his generals who was a German, the latter later repeated from the Bible: "The hand of the Lord was upon me, etc." The first person continued, saying that history knew only of two royal wallopers, Peter I. and the late King of Prussia, the father of the present King. Later he began to praise Charles XII., the King of Sweden; I told him that Voltaire had written that Charles XII. deserved to be the first soldier in Peter the Great's army. Upon this his Highness asked whether it was really so. The speaker answered his Highness that it was very likely written that way, but that it was nothing but mere flattery.

When I later spoke of the Emperor's letters, which he had

written from abroad to his ministers, and remarked that for
the correct understanding of his time it was necessary to
have these letters, and that I possessed many of them, and
so forth, the first speaker did not deign to make any other
remarks thereupon except that these letters were very funny
because the Emperor often addressed them to " Min Her Ad-
miral," and signed them " Piter." I found it difficult to dis-
semble my dissatisfaction, and to subdue my excitement.

I leave it to the whole intelligent and unbiassed world
whether it is proper to let his Imperial Highness, the heir
apparent of the Russian throne, and a great-grandchild of
Emperor Peter the Great, to be a witness to such malicious
remarks. Xenophon has represented in his Cyrus a perfect
king, and his rule a beneficent rule, and an example for the
emulation of the monarchs of future generations. Senseless
historians in many points contradict Xenophon's history,
and try to point out the weaknesses of his hero. But clever
and far-sighted men care very little whether Cyrus was
really such as Xenophon has painted him, or otherwise,
and extol the historian for having given us a perfect model
for kings, and they adduce his wise rule as an example for
them to follow. Thus, too, many other monarchs, whose
great deeds history has preserved to our own days, are
adduced as an example. Is it not necessary to present to
his Highness the praiseworthy deeds of famous heroes, in
order to rouse in him the desire and noble impulse of emulating them? That seems to be evident and incontrovertible.
Now, whose deeds will awaken in him a greater attention,
will produce a stronger effect upon him, and are more important for his knowledge, than the deeds of Emperor Peter
the Great of blessed memory? They are esteemed great and
glorious in the whole subsolar world, and are proclaimed
with ecstasy by the lips of the sons of Russia. The Grand
Duke, his Highness's own grandchild, was born in the same
nation, and by the decree of God will in time be the ruler of
the same nation.

If there had never been on the Russian throne such an
incomparable man as was his Highness's great ancestor, it

would be useful to invent him, for his Highness's emulation. But we have such a famous hero,—and what happens? I do not mean to say that the Emperor Peter the Great was free from imperfections. Who of mortals is? As many great men as history knows have all been subject to certain weaknesses. But when they are used as examples, we must not sermonise about their vices, but about their virtues. Vices may either entirely be passed over in silence, or they may be mentioned, but only incidentally, with the remark that the ruler who is taken as a model tried his best to free himself from them and that he overcame them. And the very opposite has happened. . . .

At table Prince Baryatínski remarked that during his stay in Sweden he had heard that all the wearing apparel, sword, boots and everything else that had belonged to King Charles XII. was preserved in the arsenal. I retorted that in our Museum are preserved the wearing apparel and other belongings of Peter the Great, but that we naturally had more reason to keep these things than the Swedes, because the one defended his country and brought it to a flourishing condition, while the other had brought his to such ruin that even to the present day it has not been resuscitated, and that, of course, not one intelligent Swede could mention the name of Charles XII. without disgust. Prince Sergyéich assented to this. Then the conversation turned to Keissler's travels, and then to the academic translators Teplóv, Golubtsóv and Lébedev. I said that they knew and translated Russian well. The first speaker remarked to that: "And yet they all died the same death, namely, from drinking." Thereupon the Grand Duke turned to me and said: "Now, you hear that yourself. I suppose that is not a lie?" I answered that I did not know them intimately, that I was not acquainted with the manner of their demise, and that equally I did not know where that gentleman got his information.

February 28, 1765.—His Highness arose at eight o'clock. After having dressed himself, he sat down to his customary studies. After his lesson he looked with me carefully at the

road map to Moscow, and recollected where and how we
passed the time on our last journey thither. I read to his
Highness Vertot's *History of the Order of Maltese Knights.*
Then he amused himself with his toys, and, attaching to his
cavalry the flag of the admiralty, imagined himself a Maltese
Knight. At ten o'clock we sat down to breakfast. We
spoke of Moscow and dramatic performances. We were
about to rise from table, when someone, I do not remember
who, asked for butter and cheese. The Grand Duke became
angry at the butler and said: "Why did you not put it on
the table before?" and then turning to us: "They simply
steal the things for themselves!" We all armed ourselves
against the Grand Duke and told him in French how bad it
was to insult in this way a man of whom he could not know
whether he was guilty or not.

When we left the table, this sermon was continued. Mr.
Osterwald and I told his Highness in strong terms how bad
his action was, and how easily he could cause those people
to hate him. Then our conversation turned to the labours
that an Emperor must undertake. His Highness remarked
among other things: "But an Emperor cannot work all the
time! He needs also some rest, and his amusements." To
this I retorted to the Grand Duke: "No one demands that
an Emperor should never have any rest, for that is above
human strength, and an Emperor is just such a man as
anybody else; only he has been exalted to his position by
God for his nation, and not for himself; that, consequently,
he must use all his endeavour in the welfare and advancement of his nation; that his amusements and pleasures ought
to consist in his knowledge and vivid representation of the
great mass of his subjects who through his labours and cares
enjoy well-being and numberless advantages, and of the
flourishing condition of his country as the result of his work,
and how his name will in just glory redound to the future
generations." These are the exact words which I spoke to
his Highness. He listened to them very attentively.

September 20, 1765.—The birthday of his Imperial Highness; he is eleven years old. His Highness arose a little

after seven. . . . I was not yet all dressed, when he appeared in my room, took me by my hand and began to walk around with me. I congratulated the Tsarévich upon his birthday, and explained to him my wishes in regard to him, which were similar to those of all the faithful sons of the country. Having dressed himself, he went into the yellow room. His Reverence, Father Platón, addressed to the Tsarévich a short congratulation, in which he presented very strongly and wittily our wishes and hopes in the progress of his Highness's studies. Then his Highness went into the interior apartments to the Empress, and from there with her Highness to church. At the end of the liturgy, Father Platón spoke a sermon on the theme: " Settle it therefore in your hearts, not to meditate before what ye shall answer " (Luke xxi. 14). The whole sermon was beautiful. But especially the final address to her Highness and the Grand Duke visibly moved the hearts of all. Many eyes were seen in tears. . . . The Empress went from church to her inner apartments, and his Highness followed her. As we were there admitted to kiss her hand, she said among other things: " Father Platón does with us what he wants. If he wants us to weep, we weep; if he wants us to laugh, we laugh."

The Satirical Journals (1769-1774), and Nikoláy Ivánovich Nóvikov. (1744-1818.)

The first attempt at a periodical was made as early as the year 1728, when literary essays were regularly added to the news of the day in the *St. Petersburg Gazette*, but the first literary journal was established in 1759 by Sumarókov under the name of *The Industrious Bee*. The example of Russia's first littérateur was at once imitated by a number of private individuals, and magazines became common, though their life was nearly always very short. In 1769 there was issued by Grigóri Kozítski, under Catherine's supervision, the first satirical journal, under the name of *All Kinds of Things*. During the time of reforms, satire appears as a natural weapon of attack against the old order of things, and there was, therefore, nothing unusual in the popularity which this and the following satirical journals attained. There is, however, also another reason for their appearance. The English *Spectator, Tatler* and *Rambler* were at that time well known in Russia, and the literary part of the *St. Petersburg Gazette* brought out a large number of translations from these English journals. *All Kinds of Things* shows plainly the influence of Addison in the tone of playful censure which was to Catherine's liking and which it cultivated.

Of the several satirical periodicals that followed, the *Hell's Post; or, Correspondence between the Lame and the Halt Devils,* by F. Émin, and the famous *Drone*, by N. I. Nóvikov, may be mentioned. The name of the latter is evidently chosen in contradistinction to Sumarókov's *Industrious Bee*, and its editor, of whose imposing personality we shall speak later, belonged to that enlightened class of men who were in sympathy with the most advanced reforms, but had no love for the flimsy Voltairism which pervaded Russian society, and, like the Slavophile Shcherbátov (see p. 287), thought he discerned some stern virtues in the generations preceding the reforms of Peter the Great. He therefore set out to scourge vice wherever he found it. The satirical journals were divided into two camps: some clung to the mild and harmless satire of *All Kinds of Things*, the others took the *Drone* for their model. When the collaboration of Catherine in the first became known, Nóvikov found it necessary to desist from his attacks, to avoid the displeasure of the Empress, and soon his journal stopped entirely. He later edited for a short time the *Painter* and the *Purse*, but in 1774 all satirical journals ceased to exist. The most important of these journals has been the *Painter*, from which a generation of writers drew subjects for their satire or comedy.

Nóvikov's early education was received at the Gymnasium connected with the Moscow University; he was excluded from it in 1760 for laziness and insufficient progress. He soon drifted into literature, and directed his attention to the dissemination of useful knowledge among the people. He developed a prodigious activity from 1772 to 1778, publishing a large number of chronicles and documents dealing with Russian antiquity. In 1779 he rented the University press for ten years, published in three years more books than had been issued by that institution in the preceding twenty-four years of its existence, opened bookstores all over Russia and encouraged and protected a whole generation of young writers. He was a zealous Mason, and in that capacity practised a most generous philanthropy by using the very great income from his venture for the establishment of charities and schools. Catherine was never favourable to the Masons and other mystics who had got a firm foothold in St. Petersburg and Moscow, and when the French Revolution had broken out, she suspected such men as Radíshchev (see p. 361) and Nóvikov of belonging to a secret society whose object was the overturning of the existing order of things. At first she ordered the metropolitan Platón to examine into the soundness of Nóvikov's religious views, but the enlightened prelate reported: "I implore the all-merciful God that not only in the flock which has been entrusted by God and you to me, but in the whole world there should be such good Christians as Nóvikov." Nevertheless, Catherine later found an excuse for seizing Nóvikov and imprisoning him in the fortress of Schlüsselburg, from which he was released by Emperor Paul, who is said with tears in his eyes and upon his knees to have begged Nóvikov's forgiveness for his mother's cruelty to him. He passed the rest of his days in his estate of Tikhvín.

FROM "ALL KINDS OF THINGS"

I lately went to dine in a Moscow suburb with a friend of mine. To my great displeasure I found the house in great sorrow because his wife had had a bad dream which threatened some danger to him, her and their children. We seated ourselves at the table. Their youngest boy, who was sitting at the end of the table, began to cry: "Mamma, I shall begin my problems on Monday." "On Monday!" exclaimed his mother: "The Lord preserve us! Nobody begins anything new on Monday. Tell the deacon to begin on Tuesday." The lady of the house asked me to pass her the salt. I hastened to do her the favour, but, being timid and overzealous, I dropped the salt-cellar in passing it. She trembled when she saw the mishap, and immediately remarked that the salt was spilled in her direction. Collecting herself again, she sighed and said to her husband: "My darling, misfortune never comes single. You will remember that the dove-cot broke down the same day our servant girl spilled the salt on the table." "Yes, I remember," said her husband, "and next day we received the news of the battle of Zorndorf." I managed to finish my dinner, though with a heavy heart. The dinner being over, I accidentally placed my knife and fork crosswise on my plate. The hostess asked me to put them together. I soon learned from the lady's behaviour that she looked upon me as an odd fellow and foreboder of misfortunes.

Gentlemen:—He who writes *All Kinds of Things* ought not to disdain anything. In this hope I, though a common labourer, take up the pen without hesitation, thinking that you might find something of interest in what I write. I have no intricate style, but write simply, just as I think.

I am a silversmith. Though I was not born here, I love Russia. I am not the only German whom it supports. The Lord may grant all to feel as gratefully to Russia, but people feel differently about that. I work for many people, among them for a French teacher. You know there are bushels of them in Moscow. The one I am telling you about came to his profession in a strange manner. He was originally a shoemaker. Suddenly he was seized by the spirit of heroism, or, to tell the truth, indolence and starvation compelled him to enlist as a soldier. After the battle of Rossbach, he fled in company with many others. He worked in many capacities, wandering about from place to place, and finally reached Russia, where he developed the proper qualifications for a coachman. But he soon grew tired of sitting on the coachman's seat, and had a strong desire of getting inside the carriage. He found no easier way of accomplishing his ambition than by becoming a teacher, emulating in this the example of many of his countrymen who, some from the box, like him, others from the footman's stand, have found their way into the carriage. And he succeeded. Thus a lazy shoemaker, runaway soldier and bad coachman was turned into a first-class teacher. At least he appears to me to be good because he pays promptly for my work and does not feed me, as other gentlemen do, with to-morrows.

SOUND REASONING ADORNS A MAN

My teacher made me once a present of a doll on my name-day, accompanying it with the following noteworthy words: "Every brainless man is a doll." I asked him whom he meant by the word "brainless," and he answered: "Him who obeys more his will than established rules." I wanted to know why. He said: "Will without rule is licence, and licence is injurious to oneself and his neighbour, whereas rules have been established in life in order to curb harmful lusts." I sighed and said: "Oh, I see, then our neighbour committed an act of licence, and did not obey the established rules, when he took away our meadows so that our cattle are starving." " Our neighbour," he answered with a smile, " has his own rules. He belongs to the class of people who say every morning: ' Lord, I am in need of everything, but my neighbour is in need of nothing.' "

We paid such a high salary to this teacher that my step-mother found it necessary to dismiss him, in order to add one hundred roubles to the cook's wages, and another cheaper teacher was hired for me. He belonged to the class of people who write in their will that they are to be buried without being washed. His affection for his ungrateful country was so strong that he always had the name of Paris in his mouth, in spite of the fact that he had been driven out of his country with the coat of arms of a full-blown lily imprinted on his back.[1] He knew by heart the names of all the streets of Paris, and the external walls of all the prominent buildings of that city were familiar to him, but he had never had the courage to enter them. He was so adorned with wisdom that he knew everything without having studied anything. He had an absolute contempt for everything that did not transpire in France. For other things he had no mind, for frequently, in a fit of abstraction, he put other people's property into his pockets, the result of which was a certain misunderstanding, as he called it, between him and the police. The police proved that he had stolen, but he affirmed the word " steal " was the invention of crass ignorance, and that an honest man must defend his honour from the police by means of the rapier. So he invited the commissary of police to fight a duel with him. The latter not being as good a talker as he was wont to stick to incontrovertible proofs, ordered my mentor to be cast into prison.

[1] French criminals had the lily burnt upon their backs, hence they wanted to be buried unwashed, that their disgrace should not become apparent.

My mother was quite put out about him, for she said she did not know where to get another cheap teacher like him. However, there arrived at that time some guests at our house who assured her that that very day there had arrived in Moscow the coachman of the French ambassador, with his scullion, hair-dresser, courier and lackey, who did not wish to return with him, and that for the common good of the people of Moscow they had the intention of imparting their arts to those who wanted to be instructed for a reasonable consideration, though somewhat higher than the price they had received in the stable, kitchen, kennel, or for blackening shoes and making wigs.

I once went to see my friend and, as he was not at home, went to his wife's apartments. She had stepped down into the nursery. As I am quite at home there, I went down into the nursery myself and found her surrounded by her four children. The smallest boy started crying; to pacify him, his mother made him beat the nurse with a handkerchief. She pretended she was crying, while the mother kept on repeating : " Beat her, my darling, beat well the stupid nurse! She had no business annoying baby." The child was trying to strike the nurse hard; and the harder he struck her, she feigned weeping harder, whereat the child smiled. A little while later, another child fell down. The mother told it to spit on the floor and to kick the place where it had stumbled. When I remarked that it was not good education to allow the child to do that, she answered me: " My friend, you are always philosophising. As if we had not been brought up in the same way! Why should it be different with these babies?" Then I heard the whining of a dog. I looked around and saw a third child pinching a pup, while another child was frightening a canary bird by striking with his hands against the cage: the poor little bird flitted about distressed from one corner to another. I lost my patience, and told their mother: " You are making tyrants of these children, if you do not teach them to respect man and beast. I 'll tell your husband so!" and I slammed the door as I went out.

FROM THE "DRONE"

RECIPE FOR HIS EXCELLENCY, MR. LACKSENSE

This nobleman suffers from a quotidian fever of boasting of his family. He traces his family tree to the beginning of the universe, and hates all those who cannot prove their aristocratic blood at least five hundred years back, and loathes to speak with those whose nobility is only a hundred years old or less. He shakes with fever the moment somebody mentions burghers or peasants in his presence. In opposition to the modern current appellation, he does not even honour them with the name "low-born," but in the fifty years of his fruitless life he has not yet been able to find a proper term for them. He does not travel to church nor in the streets, for fear of a dead faint which would unavoidably fall upon him the moment he met an ignoble man. Our patient complains hourly against fate for having destined him to share the same air, sun and moon with the common people. He wishes there were no other beings on the whole globe but aristocrats, and that the common people should all be annihilated. He had repeatedly handed in projects to that effect, and they had been highly praised for the good and novel ideas contained therein, though many rejected them, because the inventor demanded three million roubles in advance in order to execute his plans.

Our aristocrat hates and loathes all the sciences and arts, and regards them as a disgrace for any noble gentleman. In his opinion a blueblood can know everything without having learned it; but philosophy, mathematics, physics and all the other sciences are trifles that are below a nobleman's attention. Books of heraldry and letters patent that have just escaped the dust-pile and mould are the only books which he continually reads by spelling out. Alexandrian sheets, on which the names of his ancestors are written in circles, are the only pictures with which his house is adorned. But to be short; the trees by which he illustrates the descent of his family have many a dry limb, but there is no more rotten twig upon them than he himself is, and in all his family coats of arms there is not such a beast as is his Excellency. However, Mr. Lacksense thinks differently of himself, and worships himself as a great man in mind, and as a small god in his nobility. To make the whole world believe the same way, he tries to differ from all others, not by useful and glorious deeds, but by magnificent houses, carriages and liveries, though he spends on his foolishness all his income that ought to support him ten years hence.

Recipe, to cure Mr. Lacksense of his fever.—It is necessary to inoculate the sick man with a good dose of common sense and philanthropy, in order to kill in him his empty superciliousness and the lofty contempt for other people. Noble descent is, indeed, a great privilege, but it will always be dishonoured if it is not fortified by personal worth and noble services to your country. Meseems it is more laudable to be a poor yeoman or burgher and a useful member of society than a distinguished drone who is known only for his stupidity, his house, carriages and liveries.

THE LAUGHING DEMOCRITOS

Bah! There is the miser in his rags and tags, who has all his life been hoarding money and squandering his conscience; who is dying from hunger and cold; who teaches his servants to eat to live, that is, not more than is necessary to keep body and soul together; who is known far and wide for his unlawful usury; who has imposed upon himself and all his slave cattle a whole year's fast; who in winter heats his miserable hut only once a week; who is ready to sell himself for a dime, and who has forty thousand roubles, in order to leave them after his death to his stupid nephew, that seventeen-year-old wretch who in miserliness and unscrupulous usury has surpassed his uncle of sixty years; who steals money from himself and takes a fine from himself for this theft; and who does not want to get married all his life, only not to spend his income on his wife and children. Oh, they deserve being laughed at. Ha, ha, ha!

Meseems I see his opposite. Of course, it is Spendthrift?

Certainly. Oh, that young man has not the vices of his father, but he is infested by other vices, not less objectionable. His father hoarded money by unlawful exactions, and he spends it recklessly. His miserly father consumed in one month what he ought to have eaten in one day; Spendthrift, on the contrary, devours in a day what he ought to eat up in a year. The other walked in order not to spend money for the feeding of the horses; this one keeps six carriages and six tandems, not counting the saddle and sleigh horses, only that he may not get tired of travelling all the time in one and the same carriage. The other wore for twenty years the same miserable caftan; while to Spendthrift twenty pairs a year seem too little. In short, his father collected a great treasure through all illegal means, usury, maltreatment of his kin, and ruin of the helpless; but Spendthrift ruins himself and lavishes on others: they are both fools, and I laugh at both. Ha, ha, ha, ha!

Who is galloping there so swiftly? Bah! it is Simple. He is hurrying to some aristocratic house, to show there his stupidity. Simple glories in visiting distinguished people. He goes to see them as often as possible and, to please them, makes a fool of himself, then boasts to others of the influence he has there. He takes part in their conversations and, though he knows nothing, thinks he is posing as a wise man; he reads books, but he does not understand them; goes to the theatre, criticises the actors and, repeating what he has heard elsewhere, speaks authoritatively: this actor is good, that one is bad. He tells distinguished people all kinds of jokes, and wants to be cutting in his remarks, though he never adapts them to the occasion; in short, Simple tries to convince himself that his acts are intelligent, but others think that they are silly. Ha, ha, ha!

Hypocrite steps humbly out of church and distributes to the poor that surround him a farthing each, and counts them off on his rosary. As he walks along, he mumbles his prayers. He turns his eyes away from women, and shades them with his hands, for he avers he would take them out if they tempted him. Hypocrite sins every minute, but he appears as a righteous man that walks over a path strewn with thorns. His simulated prayers, piety and fasts in no way keep him from ruining and oppressing his like. Hypocrite has stolen thousands, and he gives them away by farthings. By such appearances he deceives many. He hourly preaches the nine virtues to young people, but in the sixty years of his life he has never carried out one himself. Hypocrite always walks humbly and never turns his looks to heaven, for he cannot hope to deceive those that abide there; but he looks upon the earth whose inhabitants he cheats. Ha, ha, ha!

FROM "HELL'S POST"

LETTER FROM HALT TO LAME

Last evening I took a walk in the park where nearly the whole town disports itself twice a week. I seated myself with a friend on a bench: four men, all acquaintances of my friend, passed by us; one of them was an ex-officer who had left the service, in order that he may not serve the Tsar, that he may cheat the world and become rich through illegal means. All the pettifoggers and the minor officials at the court of justice, and all the large litigators are known to him. He hardly ever goes out of the Land Office, and even in other places there appears almost every day a complaint of his. All the doubtful villages are his, and he frequently makes application for them, proving that they once belonged to his ancestors. He has no end of genealogies in his pocket, and upon request can prove his descent from any family he pleases. He buys promissory notes at a great discount, and gets the money from the creditor with all the interest due thereupon. If anybody borrows money from him, he never asks more than five kopeks from the rouble a month, and he deducts the interest in advance.

FROM LAME TO HALT

A certain secretary of a government office in this town

got himself into trouble by taking bribes, but he very soon freed himself through his cunning. Although many orders explicitly demand that no bribes should be received by officers, yet they insist that it is superhuman to receive nothing from complainants. Many people of that class, however, do not submit to the common weakness of the office, and live on their incomes and salaries, but they have always empty pockets. Scribe S. is much richer than Secretary V. because the one sells every step of his, while the other attends to the affairs under his charge for nothing. Now many of these gentlemen have discovered a secret of stealing in a diplomatic way, that is, they no longer take bribes themselves, but send the complainant to their wives, who receive them very graciously. If he is a merchant, she asks for some stuffs or velvet for a dress. When the goods have been brought to her house, she says to the merchant: " My friend, come again in a few days, and I will pay you!" The merchant knows what that means and, being in need of her husband, goes home and for ever bids good-bye to the goods he has furnished. If the complainant is a nobleman, the officer's wife tells him that she has no servant-girl, or boy, and that she is compelled to do all the work herself; and the complainant, having of necessity learned this conventional language, answers her as she wants to be answered. Thus, in the taking of bribes there has been produced this change: formerly the husband was dishonest, now his wife helps him. But there are some officials who are even more cunning and who steal in an honourable manner. They invite the complainant who has any dealing with them to dinner, after which they sit down and play cards with him. When they lose, they assume a very angry look, but when they win, they look exceedingly satisfied: this language the complainants have soon learned to understand. To please the host, they throw off trumps and, losing to the host, say two hundred roubles or as much as the host expects for the case in hand, receive the next day a favourable decision for it. Even the merchants have become refined and frequent the houses of officials to play cards with them.

FROM THE "PAINTER"

To My Son Falaléy:—

Is that the way you respect your father, an honourably discharged captain of dragoons? Did I educate you, accursed one, that I should in my old age be made through you a laughing-stock of the whole town? I wrote you, wretch, in order to instruct you, and you had my letter published. You fiend, you have ruined me, and it is enough to make me insane! Has such a thing ever been heard, that children should ridicule their parents? Do you know that I will order you to be whipped with the knout, in strength of ukases, for disrespect to your parents! God and the Tsar have given me this right, and I have power over your life, which you seem to have forgotten. I think I have told you more than once that if a father or mother kills a son, they are guilty only of an offence against the church.[1] My son, stop in time! Don't play a bad trick upon yourself: it is not far to the Great Lent, and I don't mind fasting then. St. Petersburg is not beyond the hills, and I can reach you by going there myself.

Well, my son, I forgive you for the last time, at your mother's request. If it were not for her, you would have heard of me ere this, nor would I have paid attention to her now, if she were not sick unto death. Only I tell you, look out: if you will be guilty once more of disrespect to me, you need not expect any quarter from me. I am not of Sidórovna's[2] kind: let me get at you, and you will groan for more than a month.

Now listen, my son: if you wish to come into my graces again, ask for your resignation, and come to live with me in the country. There are other people besides you to serve in the army. If there were no war now, I should not mind your serving, but it is now wartime, and you might be sent into the field, which might be the end of you. There is a proverb: "Pray to God, but look out for yourself"; so you

[1] For which the punishment would be a penance of fasting.
[2] His wife's name.

had better get out of the way, which will do you more good.
Ask for your discharge and come home to eat and sleep as
much as you want, and you will have no work to do. What
more do you want ? My dear, it is a hard chase you have
to give after honour. Honour! Honour! It is not much
of an honour, if you have nothing to eat. Suppose you will
get no decoration of St. George, but you will be in better
health than all the cavaliers of the order of St. George.
There are many young people who groan in spite of their
St. George, and many older ones who scarcely live: one has
his hands all shot to pieces, another his legs, another his
head: is it a pleasure for parents to see their sons so disfigured ? And not one girl will want you for a husband.

By the way, I have found a wife for you. She is pretty
well off, knows how to read and write, but, above all, is a
good housekeeper: not a blessed thing is lost with her.
That's the kind of a wife I have found for you. May God
grant you both good counsel and love, and that they should
give you your dismissal! Come back, my dear: you will
have enough to live on outside of the wife's dowry, for I
have laid by a nice little sum. I forgot to tell you that
your fiancée is a cousin of our Governor. That, my friend,
is no small matter, for all our cases at law will be decided in
our favour, and we will swipe the lands of our neighbours
up to their very barns. I tell you it will be a joy, and they
won't have enough land left to let their chickens out. And
then we will travel to the city, and I tell you, my dear
Falaléy, we are going to have a fine time, and people will
have to look out for us. But why should I instruct you ?
You are not a baby now, it is time for you to use your
senses.

You see I am not your ill-wisher and teach you nothing
but that is good for you and that will make you live in greater
comfort. Your uncle Ermoláy gives you the same advice;
he had intended to write to you by the same messenger.
We have discussed these matters quite often, while sitting
under your favourite oak where you used to pass your time
as a child, hanging dogs on the branches, if they did not

hunt well for the rabbits, and whipping the hunters, if their
dogs outran yours. What a joker you used to be when you
were younger! We used to split with laughter looking at
you. Pray to God, my friend! You have enough sense to
get along nicely in this world.

Don't get frightened, dear Falaléy, all is not well in
our house: your mother, Akulína Sidórovna, is lying on her
death-bed. Father Iván has confessed her and given her the
extreme unction. It is one of your dogs that was the cause
of her ailment. Somebody hit your Nalétka with a stick of
wood and broke her back. When she, my little dove, heard
that, she fainted away, and fell down like dead. When she
came to again, she started an inquiry into the matter, which
so exhausted her that she came back scarcely alive, and
had to lie in bed. Besides, she emptied a whole pitcher of
cold water, which gave her a fever. Your mother is ill, my
friend, very ill! I am waiting every minute for God to take
her soul away. So I shall have to part, dear Falaléy, from
my wife, and you from your mother and Nalétka. It will
be easier for you to bear the loss than for me: Nalétka's pups,
thank the Lord! are all alive. Maybe one of them will take
after his mother, but I shall never have such a wife again.

Alas, I am all undone! How can I ever manage to look
after all things myself? Cause me no more sorrow, but
come home and get married, then I shall at least be happy
to have a daughter-in-law. It is hard, my dear Falaléy, to
part from my wife, for I have got used to her, having lived
with her for thirty years. I am guilty before her for having
beaten her so often in her lifetime; but how could it be otherwise? Two pots staying a long time together will get
knocked a great deal against each other. Indeed it could
not be otherwise: I am rather violent, and she is not yield-
ing; and thus, the least thing gave occasion for fights.
Thank the Lord! she was at least forgiving. Learn, my
son, to live well with your wife; though we have had many
a quarrel, yet we are living together, and now I am sorry
for her. It's too bad, my friend, the fortune-tellers cannot
do your mother any good: there have been a lot of them here,

but there is no sense in it, only money thrown away. And now I, your father, Trifón, greet you and send you my blessing.

My Darling Falaléy Trifónovich:—
What kind of tricks have you been playing there, darling of my heart? You are only ruining yourself. You have known Pankrátevich ere this, so why don't you take care of yourself? If you, poor wretch, got into his hands, he would maim you beyond mercy. There is no use denying it, Falaléy, he has a diabolical character, the Lord forgive me for saying so! When he gets into a temper, all my trying to soothe him does no good. When he begins to yell, it 's a shame to leave the holy images in the room. And you, my friend, just think what you have done! You have given his letter to be published! All his neighbours are now making fun of him: "A fine son you have! He is ridiculing his father." They say a great deal more, but who can know all that the evil-minded people say? God help them, they have their own children to look to, and God will pay them their due. They always find fault with somebody else's children, and think that theirs are faultless: well, they had better take a closer look at their own children!
Take good care of yourself, my friend, and don't anger your father, for the devil could not get along with him. Write him a kind letter, and lie yourself out of the affair: that would not be a great sin, for you would not be deceiving a stranger. All children are guilty of some misbehaviour, and how can they get along without telling their fathers some lie? Fathers and mothers do not get very angry with children for that, for they are of necessity their friends. God grant you, darling of my heart, good health!
I am on my death-bed; so do not kill me before my time, but come to us at once, that I may have my last look at you. My friend, I am feeling bad, quite bad. Cheer me up, my shining light, for you are my only one, the apple of my eye, —how can I help loving you? If I had many children, it would not be so bad. Try to find me alive, my dear one:

I will bless you with your angel, and will give you all my money which I have hoarded up in secret from Pankrátevich, and which is for you, my shining light.

Your father gives you but little money, and you are yet a young boy, and you ought to have dainty bits and a good time. You, my friend, are yet of an age to enjoy yourself, just as we did when we were young. Have a good time, my friend, have a good time, for there will later come a time when you will not think of enjoyment. My dear Falaléy, I send you one hundred roubles, but don't write father about it. I send it to you without his knowledge, and if he found it out, he would give me no rest. Fathers are always that way: they only know how to be surly with their children, and they never think of comforting them. But I, my child, have the heart not of a father, but of a mother: I would gladly part with my last kopek, if that would add to your pleasure and health.

My dear Falaléy Trifónovich, my beloved child, my shining light, my clever son, I am not feeling well! It will be hard for me to go away from you. To whose care shall I leave you? That fiend will ruin you; that old brute will maim you some day. Take good care of yourself, my shining light, take the best care you can of yourself! Leave him alone, for you can't do anything with that devil, the Lord forgive me for saying so! Come to our estate, my dear one, as soon as you can. Let me get a look at you, for my heart has the presentiment that my end has come. Good-bye, my dear one, good-bye, my shining light: I, your mother Akulína Sidórovna, send you my blessing and my humblest greeting, my shining light. Good-bye, my dove: do not forget me!

Denís Ivánovich Fon-Vízin. (1744-1792.)

Denís Fon-Vízin tells us in his *Confession* (given below) what his early education was. Even the Moscow University was filled with ignorant, corrupt teachers, and in the country the conditions were naturally much worse. Nor could it have been different in the early part of Catherine's reign. The older generation was steeped in ignorance and superstition, and the upper classes, who carried Voltaire and liberalism on their lips, ranted of a culture of the heart, which was nothing else than an excuse for extreme superficiality, as something superior to culture of the mind. Such a period is naturally productive of characters for comedy and satire. Fon-Vízin, who had the talent for satirical observation, was himself a product of the superficiality of his time. In his letters from abroad he assumed a haughty air of Russian superiority over matters French, German and European in general, aiding in the evolution of a sickly Slavophilism which a Russian critic has characterised as "subacid patriotism." Unfortunately for their originality, most of these attacks on the French and Germans are taken from French and German sources.

Fon-Vízin wrote two comedies, *The Brigadier* and *The Minor*, both of which are regarded as classical. Neither the subjects nor the plots are original. They follow French plays; but Fon-Vízin has so excellently adapted them to the conditions of his time, and has so well portrayed the negative characters of contemporary society, that the comedies serve as an historical document of the time of Catherine II. How true to nature his Ciphers, Beastlys, Uncouths and Brigadiers are may be seen from a perusal of contemporary memoirs and the satirical journals. These give an abundance of such material, and indeed Fon-Vízin has made ample use of them. As there were no positive characters in society, so the characters of his plays that stand for right and justice are nothing more than wordy shadows.

In *The Minor*, of which the first act is here translated, the author gives a picture of the lower nobility, who had not yet outgrown the barbarism of the days preceding Peter's reforms, though anxious to comply, at least outwardly, with the imperative demands of the Government. Peter the Great had promulgated a law that all the children of the nobility must immediately appear to inscribe themselves for service. These "minors" had to present a proof or certificate that they had received instruction in certain prescribed subjects. Without that certificate they could not enter any service, or get married. Up to the time of Catherine II. there were issued laws dealing with such "minors." Mitrofán, the "minor" of the play, has become the nickname for every grown-up illiterate son of the nobility.

THE MINOR

ACT I., SCENE I.   MRS. UNCOUTH, MITROFÁN, EREMYÉEVNA

Mrs. Uncouth (examining Mitrofán's caftan). The caftan is all ruined. Eremyéevna, bring here that thief Tríshka! (*Exit Eremyéevna.*) That rascal has made it too tight all around. Mitrofán, my sweet darling, you must feel dreadfully uncomfortable in your caftan! Go call father. (*Exit Mitrofán.*)

SCENE 2. MRS. UNCOUTH, EREMYÉEVNA, TRÍSHKA

Mrs. Uncouth (to Tríshka). You beast, come here. Did n't I tell you, you thief's snout, to make the caftan wide enough? In the first place, the child is growing; in the second place, the child is delicate enough, without wearing a tight caftan. Tell me, you clod, what is your excuse?

Tríshka. You know, madam, I never learned tailoring. I begged you then to give it to a tailor.

Mrs. Uncouth. So you have got to be a tailor to be able to make a decent caftan! What beastly reasoning!

Tríshka. But a tailor has learned how to do it, madam, and I have n't.

Mrs. Uncouth. How dare you contradict me! One tailor has learned it from another; that one from a third, and so on. But from whom did the first tailor learn? Talk, stupid!

Tríshka. I guess the first tailor made a worse caftan than I.

Mitrofán (running in). I called dad. He sent word he 'll be here in a minute.

Mrs. Uncouth. Go fetch him by force, if you can't by kindness.

Mitrofán. Here is dad.

SCENE 3. THE SAME AND UNCOUTH

Mrs. Uncouth. You have been hiding from me! Now see yourself, sir, what I have come to through your indulgence! What do you think of our son's new dress for his uncle's betrothal? What do you think of the caftan that Tríshka has gotten up?

Uncouth (timidly stammering). A li-ittle baggy.

Mrs. Uncouth. You are baggy yourself, you wiseacre!

Uncouth. I thought, wifey, that you thought that way.

Mrs. Uncouth. Are you blind yourself?

Uncouth. My eyes see nothing by the side of yours.

Mrs. Uncouth. A fine husband the Lord has blessed me with! He can't even make out what is loose and what tight.

Uncouth. I have always relied upon you in such matters, and rely even now.

Mrs. Uncouth. You may rely also upon this, that I will not let the churls do as they please. Go right away, sir, and tell them to flog——

SCENE 4.   THE SAME AND BEASTLY

Beastly. Whom? For what? On the day of my betrothal! I beg you, sister, for the sake of the celebration, put off the flogging until to-morrow, and to-morrow, if you wish, I 'll gladly take a hand in it myself. My name is not Tarás Beastly, if I don't make every offence a serious matter. In such things my custom is the same as yours, sister. But what has made you so angry?

Mrs. Uncouth. Here, brother, I 'll leave it to you. Mitrofán, just come here! Is this caftan baggy?

Beastly. No.

Uncouth. I see now myself, wifey, that it is too tight.

Beastly. But I don't see that. My good fellow, the caftan is just right.

Mrs. Uncouth (to Tríshka). Get out, you beast! (*To Eremyéevna.*) Go, Eremyéevna, and give the child his breakfast. I am afraid the teachers will soon be here.

Eremyéevna. My lady, he has deigned to eat five rolls ere this.

Mrs. Uncouth. So you are too stingy to give him the sixth, you beast? What zeal! I declare!

Eremyéevna. I meant it for his health, my lady. I am looking out for Mitrofán Teréntevich: he has been ill all night.

Mrs. Uncouth. Oh, Holy Virgin! What was the matter with you, darling Mitrofán?

Mitrofán. I don't know what, mamma. I was bent with pain ever since last night's supper.

Beastly. My good fellow, I guess you have had too solid a supper.

Mitrofán. Why, uncle! I have eaten hardly anything.

Uncouth. If I remember rightly, my dear, you did have something.

Mitrofán. Not much of anything: some three slices of salt bacon, and five or six pies, I do not remember which.

Eremyéevna. He kept on begging for something to drink all night long. He deigned to empty a pitcher of kvas.

Mitrofán. And even now I am walking around distracted. All kinds of stuff passed before my eyes all night long.

Mrs. Uncouth. What kind of stuff, darling Mitrofán?

Mitrofán. At times you, mamma, at others—dad.

Mrs. Uncouth. How so?

Mitrofán. No sooner did I close my eyes, than I saw you, mamma, drubbing dad.

Uncouth (*aside*). It is my misfortune, the dream has come to pass!

Mitrofán (*tenderly*). And I felt so sorry.

Mrs. Uncouth (*angrily*). For whom, Mitrofán?

Mitrofán. For you, mamma: you got so tired drubbing dad.

Mrs. Uncouth. Embrace me, darling of my heart! Son, you are my comfort.

Beastly. I see, Mitrofán, you are mother's son and not father's.

Uncouth. I love him anyway as becomes a father: he is such a clever child, such a joker! I am often beside myself with joy when I look at him, and I can't believe that he is my own son.

Beastly. Only now our joker looks a little gloomy.

Mrs. Uncouth. Had I not better send to town for the doctor?

Mitrofán. No, no, mamma. I 'll get well myself. I 'll run now to the dove-cot, maybe——

Mrs. Uncouth. Maybe God will be merciful. Go, have a good time, darling Mitrofán. (*Exeunt Mitrofán and Eremyéevna.*)

SCENE 5.   MRS. UNCOUTH, UNCOUTH, BEASTLY

Beastly. Why do I not see my fiancée? Where is she? The betrothal is to be this evening, so it is about time to let her know that she is to be married soon.

Mrs. Uncouth. There is time for that, brother. If we were to tell her that ahead of time, she might get it into her head that we are reporting to her as to a superior person. Although I am related to her through my husband, yet I love even strangers to obey me.

Uncouth (to Beastly). To tell the truth, we have treated Sophia like a real orphan. She was but a baby when her father died. It is now half a year since her mother, who is related to me by marriage, had an apoplectic fit——

Mrs. Uncouth (as if making the sign of the cross). The Lord be with us!

Uncouth. —which took her to the other world. Her uncle, Mr. Conservative, has gone to Siberia, and as there has been no news from him for some years we regard him as dead. Seeing that she was left alone, we took her to our village, and we watch her property like our own.

Mrs. Uncouth. What makes you talk so much to-day, husband? My brother might think that we took her to our house for our own interest.

Uncouth. How could he think so? We can't move up Sophia's property to ours.

Beastly. Even if her movable property has been removed, I won't go to law for that. I don't like the law courts, and I am afraid of them. No matter how much my neighbours have insulted me, no matter how much damage they have done me, I have never had any litigations with them. Rather than have trouble with them, I make my peasants suffer for the damages my neighbours do me, and that's the end of it.

Uncouth. That is so, brother. The whole district says that you are a great hand at getting work out of your peasants.

Mrs. Uncouth. I wish, brother, you would teach us to do likewise, for since we have taken everything away from the peasants that they had, there is nothing left with them which we can carry off. It 's a real misfortune!

Beastly. I don't mind, sister, giving you a lesson, only first marry me to Sophia.

Mrs. Uncouth. Have you really taken a liking to the girl?

Beastly. No, it is not the girl I like.

Uncouth. Then it is her adjoining villages?

Beastly. Not even her villages; but that which is to be found in her villages, and for which I have a great passion.

Mrs. Uncouth. What is it, brother?

Beastly. I like the pigs, sister. Down our way there are some very big pigs: why, there is not one among them that if it stood up on its hind legs would not be a head taller than any of us.

Uncouth. Now, brother, this is a wonderful family resemblance. Our dear Mitrofán is just like his uncle: he has had the same passion for pigs ever since babyhood. He was only three years old when he would tremble with joy every time he saw a pig.

Beastly. Truly wonderful! All right: Mitrofán loves pigs because he is my nephew. There is some resemblance there. But why have I such a passion for pigs?

Uncouth. There must be some resemblance there too, that 's what I think.

SCENE 6. THE SAME AND SOPHIA

(*Sophia enters holding a letter in her hand and looking cheerful.*)

Mrs. Uncouth (*to Sophia*). Why so merry, dear? What has made you so happy?

Sophia. I have just received some joyful news. My uncle, of whom we have not heard for a long time, whom I love and honour like my father, arrived in Moscow a few days ago. This is the letter I have just received from him.

Mrs. Uncouth (*frightened, angrily*). What, Conservative, your uncle, is alive? And you think it right to jest about his resurrection? A fine story you have invented!

Sophia. Why, he never was dead.

Mrs. Uncouth. He did not die! Why could he not have died? No, madam, that is your invention. You are trying to frighten us with your uncle, that we might give you your liberty. You judge like this: " My uncle is a clever man; he seeing me in other people's hands, will find a way of rescuing me." That 's what you are happy about, madam. But your joy is all in vain: of course, your uncle has never thought of rising from the dead.

Beastly. Sister, but if he never died?

Uncouth. God be merciful to us, if he did not die.

Mrs. Uncouth (to her husband). How not dead? You are talking nonsense. Don't you know that I have had people remember him in their prayers for the rest of his soul? Is it possible my humble prayers have never reached heaven? (*To Sophia.*) You let me have that letter! (*Almost tears it out of her hand.*) I will wager anything that it is some love letter, and I can guess from whom. It 's from that officer that was trying to marry you, and whom you were ready to marry yourself. Who is that rascal that dares hand you letters without telling me first about them? I 'll get at him! That 's what we have come to: they write letters to girls! And girls know how to read!

Sophia. Read it yourself, madam: you will see that there can be nothing more harmless than that letter.

Mrs. Uncouth. " Read it yourself! " No, madam! Thank the Lord, I have not been educated that way! I may receive letters, but I order others to read them to me. (*To her husband.*) Read it!

Uncouth (looking at it for some time). It 's more than I can read.

Mrs. Uncouth. I see, they have educated you like a fair maiden. Brother, be so kind as to read it.

Beastly. I? I have never read a line since I was born! God has saved me that annoyance.

Sophia. Let me read it to you.

Mrs. Uncouth. I know you will read it, but I don't trust you. There! Mitrofán's teacher will soon be here, so I 'll tell him——

Beastly. So you have begun to teach your son reading?

Mrs. Uncouth. Oh, my brother! He has been studying these four years. It shall not be laid to our door that we are not giving Mitrofán an education: we pay three teachers for it. The deacon from Pokróv, Carouse, comes to him for reading and writing. Arikmethick he studies with an ex-sergeant, Cipher. They both come from town, which is only two miles from us. French and all the sciences he takes from a German, Adam Adámych Bluster. He gets three hundred roubles a year. We let him eat at table with us; our peasant women wash his linen; if he has to travel anywhere, he gets our horses; at the table he always has a glass of wine, and at night a tallow candle, and Fomká fixes his wig for nothing. To tell the truth, we are satisfied with him, for he does not drive our child. I don't see, anyway, why we should not fondle Mitrofán as long as he is a minor. He will have to suffer enough some ten years hence, when serving the Government. You know, brother, some people have luck from their birth. Take our family of Uncouths: they get all kinds of advancements while lying softly on their sides. With what is our Mitrofán worse than they? Ah, there is our dear guest.

SCENE 7.   THE SAME AND TRUTHFUL.

Mrs. Uncouth. Brother, I recommend to you our dear guest, Mr. Truthful; and to you, sir, I recommend my brother.

Truthful. Am glad to make your acquaintance.

Beastly. Very well, sir. What is your name? I did not quite hear it.

Truthful. My name is Truthful, so that you may hear it.

Beastly. Where born, sir? Where are your villages?

Truthful. I was born in Moscow, if you must know that, and my villages are in this province.

Beastly. And may I ask you,—I do not know your name and patronymic,—are there any pigs in your villages?

Mrs. Uncouth. Now, stop, brother, asking about your pigs. We had better talk about our trouble. (*To Truthful.*)

Listen, sir! By God's command we have taken this maiden upon our hands. She deigns to receive letters from her uncles: you see, her uncles write to her from heaven. Do us the kindness, sir, and read us this letter aloud.

Truthful. Excuse me, madam, I never read letters without the permission of those to whom they have been addressed.

Sophia. On the contrary, I beg you to do me the favour.

Truthful. If you so order. (*He reads.*)

"Dear niece! My affairs have compelled me to live for some years away from my relatives, and the great distance has deprived me of the pleasure of hearing any news from you. I am now living in Moscow after having been for some years in Siberia. I am a living example that it is possible by work and honesty to gain some wealth. By these means, fortune smiling upon me, I have saved up enough to have ten thousand roubles yearly income——"

Beastly and the Uncouths. Ten thousand!

Truthful (*reads*). "Of which I make you, dear niece, my sole heiress——"

Mrs. Uncouth. You an heiress!
Uncouth. Sophia an heiress!   } (*All together.*)
Beastly. Her an heiress!

Mrs. Uncouth (*hastening to embrace Sophia*). I congratulate you, Sophia! I congratulate you, my darling! I am beside myself with joy! Now you need a husband. I, I could not wish a better bride for my Mitrofán. That's what I call a fine uncle! A real father! I always thought that God was taking care of him, that he was still alive.

Beastly (*stretching out his hand*). Well, sister, let us settle it right away.

Mrs. Uncouth (*whispering to Beastly*). Wait, brother, first we have to ask her whether she wants you.

Beastly. What a question! Or do you really want to report to her as to a superior person?

Truthful. Do you want me to finish the letter?

Beastly. What for? Even if you were to keep on reading for five years you could not read out of it anything better than ten thousand.

Mrs. Uncouth (to Sophia). Sophia, my darling! Come with me to my sleeping-room. I have some important matter to talk to you about (*leading Sophia out*).

Beastly. Pshaw! I see there is not much chance for a betrothal to-day!

SCENE 8.   TRUTHFUL, UNCOUTH, BEASTLY, A SERVANT

Servant (to Uncouth, out of breath). Sir, sir! Soldiers have come; they have stopped in our village.

Uncouth. There is a misfortune! They will ruin us completely.

Truthful. What frightens you so?

Uncouth. Oh, I have seen terrible things, and I am afraid to show up before them.

Truthful. Don't be afraid. Of course, an officer is leading them, and he will not permit any insolence. Come, let us go to him. I am confident you are unnecessarily frightened. (*Truthful, Uncouth and Servant exeunt.*)

Beastly. They have all left me alone. I think I'll take a walk in the cattle yard.

End of Act I.

AN OPEN-HEARTED CONFESSION OF MY ACTS AND THOUGHTS

My parents were pious people, but as in our childhood they did not wake us for the morning service, there was a night service held in our house every church holiday, as also in the first and last weeks of Lent. As soon as I learned to read, my father made me read at the divine services. To this I owe whatever knowledge of Russian I possess, for, reading the church books, I became acquainted with the Slavic language, without which it is impossible to know Russian. I am thankful to my father for having watched carefully my reading: whenever I began to read indistinctly, he would say to me: "Stop mumbling! or do you imagine God is pleased with your muttering?" But more than that:

whenever my father noticed that I did not understand the passage that I had just read, he undertook the labour of explaining it to me,—in short, he showed endless care in my instruction. As he was not able to hire teachers of foreign languages for me, he did not delay, I may say, a day to place me and my brother in the University as soon as it was founded.

Now I shall say something of the manner of instruction at our University. Justice demands that I should state at the start that the University of to-day is quite a different thing from what it was in my days. Both the teachers and students are of a different calibre, and however much the school was then subject to severe criticism, it now deserves nothing but praise. I shall relate, as an example, how the examination was conducted in the lower Latin class. The day before the examination we were being prepared. Here is what was done: our teacher came in a caftan that had five buttons, while his vest had only four. This peculiarity surprised me much, and I asked the teacher for the cause of it. "My buttons seem to amuse you," he said, "but they are the guardians of your honour and of mine: those on the caftan stand for the five declensions, and on the vest for the four conjugations. And now," he proceeded, as he beat the table with his hand, "be all attentive to what I have to say! When they shall ask you for the declension of some noun, watch what button I am touching: if you see me holding the second button, answer boldly 'The second declension.' Do similarly in regard to the conjugations, being guided by the buttons on my vest, and you will never make a mistake." That is the kind of an examination we had!

O you parents who take pleasure in the reading of gazettes, when you find the names of your children mentioned in them as having received prizes for diligence, listen what I got a medal for! Our inspector had a German friend who was made a professor of geography. He had only three students. As this teacher was more stupid that our Latin teacher, he arrived at the examination in a full complement of buttons, and we were consequently examined without preparation. My companion was asked: "Where does the Vólga flow to?" "Into the Black Sea," was his answer. The same question was put to my other schoolmate. "Into the White Sea," was his answer. Then they asked me the same question. "I don't know," I said with such an expression of simplicity, that the examiners unanimously voted to give me a medal. Now, I did not in the least earn this medal for any geographical knowledge, though I deserved it for an illustration of practical morals.

However it may be, I owe the University a grateful recognition: I learned there Latin, and thus laid the foundation for some of my sciences. I also learned there some German, and especially acquired a taste for literary studies. A love for writing was developed in me very early in my childhood, and I practised for many years translating into Russian.

At that time our director had taken it into his head to journey to St. Petersburg with a few of his students, in order to show the founder of the University the fruits of his school. I do not know how, but my brother and I were among the number of the chosen pupils. The director started for St. Petersburg in the winter with his wife and ten of us youngsters. This was the first, and consequently a difficult, journey for me and my companions, but I must make a grateful acknowledgment of the kind attention we received from our director and which alleviated our hardships. He and his wife looked after us as after their children. When we arrived in St. Petersburg, my brother and myself stopped at the house of an uncle of ours. A few days later, our director presented us to the curator. This esteemed gentleman, whose deserts Russia must not forget, received us very kindly. He took hold of my hand and led me to a man whose appearance had attracted my respectful attention. That was the immortal Lomonósov. He asked me what I had learned. "Latin," said I. Then he began to speak with great eloquence of the importance of the Latin language.

After dinner of the same day we were at Court, it being a reception day, but the Empress did not appear. I was wonder-struck by the magnificence of the Empress's palace. All around us was sparkling gold, a gathering of men in blue and red ribbons, a mass of beautiful women, an enormous orchestra,— all that bewildered and blinded me, and the palace appeared to me to be the dwelling-place of a super-human being. Indeed, it could not have been otherwise, for I was then only fourteen years old, had never seen any-thing, and everything appeared to me new and charming. Having returned to the house, I asked my uncle whether they had often receptions at Court, to which he answered: "Almost every Sunday." I decided to stay in St. Peters-burg as long as possible, in order to see more of the Court. This desire was the result of curiosity and impulse : I wanted to enjoy the magnificence of the Court and hear agreeable music. This desire soon subsided, and I began to pine for my parents, whom I became impatient to see. The day I received letters from them was for me the pleasantest of all, and I went often to the post to ask for them.

Nothing delighted me in St. Petersburg so much as the theatre, which I saw for the first time in my life. They were playing a Russian comedy, *Henry and Pernilla*, and I re-member it as if it happened to-day. I saw there Shúmski, who so amused me with his jokes that I lost all sense of propriety and laughed as loud as I could. It is almost im-possible to describe the feelings which the theatre aroused in me. The comedy which I saw was quite stupid, but I looked upon it as the production of the greatest mind, and upon the actors as great people, whose acquaintance I regarded as the greatest happiness. I almost went insane when I found out that these actors frequented the house of my uncle, where I was living. After a little while I there became acquainted with our famous actor, Iván Afanásevich Dmitrévski, an honourable, clever and cultured gentleman, whose friendship I am enjoying even now.

Standing once in the pit, I struck up an acquaintanceship with the son of a distinguished gentleman, who had taken a fancy to my face. As soon as he received a negative answer to his question whether I knew French, he suddenly changed and became cold to me. He looked upon me as an ignoramus and badly educated man, and began to make fun of me. When I noticed from his manner of speech that he did not know anything else but French, which he spoke badly, I made such a biting repartee, that he stopped his raillery, and invited me to his house; I answered politely, and we parted as friends. But I learned from this how necessary it was for a young man to know French; so I began to study the language in earnest, continuing at the same time the study of Latin, in which language I heard the lectures on logic by Professor Sháden, who was then rector. This learned man has the rare gift of lecturing and expounding so clearly that we all made palpable progress, and my brother and I were soon admitted as real students. All that time I did not stop practising translations from German into Russian; among other things I translated *Seth, the Egyptian King*, but not very successfully. My knowledge of Latin was exceedingly useful to me in my study of French. In two years I could understand Voltaire, and I began translating in verse his *Alzire*. That translation was nothing more than a youthful error, nevertheless there are some good verses in it.

LETTERS TO COUNT P. I. PÁNIN, DURING HIS FIRST JOURNEY ABROAD

MONTPELLIER, November 22 (December 3), 1777.

. . . I found this city (Leipsic) full of learned men. Some of these regard it as their chief desert that they are able to talk in Latin, which, by the way, five-year-old children were able to do in the days of Cicero. Others soar in thoughts in the sky, and are ignorant of what goes on upon earth. Others again are strong in artificial logic, having an extreme absence of natural logic. In short, Leipsic proves beyond controversy that learning does not beget common sense. I left these pedants, and went to Frankfurt-on-the-Main. This city is celebrated for its antiquities, and is noteworthy from the fact that the Roman Emperor is chosen here. I was in the election room from which he issues to the people. But its antiquity consists merely in being old: all I saw there were four empty walls in an old building. They showed me also the famous so-called La Bulle d'Or of Emperor Charles IV., which was written in the year 1356, and I was also in the Imperial Archives. But it was hardly worth my while to climb up garrets and down cellars, in order to see the relics of a rude age. From Frankfurt I travelled through German principalities: every step a new principality. I saw Hanau, Mainz, Fulda, Sachsen-Gotha, Eisenach and a few other principalities of minor princes. I found the roads frequently not paved, but I had nevertheless to pay dearly for the pavement. When they pulled me out of a bog and asked pavement money of me, I had the courage to ask them: "Where is it?" To which they answered me that his Majesty, the reigning prince, had the intention of having the roads paved, but that at the present he was only collecting toll. Such justice in regard to strangers has led me to make my own conclusions in regard to their relations with their subjects, and I did not at all wonder when from every hut there came out a crowd of beggars and followed my carriage. . . .

From here I went into France, and reached the famous city of Lyons. In this country the roads are very good; but in the cities the streets are so narrow and are so badly kept that I cannot understand how people with their five senses manage to live in such dirt. It is evident that the police does not interfere with it. To prove this I shall take the liberty of telling your Highness an occurrence. I was walking in the finest and largest street in Lyons (which, however, cannot compare with our by-streets), and saw in bright daylight burning torches and a crowd of people in the middle of the street. Being near-sighted, I naturally thought it was some elegant funeral. Upon approaching nearer out of curiosity, I saw how great my mistake was: Messrs. Frenchmen had simply stuck a pig and were singeing it in the middle of the street! The stench, dirt and a crowd of leisure people who were watching the operation compelled me to take another street. I have not yet seen Paris, so I do not know whether my olfactories will suffer there less; in any case, all the French cities which I have so far seen are badly off as to their cleanliness.

PARIS, March 20 (31), 1778.

. . . Voltaire's arrival in Paris produced the same effect on the people here as if a divinity had come down upon earth. The respect shown to him in no way differs from worship. I am confident that if his deep old age and ailments did not oppress him, and he wished to preach now some new sect, the whole nation would at once turn to him. Your Excellency will form your own opinion from what follows whether one can come to any other conclusion from the reception the public gave him.

When he arrived here, the poets who are devoted to him began to write poems in his honour, while those who hate him sent him anonymous satires. The first are printed, but not the other, for the Government has by a special rescript forbidden to print anything that might be prejudicial to Voltaire. This consideration is shown him as much for his great talents as for his advanced age. This man of eighty-five years has composed a new tragedy, *Irene and Alexis Comnenus*, which has been performed. Although it can by no means be compared to his former plays, yet the public received it with rapture. The author being ill, he was not present at the first presentation. It is only the first time yesterday that he has driven out: he was in the Academy, then in the theatre, where they purposely gave his new tragedy.

As he drove out from his house, the carriage was accompanied as far as the Academy by an endless throng of people who kept up applauding. All the academicians came out to meet him. He was seated in the president's chair and, waiving the customary voting, was elected by acclamation to be president for the April quarter. As he walked down the staircase and took his seat in the carriage, the populace

demanded vociferously to take off hats. From the Academy
to the theatre he was accompanied by the people's cheering.
When he entered his box, the audience applauded repeatedly
with indescribable rapture, and a few minutes later the oldest
actor, Brisard, stepped into his box with a wreath which he
placed on Voltaire's head. Voltaire immediately took the
wreath off and with tears of joy spoke aloud to Brisard: "Ah,
Dieu! vous voulez donc me faire mourir!" The tragedy was
played with much greater perfection than at any previous
performance. At its conclusion there was a new spectacle.
All the actors and actresses surrounded Voltaire's bust and
adorned it with laurel wreaths. This homage was followed
by the people's applause, which lasted nearly fifteen minutes.
Then Madame Vestrice, who had played Irene, turned towards Voltaire and read some laudatory verses. To show
their appreciation, the public demanded that the verses be
read again, and they applauded wildly. As soon as Voltaire
seated himself in his carriage, the people stopped the coachman and cried: "Des flambeaux, des flambeaux!" When
the torches were brought, they ordered the coachman to
drive at a slow pace, and an endless crowd accompanied him
to his very house with torches, crying all the time: "Vive
Voltaire!" Voltaire has received many an ovation in his
lifetime, but yesterday was, no doubt, the best day of his
life, which, however, will soon come to an end. Your Excellency will see how he now looks from his portrait which I
here enclose and which is a very good likeness of him.

Ermíl Ivánovich Kostróv. (1750-1796.)

Kostróv was the son of a peasant. He studied in a seminary and
began to write verses early, first under the influence of Lomonósov,
in the pseudo-classic style,—later, under the influence of Derzhávin,
he cultivated a simpler and better language. His chief services to
Russian literature are his translations of Apuleius, Ossian, and the
Iliad. The ode which is given here marks the turning-point in his
manner of writing, and at the same time indicates how great was the
change brought about by Derzhávin's *Felítsa* (see p. 378) in Russian
poetry.

LETTER TO THE CREATOR OF THE ODE IN
PRAISE OF "FELÍTSA, THE KIRGÍZ-KAYSÁK
PRINCESS"

Singer, to whom with a gentle smile the Muse has lately
brought from the Parnassian heights a wreath, I hanker for
your friendship and union with you.   Moscow is my habitation, you sing the Neva stream.   But not the distant roads,
nor mounts, nor hills, nor forests, nor rivers shall impede
my zeal to you, which to Petropolis shall be borne, to issue
in your breast and ears: not impossible to Muses is what the
Muses will.

Tell me, I pray, how without a lyre, nor violin, not even
having saddled the Parnassian steed, you have sung so
sweetly Felítsa's acts, and her crown's life-giving beams?
You evidently have walked all streets and byways on Pindus'
heights and in the grassy vale of the pure Muses, and to
glorify, console, make happy, amuse the Princess, you have
discovered a new, untrodden path.   Having discovered it,
you ran it at will, and neither stump nor stone e'er tripped
you, but all appeared to you a grassy mead, and your caftan
was nowhere rent by thorns.   Proclaiming the praises of
the Princess, recounting the pleasures of the bashaws, you
played the bagpipe, yet sang enticingly withal.

Disdaining the evil conscience of the envious, you onward
bore, which boldness seeing, Parnassus wound a wreath for
you.   Their flowing hair descending on their arms, disport-
ing on their pink-white breasts and cheeks, the forms of
fairy nymphs from the Neva rose; gently waving on the
crests, they listened intent to you, and praised the beautiful
innovation of your verse.   In token of their heartfelt tribute,
they clapped their hands in ecstasy, then disappeared into
the crystal depths.

By easy post Felítsa's praise was borne to Moscow, to the
delight of all the hearts, and all who read have sung your
praise, and arbiters of taste have wound a wreath for you.
They have read it a hundred times, yet listen gladly,
with attention, when someone in their presence reads it

again, and cannot assuage their spirits, nor satisfy their captive ears, while listening to its sportive jests. Just so a garden, with charming shrubs and shade of trees, planted on a hill above a stream of limpid waters, though it be well known to us, though known the taste of every fruit therein, though familiar to us its every path, yet drawn by a mysterious feeling, we hasten to walk in it once more, and turn our glances all about us, to discover something new, though we have seen it all before.

Our ears are almost deaf from the vociferous lyric tones, and, meseems, 't is time to come down from the clouds, lest, forgetful of the law of equilibrium, and flying from the heights, one break his arms and legs: no matter what our endeavour be to rise on high, Felítsa's deeds will still be higher. She likes simplicity of style, so 't were better, treading that road in modesty, to raise our voice to her. Dwelling on Parnassus in union with the nymphs, I have thrummed the sonorous harp, while praising the Kirgíz-Kaysák Princess, and have only earned cold praises. All lauded there my verses, flattered me, though themselves were but amused; and now they have the honour in oblivion to lie: 't is evident high-soaring odes are out of fashion.

Above us you have risen through your simplicity! Write, as formerly, again a letter to your neighbour; you have well depicted his luxurious mind, how he invites a hungry mob to dinner, games and luxuries on the tables; or, loving Nature's beauties, sing of the crystal waters, as once you sang the Spring of Grébenev. This spring, flowing through the valley, even now is pleasing to me: whenever I slaked my thirst, a ray of joy shone to me.

But to you, who preside most wisely, leader of the Muses, their labours' judge, listening to their sweet thunderous music, to you this honour and praise is due, because, burning with zeal and inventive of new paths, you labour to advance our native tongue. It is majestic, sweet and rich, thunderous, elate, liquid and strong, and great is your work of its perfection. Encouraged by you, the lovers of the sciences have with heartfelt zeal walked on the glorious path:

we see the fair Russian diction in their labours, and its progress in him who has extolled you.

I shall say it without hesitation: you emulate Minerva, and bring your rest as a sacrifice to the Muses, and the glory of your country is your pleasure and consolation. Your exploits are enviable to men. With Felítsa's beloved, precious name, with Felítsa's praise and the laudation of her wise acts the beginning of these labours has been adorned, and has brought joy and rapture to its readers. Blessed is that beginning where her resplendent name appears, and the end is crowned with success. To him who thus has glorified Felítsa, and has given a new flavour to his verses, honour and glory from the depth of our hearts!

Alexander Nikoláevich Radíshchev. (1749–1802.)

In 1765 Catherine II. sent twelve young men to Leipsic to be educated in the University; among the number was Radíshchev. He studied philosophy under Platner, and for his own amusement took a full course in medicine. Upon his return he was attached to the Kómmerz-Kolleg, a kind of Department of Finance, where he distinguished himself for his unexampled honesty and gained the love of its President, Count Vorontsóv, whom he had the courage to oppose in a decision at law, in order to save some innocent men from transportation to Siberia. When he was later put in charge of the Customs House of St. Petersburg, he discovered that the considerable traffic with England demanded a knowledge of English, if he wished to dispense with a translator; accordingly at the age of thirty he acquired the English language and began to read its literature, which exerted a great influence upon him.

In 1790 he wrote his *Journey from St. Petersburg to Moscow*, which he distributed among his friends, though it had not been approved by the censor. This work, written in the style of Sterne's *Sentimental Journey*, is not only remarkable as a piece of literature, but also as a political pamphlet. It attacks the institution of Russia in the light of the most advanced liberalism of France and North America. Radíshchev advocated in no unmistakable terms the liberation of the serfs, almost half a century before Turgénev. When Catherine II. read the book, she exclaimed: "He is a Martinist. He is worse than Pugachév, he praises Franklin." Radíshchev was banished to Siberia. There he devoted himself to literature, wrote his *Ode to Liberty*, which is the forerunner of all the poems of liberty by Rylyéev, Ogarév, Odoévski, and a few longer poems in a lighter vein. Emperor Paul pardoned him, and Emperor Alexander advanced him to higher honours. When an acquaintance of his accused him of returning to his youthful ideals and warned him of subjecting himself to the danger of another banishment, he committed suicide in a moment of despondency.

JOURNEY FROM ST. PETERSBURG TO MOSCOW

DEPARTURE

After having taken supper with my friends, I took my seat in the kibítka. The driver drove the horses at full gallop, as was his wont, and in a few minutes we were outside the city. It is hard to part, even for a short time, from those who have become necessary to us at every moment of our existence. It is hard to part,—but happy is he who can part without smiling, for love or friendship is his consolation. You weep as you say "good-bye"; but think of your return,—and let your tears dry up at this thought, as dries up the dew before the face of the sun. Happy is he who weeps, hoping to be consoled! Happy is he who sometimes lives in the future! Happy is he who lives in meditation! His existence is enriched; his joy is multiplied, and calm assuages the gloom of his pining, generating images of happiness in the mirrors of his contemplation.

I lay in the kibítka. The tinkling of the post bell was monotonous to my ears, and finally brought to me beneficent Morpheus. The grief of my parting persecuted me in my deathlike state, and painted me to my imagination as forlorn. I saw myself in a spacious vale which had lost all its amenity and greenness of leafage through the hot rays of the sun. There was not a spring to offer coolness, nor treeshade to protect from the heat. I was a hermit, left in the midst of Nature! I shuddered. "Miserable man!" I sighed, "where are you? What has become of all that has enticed you? Where is all that has made your life agreeable? Is it possible that the pleasures which you have tasted are only an idle dream?"

Luckily there was a deep rut in the road, and my kibítka,

getting into it, jostled me and woke me up. The kibítka stopped. I raised my head and saw three habitations in a barren spot.

" What is that ? " I asked my driver.

" A post station."

" Where are we ? "

" In Sofíya," and he unhitched the horses.

SOFÍYA

All around me was silence. I was absorbed in contemplation and did not notice that the kibítka had been standing quite a while without the horses. My driver broke my meditation:

" Master, father, some money for a drink! "

This tax is illegal, but no one objects to paying it, in order that he may be able to travel at his ease; the twenty kopeks I gave him were a good investment. Who has travelled by post knows that a passport is a precaution without which any purse, unless it be a general's, will have to suffer. I took it out of my pocket and went with it, as people sometimes go with the cross for their defence.

I found the Post Commissary snoring. I touched his shoulder.

" Whom does the devil drive so ? What a miserable habit to depart from the city at night ? There are no horses here, —it 's too early yet. Go into the inn and drink tea, or go to sleep! "

Having said that, the Commissary turned to the wall, and went to snoring again. What was I to do ? I once more shook the Commissary by his shoulder.

"What is the matter with you ? I told you there are no horses! " and, covering himself with the blanket, the Commissary turned away from me.

If the horses are all engaged, I thought to myself, then it is not right for me to disturb the Commissary's sleep. But if there are any horses in the stable . . . I made up my mind I would find out whether the Commissary told the truth. I went into the yard, hunted up the stable and found some twenty horses in it. It is true, one could count the bones on them, yet they would have taken me to the next station. From the stable I returned to the Commissary, and shook him harder than before, for I felt I had a right to do so, having discovered that he had told a lie. He jumped up from his bed and without opening his eyes asked who had arrived. " I . . ." But coming to his senses, and noticing me, he said:

" Young man, you are evidently in the habit of commanding drivers of olden days, when they used to beat them with sticks. Well, that won't work now-a-days." The Commissary lay down angrily in his bed again. I had really a desire to treat him like one of those drivers when they were discovered cheating; but my generosity to the city driver caused the Sofíya drivers to hurry up and hitch the horses to the kibítka. Just as I was getting ready to commit a crime on the back of the Commissary, the bells were heard in the yard. I remained a good citizen, and thus twenty kopeks saved a peaceable man from an inquest, my children from an example of incontinence in anger, and I discovered that reason is a slave to impatience.

The horses carried me away. The driver started a song which, as usual, was a doleful one. He who knows the tunes of Russian popular songs will admit that there is something in them that speaks of sadness of spirit. Nearly all the tunes of such songs are in the minor key. In this musical inclination of the popular ear one may find a solution of the trend of his actions. In it one may discover the condition of the nation's soul. Look at a Russian! You will always find him lost in meditation. If he wants to drive away ennui, or, as he calls it, have a good time, he goes to the inn. In his intoxication he is impulsive, bold, quarrelsome. If anything takes place not to his liking, he at once starts a brawl or fight. A churl who goes into the inn with a downcast look and returns from it covered with blood from having had his ears boxed may throw a light on many an enigmatic point in Russian history.

My driver was singing. It was three o'clock in the morning. As before the bell, so now his song put me to sleep: "O Nature! Having swathed man at his birth in the winding-sheets of sorrow, dragging him all his life over the forbidding crags of fear, ennui and sadness, you have given him sleep as a consolation. You fall asleep, and all is at an end! Unbearable is the awakening to the unfortunate man. Oh, how acceptable death is to him! And if it is the end of sorrow. . . . All-kind Father! Wilt Thou turn away Thy look from him who ends his life in a manly way? To Thee, the source of all goodness, this sacrifice is brought. Thou alone givest strength when creation trembles and is convulsed. It is the voice of the Father, calling His child unto Himself! Thou hast given me life, to Thee I return it: upon earth it has become useless."

TOSNÁ

When I left St. Petersburg I thought I would find a very good road. All those who have travelled upon it after the Emperor have thought so. It had been such, indeed, but only for a short time. The dirt which had been put upon the road in dry weather in order to make it even had been washed by the rains, forming a swamp in the summer, and made it impassable. Fearing bad weather, I got out of the kibítka and went into the post station, intending to take a rest. In the room I found a traveller who was sitting behind a long, common peasant table in the nearer corner and was turning over some papers. He asked the Post Commissary to give him horses as soon as possible. To my question who he was, I learned that he was a pettifogger of the old style, and that he was going to St. Petersburg with a stack of torn papers which he was then examining. I immediately entered into a conversation with him, and here is what he said:

"Dear sir,—I, your humble servant, have been a Registrar in the Archives of the Estates, where I had an opportunity to make good use of my position: by assiduous labour

I have collected a genealogy, based on clear documentary proof, of many Russian families, and I can trace their princely or noble origin several centuries back. I can reinstate many a man in his princely dignity, by showing his origin from Vladímir Monomákh, or even from Rúrik. Dear sir," he continued, as he pointed to his papers, "all Great-Russian nobles ought to purchase my work, paying for it more than for any other wares. But with the leave of your High Birth, Noble Birth, or High and Noble Birth, for I do not know how to honour you, they do not know what they need. You know how the orthodox Tsar Feódor Aleksyéevich of blessed memory has injured the Russian nobility by doing away with the prefecture. That severe legislation placed many honourable princely and royal families on a level with the Nóvgorod nobility. But the orthodox Emperor Peter the Great has entirely put them in the shade by his Table of Ranks. He opened the way to all for obtaining the title of nobility through military and civil service, and he, so to say, has trampled the old nobility in the dirt. Our Most Gracious Mother, now reigning, has confirmed the former decrees by her august Law of the Nobility, which has very much disquieted all our higher nobles, for the old families are placed in the Book of the Nobility lower than the rest. There is, however, a rumour that there will soon be issued a supplementary decree by which those families that can trace their noble origin two or three hundred years back will be granted the title of Marquis or something like it, so that they will have some distinguishing feature from the other families. For this reason, dear sir, my work must be acceptable to all the old nobility. But there are rascals everywhere. In Moscow I fell in with a company of young gentlemen to whom I proposed my work, in order to be repaid through their kindness at least for the paper and ink wasted upon it. But instead of kindness they heaped raillery upon me; so I left that capital from grief, and am on my way to St. Petersburg, where there is more culture."

Saying this, he made a deep bow, and straightening him-

self up, stood before me with the greatest respect. I understood his thought, took something out of my purse and,
giving it to him, advised him to sell his paper by weight to
peddlers for wrapping paper, for the prospective marquisates
would only turn people's heads, and he would be the cause
of a recrudescence of an evil, now passed in Russia, of boasting of old genealogies.

LYUBÁNI

I suppose it is all the same to you, whether I travelled in
summer or winter, especially since it is not uncommon for
travellers to travel both summer and winter, starting out in
a sleigh and returning in a wheel carriage. The corduroy
road wore out my sides. I crawled out of the kibítka, and
started on foot. While I was lying in the kibítka, my
thoughts were directed to the immeasurableness of the world,
and while my soul flitted away from the earth, it seemed
easier to bear the jostling of the carriage. But spiritual
exercises do not always distract our corporeality, and it was
in order to save my sides that I went on foot.

A few steps from the road I noticed a peasant who was
ploughing his field. It was warm; I looked at my watch: it
was twenty minutes to one. I left the city on Saturday, so
it was Sunday then. The peasant that was ploughing evidently belonged to a landowner that did not receive any tax
from him. The peasant was ploughing with great care;
evidently the field did not belong to the master. He was
turning the plough with remarkable ease.

"God aid you!" I said as I approached the ploughman,
who did not stop but finished the furrow he had begun.

"God aid you!" I repeated.

"Thank you, sir!" said the ploughman as he cleaned the
ploughshare and transferred the plough to a new furrow.

"You are, of course, a dissenter, since you work on Sunday."

"No, sir, I make the correct sign of the cross," he said,
and showed me his three fingers put together; "but God is

merciful and does not want a person to starve, as long as he has a family and sufficient strength.''

'' Have you not any time to work during the week, that you work on a Sunday, and at that in a great heat ? ''

'' In the week, sir, there are six days, and we have to work for the manor six times a week, and in the evening we haul the hay from the meadows, if the weather is good; and on holidays the women and girls go to the woods to gather mushrooms and berries. God grant a rain this evening,'' he added as he made the sign of the cross. '' Sir, if you have any peasants, they are praying for the same.''

'' I have no peasants, my friend; and so nobody curses me. Have you a large family ? ''

'' Three sons and three daughters. My eldest is ten years old.''

'' How do you manage to get enough grain, if you have only the Sundays to yourself ? ''

'' Not only the Sundays,—the nights are ours too. We need not starve, if we are not lazy. You see, one horse is resting; and when this one gets tired, I 'll take the other, and that 's the way I make my work count.''

'' Do you work the same way for your master ? ''

'' No, sir! It would be sinful to work the same way; he has in his fields one hundred hands for one mouth, and I have but two hands for seven mouths, if you count it up. If you were to work yourself to death at your master's work, he would not thank you for it. The master will not pay the capitation tax; he will let you have no mutton, no hempen cloth, no chicken, no butter. Our people are fortunate in those places where the master receives a rent from the peasant, particularly without a superintendent! It is true, some good masters ask more than three roubles for each soul, yet that is better than tenant labour. They are now getting in the habit of letting farms out to renters who, being poor, flay us alive. They do not give us our own time, and do not let us go out in the winter to work for ourselves, because they pay our capitation tax. It is a devilish idea to let one's peasants do work for somebody else! There is at least a chance of complaining against a superintendent, but to whom is one to complain against a tenant?"

"My friend! You are mistaken: the laws do not permit to torture people."

"Torture, yes! But, sir, you would not want to be in my hide!" In the meantime the ploughman hitched another horse to his plough and, bidding me good-bye, began a new furrow.

The conversation with this agriculturist awakened a multitude of thoughts in me. Above all, I thought of the inequality of the peasant's condition. I compared the crown peasants with those of the proprietors. Both live in villages, but while the first pay a stated tax, the others have to be ready to pay whatever the master wishes. The first are judged by their peers; the others are dead to the laws, except in criminal matters. A member of society only then is taken cognisance of by the Government that protects him when he violates the social bond, when he becomes a criminal! That thought made all my blood boil. Beware, cruel proprietor! On the brow of every one of your peasants I see your condemnation!

Absorbed in these thoughts I accidentally turned my eyes to my servant, who was sitting in front of me in the kibítka and was shaking from side to side. I felt a sudden darkness come over me, which passed through all my blood and drove a burning feeling upwards and made it spread over my face. I felt so heartily ashamed of myself, that I wanted to cry. "In your anger," I said to myself, "you attack the cruel master who maltreats his peasants in the field; and are you not doing the same, or even worse? What crime did your poor Petrúshka commit that you do not allow him to enjoy the comfort of our misfortunes, the greatest gift of Nature to the unfortunate man,—sleep? 'He receives his pay, his food and dress; I never have him whipped with a scourge or sticks.' O you kind man! You think that a piece of bread and a rag give you the right to treat a being that resembles you as a top? You are merely boasting that you do not very often whip it as it is whirling about. Do you know what is written in the first law of each man's heart? ' If I strike anyone, he has the right to strike me also.' Remember the day when Petrúshka was drunk and did not dress you fast enough! Remember how you boxed his ears! Oh, if he had then, drunk as he was, come to his senses, and had answered your question in a befitting manner! Who has given you the right over him? The law! Law! And you dare besmirch that sacred name! Wretch! . . .'' Tears flowed from my eyes, and in this condition the post horses brought me to the next station.

Alexander Onisimovich Ablesímov. (1742–1783.)

Ablesímov was a frequent contributor to several periodical publications; his contributions present no special interest, but he gained a great reputation by his comic opera *The Miller*, which, though it is an imitation of a foreign original, was the first play to introduce a popular element, taken directly from the life of the people. The public hailed this comedy as a new departure; it was given to crowded houses twenty-seven times in succession, and a number of imitations appeared with the same element of sorcery and country life for their background.

THE MILLER

ACT I

The stage represents on one side a forest, with small villages in the distant hills, and on the other a mill, and nearby a waggon with sacks. In front of it is a tree.

SCENE I

Miller (alone. He is planing a board and sings, only the song is without words and music. Then he says): What song is that? . . . Oh, yes: '' How our night from midnight '' . . . that 's it . . . *(he begins to sing that tune, continuing his work).*

> How our night from midnight,
> From midnight to white day . . .

What a downpour it has been, and now it has stopped !
(*He sings again, and continues his song.*)

> 'T was at the dawn, the early one,
> At the fall of the shining moon . . .

How it did blow! I declare, it did blow; why, it almost
tore my mill down. I would have been left with nothing.
It has done some damage,—thanks to the Lord, not much
damage. Did I say not much damage? Well, I have enough
to do to fix it up. (*Putting the level to the board.*) It 'll
come out all right, and all will go well again. (*Advancing towards the orchestra.*)   I have to laugh every time I
think of it; they say that a mill cannot exist without a
wizard, and that a miller is n't just a man like anybody else:
he is on speaking terms with the house-spirit, and the house-
spirits live in their mills like devils . . . ha, ha, ha, ha!
What bosh! Am I not a miller through and through? I
was born, brought up, and have grown old in the mill, and
yet I have never laid my eyes on a house-spirit. Now, to
tell the gospel truth, it 's just this: if you are a shrewd fellow and a good hand at cheating, that sorcery business is a
good thing. . . . Let them prattle what they please,
but we earn our bread by our profession.

> Who by cheating makes a living,
> Him at once all call a gipsy,
> And you gain through gipsy dealings
> The reputation of a wizard.
> Even in that way the witches
> Make a living by deception.
> There 's a big lot of these rascals:
> Some of them bespeak the water,
> Others turn the sieve for people,
> And through such tricks make a living!
> Just like me, sinful man! . . .

SCENE 2.   FILIMÓN AND THE FORMER

Miller (*noticing him*). Ah! I am getting a guest.   I 'll earn
a penny this day. (*To Filimón.*) Godspeed, young man!

Filimón. My respects, old man.

Miller. Whence come you, whither tend you?

Filimón. Not farther than my business takes me.

Miller. Of your own will, or by compulsion?

Filimón. I am looking for horses: my roan and grey have gotten away from me; they are fine horses, such fine horses. (*Aside.*) He is a fortune-teller: I 'll try my fortune with him. (*To the Miller.*) Say, old man, I want to ask you——

Miller. What is it you want? As you please, I am at your service.

Filimón. That 's good! And I 'll pay you for it. Tell me my fortune: shall I find my horses?

Miller. Shall you find your horses?

Filimón. That 's it, old man. I am very anxious to find out about them.

Miller. Now, how about that; is there going to be anything? (*Stretches out his hand to him.*)

Filimón. First tell me, old man, and then we 'll see.

Miller (*turns away from him, and angrily begins a song*):

> Tell the fortune:
> As the guess is,
> So is the pay.

Filimón. But, old man, I expect to pay you.

Miller.
> 'T is with a promise
> As with a chair:
> If you sit and do not eat,
> Then your belly is not full.

Filimón. Believe me, I am not lying to you.

Miller.
> If it 's so,
> All this talking is in vain;
> Take out your purse,
> Don't talk uselessly,
> Count out the money.
> (*Puts out his hand, and looks in his eyes.*)

Filimón. Well, I don't care: I 'll give you some money in advance.

Miller. Only this?

Filimón. It will do for the present; what more do you want?

Miller (aside). You won't get off with less than half a rouble.

Filimón. What are you going to tell me now?

Miller. What is it now, early in the morning?

Filimón. Not very late yet, the sun has not yet set behind the woods.

Miller. Turn three times around, towards the sun.

Filimón. What for?

Miller. That 's what I need in my sorcery.   Do as you are told!

Filimón. To please you, I 'll turn around. (*Turns around once.*)

Miller. Once more, towards the sun.

Filimón (turning around). Here it is, and towards the sun.

Miller. Now stand against this tree.   (*Filimón is about to start for the tree, but the Miller says*): No, no, stop!   Have you a kerchief?

Filimón (taking out his handkerchief). Here it is.

Miller. Close your eyes tight, and tie your kerchief over them.   That 's all right!   Now listen: you must stand quiet, and don't move from the spot, nor speak a word to anyone, while I go and see the elder.

Filimón (does all the Miller commands him to do). But suppose someone should come and ask me why I am standing there, and why my eyes are tied up?

Miller. Not a word to anybody; but you may grumble to yourself.

Filimón. May I sing a song?

Miller. You will frighten all.   No, you must not.

Filimón (aside). What is it all going to be?

Miller. Stand still and don't move!

Ippolít Fédorovich Bogdanóvich. (1743–1803.)

Ippolít Bogdanóvich, the son of a minor official, entered the mathematical school connected with the Senate ; at fourteen years of age he began to study at the University and to write verses under the guidance of Kheráskov. He then served as secretary of legation in Saxony, and later was connected with the Government Archives. His reputation rests only on his *Psyche*, which is a paraphrase in verse of La Fontaine's *Les amours de Psyché et de Cupidon*, itself an imitation of an episode in Apuleius's *Golden Ass*. It is a mock-heroic in the style of Máykov's *Eliséy* (see p. 263), and was immensely popular at the end of the eighteenth century, and even Dmítriev, Púshkin and Byelínski found pleasure in reading it. There are traces in his poems of an intimate acquaintance with the Russian popular literature, from which are introduced many characters. The poem found so many admirers because it was an expression of the reverse side of the philosophy of the eighteenth century, with its frivolity and superficiality.

PSYCHE

FROM BOOK I

The goddess donned her ancient gala dress, and seated in the shell, as they paint in pictures, glided over the waters on two large dolphins.

Cupid, bestowing his imperious look, bestirred all Neptune's court. The frisky waves, perceiving Venus, swam after her, replete with merriment. The watery tribe of Tritons issues to her from the abysses of the waters: one dives all about her and pacifies the wanton waves; another, whirling in the depths, gathers pearls at the bottom and drags forth all the secrets of the sea to place before her feet. One, struggling with the monsters, forbids them to disport nearby; another, briskly leaping into the coachman's seat, scolds loudly those he meets and orders them to stand aside; he proudly holds the lines, and steers his path away from rocks, and crushes impudent monsters. One, with trident, precedes her on a whale and drives all far out of the way; he casts about him his angry looks and, that all may know his will, loudly blows a coral horn; another, having come to the goddess from distant regions, bears before her a bit from a crystal mountain instead of a mirror. This sight refreshes her pleasure and the joy upon her brow.

"Oh, if this sight," proclaims he, "for ever remained in this crystal!" But the Triton's wish is vain: that vision will disappear like a dream, and nothing will remain but the stone, and in the heart a fatal flame which will consume him. Another has joined the retinue of the goddess, and protects her from the sun and cools the sultry beam by sending upwards a stream of water. Meanwhile sirens, sweet singers, sing verses in her honour, and mingle fiction with truth in their attempt to extol her: some dance before her; others, anticipating her wishes, are present to serve her, and with fans waft coolness to the goddess; others, borne on the crests, breathe heavily in travelling post from fields, beloved by Flora, and bring her flowery wreaths. Thetis herself has sent them for small and great services, and wishes only that her husband stay at home. The weather being most favourable, the storms dare not annoy her, and only the Zephyrs are free to fondle Venus.

FROM BOOK II

Psyche awoke from her sleep not sooner than midday past, nay, one hour after midday. All serving-maids came to dress the princess, and brought with them forty garments and all that with them went. For that day Psyche designated the simplest of all gowns, for she hastened as soon as possible to inspect the marvels of the palace. I shall follow in the princess's track and shall present the mansion to you, and describe all in detail that could amuse her.

At first Psyche visited the rooms, nor left a corner in them where she did not pass a while; thence to the conservatory and to the balcony; thence on the veranda, and down, and out, to inspect the house from all sides. A bevy of girls were slow in following her; only the Zephyrs were fast enough, and they guarded her, lest running she should fall. Two or three times she inspected the house from within and from without. Meanwhile the Zephyrs and

Cupids pointed out the architecture to her and all the marvels of nature, which Psyche was anxious to inspect. She wished to see all, but knew not where to begin, for her eyes were distracted now by one thing, now by another. Psyche would fain have looked at everything, but running around so much, she soon became fatigued.

While resting herself, she looked at the statues of famous masters: those were likenesses of inimitable beauties, whose names, in prose and verse, in various tales, both short and long, reign immortally among all the nations and through all the ages: Calisto, Daphne, Armene, Niobe, Helen, the Graces, Angelica, Phryne, and a multitude of other goddesses and mortal women appeared before her eyes in lifelike form, in all their beauty arrayed along the wall. But in the middle, and right in front of them, Psyche's image stood on an elevated pedestal and surpassed them all in beauty. Looking at it, she herself fell to wondering, and, beside herself with wonderment, stopped: then you might have perceived another statue in her, such as the world had never seen.

Psyche would have stayed there a long time, looking at her image that held sway over her, if her servants who were with her had not pointed out in other places, for the pleasure of her eyes, other likenesses of her beauty and glory: up to her waist, her feet, her lifelike form, of gold, of silver, of bronze, of steel, her heads, and busts, and medals; and elsewhere mosaic, or marble, or agate represented in these forms a new splendour. In other places Apelles, or the god of artists who with his hand had moved Apelles's brush, had pictured Psyche in all her beauty, such as no man could have imagined before.

But does she wish to see herself in pictures? Here, Zephyrs bring her Pomona's horn and, strewing flowers before her, disport with her in vales; in another, she with mighty buckler in her hands, dressed as Pallas, threatens from her steed, with her fair looks more than with her spear, and vanquishes the hearts through a pleasant plague. There stands Saturn before her: toothless, baldheaded and grey, with new wrinkles on his old face, he tries to appear young: he curls his sparse tufts of hair, and, to see Psyche, puts on his glasses.   There, again, she is seen like a queen, with Cupids all around her, in an aërial chariot: to celebrate fair Psyche's honour and beauty, the Cupids in their flight shoot hearts; they fly in a large company, all carrying quivers over their shoulders, and, taking pride in her beautiful eyes, raise their crossbows and proclaim war to the whole world.   There, again, fierce Mars, the destroyer of the law of peace, perceiving Psyche, becomes gentle of manner: he no longer stains the fields with blood, and finally, forgetting his rules of war, lies humbled at her feet and glows with love to her.   There, again, she is pictured among the Pleasures that precede her everywhere and by the invention of varied games call forth a pleasant smile upon her face.   In another place the Graces surround the princess and adorn her with various flowers, while Zephyr, gently wafting about her, paints her picture to adorn the world with; but, jealous of licentious glances, he curbs the minds of the lovers of licentiousness, or, perchance, shunning rebellious critics, hides in the painting the greater part of her beauties, though, as is well known, before Psyche those beauties of themselves appear in the pictures.

In order that various objects, meeting her eyes, should not weary her, her portraits alone were placed upon the wall, in simple and in festive gowns, or in masquerade attire. Psyche, you are beautiful in any attire: whether you be dressed as a queen, or whether you be seated by the tent as a shepherdess.   In all garments you are the wonder of the world, in all you appear as a goddess, and but you alone are more beautiful than your portrait.

Gavriíl Románovich Derzhávin.   (1743–1816.)

Derzhávin was born near Kazán, deriving his descent from a Tartar Murza, and passed his childhood in the east, in the Government of Orenbúrg. His early education was very scanty. In his fourteenth year his mother hastened with him to Moscow to enter him for future service as the son of a nobleman ; but, her means being exhausted, she returned with him to Kazán, where she placed him in the newly opened Gymnasium. Even here the lack of good teachers precluded his getting any thorough instruction; his only positive gain was a smattering of German, which was to help him later in acquainting himself with the productions of the German Muse. In 1762 he entered the regiment of the Transfiguration (Preobrazhénski) as a common soldier. Whatever time he could call his own in the crowded and dingy barracks in which he passed eight years of his life he devoted to reading and to imitations of Russian and German verse. In 1772 he was made a commissioned officer, and was employed to quell the Pugachév rebellion.

It was only in 1779 that Derzhávin began to write in a more independent strain; one of the best odes of this new period is his *Monody on the Death of Prince Meshchérski*. But the one that gave him his greatest reputation was his *Felítsa*, with which began a new epoch in Russian poetry. Lomonósov, Sumarókov, Tredyakóvski, and a number of minor poets had flooded Russian literature with lifeless odes in the French pseudo-classic style, written for all possible occasions, and generally to order. Just as a reaction was setting in against them in the minds of the best people, Derzhávin proved by his *Felítsa* that an ode could possess other characteristics than those sanctioned by the French school. In 1782 he occupied a position in the Senate under the Procurator-General Vyázemski. He had an exalted opinion of Catherine, whom he had not yet met, and he spoke with full sincerity of her in his ode. The name *Felítsa* was suggested to him by the princess in her moral fable (see p. 276 *et seq.*). The chief interest in the ode for contemporary society lay in the bold attacks that Derzhávin made on the foibles of the dignitaries. Its literary value consists in the fact that it was the first attempt at a purely colloquial tone of playful banter, in a kind of poetic composition formerly characterised by a stilted language, replete with Church-Slavic words and biblical allusions. Numerous are the references made by the poets of the day to the Singer of *Felítsa* (see p. 358 *et seq.*); they all felt that Derzhávin had inaugurated a new era, that the period which had begun with Lomonósov's *Capture of Khotín* was virtually over.

Catherine made Derzhávin Governor of Olónetsk, and later of Tambóv; but neither in these high offices, nor later, when Paul appointed him Chief of the Chancery of the Imperial Council, and Alexander I. made him Minister of Justice, was he successful. His excitable temperament, combined with a stern love of truth which brooked no compromise, made him everywhere impossible. Of the many productions which he wrote after *Felítsa*, none gained such wide popularity as his *Ode to God*. Though parts of it bear strong resemblance to similar odes by Klopstock, Haller, Brockes, and to passages in Young's *Night Thoughts*, yet the whole is so far superior

to any of them that it soon was translated into all European languages, and also into Japanese; there are not less than fifteen versions of it in French. Derzhávin lived to hear Púshkin recite one of
his poems and to proclaim him his spiritual successor. The following translations of Derzháviu's poems in English are known to me:

*God, On the Death of Meshcherski, The Waterfall, The Lord and
the Judge, On the Death of Count Orlov, Song (The Little Bee)*, in
Sir John Bowring's *Specimens of the Russian Poets*, Part I.; *To a
Neighbour, The Shipwreck, Fragment, ib.*, Part II.; *To God, The
Storm*, in William D. Lewis's *The Bakchesarian Fountain*, Philadel-
phia, 1849; *The Stream of Time*, in J. Pollen's *Rhymes from the
Russian; Drowning*, by N. H. Dole; *Ode to the Deity*, by J. K.
Stallybrass, in The Leisure Hour, London, 1870, May 2; *Ode to
God*, by N. H. Dole, in The Chautauquan, vol. x; *On the Death of
Meshcherski*, in C. E. Turner's *Studies in Russian Literature*, and
the same in Fraser's Magazine, 1877.

ODE TO THE DEITY

O Thou infinite in being;
   Living 'midst the change of all;
Thou eternal through time's fleeing;
   Formless—Three-in-one withal!
Spirit filling all creation,
Who hast neither source nor station;
   Whom none reach, howe'er they plod;
Who with Thine existence fillest,
Claspest, mouldest as Thou willest,
   Keepest all; whom we call—God!

Though the lofty mind could measure
   Deepest seas, and count the sand,
Of the starry rays the treasure,
   Thou no number hast, no strand!
Highest souls by Thee created,
To Thy service consecrated,
   Ne'er could trace Thy counsels high;
Soon as thought to Thee aspireth,
In Thy greatness it expireth,
   Moment in eternity.

Thou didst call the ancient chaos
　From eternity's vast sea:
On Thyself, ere time did ray us,
　Thou didst found eternity.
By Thyself Thyself sustaining,
From Thyself unaided shining,
　Thou art Light—light flows from Thee;
By Thy words all things creating,
Thy creation permeating,
　Thou wast, art and aye shalt be.

All existence Thou containest
　In Thee, quick'nest with Thy breath;
End to the beginning chainest;
　And Thou givest life through death.
Life as sparks spring from the fire,
Suns are born from Thee, great sire:
　As, in cold clear wintry day,
Spangles of the frost shine, sparkling,
Turning, wavering, glittering, darkling,
　Shine the stars beneath Thy ray.

All the million lights, that wander
　Silent through immensity,
Thy behests fulfil, and squander
　Living rays throughout the sky.
But those lamps of living fire,
Crystals soaring ever higher,
　Golden waves in rich array,
Wondrous orbs of burning ether,
Or bright worlds that cling together,
　Are to Thee as night to day.

Like a drop in sea before Thee
　Is the firmament on high:
What 's the universe of glory,
　And before Thee what am I ?
In yon vast aërial ocean

Could I count those worlds in motion,
   Adding millions to them—aught
I could fancy or decipher,
   By Thy side is but a cipher;
     And before Thee I am—naught!

Naught! And yet in me Thou rayest,
   By Thy gift and through Thy Son:
In me Thou Thyself portrayest,
   As in one small drop the sun.
Naught! Yet life I feel throughout me,
And, content with naught about me,
   Upward fly with eager heart.
That Thou art, my soul supposes,
Tries, and with this reas'ning closes:
   " Sure I am, hence Thou too art."

Yes, Thou art—all nature tells me;
   Whispers back my heart the thought;
Reason now to this impels me:
   Since Thou art, I am not naught!
Part of Thine entire creation,
Set in nature's middle station
   By Thine order I abide;
Where Thou endest forms terrestrial
And beginnest souls celestial,
   Chains of beings by me tied.

I 'm the link of worlds existing,
   Last high grade of matter I,
Centre of all life subsisting,
   First touch of divinity.
Death to dust my body sunders:
In my mind I wield the thunders.
   I 'm a king, a slave to Thee:
I 'm a worm, a god! Whence hither
Came I, wonderful? Oh, whither?
   By myself I could not be.

Thine am I, Thou great Creator,
   Outcome of Thy wisdom sole;
Fount of life, blest conservator;
   Of my soul the king and soul!
Needful to Thy just decreeing
Was it that my deathless being
   Pass to Thee through death's abyss:
That my soul, in body vested,
Wend, by death refined and tested,
   Father, to Thy deathlessness.

Traceless One, unfathomable!
   Now I cannot see Thy face:
My imagining 's too feeble
   E'en Thy shadow here to trace;
But, if we must sing Thy glory,
Feeble mortals, to adore Thee
   In a worthy attitude,
We must rise to Thee to wreathe Thee,
Lost in distance far beneath Thee,
   And—shed tears of gratitude.
   —Translated by J. K. Stallybrass, in The Leisure
         Hour, London, 1870, May 2.

MONODY ON PRINCE MESHCHÉRSKI [1]

O iron tongue of Time, with thy sharp metallic tone,
Thy terrible voice affrights me:
Each beat of the clock summons me,
Calls me and hurries me to the grave.
Scarcely have I opened my eyes upon the world,
Ere Death grinds his teeth,
And with his scythe, that gleams like lightning,
Cuts off my days, which are but grass.

---

[1] Alexander Ivánovich Meshchérski was the president of the St. Petersburg magistracy, and later served in the Chief Customs Chancery. Both he and his friend Perfílev, mentioned at the end of the monody, led a life of luxury.

Not one of the horned beasts of the field,
Not a single blade of grass escapes,
Monarch and beggar alike are food for the worm.
The noxious elements feed the grave,
And Time effaces all human glory;
As the swift waters rush towards the sea,
So our days and years flow into Eternity,
And empires are swallowed up by greedy Death.

We crawl along the edge of the treacherous abyss,
Into which we quickly fall headlong:
With our first breath of life we inhale death,
And are only born that we may die.
Stars are shivered by him,
And suns are momentarily quenched,
Each world trembles at his menace,
And Death unpityingly levels all.

The mortal scarcely thinks that he can die,
And idly dreams himself immortal,
When Death comes to him as a thief,
And in an instant robs him of his life.
Alas! where fondly we fear the least,
There will Death the sooner come;
Nor does the lightning-bolt with swifter blast
Topple down the towering pinnacle.

Child of luxury, child of freshness and delight,
Meshchérski, where hast thou hidden thyself?
Thou hast left the realms of light,
And withdrawn to the shores of the dead;
Thy dust is here, but thy soul is no more with us.
Where is it? It is there. Where is there? We know not.
We can only weep and sob forth,
Woe to us that we were ever born into the world!

They who are radiant with health,
Love and joy and peace,
Feel their blood run cold

And their souls to be fretted with woe.
Where but now was spread a banquet, there stands a coffin:
Where but now rose mad cries of revelry,
There resounds the bitter wailing of mourners;
And over all keeps Death his watch,—

Watches us one and all,—the mighty Tsar
Within whose hands are lodged the destinies of a world;
Watches the sumptuous Dives,
Who makes of gold and silver his idol-gods;
Watches the fair beauty rejoicing in her charms;
Watches the sage, proud of his intellect;
Watches the strong man, confident in his strength;
And, even as he watches, sharpens the blade of his scythe.

O Death, thou essence of fear and trembling!
O Man, thou strange mixture of grandeur and of nothingness!
To-day a god, and to-morrow a patch of earth:
To-day buoyed up with cheating hope,
And to-morrow, where art thou, Man?
Scarce an hour of triumph allowed thee
Ere thou hast taken thy flight to the realms of Chaos,
And thy whole course of life, a dream, is run.

Like a dream, like some sweet vision,
Already my youth has vanished quite.
Beauty no longer enjoys her potent sway,
Gladness no more, as once, entrances me,
My mind is no longer free and fanciful,
And all my happiness is changed.
I am troubled with a longing for fame;
I listen; the voice of fame now calls me.

But even so will manhood pass away,
And together with fame all my aspirations.
The love of wealth will tarnish all,
And each passion in its turn
Will sway the soul and pass.
Avaunt, happiness, that boasts to be within our grasp!

All happiness is but evanescent and a lie:
I stand at the gate of Eternity.

To-day or to-morrow we must die,
Perfílev, and all is ended.
Why, then, lament or be afflicted
That thy friend did not live for ever?
Life is but a momentary loan from Heaven:
Spend it then in resignation and in peace,
And with a pure soul
Learn to kiss the chastening rod.

    —From C. E. Turner's *Studies in Russian Literature*,
        and the same in Fraser's Magazine, 1877.

FELÍTSA [1]

Godlike queen of the Kirgíz-Kaysák horde,[2] whose incomparable wisdom discovered the true path for the young Tsarévich Khlor, by which to climb the high mountain where grows the rose without prickles, where virtue dwells that captivates my soul and my mind! Oh, teach me how to find it!

Instruct me, Felítsa, how to live voluptuously, yet justly; how to tame the storm of passions, and be happy in the world. Your voice enthuses me, your son guides me, but I am weak to follow them. Disturbed by worldly cares, I control myself to-day, to-morrow am a slave of my caprices.

You do not emulate your Murzas,[3] and frequently go on foot; the simplest food is served at your table. You disdain your rest, and read and write by the tallow dip, and from your pen flows bliss to all the mortals.[4] Nor do you play cards, like me, from morning until morning.[5]

You do not care overmuch for masquerades, and do not

[1] See Catherine II.'s *Prince Khlor*, p. 280.

[2] Catherine had some villages in the Government of Orenbúrg, near the settlements of the Kirgíz-Kaysák horde,—hence the name given her by Derzhávin.

[3] Tartar chiefs, but courtiers are meant here.

[4] Through the promulgation of her laws.

[5] Derzhávin was much addicted to gambling in his early life, and had even tried to mend his fortune by cheating.

set your foot into a club. You keep old customs and habits, and make no Don Quixote of yourself. You do not saddle the steed of Parnassus,[1] do not attend the séances, to see spirits,[2] do not go to the East[3] from your throne; but, walking on the path of humility, your gracious soul passes an even tenor of useful days.

But I sleep until noon, smoke tobacco and drink coffee. I change the work-days into holidays, and live in a whirl of chimerical thoughts: I now take booty from the Persians, now direct my arrows to the Turks; now, imagining myself to be the Sultan, I make the world tremble with my looks; or, suddenly attracted by a sumptuous garment, I hasten to the tailor for a new caftan.[4]

Or I am at a sumptuous feast, where they celebrate in my honour, where the table sparkles with its silver and gold, where there are a thousand different courses,—here the famous Westphalian bacon, there slices of Astrakhán fish, there stand the pilau and the cakes,—I drink champagne after my waffles and forget everything in the world 'midst wine, sweetmeats and perfumes.

Or, 'midst a beautiful grove, in an arbour, where the fountain plashes, by the sound of a sweet-voiced harp, where the zephyr scarcely breathes, where everything inclines to luxury, and entices the mind to joy, and the blood becomes now languid, now flows warm, inclining upon a velvet divan, I rouse the tender feelings of a young maiden, and inspire her heart with love.

Or, in a magnificent tandem, in a gilded English carriage, I drive with a dog, a fool, or friend, or fair maiden to the Swings, or stop at the taverns to drink mead; or, when I get tired of that, for I am inclined to change, fly, with my cap posed jauntily, on a mettled steed.

[1] Catherine was not successful as a versifier.
[2] She loved neither Masons nor Martinists, who were a kind of precursors of the modern spiritualists.
[3] Name of a Masonic lodge.
[4] The reference is to Potémkin, his dreams of conquering India and Persia, his foppery, his sumptuous feasts.

Or I delight my soul with music and singers, the organ and flute, or boxing and the dance.[1] Or, dropping all care of business, go on the chase, and take pleasure in the barking of the hounds[2]; or, on the banks of the Nevá, enjoy at night the sound of horns and the rowing of agile oarsmen.[3]

Or, staying at home, pass my time playing " Old Maid " with my wife; or we climb together into the dove-cot, or, at times, play Blindman's Buff with her, or sváyka,[4] or have her examine my head; or I love to pore over books, to enlighten my mind and heart, that is, I read *Pulicane* and *Bovo*,[5] or yawn and fall asleep over the Bible.

Such are my debauches, Felítsa! But the whole world resembles me, no matter if one passes for a sage: every man is a living lie. We travel not by the paths of light, we run after the whims of pleasure. 'Twixt the Indolent and the Choleric,[6] 'twixt vanity and vice, one seldom finds the straight road to virtue.

Suppose we have found it! How are we weak mortals not to blunder, where even Reason stumbles and follows after passions, where learned ignoramuses bedim our heads as the mist bedims the wanderers? Temptation and flattery dwell everywhere, and luxury oppresses all the pashas. Where, then, dwells virtue? Where grows the rose without prickles?

It becomes you alone, O Empress, to create light from darkness, dividing chaos harmoniously in spheres, to firmly unite them by a common bond; you alone can bring forth concord out of discord, and happiness out of violent passions:

[1] Characterisation of A. G. Orlóv.

[2] P. I. Pánin.

[3] Allusion to S. K. Narýshkin, who had introduced wind instruments, where each player played but one note.

[4] A game which consists of throwing a large nail into a ring.

[5] Famous popular novels much in vogue in all Europe ; the latter is the English *Bevys of Hamptoun ;* the allusion is here to the rude manners of Prince Vyázemski.

[6] Lentyág and Bryúzga of Catherine's *Prince Khlor,* by whom she meant Potémkin and Vyázemski.

thus the sailor, crossing the sea, catches the gale in his sails and safely guides his ship.

You alone hurt not, nor injure anyone; though you may connive at stupidity, you tolerate no mean act; you treat peccadillos with condescension. You do not choke people, as the wolf chokes the sheep, but you know their worth: they are subject to the will of kings, but more to righteous God who lives in their laws.

You judge soundly of merits, and mete out honour to the deserving: you deem him not a prophet who merely makes rhymes. And as for that entertainment of the mind,—the honour and glory of good caliphs, the lyric strain to which you condescend,— poetry is pleasing to you, acceptable, soothing, useful,—like a refreshing lemonade in summer.

Rumour tells of you that you are not in the least haughty, that you are pleasant in business and in jest, agreeable in friendship and firm; that you are indifferent to misfortune, and so magnanimous in glory that you refused to be called "Wise." [1] Again, they justly say that one may always tell you the truth.

This, too, is an unheard-of thing and worthy of you alone: you permit the people boldly to know and think all, [2] openly or in secret; nor do you forbid them to say of you what is true or false; and you are always prone to forgive those crocodiles, the Zoiluses of all your benefactions.

Rivers of joyful tears stream from the depth of my heart. Oh, how happy the people must be there with their fate,

[1] In 1767 the Senate and deputies, who had been invited to present a project for a new code of laws, proposed a title for the Empress "Great, Most Wise, and Mother of the Country," but she declined it.

[2] This and the following lines refer to the reign of Empress Anna, when the least inattention to the minutest details of Imperial prerogatives brought about the severest persecution: it was sufficient not to empty a beaker which was drunk to her health, or to scratch out or correct her name in a document, or to drop a coin with her picture upon it, in order to be immediately denounced to the secret police. Then follows the reference to the ice palace in which the marriage of the Court fool, Prince Golítsyn, was celebrated; the other Court fools of the day were the Princes Volkónski and Apráksin.

where a meek, peaceful angel, clad in porphyry splendour, wields the heaven-sent sceptre! There one may whisper conversations and, without fearing punishment, at dinners not drink the health of kings.

There one may erase Felítsa's name in the line, or carelessly drop her portrait on the ground. There they do not celebrate preposterous weddings, and steam people in ice baths, and pull the mustaches of dignitaries; princes do not cackle like sitting hens, nor favourites laugh loud at them and smear their faces with soot.

You know, O Felítsa, the rights of men and kings. While you enlighten the manners, you do not turn men into fools. In your moments of rest you write fables for instruction and teach the alphabet to Khlor: "Do no wrong, and you will cause the bitterest satirist to become a hated prevaricator."

You are ashamed to be called great, lest you be feared and hated: it becomes only a wild she-bear to tear animals and suck their blood. Need one have recourse to the lancet, unless in extreme fever, when one can get along without it? And is it glorious to be a tyrant, a great Tamerlane in cruelty, where one is great in goodness, like God?

Felítsa's glory is the glory of a god who has calmed strife, who has covered, dressed and fed the orphaned and the poor; whose radiant eye emits its light to fools, cowards, ungrateful people and the just, and enlightens alike all mortals, soothes, cures the sick,—does good for good's sake;

Who has given the liberty to travel to other lands, has permitted his people to seek gold and silver; who makes the waters free, and does not prohibit cutting down the woods; who orders to weave, and spin, and sew; who, freeing the mind and the hands, orders to love commerce and the sciences, and to find happiness at home;

Whose law and hand distribute favours and justice. Announce, wise Felítsa, where is the villain separated from the honest man? Where does old age not go a-begging, and merit find its bread? Where does revenge not drive anyone? Where dwells conscience with truth? Where shine virtues?—if not at your throne?

But where does your throne shine in the world? Where do you flourish, celestial branch? In Bagdad, Smyrna, Cashmir? Listen: wherever you may live and my praises reach you, think not that I wish a hat or caftan for them. To feel the charm of goodness is for the soul a wealth such as even Crœsus did not possess.

I pray the great prophet that I may touch the dust of your feet, that I may enjoy the sweet stream of your words and your look. I entreat the heavenly powers that they extend their sapphire wings and invisibly guard you from all diseases, evils and ennui, that the renown of your deeds may shine in posterity like stars in the heavens.

FROM "THE WATERFALL"

Lo! like a glorious pile of diamonds bright,
Built on the steadfast cliffs, the waterfall
Pours forth its gems of pearl and silver light:
They sink, they rise, and sparkling cover all
With infinite refulgence; while its song,
Sublime as thunder, rolls the woods along,—

Rolls through the woods,—they send its accents back,
Whose last vibration in the desert dies:
Its radiance glances o'er the watery track,
Till the soft wave, as wrapt in slumber, lies
Beneath the forest shade; then sweetly flows
A milky stream, all silent, as it goes.

Its foam is scattered on the margent bound,
Skirting the darksome grove. But list! the hum
Of industry, the rattling hammer's sound,
Files whizzing, creaking sluices, echoed come
On the fast-travelling breeze! Oh no, no voice
Is heard around but thy majestic noise!

When the mad storm-wind tears the oak asunder,
In thee its shivered fragments find their tomb;
When rocks are riven by the bolt of thunder,

As sands they sink into thy mighty womb:
The ice that would imprison thy proud tide
Like bits of broken glass is scattered wide.

The fierce wolf prowls around thee—there it stands
Listening,—not fearful, for he nothing fears:
His red eyes burn like fury-kindled brands,
Like bristles o'er him his coarse fur he rears;
Howling, thy dreadful roar he oft repeats,
And, more ferocious, hastes to bloodier feats.

The wild stag hears thy falling waters' sound,
And tremblingly flies forward,—o'er her back
She bends her stately horns, the noiseless ground
Her hurried feet impress not, and her track
Is lost among the tumult of the breeze,
And the leaves falling from the rustling trees.

The wild horse thee approaches in his turn:
He changes not his proudly rapid stride;
His mane stands up erect, his nostrils burn,
He snorts, he pricks his ears, and starts aside;
Then rushing madly forward to thy steep,
He dashes down into thy torrents deep.

> —From Sir John Bowring's *Specimens of the
> Russian Poets*, Part I.

THE STORM

As my bark in the restless ocean
  Mounts its rough and foaming hills,
Whilst its waves in dark commotion
  Pass me, hope my bosom fills.

Who, when warring clouds are gleaming,
  Quenches the destructive spark?
Say what hand, what safety's beaming,
  Guides through rocks my little bark?

Thou, Creator, all o'erseeing,
  In this scene preserv'st me dread!

Thou, without whose word decreeing
Not a hair falls from my head!

Thou in life hast doubly blest me,
All my soul to Thee 's revealed, —
Thou amongst the great hast placed me, —
Be 'midst them my guide and shield!
—From W. D. Lewis's *The Bakchesarian Fountain.*

THE STREAM OF TIME [1]

The stream of time, with onward sweep,
Bears off men's works, all human things,
And plunges o'er Oblivion's steep
Peoples and kingdoms with their kings.
If for a space amidst the swirl
The lyre of trumpet some sustain,
They 're swept at last in ceaseless whirl,
And none escape Fate's common main.
—From John Pollen's *Rhymes from the Russian.*

Yúri Aleksándrovich Neledínski-Melétski.
(1752-1829.)

After finishing his education in the University of Strassburg, Neledínski occupied various posts in the army and with legations. In 1800 he was made a Senator. He distinguished himself in literature by his simple, deep-felt songs, two of which, given below, have become enormously popular. His other poems and translations from French authors are now forgotten.

Sir John Bowring has translated his "Under the oak-tree, near the rill," "To the streamlet I'll repair," and "He whom misery, dark and dreary"; the latter is the same as Lewis's "He whose soul from sorrow dreary."

SONG

To the streamlet I 'll repair,
Look upon its flight and say:
" Bear, O fleeting streamlet, bear
All my griefs with thine away!"

[1] The last verses Derzhávin wrote.

Ah, I breathe the wish in vain!
  In this silent solitude
Counted is each throb of pain:—
  Rest is melancholy's food.

Waves with waves unceasing blend,
  Hurrying to their destiny:
E'en so thoughts with thoughts, and tend
  All alike to misery.

And what grief so dark, so deep
  As the grief interred within,
By the friend, for whom I weep,
  All unnoticed, all unseen?

Yet, could I subdue my pain,
  Soothe affection's rankling smart,
Ne'er would I resume again
  The lost empire of my heart.

Thou, my love, art sovereign there!
  There thou hast a living shrine:
Let my portion be despair,
  If the light of bliss be thine.

Loved by thee, oh, might I live,
  'Neath the darkest, stormiest sky:
'T were a blest alternative!
  Grief is joy, if thou be nigh.

Every wish and every pray'r
  Is a tribute paid to thee:
Every heart-beat—there, oh there,
  Thou hast mightiest sovereignty.

To thee, nameless one! to thee
  Still my thoughts, my passions turn;
'T is through thee alone I see,
  Think, and feel, and breathe, and burn.

If the woe in which I live
  Ever reach thy generous ear,
Pity not, but oh, forgive
  Thy devoted worshipper!

In some hour of careless bliss
  Deign my bosom's fire to prove;
Prove it with an icy kiss,—
  Thou shalt know how much I love!
            —From Sir John Bowring's *Specimens of
                  the Russian Poets*, Part I.

STANZAS

He whose soul from sorrow dreary,
  Weak and wretched, naught can save,
Who in sadness, sick and weary,
  Hopes no refuge but the grave;
On his visage Pleasure beaming
  Ne'er shall shed her placid ray,
Till kind fate, from woe redeeming,
  Leads him to his latest day.

Thou this life preservest ever,
  My distress and my delight!
And, though soul and body sever,
  Still I 'll live a spirit bright;
In my breast the heart that 's kindled
  Death's dread strength can ne'er destroy,
Sure the soul with thine that 's mingled
  Must immortal life enjoy.

That inspired by breath from heaven
  Need not shrink a mortal doom,
To thee shall my vows be given
  In this world and that to come.
My fond shade shall constant trace thee,
  And attend in friendly guise,
Still surround thee, still embrace thee,
  Catch thy thoughts, thy looks, thy sighs.

To divine its secret pondering,
   Close to clasp thy soul 't will brave,
And if chance shall find thee wandering
   Heedless near my silent grave,
E'en my ashes then shall tremble,
   Thy approach relume their fire,
And that stone in dust shall crumble,
   Covering what can ne'er expire!
—From W. D. Lewis's *The Bakchesarian Fountain*.

Mikhaíl Nikítich Muravév. (1757–1807.)

Muravév was an alumnus of the Moscow University, and early distinguished himself for his intimate knowledge of the ancient and
many modern languages. In 1785 he became the instructor of Alexander and Constantine, and when the first ascended the throne,
Muravév was made Senator, and later Curator of the Moscow University. He not only did much for the cause of education in Russia,
but himself educated a new generation of writers, among them
Bátyushkov ; through his efforts Karamzín was made historiographer,
and the Archives were opened to him. In his prose and poetry,
Muravév was himself a follower of the pseudo-classic school, with an
addition of sentimentalism, through Karamzín's influence. In his
classicism, however, he differs from all his contemporaries in that
he drew directly from the ancient sources, with which he was intimately acquainted.

Sir John Bowring translated Muravév's *To the Goddess of the
Neva, Boleslav*, and " She bent her head, and her tears that fell."

TO THE GODDESS OF THE NEVÁ

Glide, majestic Neva! Glide thee,
   Decked with bright and peaceful smiles;
Palaces are raised beside thee,
   'Midst the shadows of the isles.

Stormy Russian seas thou bindest
   With the ocean—by the grave
Of our glorious Tsar thou windest,
   Which thy graceful waters lave.

And the middle-ocean's surges
  All thy smiling naiads court;
While thy stream to Paros urges,
  And to Lemnos' classic port.

Hellas' streams, their glory shaded,
  See the brightest memories fade;
Glassy mirrors—how degraded!
  Dimmed by Kislar Aga's shade.

While thy happier face is bearing
  Ever-smiling images,
On thy busy banks appearing
  Crowds in gaiety and peace.

Thames' and Tagus' gathering prizes,
  Spread their riches o'er thy breast,
While thy well-known banner rises,
  Rises proudly o'er the rest.

In thy baths what beauties bathe them,
  Goddesses of love and light;
There Erota loves to swathe them
  In the brightest robes of night.

Cool thy smiling banks at even,
  Cool thy grottoes and thy cells,
Where, by gentle breezes driven,
  Oft the dancing billow swells.

Then thou gatherest vapours round thee,
  Veil'st thee in thy twilight dress;
Love and mirth have now unbound thee—
  Yield thee to thy waywardness.

Thou dost bear the dying over,
  Weary of this earthly dream;
And with awful mists dost cover
  All the bosom of the stream.

With thy car thou troublest never
  The calm silence of the deep;
Sirens dance around thee ever,
  Laughing o'er thy quiet sleep.

Peaceful goddess! Oft the singer
  Sees thee in his ecstasy,
On the rock he loves to linger,
  Sleepless,—then he meets with thee.
          —From Sir John Bowring's *Specimens of the
          Russian Poets*, Part II.

Vasíli Vasílevich Kapníst. (1757-1824.)

Kapníst, the son of a brigadier, entered the army as a corporal in
1771, and was made a commissioned officer in 1775, but he soon retired to his native village of Obúkhovka in the Government of Kíev,
which he later described in the manner of Horace. He was elected
a Representative of the Nobility of his district, later (upon his return
to St. Petersburg), became a member of the Academy, and rose to
many other honours. He early distinguished himself by translations
and imitations of Horace, in which he devoted a closer attention to
perfect form than any of his contemporaries, so that, but for a somewhat antiquated language, he is read with pleasure even at the
present time. His chief reputation with his contemporaries was
earned by the comedy *The Pettifoggery*, which had a phenomenal
success, and was only superseded by Griboyédov's *Intelligence Comes
to Grief* and Gógol's *The Revizór*. Like all the great comedies of
Russia, *The Pettifoggery* deals with the negative sides of social life,
and lays bare the corruption of officialdom. The plot of the play is
as follows : Pettifog devises a plan by which he is to get hold of the
property of Squareman. The latter is named in his certificate of
birth Theodotos ; his father left his estate to this Theodotos, but he
naming himself Deodatus (Bogdán), Pettifog argues before the judges
that Deodatus is another unlawful holder of that estate, and that it
ought to revert to himself, as a distant relative of the deceased man.
To make his case sure he bribes the judges, Gurgle, Snare, Gladly
and Wordy, and the Procurator Grab and Secretary Talon, and sues
for the hand of Sophia, the daughter of the Presiding Judge Casetwister. All, however, ends well, for Pettifog is denounced to the
Senate and put in gaol, and the judges are turned over to the
criminal court, while Squareman marries Sophia, his old sweetheart.
The verses at the end of Act III., Scene 6, "Take, you'll learn the

art with ease," went like wild-fire through all Russia, and became the byword for the large host of bribers.

Sir John Bowring has translated his *On Julia's Death*, also reprinted in F. R. Grahame's *The Progress of Science, Art and Literature in Russia*.

FROM "THE PETTIFOGGERY"

ACT III., SCENE 6. FÉKLA, SOPHIA, ANNA, CASETWISTER, PETTIFOG, GURGLE, SNARE, GLADLY, WORDY, GRAB, TALON AND SLY (tipsy, playing cards)

Talon. They have picked me clean.

Gurgle. Well! We are not picking your own feathers.

Pettifog. My dear friend, always grab the jack-pot!

Talon. A well-born man grabs all in splendid style.

Wordy (*to Pettifog*). Your intimate has been flaying us.

Pettifog. That's proper. (*To Sly.*) You had better rise. (*To Casetwister.*) Will you not let him mix a punch for us? He is a great hand at it.

Casetwister. Very well.

Gurgle. That's right, for the young beauty has been watering us as from a trough. . . .

Sly (*walking up to Anna*). There is some brandy in the basket.

Fékla. His goose is cooked.

Pettifog. That's so.

Casetwister. Whose?

Pettifog. Mine.

Gurgle. That accursed Theodotos has done it all.

Gladly (*to Grab, who has been looking into his cards*). Leave my ca-ca-ca——

Grab (*putting his hand on his mouth*). Stop your cawing.

Wordy. Say, Sly, stop courting her.

Casetwister. Anna, why have you run away from us? You had better serve us the new punch; we will be obliged to you.

Fékla (*to Anna*). Hurry up.

(*Anna serves to the guests punch and wine, while Fékla gives her privately some signs : the guests are getting drunk.*)

Snare. Oh, oh, we are getting there!

Pettifog. Eh?

Wordy (*pointing to Sly*). Ask him.

Sly. Sir, the trouble is, it 's all gone.

Pettifog. Keep it up; here is the wherewithal (*throws a purse to him*).

Gurgle. The trouble is all with Theodotos.

Pettifog. It is easy for you to have your fun with Theodotos; but it 's I who am having the trouble with him.

Casetwister. What of it? If it is true that through conspiracy Deodatus has gotten away with Theodotos's property, there is a law for such a case.

Talon. I have already given the order to find the laws that cover the case.

Casetwister. I suppose there are some statutes?

Talon. Lots of them, sir.

Wordy. And also some decrees?

Talon. There are.

Gurgle. And, of course, there must be a special ukase.

Talon. There are several.

Grab. But clearest of all it is in the Institutes; you will find it in the chapter where . . . about it——

Snare. Rather dark.

Wordy. It 's an ace and a jack.

Casetwister. And then we may apply the law of false pretences?

Talon. Of course, we may, sir! It fits the case.

Gurgle. And we bring the Reglement in accord with the Institutes. . . .

Talon. Then all will agree with the above-mentioned ukase.

Gurgle. That 's it. You see, you can easily pass sentence.

Casetwister. Theodotos is out of the question. Deodatus is certainly a villain; so we will take Theodotos's property and give it where it belongs. That 's my opinion.

Gurgle. Mine too.

Snare. And mine.

Wordy. And mine.

Gladly. A-a-and mine.

Grab. I agree with that unanimous opinion.

Pettifog. Thank you all.

Casetwister. 'T is not hard to pick the laws.

Anna (*aside, as she picks up the cards on the ground*). And I will pick the cards.

Casetwister. Where is the punch?

Fékla. Anna! Be quick about it, and serve them often all around, and ask their favour.

Gurgle. Oh, we will soon ask hers.

Casetwister. Let 's have a song.

Wordy. Let 's throw away the cards: the queen has forsaken me.

Snare. You deal with a heavy hand.

Casetwister (*to Grab*). Dear Procurator! You have a good voice: give us a song!

Grab. Most gladly, but I have no voice.

Casetwister. The best way you can.

Gurgle. We will sing the refrain.

Grab (*sings*).

> Take, you 'll learn the art with ease!
> Take whatever you can seize!
> God for this your hands did make,
> That you may take!

(*All repeat :* Take, take, take!)

(*Sophia shuts her ears and goes away.*)

ACT IV., SCENE 6.   CASETWISTER, FÉKLA AND TALON

Casetwister (*to Talon*). But hear, my dear. The rumour must be false that some meddler has denounced us to the Senate for taking bribes and for deciding wrongly cases at law.

Talon. I declare! What bad luck is that?

Casetwister. I could not find out all. But you, my friend, tell me in truth what case it was we decided so wrongly that we did not cover our tracks? I can't think of any.

Talon (scratching his spine). Even if I were to go to confession, I could not think of any.

Fékla. But that's impossible.

Casetwister. I beg you, wife, leave us alone! We know affairs better than you.

Fékla. Indeed, I know as well as you. Is it not my business to receive things and look after them? But may the wrath of the Lord strike me on the spot, if my right hand knows what my left hand takes.

Casetwister (to Talon). Say: it just occurs to me that there was quite a disturbance about the note whose endorsement I ordered to have scratched.

Talon. O sir, there is no cause for your worry there. I myself did the scratching. The defendant suspected the plaintiff of changing the endorsement. You decided the case properly according to the laws, and ordered the note to be destroyed.

Fékla (to Casetwister). Well, you have done no more wrong there than I.

Talon. Besides, you did not scratch the note, but only clean paper.

Fékla. Then where is your guilt? What sin is there in scratching mere paper? None at all.

Casetwister. So much the better.

Talon. There is something else that occurs to me. Do you remember the lawsuit for Simple's estate? Pettifog, who had really nothing to do with the case and had forgotten the name of Simple in the lawsuit, contrived cunningly to sue Trickster, who had also not the slightest right to the estate. We did not bother about finding out whose the village in question was, and without further investigation, in the absence of Simple, disposed of the lawsuit by adjudging another's property to the contending parties, which they proceeded at once to divide among themselves. I can't imagine what Simple is going to say about it.

Casetwister. Let him say whatever he pleases, since he has paid so little attention to it. Why should we worry about him now? We are the judges. 'T is our duty to know only that which is presented for our consideration on paper. What right have we to know that the estate under contention does not belong to the contending parties, but to someone else? We should have to have some written proof of that; in absence of the same, we simply must decide a lawsuit between two parties strictly according to the laws. We cannot help it if both were contending for something that did not belong to them.

OBÚKHOVKA

At peace with my neighbours and relatives, at peace with my conscience, in love with my beloved family, I here with my joys alone measure the stream of quiet days.

My cosey house with straw-thatched roof is all I want, neither too low, nor too high; there is a nook in it for friendship, and indolence has forgot to put a lock on the door, to notabilities unknown.

By a mount from the north protected, it stands upon a grassy hill, and looks into groves and distant meadows, while Psel, winding like a serpent, babbles as it tends towards the mills.

Nearby, the favourite child of nature, a vast shadowy forest, surrounds it on all sides with its thick tree-tops, without encroachment on the free expanse.

Before it, and on a small eminence, art, to please our eyes, having given a gentle slope to abrupt mounds, has on a modest elevation raised a modest temple to moderation.

Moderation, O heavenly friend, be ever my companion! You lead men to happiness; but your altar, not known to all, is hidden from the boastful rich.

You have taught me from earliest youth not to seek honour nor gold, without pinions not to fly upwards, and in the glowworm not to show the light to the wonderment of the world.

With you, the dearest one to me in the world, I treasure my fate; whithersoever I glance with you, in every object I discover a new charm.

As I walk down the hill, the arbour covered by the dense shade of trees calls the tired one, through the forest that bends into a vault, to rest, and mirrors itself in the crystal stream below.

Coolness reigns here for ever and refreshes the feelings and the mind, while the gentle, incessant murmur of the impetuous waterfall induces sleep amidst sweet thoughts.

There suddenly twenty wheels begin to turn, and circle hastens after circle; diamonds, opals, hyacinths, rain down from gleaming bows, while pearls beat underneath in clouds.

Thus the vision of happiness moves the passions, and with them the whole world is in motion. Fortunate he who gets away from them, for they crush all, tear all in pieces that passes under their millstone.

Let us go, before it grows dark, to rest upon the nearby island; a covered way leads to it, where the rays of the sun dare not glide through the dark foliage.

There I shall sit down under a mossy elm, leaning against a mighty trunk. Alas, not long, upon a hot day, will its leafy top carpet for me a hospitable shade!

Already it has inclined its brow upon the water that has undermined the steep bank; already it looks into the gloomy depth,—and soon, in stormy weather, it will fall with upturned roots into the water.

Thus in the world all is carried away by the stream of time amidst an eternal strife; thus ancient altars have fallen; thus kingdoms and kings have fallen, with the pillars of their thrones.

But to disperse painful thoughts, let us walk the path to the forest-covered hill where Phœbus with brilliant beam reflects from the zenith a mighty shade.

I see a modest plain with a hedge of crimson bushes: there Flora, the tender mother of the gardens, has scattered her basket full of fragrant flowers.

Farther off, in the realm of Pomona, fruit burdens the trees; beyond is the vineyard of Bacchus, where, filled with nectar juice, gleam amber clusters.

Is it possible to picture all the beauties of nature, and all its charm? To weld there the distance with the horizon, to adorn here the vales with flocks, and nap it with the golden harvest?

No, no! Abandon the vain endeavour! Already the sun has disappeared behind the mountain; already above the ethereal azure, 'twixt clouds, twinkle bright stars and glisten on the waves of the river.

I ascend the hill. The golden moon has swum out on a gentle cloud, and, glinting through the bluish cirrus, leaves behind it a gleaming path above the liquid glass.

Oh, how dear that place is to me when the satellite of the night comes, in all her beauty, to weld with the dream of a pining soul the remembrance of bright days!

ON JULIA'S DEATH

The evening darkness shrouds
  The slumbering world in peace,
And from her throne of clouds
  Shines Luna through the trees.
My thoughts in silence blend,
  But gathered all to thee:
Thou moon! the mourner's friend,
  Oh, come and mourn with me!

Upon her grave I bow,
  The green grave where she lies:
Oh, hear my sorrows now,
  And consecrate my sighs!
This is her ashes' bed,—
  Here her cold relics sleep,—
Where I my tears shall shed,
  While this torn heart can weep.

O Julia! Never rose
  Had half the charms of thee!
My comfort, my repose,—
  Oh, thou wert all to me!

But thou art gone, and I
   Must bear life's load of clay,—
And pray, and long to die,
   Though dying day by day.

But I must cease to sing,
   My lyre all mute appears.
Alas! Its plaintive string
   Is wetted with my tears.
Oh! Misery's song must end,—
   My thoughts all fly to thee:—
Thou moon! The mourner's friend,
   Oh, come and mourn with me!

> —From Sir John Bowring's *Specimens of
> the Russian Poets*, Part II.

Adrián Moyséevich Gribóvski. (1766–1833.)

Gribóvski was a Little-Russian by birth. In 1784 he was secretary to Derzhávin, the poet, who was then Governor of Olónetsk. Then he served under Potémkin, and after his death in 1791 he entered the service of Count Zúbov, Catherine's favourite. In 1795 he was Catherine's Secretary of State. Like so many Russian Memoirs of the eighteenth century, Gribóvski's *Memoirs* not only throw light on contemporary events, but are of great importance for a correct appreciation of the literature of the time. What Gribóvski reports of the simplicity of Catherine's private life forms the subject of Derzhávin's *Felítsa* (see p. 385 *et seq.*).

FROM HIS "MEMOIRS"

The Empress's [Catherine II.] manner of life was of late years the same: In the winter she resided in the large Winter Palace, in the middle story, above the right, smaller entrance. Her own rooms were few. Upon ascending a small staircase, one entered into a room where, for the immediate dispatch of the Empress's orders, there stood behind a screen a writing table with writing material for the secretaries of state and other officers. This room faced a small court, and from it you passed into the boudoir, with its windows on the Palace Square. Here stood a toilet table.

Of the two doors in this room, the one to the right led into the diamond room, the other, to the left, into the sleeping-room, where the Empress generally received her reports. From the sleeping-room one passed straight into the interior boudoir, and to the left—into the study and mirror room, from which one way led into the lower apartments, and the other, over a gallery, into the so-called Neighbouring House. In these apartments the Empress lived until spring, but sometimes she removed earlier to the Tauric Palace, which had been built by Prince Potémkin on the bank of the Nevá.

The main building of this latter palace was only one story high, on purpose, it seems, that the Empress should not be annoyed by staircases. Here her rooms were larger than in the Winter Palace, especially the study in which she received the reports. In the first days of May she always went incognito to Tsárskoe Seló, and from there she returned, also incognito, in September to the Winter Palace. Her apartments in Tsárskoe Seló were quite large and tastefully furnished. All know the magnificent gallery in which the Empress frequently took a walk, particularly on Sundays when the park was filled with a large crowd of people that used to come down from St. Petersburg. She received the reports in the cabinet, or in the sleeping-room.

The Empress's time and occupations were arranged in the following manner: She rose at seven, and was busy writing in her cabinet until nine (her last work was on the Senate Regulations). She once remarked in her conversation that she could not live a day without writing something. During that time she drank one cup of coffee, without cream. At nine o'clock she passed into the sleeping-room, where almost in the entrance from the boudoir she seated herself in a chair near the wall. Before her stood a table that slanted towards her and also to the opposite direction, where there was also a chair. She then generally wore a sleeping-gown, or capote, of white gros de Tours, and on her head a white crêpe bonnet which was poised a little towards the left. In spite of her sixty-five years, the Empress's face was still fresh, her hands beautiful, her teeth all well preserved, so that she spoke distinctly, without lisping, only a little masculinely. She read with eyeglasses and a magnifying glass. Having once been called in with my reports, I found her reading in this way. She smiled and said to me: "You, no doubt, do not need this apparatus! How old are you?" And when I said: "Twenty-six," she added: "But we have, in our long service to the Empire, dulled our vision, and now we are of necessity compelled to use glasses." It appeared to me that "we" was used by her not as an expression of majesty, but in the ordinary sense.

Upon another occasion she handed me an autograph note which contained some references for her Senate Regulations for verification, and said: "Laugh not at my Russian ortho-graphy. I will tell you why I have not succeeded in master-ing it. When I came here, I applied myself diligently to the study of Russian. When my aunt, Elizabeth Petróvna, heard of this, she told my Court mistress that I ought not to be taught any more,—that I was clever enough anyway. Thus, I could learn Russian only from books, without a teacher, and that is the cause of my insufficient knowledge of orthography." However, the Empress spoke quite cor-rect Russian, and was fond of using simple native words, of which she knew a great number. "I am very happy," she said to me, "that you know the order of the Chancery. You will be the first executor of my Regulations before the Sen-ate. But I caution you that the Chancery of the Senate has overpowered the Senate, and that I wish to free it from the Chancery. For any unjust decisions, my punishment for the Senate shall be: let them be ashamed!" I remarked that not only the Senate, but also other bureaus that are guided by the General Reglement, are hampered in the transaction of their business by great inconveniences and difficulties that demand correction. "I should like very much to see those inconveniences and difficulties of which you speak to me in such strong terms. The General Reglement is one of the best institutions of Peter the Great." Later on, I presented to her Highness my notes upon the General Reglement, which I read to her almost every afternoon of her residence

in Tsárskoe Seló in 1796, and which were honoured by her
undivided august approval. (These notes must be deposited
with other affairs in the Archives of the Foreign College.)

After occupying her seat, of which I spoke above, the
Empress rang a bell, and the valet of the day, who uninterruptedly remained outside the door, entered and, having received his order, called in the persons. At that time of the
day, the Chief Master of Police and the Secretary of State
waited daily in the boudoir; at eleven o'clock there arrived
Count Bezboródko; for the other officers certain days in the
week were set apart: for the Vice-Chancellor, Governor,
Government Procurator of the Government of St. Petersburg, Saturday; for the Procurator-General, Monday and
Thursday; Wednesday for the Superior Procurator of the
Synod and Master General of Requests; Thursday for the
Commander-in-Chief of St. Petersburg. But in important
and urgent cases, all these officers could come any other
time to report.

The first one to be called in to the Empress was the Chief
Master of Police, Brigadier Glázov. He made a verbal report on the safety of the capital and other occurrences, and
presented a note, written at the office irregularly and badly
on a sheet of paper, containing the names of arrivals and
departures on the previous day of people of all conditions
who had taken the trouble to announce their names at the
toll-house, for the sentinels stopped no one at the toll-house,
nor inquired anything of them,—in fact there existed then
no toll-gates; anybody received a passport from the Governor
at any time he asked for it, and without any pay, and could
leave the city whenever he wished: for this reason the list
of arrivals and departures never could be very long. After
the Chief Master of Police left, the Secretaries of State who
had any business had themselves announced by the valet,
and were let in one by one. I was one of them. Upon
entering the sleeping-room, I observed the following ceremony: I made a low obeisance to the Empress, to which she
responded with a nod of her head, and smilingly gave me
her hand, which I took and kissed, and I felt the pressure

of my own hand; then she commanded me to take a seat. Having seated myself on the chair opposite, I placed my papers on the slanting table, and began to read. I suppose the other reporting officers acted in the same way, when they entered the room of the Empress, and that they met with the same reception.

About eleven o'clock the other officers arrived with their reports, as mentioned above, and sometimes there came Field-Marshal Count Suvórov Rýmnikski, who then, after the conquest of Poland, resided at St. Petersburg. When he entered, he first prostrated himself three times before the image of the Holy Virgin of Kazán, which stood in the corner, to the right of the door, and before which there burned an undying lamp; then he turned to the Empress, prostrated himself once before her, though she tried to keep him from it, and, taking him by the hand, lifted him and said: "Mercy! Alexander Vasílevich, are you not ashamed to act like that?" But the hero worshipped her and regarded it as his sacred duty to express his devotion to her in that manner. The Empress gave him her hand, which he kissed as a relic, and asked him to seat himself on the chair opposite her; two minutes later she dismissed him. They used to tell that Count Bezboródko and a few others prostrated themselves in the same way before her, but not before the Holy Virgin.

At these audiences in the Winter and Tauric Palaces, the military officers wore uniforms, with their swords and shoes, but boots on holidays; civil officers wore during week-days simple French coats, but on holidays gala dresses; but at Tsárskoe Seló, both the military and civilians wore dress-coats on week-days, and only on holidays the former put on uniforms, and the latter French coats with their swords.

The Empress was busy until noon, after which her old hair-dresser, Kozlóv, dressed her hair in her interior boudoir. She wore her hair low and very simple; it was done up in the old fashion, with small locks behind her ears. Then she went into the boudoir, where we all waited for her; our society was then increased by four spinsters who came to serve the Empress at her toilet.   One of them, M. S. Aleksyéev, passed some ice to the Empress, who rubbed her face with it, probably in order to show that she did not like any other washes; another, A. A. Polokúchi, pinned a crêpe ornament to her hair, and the two sisters Zvyerév handed her the pins. This toilet lasted not more than ten minutes, and during that time the Empress conversed with some one of the persons present, among whom there was often the Chief Equerry, Lev Sergyéevich Narýshkin, and sometimes Count Strogonóv, who were her favourite society.   Having bid the company good-bye, the Empress returned with her maids into the sleeping-room, where she dressed herself for dinner, with their aid and with the aid of Márya Sávishna, while we all went home.   On week-days the Empress wore simple silk dresses, which were all made almost according to the same pattern, and which were known as Moldavian; the upper garment was usually of lilac or greyish colour, and without her decorations,— her lower garment white; on holidays she wore a brocade gown, with three decorations— the crosses of St. Andrew; St. George and St. Vladímir, and sometimes she put on all the sashes that belong to these decorations, and a small crown; she wore not very high-heeled shoes.

Her dinner was set for two o'clock.   During the week there were generally invited to dinner, of ladies, the Maid of Honour Protásov and Countess Branítski; of gentlemen, Adjutant-General P. V. Pássek, A. A. Narýshkin, Count Strogonóv, the two French emigrants, the good Count Esterházy and the black Marquis de Lambert, at times Vice-Admiral Ribas, Governor-General of the Polish provinces Tutolmín, and finally the Marshal of the Court, Prince Baryatínski.   On holidays there were invited also other military and civil officers who lived in St. Petersburg, down to the fourth class, and, on special celebrations, down to the sixth class.   The ordinary dinner of the Empress did not last more than an hour.   She was very abstemious in her food: she never breakfasted, and at dinner she tasted with moderation of not more than three or four courses; she drank only a glass of Rhine or Hungarian wine; she never ate supper. For this reason she was, in spite of her sixty-five years and industrious habits, quite well and lively. At times, indeed, her legs swelled and sores were opened up, but that only served to purify her humours, consequently was advantageous for her health. It is asserted that her death took place solely through the closing up of these sores.

After dinner all the guests immediately departed. The Empress was left alone: in summer she sometimes took a nap, but in winter never. She sometimes listened, until the evening assembly, to the foreign mail which arrived twice a week; sometimes she read a book, or made cameo imprints on paper; this she did also during the reading of her mail by P. A., or Count Markóv, or Popóv; but the latter was rarely invited to read, on account of his poor pronunciation of French, though he was nearly always present in the secretary's room. At six o'clock there assembled the aforementioned persons, and others of the Empress's acquaintance whom she specially designated, in order to pass the evening hours. On Hermitage days, which were generally on Thursdays, there was a performance, to which many ladies and gentlemen were invited; after the performance they all went home. On other days the reception was in the Empress's apartments. She played rocambole or whist, generally with P. A., E. V. Chertkóv and Count Strogonóv; there were also card-tables for the other guests. At ten o'clock the Empress retired to her inner apartments; at eleven she was in bed, and in all the rooms reigned a deep silence.

Gavrílo Petróvich Kámenev. (1772–1803.)

Kámenev wrote very few poems, and his reputation rests on his ballad *Gromvál*, which is remarkable for its flowing verse, the first two lines being in dactylic measure, and the last two lines of each stanza in anapests. Its main importance, however, lies in the fact that it was the first successful attempt at Romantic verse in the Russian language. Púshkin said of him: "Kámenev was the first in Russia who had the courage to abandon the classic school, and we Russian Romantic poets must bring a fitting tribute to his memory."

GROMVÁL

In my mind's eye I rapidly fly, rapidly piercing the dimness of time; I lift the veil of hoary antiquity, and I see Gromvál on his good horse.

The plumes wave upon his helmet, the tempered arrows clang in his quiver; he is borne over the clear field like a whirlwind, in burnished armour with his sharp spear.

The sun is setting behind the mountains of flint, the evening is descending from the aërial heights. The hero arrives in the murky forest, and only through its tops he sees the sky.

The storm, shrouded in sullen night, hastens to the west on sable pinions; the waters groan, the oak woods rustle, and centennial oaks creak and crack.

There is no place to protect oneself against the storm and rain; there is no cave, no house is seen; only through the dense darkness now glistens, now goes out, through the branches of the trees, a little fire in the distance.

With hope in his heart, with daring in his soul, slowly travelling through the forest towards the fire, the hero arrives at the bank of a brook, and suddenly he sees nearby and in front of him a castle.

A blue flame gleams within and reflects the light in the flowing stream; shadows pass to and fro in the windows, and howls and groans issue dully from them.

The knight swiftly dismounts from his horse and goes to the grass-covered gate; he strikes mightily against it with his steel spear, but only echoes in the forest respond to the knocking.

Immediately the fire within the castle goes out, and the light dies in the embrace of darkness; the howls and groans grow silent, too; the storm increases, the rain is doubled.

At the powerful stroke of his mighty hand the firmness of the iron gates gives way: the latches are broken, the hinges creak, and fearless Gromvál goes in.

He unsheathes his sword, ready to strike, and, groping,

goes into the castle. Quiet and gloom lie over all, only through the windows and chinks the whirlwind whistles.

The knight cries out in anger and in grief: "Ferocious wizard, greedy Zlomár! You have compelled Gromvál to wander over the world, you have stolen Rognyéda, his companion!

"Many a kingdom and land have I passed, have struck down mighty knights and monsters, have vanquished giants with my mighty hand, but have not yet found my beloved Rognyéda!

"Where do you dwell, evil Zlomár? In wild mountain fastnesses, in caves, in forests, in murky underground passages, in the depth of the sea do you hide her from my view?

"If I find your habitation, wicked magician, evil sorcerer, I will drag Rognyéda out of her captivity, I will pull out your black heart from your breast."

The knight grows silent, and sleep comes over him. Fatigue and night make him a bed. Without taking off his armour, in the breastplate and helmet, he kneels down and falls into a deep sleep.

The clouds hurry away, and the storm dies down, the stars grow dim, the east grows light; the morning star awakes, Zimtsérla blooms like a crimson rose, but Gromvál is still asleep.

The sun rolls over the vault of heaven, at noon glows with its heated rays, and the pitch of the pines waters through the bark, but sleep still keeps Gromvál in its embrace.

The forerunner of the night with olive brow glances from the east upon the forest and fields, and from an urn sprinkles dew upon the sward; but sleep still keeps Gromvál in its embrace.

Night, with cypress crown upon its head, in a garment woven of darkness and stars, walks frowning, over stairs, to its throne; but sleep still keeps Gromvál in its embrace.

Clouds congest in the vault of heaven, darkness grows thick, midnight comes on; the hero, awakening from his deep sleep, wonders when he sees not the crimson dawn.

Suddenly peals roar in the castle like thunder; the walls

shake, the windows rattle, and, as lightnings rapidly flash in the darkness, the hall is made bright with a terrible fire.

All the doors bang loud as they open: in white shrouds, with candles in their hands, shadows appear; behind them skeletons carry in their bony hands an iron coffin.

They place the coffin in the vast hall; immediately the lid flies off, and the wizard Zlomár, O horrible sight! lies breathless within, with open eyes.

The floor opens wide, and a hellish fire rises up in a howling whirlwind and thunder, and, embracing the iron coffin, heats it to a white glow; Zlomár sighs the heavy sigh of Gehenna.

In his wild, fierce, bloodshot eyes terror is painted, despair and grief; from his mouth black foam boils in a cloud, but the magician lies motionless, like a corpse.

The ghosts and skeletons, taking each other's hands, yell, howl, laugh, whistle; raving in rapturous orgy, they dance a hellish dance around his coffin.

Midnight passes in a terrible entertainment, and their groans and howls thunder ever more horrible. But scarcely has the herald of morning crowed three times, when ghosts, skeletons and coffin suddenly disappear.

There is darkness as in the grave, and quiet all around; in the forest nearby is silence and gloom. Gromvál perplexed, marvels at the appearance, and wondering does not believe himself.

Suddenly a magic flute is heard, and the sound of the harp strikes his ears: the vault of the hall bursts open, and a rose-coloured beam, with its soft light, dispels dense night.

In a light cloud of fragrant vapours, as if a fresh breeze were blowing and a swan gently gliding high up in the air, a sorceress softly descends into the hall.

Purer than the lily is her garment; her girdle shines on her waist like hyacinth; like the twinkle of the gold-gleaming eastern star, merriment beams in her eyes.

With a pleasant voice Dobráda speaks: "Sad knight, submit to your fate! Zlomár is no longer; fate has for ever cleared the world from that wrongdoer.

" Into the abyss of hell he has been hurled for ever; the jaws of Gehenna have swallowed him; with the gurgling of the lava and the roar of the fire, the abyss alone will hear his howl and groan.

"Death, transgressing the law of nature, has not deprived the magician's body of feeling: the shades of persons by him destroyed nightly torment him here in the castle.

" Knight, hasten to your Rognyéda! To the south of the forest, in a sandy plain, in a steel prison of Zlomár's castle, two winged Zilants watch her.

"Accept this magic horn from me; it has the power to close the jaws of monsters. But listen! You cannot save Rognyéda without shedding her blood,—thus the fates have decreed."

The magic strings sound again; the cloud is wafted upwards with Dobráda. Struck dumb by this speech, and beside himself, Gromvál, like a statue of stone, follows her with his glances.

Holding the emerald horn in his hand, in bitter resentment, the hero exclaims: " Ill-starred gift of the faithless sorceress, you promise happiness to me by the death of Rognyéda!

" No! I tremble at the very thought, and my heart flies a sacrifice to her. But, Gromvál, obey the dictum of fate, and hasten to destroy Zlomár's sorcery.

" If you cannot save Rognyéda, lay the castle in ruins, vanquish the Zilants,—shed your heroic blood for her, and crown your love with an heroic death!"

A beautiful morning with radiant beam gilds the tops of century oaks. Turning his horse to the midday sun, our knight leaves both the castle and forest.

Ravines, cliffs, rapids, crags, groan under the heavy beats of the hoofs; dense dust like a cloud and whirling in a pillar flies upwards where Gromvál races.

Through the gloomy pass of a rocky mount the knight rides into a vast steppe: an ocean of sand spreads before his view, and in the distance, it seems mingled with the sky.

No wind stirs the sandy waves; heat breathes there its

pestiferous breath; no shrubs rustle there, nor brooks babble: all is quiet and still as in the cemetery at midnight.

Through that wilderness, those terrible fields, no road leads, no tracks are seen; only in the east one can discern a steep mountain, and upon it a mighty castle stands out black in the distance.

Struggling three days with thirst and heat, the hero passes the barrier of death; on his worn-out steed, and in a bloody perspiration, he slowly reaches the foot of the mountain.

Over slippery paths on overhanging cliffs that threaten to crash down into the valley, slowly ascending the narrow footpath above an abyss, Gromvál reaches the top and castle.

Zlomár has built this castle with the power of Gehenna and the spirits of Hell. The turrets that tower above black cliffs announce destruction and evil death.

With Rognyéda in his heart, with bravery in his soul, Gromvál, like a fierce storm, breaks the hinges of the cast-iron doors, and with his tempered spear enters the terrible castle.

Furious he advances,—under his mighty heel dead bones and skulls crack; ravens, birds of the night and bats are awakened in the mossy crevices of the walls.

They hover like a cloud above the castle, and their terrible cries shake the air; the Zilants, hearing Gromvál's arrival, begin to howl and whistle, and flap their wings.

Opening their jaws, they fly against him; their stings issue from their mouths like spears; they rattle their scales, bending their tails, and stretch out their destructive claws from their feet.

The hero blows his emerald horn,— the sound deafens them, and they fall like rocks; their wings are clipt, their jaws are closed; falling into a sleep of death, they lie in mounds.

In rapture the knight flies to the dungeon to embrace Rognyéda with flaming heart; but instead, an enormous door is opened, and a giant, mailed in armour, comes to meet him.

His furious glances are comets in the dark; brass is his

corselet, lead his warclub; grey moss of the bog is his beard, a black forest after the storm the hair on his head.

Swinging his club with a terrible might, the giant lets it fall on Gromvál and strikes his valiant head: the echo shakes, reverberating through the castle.

The helmet clangs and is shattered to pieces; sparks issue from his dark eyes. From the stroke the club is bent as a bow, but Gromvál, like a rock, does not move from the spot.

The sword flashes in his heroic hand, and strikes the wretch like a thunderbolt; his strong brass would have broken to splinters, but the blade glides down his magic coat of mail.

The giant roars in evil madness, breathes flames, trembles with anger; he swells the muscles of his powerful shoulders, and threatens to crush Gromvál in his claws.

Death is unavoidable, destruction near; his terrible hands touch his corselet; but Gromvál, seizing his leg like an oak, makes him totter, and brings him to his fall.

The giant falls like a crumbling tower, and shakes all the castle with his terrible cry; the walls recede, the battlements fall; he is prostrate on the ground, and has dug a grave in the damp earth.

Grasping his throat with his mighty hand, Gromvál thrusts his sword into his jaws; the giant's teeth gnash against the steel; he roars and groans, and writhes in convulsions.

Black foam and crimson blood lash and gush from his mouth; furious with suffering, battling with death, he digs the earth with his feet, trembles, lies in the agony of death.

Mingling in a boiling stream the giant's blood wells up; a gentle vapour, rising from it in a cloud, forms the outline of fair Rognyéda.

The roses in her cheeks, the charm in her eyes, the crimson lips beckon for a kiss; her hair, falling like velvet over her shoulders, veils her swan's breast.

Gromvál marvels at this miracle: does he see a vision or a real being? Approaching her with hope and hesitation, he presses not a dream, but Rognyéda to his breast.

Filled with passionate rapture, Gromvál addresses his love with tender words: "Long, oh, long have I sought you, Rognyéda, and have, like a shadow, wandered over the wide world!"

Drawing a deep breath, she says: "The evil magician, the cunning Zlomár, impelled by his despicable passion, brought me to this enchanted castle.

"Here he touched me with his magic wand, and deprived me of memory and feelings. Falling immediately into a mysterious trance, I have ever since been shrouded in deepest darkness."

Taking Rognyéda by her hand, Gromvál softly descends to the foot of the mountain. He seats her behind him on his steed, and like an arrow flies back on the road.

Deep darkness covers the castle; thunders roar furiously in the night; stormy whirlwinds, tearing themselves away from their chains, howl, and the flinty ribs of the rock tremble.

With a terrible roar the earth bursts open, and the towers fall into the bottomless abyss; the Zilants, dungeon, giants are overthown : Gromvál has vanquished the magic of Zlomár.

Vladisláv Aleksándrovich Ózerov.   (1770–1816.)

Ózerov entered the military school when a child, left it as a lieutenant in 1788, and then was made adjutant to the director of the school, Count Anhalt, who died in 1794. His first literary venture was an *In Memoriam* to the director, written in French. He then tried himself in odes and shorter songs, of which only the *Hymn to the God of Love* rises above mediocrity. He scored his first great success in his tragedy *Œdipus at Athens*, which produced a stirring effect upon the audience. This was followed by *Fingal*, the subject being from Ossian. But the drama that most affected his generation was *Dimítri Donskóy*, which appeared opportunely on the eve of Napoleon's invasion, in 1807. The element of tearfulness, or "sentimentality," as Karamzín called it, which Ózerov was the first to introduce into the Russian tragedy, and the patriotic subject which he developed in his *Dimítri Donskóy* combined to make his plays very popular, though his verse is rather heavy and artificial.

DIMÍTRI DONSKÓY

ACT I., SCENE I. DIMÍTRI AND THE OTHER PRINCES,
BOYÁRS AND GENERALS

Dimítri. Russian princes, boyárs, generals, you who have
crossed the Don to find liberty and, at last, to cast off the
yokes that have been forced upon us! How long were we
to endure the dominion of the Tartars in our land, and, content with an humble fate, sit as slaves on our princely
throne? Two centuries had nearly passed when Heaven in
its anger sent that scourge against us; for almost two centuries the foes, now openly, now hidden, like hungry ravens,
like insatiable wolves, have been destroying, burning, plun-
dering us. I have called you here to avenge us: the time
has now come to repay the foe for our calamities. The
Kipchák horde has, like a gigantic burden, been lying on
Russian shoulders, spreading desolation and terror all
around, but now, heavy by its own weight, it has fallen to
pieces. Civil strife, dissension and all the ills which heretofore had brought the Russian land to utter weakness,
have now penetrated the horde. New khans have arisen
who have torn themselves loose from it; but the insatiable
tyrants, having barely risen, threaten our land. The most
insatiable of them and most cunning, Mamáy, the accursed
ruler of the Trans-Don horde, has risen against us in an unjust war. He is hurrying against us, and perhaps with to-
morrow's dawn will appear before our camp. But seeing
the sudden union of the Russian forces, his heart was disturbed, and his mind misgave him, so he decided to send
first an embassy to us. Friends of Dimítri, do you advise
to receive them? Or, remaining firm in our heroic intention,
shall we answer Mamáy in front of our army, when the first
bold onslaught of the Russians would resound upon the
earth and would frighten the Tartars?

Tverskóy. Let us give the answer before the army in the
field of battle! None of us, O princes, can be more anxious
than I to avenge ourselves on the inhuman foe. Whose

family can compare with the Tverskóys in misfortunes they have borne? My grandfather and his sire, after endless tortures, lay their heads in the graves through the treachery of the infidel, and their ashes groan under the power of the horde. Grand Prince of Russia, you have called us hither not to enter into parley with Mamáy, but to decide in battle and end all discord with him. . . .

Byelózerski. Oh, how happy am I to have lived to see this day, to contemplate here the concord and love among the princes, and the unanimous zeal in your hearts against the enemy! I, about to bear my age into the yawning grave, will be able to bring hope to the departed fathers, that the honour of the Russian land is to be reinstated, that her power and glory is to return. O shades of Vladímir, and you, shades of Yaroslàv, ancestral heads of princely houses! In the lap of the angels you will rejoice, as you foresee the blessed time when the disunited nation of Russian tribes, uniting with one soul into one whole, will triumphantly appear a threatening giant, and united Russia will give laws to the world! Dimítri, your victory is certain! No, never before has such an army been gathered in so far-reaching a camp, either by your grandfather Ivàn, or Simeón the Terrible, or your meek father! I, the old leader of the forces of Byelózersk, have never seen Russia lead out such numbers of bold warriors. Of all the Russian princes, Olég alone has remained in idleness at Ryazàn, and without interest in the expedition; his ear alone is deaf to the common groan. May the memory of those perish whose spirit can with quiet eye see the country's woes, or rather, let their name with disgrace and endless shame pass to late posterity! Yet, my lord, however flattering your success may be, my advice is to receive the Tartar embassy, and if we can establish peace by paying a tribute to Mamáy. . . . (*All the princes express dissatisfaction.*)

Dimítri. O Prince of Byelózersk, what do you propose? Fearing strife, to acknowledge the Tartar's power by paying a shameful tribute?

Byelózerski. To spare the priceless Christian blood. If

we conquer Mamáy, look out, the hordes will once more unite for our common woe; beware, this temporarily successful exploit will again rouse their ambitious spirit, and they will perceive at last how injurious for their ambition their strife is, which separates their khans. The murders, fire, slaughter of wives and children which the Tartars have perpetrated against us, in their opinion, give the hordes a right over us. They deem Russia to be their patrimony. Seeing our bravery, they will stop their disorders, and will soon, united, bring misery on the Russians. Rather give them a chance to weaken in their destructive discord; let us gather strength in the peaceful quiet and, warding off the chances of war, choose peace instead of useless victory.

Dimítri. Oh, better death in battle than dishonourable peace! Thus our ancestors thought, thus we, too, will think. Those times are past when timid minds saw in the Tartars a tool of Heaven, which it is senseless and improper to oppose. In our days honour and the very voice of faith arm us against the tormentors. That voice, that prophetic voice of faith, proclaims to us that an immortal crown awaits the fallen in battle, that through the grave they pass to eternal joy. O Sérgi, pastor of souls, whom the groans of fellow-citizens have so often disturbed in your hermit prayers, and whose tears have so abundantly flowed lamenting the fate of the innocent, O you who with sacred hand blessed us for the impending battle! In your hermit cell, where you pass your humble days, listen to my words: inspired by you, they will inflame the Russian hearts to seek here liberty or the heavenly crown! 'T is better to cease living, or not to be born at all, than to submit to the yoke of a foreign tribe, than with the name of payers of tribute to flatter their greed. Can we with such slavery avert our misfortunes? He who pays a tribute is weak; he who evinces a weak spirit invites arrogant lust to insult. But I am ready to receive the Khan's messenger and to bring him before the assembly of the princes, not to listen to the shameless propositions of Tartar arrogance, but to announce to him the resolve for war, that he may read valour in our brows, and, shuddering, bear terror into Mamáy's camp.

Smolénski. The whole assembly announces assent to your advice.

Dimítri. The messenger awaits the decision near the tent. You, Brénski, bring in the Tartars that have come to us!

Prince Iván Mikháylovich Dolgorúki. (1764-1823.)

Iván Mikháylovich Dolgorúki was the grandson of Prince Iván Aleksyéevich, the favourite of Peter II. (see p. 233). In 1791 he left the army with the rank of brigadier. He was then made Vice-Governor of Pénza, where he sought relief from the humdrum life of a provincial town in reading and in writing poetry. One of the first of his poems to attract attention was the envoi *To my Lackey;* he became universally known through his *My Penza Fireplace.* In 1802 he was appointed Governor of Vladímir. Not long after his return to Moscow he was forced to retire before the advancing Frenchmen. During his retreat he wrote his *Lament of Moscow.* His best poem is probably his *Legacy.* While not a poet of the first order, Dolgorúki displayed great originality and much depth of feeling. This is what he himself said of his poems: "In my poems I wished to preserve all the shades of my feelings, to see in them, as in a picture, the whole history of my heart, its agitation, the change in my manner of thinking, the progress of my thoughts in the different ages of my life, and the gradual development of my small talents. Every verse reminds me of some occurrence, or thought, or mood that influenced me at such and such a moment. . . . That is the key to the originality which many are so kind as to ascribe to my productions." *The Legacy* was translated by Sir John Bowring.

THE LEGACY

When time's vicissitudes are ended,
  Be this, be this my place of rest;
Here let my bones with earth be blended,
  Till sounds the trumpet of the blest.
For here, in common home, are mingled
Their dust, whom fame or fortune singled;
  And those whom fortune, fame passed by,
All mingled, and all mouldering;—folly
And wisdom, mirth and melancholy,
  Slaves, tyrants,—all mixt carelessly.

List! 'T is the voice of time,—Creation's
   Unmeasured arch repeats the tone;
Look! E'en like shadows, mighty nations
   Are born, flit by us, and are gone!
See! Children of a common father,
See stranger-crowds, like vapours gather;
   Sires, sons, descendants, come and go.
Sad history! Yet e'en there the spirit
Some joys may build, some hopes inherit,
   And wisdom gather flowers from woe.

There, like a bee-swarm, round the token
   Of unveiled truth shall sects appear,
And evil's poisonous sting be broken
   In the bright glance of virtue's spear.
And none shall ask, what dormitory
Was this man's doom, what robes of glory
   Wore he, what garlands crowned his brow,—
Was pomp his slave?—Come now, discover
The heart, the soul,—Delusion 's over,—
   What was his conduct?—Answer now!

Where stands yon hill-supported tower,
   By Fili, shall I wake again,
Summoned to meet Almighty Power
   In judgment, like my fellow-men.
I shall be there, and friends and brothers,
Sisters and children, fathers, mothers,—
   With joy that never shall decay;
The soul, substantial blessing beaming
(All here is shadowy and seeming),
   Drinks bliss no time can sweep away.

Friends, on my brow that rests when weary
   Erect no proud and pompous pile:
Your monuments are vain and dreary,
   Their splendour cannot deck the vile.
A green grave, by no glare attended,
With other dust and ashes blended,

Oh, let my dust and ashes lie!
There, as I sleep, Time, never sleeping,
Shall gather ages to his keeping,
   For such is nature's destiny.

My wife, my children shall inherit
   All I possessed,—'t was mine, 't is theirs;
For death, that steals the living spirit,
   Gives all earth's fragments to its heirs.
Send round no circling-briefs of sorrow,
No garments of the raven borrow;
   'T is idle charge, 't is costly pride.
Be gay, through rain and frosty weather,
Nor gather idle priests together
   To chant my humble grave beside.

Cry, orphans! Cry, ye poor! imploring
   The everlasting God, that He
May save me when I sink, adoring,
   Amidst His boundless mercy-sea.
My blessing to my foes be given,
Their curses far from me be driven,
   Nor break upon my hallowed bliss;
God needs no studied words from mortals,
A sigh may enter Heaven's wide portals,—
   He could not err, He taught us this.

No songs, no elegy,—death hearkens
   To music ne'er though sweet it be:
When o'er you night's oblivion darkens,
   Then let oblivion shadow me.
No verse will soften Hades' sadness,
No verse can break on Eden's gladness,
   'T is all parade and shifting glare:—
A stream, where scattered trees are growing,
A secret tear, in silence flowing,
   No monument as these so fair.

Such slumber here, their memory flashes
  Across my thoughts.—Hail, sister, hail!
I kiss thy sacred bed of ashes,
  And soon shall share thy mournful tale.
Thou hast paid thy earthly debts,—'t is ended,
Thy cradle and thy tomb are blended,
  The circle of thy being run;
And now in peace thy history closes,
And thy stilled, crumbling frame reposes
  Where life's short, feverish play is done.

I live and toil,—my thoughts still follow
  The idle world:—my care pursue
Dreams and delusions, baseless, hollow,
  And vanities still false, though new.
Then fly I earthly joys, I find them
Leave terror-working stings behind them:
  " Beware, beware!" experience cries;
Yet ah! how faint the voice of duty,
One smile of yonder flattering beauty
  Would make me waste even centuries.
          —From Sir John Bowring's *Specimens of*
                  the Russian Poets, Part II.

MY MOSCOW FIREPLACE

Scarcely have we seen summer, behold, winter is here!
The frosts drive us into our rooms, and will for a long time
keep us within. Nature's beauty is changed, and dimmed
by the veil of night. Oh, what shall I do? What begin?
I will move up to my dear fireplace, and will share with it,
as before, my melancholy.

Whatever countries I have been in, whether my house
was large or small, whether I paraded in high palace halls,
or retired to my apartments,—the fireplace, my winter benefactor, was everywhere the witness of my acts: whole days
I passed with it alone; pining, sorrows and annoyances, consolation, pleasure, joy,—my fireplace has experienced them
all.

Whenever I mentally survey all human lots in this world, and by the fireplace in my study judge of humanity, I with difficulty can harmonise in my imagination the opinions of happiness that are common to all. The whole world lives in a noise and din; but what does it find in place of happiness? New causes for worriment.

Kings, of their own free will, leave the throne and hasten to arms; in their elevated place they not seldom curse their lives. No matter how boyárs grow stout, they also pale in their good fortune, like their lowest slave. He in his unbounded sphere, the other in his earth hut, or cave,—both are weak against the attack.

Everywhere they have written of happiness, and will always prate about it, but they have nowhere found it. Yes, 't is difficult to attain! And I, though a simple man, can also like a philosopher aver it is within me; but where, and how to find it?—I do not know! In sorrow I suffer openly; whenever I am merry, 't is as if in a dream.

Protesting against the evil of the passions, knitting his brow, like Cato, when all is quiet in his soul, the philosopher proclaims his law: " Why be enslaved by passions? We must submit to reason. All our desires are an empty dream; all upon earth, O men, is transitory: seek eternal happiness in Heaven, for the world is vanity of vanities.

" If one dish satisfies your hunger, why have three? If you have a caftan, what is the use of five? What need is there of a pile of money? When you die, you will not take it with you. Contract the limits of your necessities, flee from the city into the country, live quietly your allotted time, with equanimity bear insults, magnanimously suffer sorrow, be more than man!"

What are you yourself, my teacher? Are you a god, or an angel in the flesh? Guardian of deep wisdom, permit me to look within you! Reveal to us not your mind alone, but your feelings, announce to us without ambiguity: are you yourself? I see, you are a vain hypocrite: you do not believe your own sermon, you are an empty-sounding cymbal.

Oh, if people all lived as reason bids them! If feelings

were more gentle, if the fount of blood did not boil,—how nice life would be! All would be peace and security, and love the tie of all the lands ; people would not devour each other; and a Frenchman, an Arab, a Mussulman would live in harmony together.

Oh, if . . . I need but place this word at the head, and my pen creates at once a new earth, nay, heaven. All kingdoms will flow with abundance, all men will be equally strong, nowhere there shall be snow, nor winter, but flowers will grow the year around, and we will not run to the fire-place,—we shall be regenerated.

Oh no! I am sorry for the fireplace! Let us leave all as it is: we cannot reproduce what my reason has evoked. Let the sphere circle around, and let each various chimera disport with every mind! The Creator will turn all for the best: to-day the chill disturbs us, but the thunder of the summer does not terrify us.

I hear at all times of the good qualities of countrymen, what beautiful lives they lead, and how the law of nature is not trampled upon by them. "Their manners," they assert, "are coarser, but their amusements are incomparably simpler than ours: they live in freedom with each other, do not drink nor eat according to the fashion." 'T is not true!

When we listen to serenades on a beautiful summer day, while limpid waterfalls make a rippling noise, and the shade of cedars protects us from the heat, the peasant hitches his horse to the plough and tears up the earth, or hauls a log, or, if it be winter, looks through dim windows, through which nothing can be seen, at the blizzard without.

Fireplace, I will not exchange you for all the treasures of the lords! You are often my consolation, and always pleasant and agreeable to me. Let sorrows be inevitable: joy is coextensive with them. You are the throne of my amusements; but I am satisfied with my books; I feel with them neither pain, nor think my room small, and I read them as my spirit prompts me.

But when I leave my book, and fix my eyes upon the fireplace, with what pleasure I recall the host of various incidents! I at once reproduce in my mind the picture of my youth, and the progress and cause of my cares; I even now, as it were, glance to the north, and south, and the capital, and the Finland border.

I accuse myself before thee, my Lord! I have in vain killed my youth; carried on the wave of habit, I have given my days and nights to dreaming. I, tossed now hither, now thither, hastened to make new acquaintances, and thought: "This is all a loan I make; some day the debt, I am sure, will be duly returned to me."

'T is time to adapt myself to the custom! I shall soon be forty years old: it is time to learn from experience that to judge people rightly, to know this world, to seek friends is a self-deception and vain endeavour of the heart. The measure of human indifference is in our days full to overflowing; ask for no examples: alas! there are too many of them.

In your presence all will praise you, but let there be an occasion for helping you, and your worth will be depreciated, or without saying a word they will walk away. If one be cunning, he will so oppress you that he will compel you to think all your life of him in tears; if he be foolish, he will, wherever he may meet you, cast a heap of stones before you and bar your way.

From all such evils my consolation art Thou, only God, God of all creation! I need nothing more, for I expect no happiness from men. A hundredfold more pleasant it is, staying at home, and not perceiving in it the temptations of the world, to live simply with your family and, modestly passing your time and vigorously communing with reason, to stir the wood in the fireplace.

Iván Ivánovich Dmítriev. (1760–1837.)

Dmítriev was born in the Government of Simbírsk, where his friend and colleague Karamzín was also born. He entered the army in 1775 as a common soldier, and did not advance to the grade of commissioned officer until 1787. During his military service he privately studied foreign languages and wrote poetry. His first collection of poems, containing *Ermák*, *What Others Say* and *The*

Little Dove, appeared in 1795. These are the best of his productions. He also wrote a number of fables that do not suffer by comparison with those of Krylóv. His shorter songs, like *The Little Dove*, have become very popular, and are part of every song-book, together with Neledínski's "To the streamlet I'll repair" and other similar songs. Dmítriev did for poetry what Karamzín was doing for prose,—he purified Russian from the dross of the Church-Slavic language, an inheritance from the days of Lomonósov, and he popularised the Romantic spirit in Russian literature. He also encouraged younger men of talent, such as Krylóv. Dmítriev rapidly rose in honours, until he was made Minister of Justice in 1810. He retired a few years later to his estates near Moscow, where he passed his days surrounded by a coterie of literary men.

The following English versions of his poems have appeared: *During a Thunder-Storm, The Tsar and the Two Shepherds, The Broken Fiddle, Over the Grave of Bogdanovich, Love and Friendship*, in Sir John Bowring's *Specimens of the Russian Poets*, Part I.; *Yermak, Moskva Rescued, To the Volga, Enjoyment*, "O had I but known before," *The Little Dove, To Chloe, ib.*, Part II.; *Counsel, The Little Dove*, in W. D. Lewis's *The Bakchesarian Fountain; Yermak, The Siskin and the Chaffinch, The Doctor, Sympathy*, in C. T. Wilson's *Russian Lyrics; The Moon*, in Fraser's Magazine, 1842 (article, *Russian Fabulists*).

THE LITTLE DOVE

The little dove, with heart of sadness,
   In silent pain sighs night and day;
What now can wake that heart to gladness?
   His mate beloved is far away.

He coos no more with soft caresses,
   No more is millet sought by him,
The dove his lonesome state distresses,
   And tears his swimming eyeballs dim.

From twig to twig now skips the lover,
   Filling the grove with accents kind,
On all sides roams the harmless rover,
   Hoping his little friend to find.

Ah! vain that hope his grief is tasting,
   Fate seems to scorn his faithful love,

And imperceptibly is wasting,
   Wasting away, the little dove!

At length upon the grass he threw him,
   Hid in his wing his beak and wept;
There ceased his sorrows to pursue him,
   The little dove for ever slept.

His mate, now sad abroad and grieving,
   Flies from a distant home again,
Sits by her friend, with bosom heaving,
   And bids him wake with sorrowing pain.

She sighs, she weeps, her spirits languish,
   Around and round the spot she goes;
Ah! charming Chloe's lost in anguish,
   Her friend wakes not from his repose!
—From W. D. Lewis's *The Bakchesarian Fountain.*

DURING A THUNDER-STORM

It thunders! Sons of dust, in reverence bow!
   Ancient of days! Thou speakest from above;
Thy right hand wields the bolt of terror now;
   That hand which scatters peace and joy and love.
Almighty! Trembling like a child,
   I hear Thy awful voice, alarmed, afraid,
I see the flashes of Thy lightning wild,
   And in the very grave would hide my head.

Lord! What is man? Up to the sun he flies,
   Or feebly wanders through earth's vale of dust:
There is he lost 'midst heaven's high mysteries,
   And here in error and in darkness lost.
Beneath the stormclouds, on life's raging sea,
   Like a poor sailor, by the tempest tossed
In a frail bark, the sport of destiny,
   He sleeps, and dashes on the rocky coast.

Thou breathest, and the obedient storm is still.
   Thou speakest,—silent the submissive wave;
Man's shattered ship the rushing waters fill,
   And the hushed billows roll across his grave.
Sourceless and endless God!   Compared with Thee,
   Life is a shadowy, momentary dream,
And Time, when viewed through Thy eternity,
   Less than the mote of morning's golden beam.

          —From Sir John Bowring's *Specimens of the*
          Russian Poets, Part I.

ERMÁK

How strange a sight is this I see,
By thee revealed, Antiquity!
Beneath the gloomy garb of night,
By the pale moonbeam's cloudy light,
I gaze upon the Irtýsh stream,
Whose waters foaming, whirling, gleam,
As on they rush with angry tide.
Two men I see, exhausted, there,
Like shadows in the murky air;
Their faces in their hands they hide.
One youthful is, the other old,
His beard hangs down with wavy fold;
Each wears a dress whose every part
With awe and wonder fills the heart;
Descending from their helmets down,
The coiling tails of serpents frown,
Mingled with owlet's bristling wing,
Their coats wild-beasts' skins borrowing.
Their breasts entire with thongs are hung,
Of flints, and rusty iron, strung;
Within each belt is firmly prest
A knife, whose edge well sharpened is;
Two drums are at their feet, I wis,
And close beside their lances rest:
They both are sorcerers of Siberian race,
And thus the meaning of their words I trace.

THE OLD MAN

" Roar on, old Irtýsh, let our cry
Along thy stream re-echoing fly;
The gods have chastening sent in ire
And poured on us misfortunes dire."

THE YOUNG MAN

" Woes, woes, upon us tenfold lour
In this our most disastrous hour."

THE OLD MAN

" O thou, whose crown three nations bore,
Their names far-spread from shore to shore!
O mighty, proud, and ancient State,
Mother of many races great!
Thy glory 's past and worn away,
No longer chief, thou must obey!"

THE YOUNG MAN

"As clouds of dust from whirlwinds hie,
So scattered quite thy people lie;
And he, Kuchúm,[1] dread of the world,
Is dead, on foreign deserts hurled."

THE OLD MAN

" The holy Shamans, forced from home,
Throughout the rugged forests roam;
For this, ye gods of earth and air,
Was it that white has grown my hair?
Tell me, was it for this that I,
Through all my life your faithful slave,
Prostrate in dust before ye lie,
And thousands for companions have ?"

THE YOUNG MAN

"And who are they have made thee fall?"

[1] Yermák defeated Kuchúm Khan in 1579; Kuchúm Khan fell into
the hands of Calmucks, who killed him.

THE OLD MAN

" From Russia come they, one and all;
Why did not plague and famine loom
Upon our land with frightful doom ?
Better if elemental wrath
Had fall'n in fury on our path,
And swallowed up Siberia's fame,
Than bow before this Ermák's name."

THE YOUNG MAN

" Of Nature's self the curse and blight,
May curses heavy on him light!
Ye streams, and mountains old, 't is he
Has flung upon you infamy!"

THE OLD MAN

"As fiery columns passing on,
As icy blasts the land upon,
All fell by his destructive tread;
Where'er his fatal arrow sped,
There life grew pale, and death's dire smart
O'ertook each timid, cowering heart."

THE YOUNG MAN

" By him deprived of mortal breath,
Our royal brother met his death."

THE OLD MAN

"As I looked on, the hero's might
Shone forth in that terrific fight;
'T was on Muhammad-Kula's [1] plain—
Such fight I ne'er shall see again.
His arrows hurtling in swift course,
His breast enkindled with strange force,
He drew from out its sheath his blade—

[1] The translator misunderstood the passage. Mehmed-Kul was the King's brother, whom Ermák made prisoner and sent to John the Terrible.

'Rather than weary life give death,
Free from captivity,' he saith,
And fierce assault upon Ermák he made.
Most terrible the sight! as clash
Their swords, the lightnings from them flash;
Blow fell on blow with frightful sounds.
They give and they receive new wounds.
They seize each other in their rage,
And dreadful combat still they wage;
Arm against arm—breast against breast—
They in their struggle know no rest;
The wild woods with their cries resound,
They dig up with their feet the ground:
From brows ran down, like hail, their sweat,
And fearfully their bosoms beat;
Their heads incline from side to side,
And thus they grapple, to each other tied,
Still struggling on; until the weight
Of Ermák seals his foeman's fate.
' The victory 's mine!'—'t is thus he cries:
' The land before me subject lies!' ' "

THE YOUNG MAN

"Accomplished is the prophecy,
That this our land should conquered be.
But shall the oppressèd sigh in vain,
And never more to freedom rise again ? "

THE OLD MAN

"Eternal is the fatal yoke:
Listen, my son!   Late yesternight
Into the silent woods I took
My way; and there, while rapturous light
Enkindled all my inmost soul,
Burnt sacrifice I offered whole,
And to the gods made fervent prayer
That they would to our aid repair:
When, suddenly, the winds arise,

From off the trees the fresh leaves fall,
The cedars groan with creaking cries,
The goats away are scattered all.
Down sank I, when, above the noise
Of the dire storm, I heard a voice
Thus speaking: ' Furious war does wage
Racha[1] 'gainst sinners; to his rage
All those who sin devoted are;
Siberia has renounced my laws,
And righteous, therefore, is the cause
Why she be subject to the fierce White Tsar.[2]
By morn and night ye shall be found
Alike in heavy fetters bound;
But Ermák's name shall never fade,
Nor of his race an end be made;
They 'neath the moon shall ever be
Eternal in their majesty.'
When ceased the voice,. the thunders loud
Rattled from out each stormy cloud;
On us has fallen Misfortune's hand,
Woe ''———

THE YOUNG MAN

"Woe to us, and our land."

Then, while they yield to deepest sighs,
They from the moss-strewn stones arise,
And while their arms again they wear,
Along the shore they disappear.
   Peace, Ermák, on thine ashes rest!
Thine image of bright silver made,
Which in Siberia's mines was laid,
Is by the crown of Russia prest.
But why speak I with hasty zeal ?
What do my foolish words reveal ?

[1] God of the Ostiaks.
[2] The Tsar of Russia ; the origin of the appellation is not certain.

We do not even know the place
Where rest thy bones in earth's embrace.
The wild beasts trample them upon,
Or Ostiaks, as they hurry on,
Chasing the antlered stag, and roe,
To bring them by their arrows low.
But, hero, from thine anger cease,
And let thy memory know peace!
Poetic genius every day,
When golden morning's beauties play,
Shall o'er thy corpse still float along,
And greet thee with triumphant song.
What matters it in any case
If to barbaric times we trace
Thy birth?   Yet thou such deeds hast done
As have thy land victorious shown.
Although thine ashes disappear,
Though e'en thy sons no likeness bear
To thee, but, their great sire forgetting,
Their livelihood in wild woods getting,
They dwell the wolves and bears amid,
Yet never shall thy name be hid.
Thou shalt with demigods find place,
From age to age, from race to race;
And ne'er shall darken thy bright ray
Until grows dark the orb of day;
When with a crash the heavens fall,
And time shall cease to be, and ruin cover all.
                    —From C. T. Wilson's *Russian Lyrics*.

WHAT OTHERS SAY

" How strange ! More than twenty years have passed since we, with mind intent and furrowed brow, have assiduously been writing odes, yet we nowhere hear praises sung to them or us! May it be that Phœbus has sent forth his stern decree that none of us should ever aspire to equal

Flaccus, Ramler [1] and all their brotherhood, or ever be renowned as they in song? What do you think? I took
yesterday the pains to compare their song and ours: in
theirs, there is not much to read! a page; if much, three
pages, and yet what joy to read! You feel—how shall I say
it?—as if you flew on wings! Judging by their briefness, you
are sure they wrote them playfully, and not labouring four
days: then why should we not be more fortunate than they,
since we are a hundred times more diligent and patient?
When one of us begins to write, he leaves all play aside,
pores a whole night over a couple of verses, sweats, thinks,
draws and burns his paper; and sometimes he rises to such
daring that he passes a whole year over one ode! And, of
course, he uses up all his intelligence upon it! And there
you have a most solemn ode! I cannot say to what species
it belongs, but it is very full,—some two hundred strophes!
Judge for yourself how many fine verses there are in it!
Besides, it is written according to the rules: at first you
read the introduction, then the argument, and finally the
conclusion,— precisely as the learned speak in the church!
And yet, I must confess, there is no pleasure in reading it.

"Let me take, for example, the odes on victories, how that
they conquered the Crimea, how the Swedes were drowned
at sea: I find there all the details of a battle, where it happened, how, when,—in short, a report in verse! Very well!
. . . I yawn! I throw it away, and open another, one
written for a holiday, or something like it: here you discover
things that a less clever mind would not have thought out
within a lifetime: 'Dawn's rosy fingers,' and 'lily of paradise,' and 'Phœbus,' and 'heaven cleft open'! So vociferous, so loud! No, it does not please, nor move our hearts
in the least."

Thus an old man of our grandfathers' times spoke yesterday to me in gentle simplicity. I, being myself a companion
of those singers, the action of whose verse he so marvelled
at, was much disturbed, nor knew how to answer him. But

[1] A German poet who translated the odes of Horace and wrote odes
of his own.

luckily, if at all that may be called luck to hear your own terrible sentence, a certain Aristarch began to speak to him.

" For this," said he, " there are many causes: I will not promise to unveil one-half of them, but some I will gladly expound to you. I myself love the language of the gods, poetry, and just as you, am little edified with ours. In former days I have much conversed in Moscow with our Pindars, and have watched them well: the greater part of them are corporals of the body-guard, assessors, officers, scribes, or dust-covered guardians of monsters in the Museum of Antiquities,—all of them busy government officials; I have often noticed that they barely have time in two days or three to make a proper rhyme, their mind being all taken up with their affairs. No sooner has a lucky thought struck them, when, lo, the clock strikes six! The carriage is waiting: 't is time for the theatre, and then to the ball, or to Lion,[1] and then 't is night. . . . When are they to call on Apollo? In the morning, no sooner has he opened his eyes, than there is a note: ' Rehearsal at five o'clock ' . . . Where? In fashionable society, where our lyric poet is to play the part of the harlequin. Is there any time left for odes? You have to learn our parts, then to ,Kroll,[2] then home again, to primp yourself and get dressed, then to the theatre, and good-bye another day. Besides, the ancients had one purpose, we another: Horace, for example, who nurtured his breast with ecstasy, what did he want? Not very much: in the æons immortality, and in Rome but a wreath of laurels or of myrtle, that Delia might say: ' He is famous ; through him I, too, am immortal!' But the aim of many of us is a present of a ring, at times a hundred roubles, or friendship with a princelet who all his life has never read anything except now and then the Court almanac, or praises from their friends to whom each printed sheet appears to be sacred.

" Considering how different their views and ours are, it may safely be asserted, without offending those mettlesome gentle-

[1] Master of masquerades at St. Petersburg.
[2] St. Petersburg tailor.

men, the alumni of the Russian Muses, that they must have
some especial taste, and different means, and a special manner in the composition of a lyrical poem; what they are I
cannot tell you, but I shall announce to you—and, truly, I
will not lie about it—what a certain poet thought of verses,
of whose works the *Mercury* and the *Observer*[1] and the book
stores and the stalls are full. 'We are born into this
world,' he thought, 'with rhymes; is it then not ridiculous
for us poets to waste our time, like Demosthenes, at the sea-
shore in a cabin, in doing nothing but reading and thinking,
and relating what we have thought out only to the noisy
waves? Nature makes the poet, and not study: he is without study learned when he becomes enthused, but science
will always remain science, and not a gift; the only necessary equipments are boldness, rhymes and ardour.'

"And this is the way the natural poet wrote an ode: barely
has the thunder of the cannon given the nation the pleasant
news that the Rýmnikski Alcides[2] has vanquished the Poles,
or that Férzen has taken their chief, Kosciuszko, captive, he
immediately grabs the pen, and, behold, the word 'ode' is
already on the paper." Then follows in one strain: "'On
such a day and year!' How now? 'I sing!' Oh no,
that's old! Were it not better: 'Grant me, O Phœbus?'
Or, better still: 'Not you alone are trod under heel, O
turban-wearing horde!' But what shall I rhyme with it
but 'snored,' or 'bored'? No, no! it will not do! I had
better take a walk, and refresh myself with a whiff of air."

He went, and thus he meditated on his walk: "The beginning never daunts the singers: you simply say what first
occurs to you. The trouble only begins when you have to
praise the hero. I know not with whom to compare him;
with Rumyántsev, with Greyg or with Orlóv? What a
pity I have not read the ancients! For it does not seem
proper to compare to the moderns. Well, I'll simply write:
'Rejoice, hero, rejoice, O thou!' That's good! But what
now? Ah, now comes the ecstasy! I'll say: 'Who has
rent the veil of eternity for me! I see the gleam of light-

---

[1] Magazines.   [2] Suvórov.

ning! From the upper world I hear, and so on.' And then? Of course: ' Many a year!' Most excellent! I have caught the plan, and thoughts, and all! Hail to the poet! All I have to do now, is to sit down and write, and boldly print!'' He hurries to his garret, scribbles, and the deed is done! And his ode is printed, and already they wrap shoeblacking in his ode. Thus has he Pindarised, and all his ilk who are scarcely capable to write a proper shop sign! '' I wish Phœbus would tell them in their dream: ' He who in Catherine's loud age of glory cannot by his eulogy move the hearts of others, nor water his sweet lyre with tears, let him throw it away, break it and know he is not a poet!' ''

END OF PART I.

INDEX

www.ingramcontent.com/pod-product-compliance
Lightning Source LLC
Chambersburg PA
CBHW050120030726
47505CB00007B/1970